Ancient Stone Sites
of New England and
the Debate Over Early
European Exploration

SECOND EDITION

ALSO BY DAVID GOUDSWARD
AND FROM MCFARLAND

*The Westford Knight and Henry Sinclair: Evidence of a 14th Century
Scottish Voyage to North America*, 2d ed. (2020)

Ancient Stone Sites of New England and the Debate Over Early European Exploration

SECOND EDITION

David Goudsward

McFarland & Company, Inc., Publishers
Jefferson, North Carolina

Library of Congress Cataloguing-in-Publication Data

Names: Goudsward, David, author.
Title: Ancient stone sites of New England and the debate over early European exploration / David Goudsward.
Description: Second edition. | Jefferson, North Carolina : McFarland & Company, Inc., Publishers, 2023 | Includes bibliographical references and index.
Identifiers: LCCN 2023033730 | ISBN 9781476690735 (print) ∞
ISBN 9781476649962 (ebook)
Subjects: LCSH: New England—Antiquities. | Historic sites—New England. | Excavations (Archaeology)—New England. | Inscriptions, Runic—New England. | Megalithic monuments—New England. | New England—Discovery and exploration—European. | New England—Discovery and exploration—Pre-Columbian. | North America—Discovery and exploration—European. | North America—Discovery and exploration—Pre-Columbian.
Classification: LCC F6 .G68 2023 | DDC 974/.01—dc23/eng/20230810
LC record available at https://lccn.loc.gov/2023033730

British Library cataloguing data are available

ISBN (print) 978-1-4766-9073-5
ISBN (ebook) 978-1-4766-4996-2

© 2023 David Goudsward. All rights reserved

No part of this book may be reproduced or transmitted in any form or by any means, electronic or mechanical, including photocopying or recording, or by any information storage and retrieval system, without permission in writing from the publisher.

Front cover image: This beehive chamber is built into the hillside of town-owned woods off Hersey Road in Danville, New Hampshire. It is a comparatively small chamber, roughly eight feet long, six feet wide, and four feet high, with a two-by-three-foot entrance pointing to the southwest. It is a drywall construction of fieldstone, covered by two capstones composed of local granite. Proponents of pre-Columbian contact note the structure's proximity to the America's Stonehenge site and similarities with other chambers across the area, and that entrance has possible alignments with the winter solstice. Opponents note the beehive is located by a road heavily trafficked since colonial times, with multiple farms along the same stretch of road as early as 1760 (author photograph).

Printed in the United States of America

McFarland & Company, Inc., Publishers
Box 611, Jefferson, North Carolina 28640
www.mcfarlandpub.com

To my wife, HEATHER BERNARD.

Her support of this project was vital,
if not always voluntary.

Acknowledgments

The following people went far beyond the call of duty to assist me in either the original edition in 2006 or this revised volume. I remain very grateful: Terry Deveau, Bobby Derie, Elizabeth Lane, Robert Stone, Malcolm Pearson, and Manuel Luciano da Silva, M.D.

Help was also provided by the following: Norm Barstow (Hadley Farm Museum, Hadley, Massachusetts), Kathleen Borelli, Jane Buchanan (M.N. Spear Memorial Library, Shutesbury, Massachusetts), Chris Cantrell (Museum Village at Old Smith's Clove, Monroe, New York), Leon Christoforo (Leominster Historical Society, Leominster, Massachusetts), Bill Darmon, Chuck Drayton, the GAR Memorial Library (West Newbury, Massachusetts), Scott Goudsward, the Groton Public Library (Groton, Connecticut), Hampton Historical Society (Hampton, New Hampshire), Carol A. Hanny, Ed Hood (Old Sturbridge Village, Sturbridge, Massachusetts), Stephen Howes (Kingman Tavern Historical Museum, Cummington, Massachusetts), Lisa Huntsha, Swenson Swedish Immigration Research Center, Augustana College, Loraine Jensen, American Association for Runic Studies, Diane Kachmar (Florida Atlantic University, Boca Raton, Florida), David Kruger (New Hampshire Society of Genealogists), Jody LaFerriere, Greg Laing (Haverhill Public Library, Haverhill, Massachusetts), Joanne Lambert, Jeannine T. Levesque (Leominster Public Library, Leominster, Massachusetts), Richard Lynch, Lynn Museum (Lynn, Massachusetts), Virginia Moore (J.V. Fletcher Library, Westford, Massachusetts), J.W. Ocker, and Vance Tiede. Thank you one and all.

Contents

Acknowledgments	vi
Introduction	1
ONE. Sacrificial Tables	3
TWO. Vineland on the Charles	17
THREE. Dighton Rock	32
FOUR. The Newport Tower	44
FIVE. America's Stonehenge on Mystery Hill	63
SIX. Celtic New England	81
SEVEN. The Westford Knight	99
EIGHT. Runic Relicts	111
NINE. The Spirit Pond Runestones	129
TEN. Thorvald's Grave	139
ELEVEN. Byzantine Connecticut	147
TWELVE. Norse Cape Cod	159
THIRTEEN. The Norse of Narragansett Bay	177
Chapter Notes	185
Bibliography	217
Index	233

Introduction

Megaliths are large stones used in various prehistoric architectures, predominantly in Western Europe during the second millennium BC. As the mysterious ancient stones of New England have become more popularized, the adjective megalithic has become more generic in usage, referring not only to the large stone constructions that comprise site features at such sites as Gungywamp, Mystery Hill, and Upton but also to the features found subsequently (astronomical alignments, inscriptions, etc.), as well as sites associated with such interests. So, even though they are not megalithic in the purest chronological or architectural sense, you will find in these pages discussions of such sites as the Newport Tower, Manana Island, and Dighton Rock.

And then there are Norse runes. Despite Scandinavian language professor Erik Wahlgren's warning that although several thousand Norse Icelanders lived on Greenland for centuries, only 40 runic inscriptions exist. Iceland has 53 inscriptions, all dated after 1200. Yet, North America has hundreds of alleged inscriptions but no verified long-term habitation.[1] A quick glance at a map demonstrates the point. Norse runes are found in diverse locations such as Minnesota, Arizona, and Oklahoma.

Archaeologist Birgitta Linderoth Wallace finds three main concentrations of claims of Norse artifacts, inscriptions, and sites.[2] New England focuses on eleventh-century voyages to Vinland. At the same time, Midwestern claims are actually post–Viking, based on the fourteenth-century dates needed to legitimize the Kensington Rune Stone. Wallace finds the Canadian Arctic cluster to be the potentially legitimate claims primarily due to their proximity to Greenland.

This book is not a comprehensive list of every site in New England associated with possible pre–Columbian contact with Europe, not just the Norse. A project of such a scope may be well beyond any person's ability to compile. By best estimates, known stone chambers alone exceed 500 in number, many of which have been destroyed by the ravages of weather and land development. Most towns in New England have at least one mysterious carving, stone structure, or odd rock that is identified as Native, Norse, or of some other origin aligning to whichever story fits the local fancy. And there may be more specious stones waiting for the unwary. Professor William H. Worrell of the University of Michigan, while rained-in during a summer vacation on Cape Cod in the 1920s, chiseled an inscription on a stone out of boredom, then buried it in the vicinity.[3] Back at the university, he gleefully admitted the prank but never told anyone where he buried it. The only reason the carving is remembered is a passing mention in the foreword of *Authenticity in Art: The Scientific Detection of Forgery*[4] that Trento noticed and pursued. Trento's article and the book are nearly 50 years old, suggesting the inscription will be forgotten again. So, when a stone is found on Cape Cod in the future, written in Amharic, a Semitic language used in Ethiopia (Worrell's specialty), it will neither be the first nor last hoax to "prove Precolumbian contact."

For this book, I have attempted to pick some of the best-known (or most notorious) sites, as well as a few lesser-known examples. What they have in common, aside from the controversy inherent in this field of study, is some reflective aspect—a stone mirror, if you will—that echoes not only the trends in research at any given point in American history but also the beliefs of the researchers.

In 1967, British archaeologist Jacquetta Hawkes wrote, "Every age has the Stonehenge it deserves—or desires." The same is true in New England—the questions about the original builders, their purposes, and messages may never be resolved to everyone's satisfaction. But as an archaeological Rorschach test, the New England stone sites continue to resonate for the ages.

CHAPTER ONE

Sacrificial Tables

Not every stone in New England with carved symbols is an ancient inscription. Sometimes it is a colonial artifact. However, there are also artifacts attributed to colonial origins that simply do not seem to fit neatly into categories. One such example is the "altar stone" or "sacrificial table."

These tables are large, flat slabs of native stone, with a groove carved on the horizontal surface, ostensibly to channel the flow of liquid. The groove leads to one edge of the stone, where a runnel directs the flow off the stone and theoretically into a container positioned beneath the stone. Although the one on Mystery Hill, North Salem, New Hampshire, is the most well-known, other examples of these oversized slabs exist.

Supporters of pre–Columbian contact with Europe suggest these stones are similar to Neolithic dolmens.[1] More conservative identifications, however, offer more recent possibilities, such as tar kilns, lye stones, and cider presses from the colonial era, which share a design similarity to these sacrificial tables.

Both proponents and opponents of a pre–Columbian origin to these "altar stones" make their identifications based on superficial similarities, not any definitive evidence. Part of the difficulty in determining the origin of these stones lies in a form of cultural amnesia—the colonial artifacts mentioned above were common farm tools of the era, so common that everyone knew their name and function and did not need to document their usage.

University of Lowell (Massachusetts) English professor and amateur archeologist Jay Pendergast was convinced eighth-century Europeans visited the Merrimack River, noting the similarity between keywords in Algonquin and Celtic. This similarity was typical of the time, popularized in the bestselling books of Barry Fell. In a 1982 article in the *Lowell Sun*, Pendergast announced he had found a settlement site on a nearby farm, "proving" his theory.[2] Pendergast poses proudly in a picture for the article with a "mysterious artifact" that he knew wasn't Indian and suspected was proof of his pre-Columbian explorers. Considering the artifact in question is clearly identifiable as a nineteenth-century lye stone, a common farm item used in the soap-making process, Pendergast's avocational archaeology skills might be suspect.

Unless an archaeologist or historian is familiar with the era and the tools, superficial similarities may actually deter proper identification. Carnegie Museum archaeologist James L. Swauger spent twenty years insisting that lye stones and tar burners found in western Pennsylvania and Ohio were Native American petroglyphs before he published an article admitting he was premature in that identification.[3]

Pine Tar Kilns

Pine tar kilns, or "tar burners," were used to extract pitch from pine trees using, as the name suggests, heat. A shallow groove was carved into the surface of a flat slab that matched the diameter of the mouth of a kettle. The kettle was packed full of slivers of pinewood, inverted over the groove, and sealed with clay. A fire was built around the kettle, and the pine resin would liquefy and collect in the groove, which then channeled the liquid into a waiting bucket.[4]

When Russia invaded Sweden as part of the Great Northern War in 1700, England lost Sweden as a primary source of tar for its fleets. England turned to a new source of tar and pitch for the English navy—the American colonies. In 1705, Parliament passed the Bounty Act, offering cash incentives to increase quantities being shipped. Bounties as high as four pounds per ton for tar and pitch and three pounds for rosin or turpentine indicate both the volume and demand for the products. By the end of hostilities in 1721, the American colonies supplied 80 percent of England's tar and pitch.[5]

Aside from the familiar maritime use of pine resin as a waterproofing agent aboard ships, pine tar had a myriad of uses on a farm. From wagon axle lubricant to livestock salves and medicinal use, pine tar was a household staple. Although pine tar processing had been a cottage industry in New England, the large size of the New England stones precludes use in household tar production.[6]

On a commercial scale, draft animals pulled fallen trees and stumps to a pit for burning. Under slow combustion, the resin was drained from the trees into wooden barrels countersunk into the ground adjacent to the pit.[7]

It is doubtful any of the New England stone tables were used as commercial tar kilns. By the time the towns associated with these stones were founded,[8] the tar production industry was located predominantly in the southern colonies, where ample supplies of longleaf pine (*Pinus palustris*) made the production of tar, pitch, and turpentine so efficient that prices had begun to spiral downward.[9] New England's "soft pine," or Eastern White Pine *(Pinus strobes)*, provided a less ample supply of pine resin and was more valuable as masts and spars for the English navy.

Lye Stones

To understand lye stones, one needs to understand soap. The process of creating soap, *saponification*, is the reaction that occurs when a fatty acid meets an alkali. Lye, a strong alkali, splits the fats into two major parts: fatty acids and glycerin. The potassium part of the lye joins with the fatty acid part of the fats. This combination is the potassium salt of the fatty acid—soap.

Two primary ingredients are required to make soap: lye and fat. Lye is created by leaching water through ashes, leaving a solution of potassium hydroxide or caustic potash, better known as lye. The original method of making lye in colonial New England was to place wood ashes in a barrel with drainage in the bottom. The barrel was then placed on a grooved wooden or stone slab. The stone, in turn, rested upon a pile of rocks or some sort of platform. To prevent ashes from seeping into the solution, a layer of straw was placed in the barrel, and the ashes placed on top. The lye was then produced by slowly pouring water over the ashes until the water, now a yellow-brown solution of caustic potash, oozed out from beneath the barrel into the groove around the stone's perimeter and drained into a storage container beneath the lip of the groove. Because of the caustic nature of the lye, wooden buckets or clay pots were used—iron or tin containers would be damaged by corrosion.

Old Sturbridge Village[10] in Massachusetts has several lye stones on public display. One with an 18-inch diameter circle stands outside the Fenno house. Another, with a 36-inch diameter circle carved into its flat surface, is used as a stepping stone outside the law office. A third lye stone is used for soap-making demonstrations outside the Freeman farm barn.[11]

This method was eventually replaced by the use of an ash hopper, which was easier to move and store. An ash hopper was basically a V-shaped wooden bin resting on a frame. The bin was wide at the top for ease in dumping in ashes and providing a larger area to add water. The bin, slanted from back to front, narrowed to a point at the bottom. Along the bottom of the container was a trough to catch the lye. The trough channeled the lye into a bucket.

To render the fat from butchered animals, it was placed in a large kettle. An equal amount of water was added. The kettle was then placed outdoors over an open fire. The foul-smelling mixture of fats and water was boiled until all of the fats had melted. More water was added, and the concoction cooled overnight. By morning, the fats had re-solidified and floated on top of the water. Any impurities would now be on the bottom of the kettle. The rendered fat and the lye solution were combined in a pot outdoors over a fire, and boiled until a thick, frothy mass formed. The process could take up to six to eight hours, depending on the volume of fats and lye and the strength of the lye solution itself.[12]

Commercial soap-making in North American colonies began as early as 1608 with the arrival of several soapmakers on the second ship from England to Jamestown. However, for decades, soap making remained essentially an unpleasant, foul-smelling household chore. This soap, it should be noted, was predominantly used for laundry, not personal cleaning purposes. Advances in chemistry and the growth of manufacturing processes made soap one of America's fastest-growing industries by 1850, but store-bought soap did not really become popular until the 1870s and 1880s, when companies such as Procter & Gamble began to aggressively advertise their mass-produced soap in various women's magazines that had been recently introduced.

The change was swift and dramatic—by the advent of the 20th century, America had changed from a nation of indifferent bathing habits to a nation obsessed with personal hygiene.[13] Lye stones and tar kilns became relics, and ash hoppers were relegated to the back of the barn. Few examples of either survive to this day.

Cider Presses

Cider[14] was a vital component of colonial life, since drinking water was, at best, a questionably safe practice.[15] However, recent studies indicate that individual homes may not have been manufacturing their own cider, as was commonly thought.[16] Based on estate inventories, barely 5 percent of the households owned cider equipment by 1774.[17] "Because the early mills required equipment that operated only once a year, farmers found it more convenient to travel considerable distances to bring their fruit to a large mill for processing into juice (sweet cider). Surplus apples could be sold or bartered to the mill owner, who would produce cider to sell. Farmers returned home and used their own method of fermentation to produce cider."[18]

After the apples were harvested, they were crushed into pomace, either employing a stone wheel in a circular trough or a hand-turned cider mill. When the pomace was adequately pulped, it was brought to the cider press. The pomace was shoveled into wooden frames with layers of straw or into cloth sacks. Additional layers were added, depending on the size and strength of the press.

A board was then lowered onto the layers of pulp, referred to collectively as the cheese. The board forced the juice from the cheese by increasing downward pressure via one or more turnscrews positioned on a frame overhead. The juice pooled on the base of the press and flowed into a groove along the perimeter of the base that directed the juice off the base and into a bucket, where it was moved into wooden casks for fermentation.

Cider presses were massive pieces of equipment. Two extant presses from the time of Jonathan Pattee's residence on Mystery Hill fill the two-story buildings that house them. Each has a massive frame of beams to hold a crossbeam above the base, through which the turnscrews pass that drive the board down into the cheese.

The Lyford-Hutchins cider press, built in Brookfield, New Hampshire, ca. 1835 and dismantled and re-erected at Old Sturbridge Village in 1985, has three turnscrews and a wooden base roughly 4½ feet square. The mill building is slightly larger than average, 26 feet × 39 feet.[19] This press is still used seasonally.

Kingman Tavern Historical Museum in Cummington, Massachusetts, has a ca. 1845 cider mill/press combination salvaged from Monson, Massachusetts. The mill building was custom-made to house the acquisition, and was built into a hillside to allow easy access to the second story. The apples are loaded on the second floor, where a chute directs them through the floor and into the grinder, which drops the pomace onto the base. This mill has two screws and is made entirely of wood, down to the gear teeth and threaded rods.

Sacrificial Table (Mystery Hill), North Salem, New Hampshire

As with all things on this hilltop in southern New Hampshire, this 4½-ton slab of bedrock granite is a lightning rod for controversy. Of the various table stones, the "sacrificial table" is the only one that can be studied in situ. As such, a number of the features associated with the placement help assess the various colonial labels attached to the artifact.

The table's perimeter is pentangular, with a flat edge to the west. Long, parallel sides, which meet a top edge comprised of unevenly angled sides that come to a point, make the stone appear to point eastward. The table rests in a manmade recess created between two stone walls and a stone chamber. The eastern point is incorporated into the western exterior wall of the "Oracle Chamber," the largest structure extant on the site. It rests a few inches below the actual roofline. The immediate area around the remaining three sides is accessible. The space on the eastern side abruptly ends at a two-story stone structure. The western side appears to have been the primary access, with a gradual incline from the surrounding bedrock near the stone. The remaining side has minimal clearance and faces a 4-foot stone wall, the terminus of a large ramp overlooking the southern side of the table, at a level that provides an unencumbered view of the stone.

The table rests on legs raising the slab 30 inches above the ground. The groove is carved more or less 11½ inches parallel from the edge of the stone and leads to a runnel that leads off the western edge. A shallow notch in the bedrock beneath the slab, measuring 10½ inches across, corresponds with the runnel, suggesting an aid for proper placement of some type of container used to collect whatever drained off the top of the slab.

There is a narrow gap in the wall beneath the table, which passes through into the Oracle Chamber. This gap is known as "the speaking tube" to reflect theoretical use in ceremonies using the Sacrificial Table. Sound projected through the tube bounces off the stone constructions, allowing the ability to place the origin of the sound. Thus, the theory goes, a religious ceremony could offer sacrifice and have the deity's voice suddenly speaking all around the table from out of nowhere, reaffirming the cleric's position as the spiritual leader.

The Sacrificial Table slab is located at the geographic center of the site. The bedrock from which the table was pried came from directly beneath the nearby

Sacrificial Table at America's Stonehenge, North Salem, New Hampshire.

astronomical center. The removal spot on the exposed bedrock can be seen beneath the astronomical viewing platform.[20] The symbolism of such a gesture is suggestive—implying that while the calendar was the most sacred aspect of the site, the sacrifice altar was important enough to use stone from that most sacred spot.[21]

Hartford, Connecticut, antiquarian William B. Goodwin coined the name "Sacrificial Table." After initially purchasing the Mystery Hill site in 1937 as the site of Vinland, Goodwin developed a theory that the site was actually the remains of *Hvitramannaland*, or *White Man's Land*, of the Icelandic sagas. Also known as *Irland it Mikla*, or *Great Ireland*, the sagas suggest an Irish settlement predated Vinland. If this were the case, the site would have been built and inhabited by ninth-century Irish Catholic colonists. Goodwin took the identification one step further, identifying the colonists as an order of monks known as *Ceilie De* or the Culdees.[22] Goodwin felt that these ascetic monks practiced a primitive form of Christianity that incorporated pagan rituals in the Christian services as a transition from pagan rites.[23] Based on the grooved table, Goodwin concluded these pagan rites included soothsaying and sacrificial ceremonies.[24] The name has remained for historical reasons (as well as the lack of a better name).

Hugh Hencken, curator of European archaeology at Harvard University's Peabody Museum, published an article in 1939 that picked apart Goodwin's Culdee theory.[25] Hencken made one of the earliest references to the Sacrificial Table being similar to a lye stone, but with the additional observation that the table was much larger in scale. William Goodwin himself provided the information on lye stones, per Hencken's footnotes in the article.[26] Goodwin had an extensive background in early colonial house inventories and would not have misidentified a lye stone.[27]

There are several logistical problems with the theory that the Mystery Hill stone was a lye stone. First and foremost, there is simply no reason to produce lye on a scale that the stone's size suggests. A formula from the time when Jonathan Pattee would have been living on the site calls for one hogshead barrel of ash, producing 15 gallons of lye, which, when added to 29 pounds of clear grease, resulted in 2 barrels (63 gallons) of soft soap.[28] The Sacrificial Table would hold 4 to 6 hogshead barrels simultaneously—enough lye to supply the entire town of North Salem with soap. Moreover, there is no indication in the local history[29] that anyone in the region was attempting to make soap commercially.

Lye stones are traditionally small enough to be moved and stored out of the way when not in use. A 4½ ton stone is not portable by any stretch of the imagination. Additionally, although the table is raised on legs, when William Goodwin began work on the site in the 1930s, the table was thought to be at ground level. Only when Goodwin's crew removed soil and debris from around the slab was it discovered that the table stood in a manmade recess, three feet off the ground. Assuming that one of Jonathan Pattee's ancestors built this table as one of the first things constructed back in the 1730s, there is still insufficient time for three feet of soil to accumulate. Based on other areas of the site, it takes about 125 years for an inch of soil to collect undisturbed on the site.[30] Three feet of soil would suggest that this lye stone had been abandoned for over 4,000 years in the past. This matches the C-14 dates at Mystery Hill but does not support a colonial lye stone theory. If the table were at ground level during the Pattee residence, a bucket could not have been placed beneath the runnel to collect the lye.

Finally, a lye stone already exists on the site. It is found near the foundation of the Pattee homestead, carved into the roof slab of a stone chamber built over by the Pattees. It has a circular groove in the stone, roughly 21 inches in circumference. Instead of a runnel off the edge of the stone, it has a metal-drilled hole through the middle of the circle that passes entirely through the 10-inch thick granite slab, draining into a narrow section of the cellar. It is an unusual design, but not an isolated example—a 1932 article in *Ohio Archaeological and Historical Quarterly* mentions a similarly designed stone.[31]

In 1955, archaeology graduate student Gary Vescelius was hired under the auspices of the Early Sites Foundation, a research organization founded by Goodwin's successor Malcolm Pearson and other interested parties, to investigate the Mystery Hill site and other related sites.

Vescelius and a three-person team completed a six-week series of excavations in the summer of 1955. His only published report was three paragraphs in Eastern States Archeological Federation's *Bulletin*.[32] By comparison, his unpublished report to Early Sites is 60 pages long.[33] He concluded that the site was less than 200 years old.

The report also includes a brief theory that identifies the Oracle Chamber as a storage location for cider barrels and the Sacrificial Table as a cider press base. This identification would not be notable except for the patently absurd continuation of Vescelius' identification, which proposes that the "speaking tube" is actually the path for a pipe from the cider press through several feet of stone walls to the barrels inside the chamber. Aside from the difficulty of maneuvering a wooden pipe through the stone wall and replacing it as needed, the cider would need to flow *uphill* at a fairly steep incline from the collection point to go through the "speaking tube." Although the chamber would make an ideal location for fermenting cider,[34] between the irregular floor surface and varying distance between walls, if it were used for cider cold storage, it was not built for that purpose.

As with the lye stone theory, the stone's original ground level position makes its use as a cider press tentative. Aside from there being no place to position a container to collect the cider, the soil level would interfere with the supporting timbers needed to support the crossbeam that holds the turnscrew(s). Goodwin's excavation of the area did not uncover any indication that soil was deposited to support a framework. Goodwin initially identified the grooved stone as a wine press,[35] later considering it could also be used for soothsaying or animal sacrifice. Goodwin never wholly abandoned the wine press theory, painting a picture of barefoot monks stomping grapes and fermenting wine for use both as sacramental wine and as a way of controlling the Indian converts "through their inherent love of alcoholic strong drink."[36]

Vescelius also states in the report that he is reasonably certain that Pattee had numerous apple trees because Pattee's cousin Richard Pattee had a large apple orchard near his house at the base of the hill. His citation is Gilbert's *History of Salem*, which also plainly shows on an accompanying map that Richard Pattee's house was on the far side of Salem, New Hampshire, on the Methuen, Massachusetts, border, not at the base of the hill.[37] Tax records for Salem indicate that Jonathan Pattee's grandfather Seth, the original owner of the property,[38] owned an acre of orchard land. The tax records do not indicate if the land was actively in use as an orchard or what fruit was being grown. Still, a plot of apple trees is not an unreasonable assumption.

Carole Shammas, in her study of colonial self-sufficiency,[39] estimates that an acre of apple trees would generate 400 bushels of apples, which in turn would render 25 gallons of cider.[40]

Assuming that the Pattee family on Mystery Hill did have an acre of apple trees in production, there was no need to have a cider press on the property. Less than a mile away on Haverhill Road stood the Edmund Adams cider mill, across from the Dow Tavern.[41]

In 2019, the sacrificial table made headlines after being vandalized. On

September 29, it was discovered that overnight, someone had damaged the slab's surface using a grinding tool, carving two lines of text into the stone. The vandal also destroyed one of the piles of rock that served as a support leg with a sledgehammer in an attempt to knock the slab over.[42] The letters across the bottom of the slab were an initialism for a motto of the conspiracist group known as QAnon. QAnon, a predominantly social media construct, was already closely monitored, and the letters were quickly identified. It was almost inevitable that someone would boast about the vandalism. The perpetrator posted a selfie on their Twitter account in front of the table wearing a QAnon shirt and a Donald Trump-branded cap. The second line of text turned out to be his Twitter handle. He was arrested in March 2021[43] and indicted in May on felony charges.[44]

The stone has been uprighted, and the carvings on the surface have been filled and blended. The site has erased evidence of that controversy. The original controversy over the origin and use of the table is still going strong.

Notown Table Stone, Leominster, Massachusetts

In the mid-1970s, the Leominster Bureau of the *Worcester Telegram* reported the disappearance of a large rock from the Notown area of Leominster. The rock was 600 to 900 pounds in weight with a groove around its flat surface. Its disappearance was discovered by a local man named Wallace E. Nash, Jr., who had first seen the stone two years earlier near one of the cellar holes that dot the forest. Nash recognized the stone as similar to the Sacrificial Table at Mystery Hill. Nash had contacted the research staff at North Salem, and at their request, he had returned to photograph the slab, only to discover it was missing.

It would later be discovered that another Leominster resident, Norman Nutting, had also found the stone. Concerned about vandalism or destruction, Nutting simply returned one night with construction equipment and moved the rock to private property.[45]

In 2002, after 30 years of on-and-off discussion, the stone was turned over to the Leominster Historical Society. It sat on the society's front lawn as plans were discussed to return the stone to its original location in the State Forest.[46] The decision was made to leave it on the Historical Society's front lawn.

Despite the uproar about the stone's discovery, disappearance, and reappearance, it was not its first time in the spotlight. The 1946 publication of William B. Goodwin's Culdee monk theory included a vast network of missionary outposts radiating out of his stone village in North Salem. The Notown grooved rock, per Goodwin's theory, was the ceremonial center for an outpost in Leominster.[47] The evidence for this outpost was somewhat scarce, which Goodwin attributed to a combination of the bellicose reaction of the local Indians to conversion attempts and subsequent colonial settlers dismantling the stone buildings that should have stood

Notown Table Stone resting on the front lawn of the Leominster Historical Society in Massachusetts, 2004. Locally it is referred to as a "chutter stone," part of a cider press.

in the area.[48] The primary evidence of this colony was the grooved slab, as well as a nearby small boulder with pictographs,[49] a stone wall leading from the grooved stone on the hilltop to a water supply in the valley below, and the proximity to the Mohican Trail.[50]

The Notown Table Stone is less than 5 feet at its widest point. From flat end to pointed end, the stone is 6 feet long, with irregular perimeter lines reminiscent of the pentangular design prevalent at Mystery Hill. The slab is roughly 11 inches thick, the groove paralleling the edge and continuing off the surface at the point. The surface within the groove is slightly convex and generally uneven. There is weathered evidence of impact dimpling near the center of the slab that is not consistent with cider press use.

The slab was originally located in the Leominster State Forest, a region that has a long history of usage by Native Americans who used local rock ledges for shelter and storage. In the early 1700s, a series of land grants awarded to the heirs of soldiers killed in the French and Indian War became an unincorporated settlement known as Notown, almost all of which is now within the boundaries of the Leominster State Forest. By 1838, Notown had ceased to exist—it was simply too isolated from neighboring communities to thrive. Notown's lands were absorbed into the towns of Leominster, Fitchburg, Westminster, and Princeton, Massachusetts. Today, forgotten cellar holes and stone walls, the Notown Reservoir, and a contested grooved slab are the only legacy of Notown.

Hadley Farm Museum slab, Hadley, Massachusetts. Note the two grooves off the edge of the stone.

Hadley Farm Museum, Hadley, Massachusetts

There are many unconfirmed reports of stone chambers and structures that were lost when the Swift River Valley was flooded to create the Quabbin Reservoir. Made to supply Boston with water, the reservoir flooded out the towns of Prescott, Enfield, Greenwich, and Dana, Massachusetts, as well as parts of seven other local communities.[51]

Hadley has one of the largest of all known sacrificial table stones, 8 feet long and 6½ feet wide. The thickness of the stone varies along the length of the stone, running from 6 to 9 inches. The groove is 2 inches wide and begins with a 90° vertical cut that grades toward the middle. The rectangular slab is made of local sedimentary rock and shows erosion damage and frost spalling on its surface.[52] It has one additional unusual feature not found on the other sacrificial tables—it is the only stone with drainage runnels off two sides, a design feature not found on cider presses, tar burners, or lye stones.

A second stone located in the Connecticut River Valley is now in the collection of Old Sturbridge Village.[53] This stone is also made of sedimentary rock and is almost square (72 inches by 76 inches). This stone slab was donated to the Sturbridge museum in 1963 by a farmer in Pascoag, Rhode Island.

Cider Mill Stone Base, Museum Village, Monroe, New York

In 1950, philanthropist and antique collector Roscoe W. Smith opened his collection of nineteenth-century farm equipment to the public. The Museum Village at Old Smith's Clove in Monroe, New York, included a cider press among the buildings filled with artifacts devoted to yesteryear. The cider mill building was an old local barn that Smith moved to the village specifically to house his cider mill. The cider press itself was purchased in 1938 near Brattleboro, Vermont. Unfortunately, the wooden base of the press had rotted away and would need to be replaced.[54]

Nineteen thirty-eight was the last year Smith could search for farm equipment in central Massachusetts' Swift River Valley; the last of the displaced locals were leaving as the Quabbin Reservoir neared completion. Not much was left standing to sell to contractors and collectors.[55] On his last trip, Smith's queries yielded a farmer who knew of a large stone base[56] in the vicinity. Smith ascertained it was in a cellar hole on property in Pelham owned by the MDWSC.[57] He made arrangements to purchase it for $10, then had the stone hauled out of the watershed area and shipped to Monroe, New York.[58]

After sitting in storage while Smith tracked down several other parts of an apple crusher needed to complete the exhibit, the various components were cobbled together into one cider milling operation as part of the museum. Early postcards from the Museum Village include one of an inaccurate portrayal of the cider mill in use with an elderly gentleman standing on the edge of the stone twisting the wooden screws downward as a lad holds a tin cup to the runnel to collect a drink.[59]

Comparing the designs of all of the tables, the stones can be grouped regionally. The three "Connecticut River Valley style" slabs (Hadley, Sturbridge, Monroe) are rectangular with squared corners, straight edges, and deep grooves indicating metal tools. All three were located initially in heavily agricultural regions, settled post-colonially. The two "Eastern style" table stones (Salem, Leominster) are pentangular with more shallow grooves and less exacting corners and sides. Whether this is indicative of different ages, different functions, or different industries is difficult to estimate since the only stone found in its original position with a clear provenience remains the Mystery Hill stone.

Foxboro Table Stone, Foxboro State Forest, Massachusetts

Goodwin also mentions a table stone in what is now the Foxboro State Forest in southeastern Massachusetts. Although Goodwin treats this Foxboro stone as interchangeable with the Leominster and North Salem stones,[60] this example is not typical of the other table stones. It sits on a bare granite knoll and is low to the ground on small stones, which provide stability rather than height. It is 8'6" × 6'10" but with only one distinct edge, which had been broken off from a larger ledge. The surface is convex and visibly uneven. The groove does not encircle the surface, merely channeling off one edge of the surface and down the side of the stone.[61]

As these stones are some of the most recognized and notorious artifacts associated with megaliths in New England, many theories have arisen, ranging from farm equipment to extraterrestrial communications.[62] Among all of the non-agrarian societal uses assigned to these altar stones, the most prevalent was espoused by Frank Glynn, a well-respected amateur archaeologist and past president of the Archaeological Society of Connecticut. Glynn was conducting research at Mystery Hill to find evidence of a correlation between the New England sites and European Bronze Age cultures. He concluded that when the cultures in Europe were compared to Mystery Hill, the most similarities were found in the megalithic culture on the islands of Malta. Glynn was so convinced of these parallels that when he discovered a grooved slab on legs at the Misrah Sinjura site in Malta, he wrote to Robert Stone at Mystery Hill, triumphantly proclaiming, "We have finally located the 'originals' for Salem's most remarkable feature—the grooved stone sacrificial table."[63]

The table at Misrah Sinjura was first discovered in 1909 and is considered the largest dolmen in Malta. The table is roughly five-sided and is larger than the New England stones, exceeding 14 feet in length and 12 feet in width[64] and supported by legs made of rough limestone blocks. Smaller blocks have been used to fill the space between the support legs, creating walls that made the underside of the roof into a small room where animals were bedded.[65] There is a flat-roofed square hut built on the top of the structure, used ostensibly for a tool shed, but it is significantly more recent than the original construction, thought to date from the first Bronze Age culture of Malta, 2500–1500 BC. The only carving on the site is the groove running around three edges of the monument's surface, which ends at a shallow cup-shaped hole.

Archaeologist James Whittall visited Malta in 1970, looking for comparative features on Maltese megalithic sites as outlined by Frank Glynn.[66] Misrah Sinjura was one of his stops. His opinion was that the Maltese table in general, and the groove in particular, looked like the altar stone at Mystery Hill.[67]

Mount Mineral Petroglyph, Shutesbury, Massachusetts

As theories range from lye kiln and cider press to Neolithic sacrificial rites, there remains one final clue that complicates discussions—a 3-foot rock found in Massachusetts just west of the Quabbin Reservoir.[68]

The rock was found by Henry Towne, who had purchased the lot at a tax sale in 1945. Towne's new property was the site of the Mount Mineral Spring Health Spa that had opened in 1867 to exploit the mineral springs on the north side of the summit. The spa had a history of failure: several fires, several foreclosures, and several owners. The newest owner was inspecting his property, apparently looking for the source of the locally famous mineral springs, when he found the carving.

The 18-inch long carving is a bell-shaped line, similar in outline to the pentangle shape of the altar tables at Mystery Hill and Leominster. Inside the bell outline is the stylized image of a man. Beneath the bell shape is a circular carving, again in a proportion suggesting a bowl where the notch beneath the sacrificial table is. The figure and the bell shape are carved in similar proportions to that of the Mystery Hill sacrificial table with a full-size man lying on it. The resemblance was so striking that it was adopted as the logo of the New England Antiquities Research Association.[69] It does not prove that the altar slabs were worthy of the sacrificial table name. It remains a tantalizing reminder that some artifacts refuse to be neatly categorized.

Mount Mineral Petroglyph, Shutesbury, Massachusetts. Carvings to the left are modern graffiti.

CHAPTER TWO

Vineland on the Charles

Ambassador Henry Wheaton used his time as *chargé d'affaires* in Denmark (1827–1835) to research the *History of the Northmen*.[1] His 1831 book claimed America had been discovered by the Norse before the voyage of Columbus. Wheaton, internationally known for his work on international law,[2] found himself in Denmark during what Oscar Falnes would later call a renaissance in Scandinavian studies.[3] Among his contacts was a Danish scholar named Carl Christian Rafn.

Rafn was preparing a publication that reproduced and translated all the Icelandic manuscripts that pertained to the Norse discovery of North America. In association with that work, he wrote to various historical societies and athenaeums requesting information on Norse ruins in North America. Rafn did not visit any of the sites he compiled from the North American groups, relying on the skills and integrity of the American scholars. Although the Norse origin of the various stone structures and carvings had been discussed elsewhere, this was the first time the awareness of the possibility had been raised to such scholarly heights.

Antiquitates Americanae[4] was published in Copenhagen in 1837 and was an immediate success. For the first time, all the Icelandic sagas were gathered in one source, with the text in Old Icelandic, Modern Danish, and Latin. It also included a section on the North American monuments and an English summary of Rafn's conclusions regarding Vinland being in New England.

Professor Rafn considered the sagas a legitimate record of a voyage of exploration to North America, supported by physical evidence of three types: structural remains, inscriptions, and place names.

Suddenly, every petroglyph, misplaced boulder, and stone structure in New England was a Norse relict. References to Norse visitations began to creep into old Yankee town histories. As one example, the 1861 *History of Haverhill, Massachusetts*[5] does not start with the city's settlement in 1640. The first chapter starts with Bjarni Herjolfsson and Leif Eriksson. It is not until the fifth chapter that Haverhill is settled, after discussions of other European explorers of New England, both before and after Columbus, as well as Pilgrims, Puritans, and local native tribes.

J. M. Mancini of University College Cork suggests that such wide mainstream acceptance of the theoretical Norse discovery of New England was a reaction by the "Anglo-Saxon elite" to the increased presence and growing political power of recent immigrants, such as the Irish, Italians, and Jews.[6] By having colonized New England 500 years before the Italian Columbus, the Vinland saga reaffirmed the social superiority of the blue-blooded families. Janet Headley of Loyola College[7] and Robin Fleming of Boston College[8] concur, noting that through Leif Eriksson, the proper Bostonians could "take back the discovery of America from a Catholic Mediterranean people and appropriate it for their imagined ancestors."[9]

Some of the writers of the time were less subtle in their endorsement, such as Marie Shipley, who triumphantly published an "exposé of the plot" to keep the Icelandic discovery of America under wraps by a pro–Columbus (i.e., Catholic) conspiracy.[10]

A replica of a Viking ship sailed from Norway to New York via Newfoundland. It was then brought to the Chicago World's Fair in 1893, which was also a commemoration of the 400th anniversary of Columbus' journey. Whether the Norse ship was there as a participant or a protest depends on which source is being read.

The Skeleton in Armor, Fall River, Massachusetts

The skeleton was found in 1832 in a gravel bank. It was near the surface, in a sitting position, wrapped in several layers of woven bark. On the chest of the remains was a metal plate, 13 inches long and roughly triangular. The chest plate appeared to have been cast, and from ⅛- to 3/32-inch in thickness. There was significant corrosion damage that prevented observers from determining any carvings on the face of the plate. Encircling the body was a belt of thin metal tubes, 4½ inches long and 3/16-inch in diameter. Near the body was a bark quiver of arrows. The arrowheads were metal, thin, flat, and triangular, with a round hole cut through near the base for attaching the head to the shaft. The immediate assumption by the press, given the metal objects and Fall River's proximity to the Dighton Rock and the Newport Tower, was that the skeleton was of a pre–Columbian explorer, buried in his bronze armor.[11]

Local historians were not convinced. Dr. Phineas W. Leland[12] pointed out that the arrangement of the corpse for burial was standard among the local natives and that parts of other skeletons were found in the general area.

There is additional historical and archaeological support for the remains being that of a proto-historic period Indian, such as John Brereton's record of Bartholomew Gosnold's voyage to the coast of New England in the spring of 1602.[13] During a trading stop on Cuttyhunk Island, southwest of Cape Cod, Gosnold's crew met a tribe of friendly natives who helped them gather a cargo of sassafras, which was in great demand in England for its medicinal value.[14] The 16-page narrative noted that these natives had a large quantity of copper that they used to decorate themselves and tip their arrows, specifically mentioning cups, earrings, breastplates, and bandoleers of copper tubes. On his voyage of 1524, Giovanni da Verrazzano also recorded[15] extensive copper use among the American Indians of present-day Rhode Island: "Both men and women have various trinkets hanging from their ears as the Orientals do; and we saw that they had many sheets of worked copper which they prize more than gold."[16]

The "bandoleer of copper tubes" matches the description of what is commonly known as "tinkling cones," named after the noise made when they strike each other. Made by rolling sheet metal into a cone, tinkling cones have been found in burials dating from the 1500s to the late 1600s.[17]

Interest in the press faded quickly, and the skeleton, reduced more or less to a local curiosity, was displayed in the local athenaeum. That might have been the end of the story except for Henry Wadsworth Longfellow.

Longfellow, the most popular American poet of the time, had been in Europe studying Scandinavian languages and literature, including the Norse sagas, and returned in 1835. During the trip, he had taken lessons in Icelandic from Carl Christian Rafn and was made a member of Denmark's Royal Society of Northern Antiquaries.[18] By the time Rafn's book came out in 1837, Longfellow was already considering a series of ballads about the Norse explorations of New England.

In 1838, Longfellow summered in Newport, Rhode Island, with field trips to both the Newport Tower and the Fall River skeleton. The end result, first published in 1841,[19] was the poem "The Skeleton in Armor." Longfellow's note on the creation of the work[20] credits the Newport Tower and the Fall River skeleton as inspiration, firmly attaching Viking origins to both as well as to Longfellow himself—when the Longfellow Bridge connecting Boston to Cambridge opened in 1906, the main piers had the carving of Viking prows on the waterline.

Longfellow has the ghost of the skeleton tell the tale of his own demise. He was a Viking who loved the daughter of King Hildebrand. When they were refused permission to marry, the lovers slipped away to the Viking's boat to escape across the sea. King Hildebrand pursued with his guards. The king's ship was faster, but the Viking swung his ship around and rammed Hildebrand's vessel, sinking it and drowning all aboard. The Viking and his maiden arrived in Narragansett Bay, where the Viking built the Newport Tower as her bower. After many years, the princess died and was buried beneath the tower. The grieving Viking dressed in his bronze armor and fell upon his spear, ending the tale of the skeleton in armor.

In short time, the skeleton was appearing in print as definitive proof of Viking explorations, including writings by such authors as Rasmus B. Anderson,[21] founder of the Department of Scandinavian Studies at the University of Wisconsin.

Part of the reason the skeleton could be so easily assimilated into a Norse identity was the lack of evidence. The atheneum and its displays were destroyed in Fall River's Great Fire of 1843. The assumption was that all the armor had been incinerated in the same fire that destroyed the body. With no evidence to test, nothing could be confirmed or refuted.

That assumption was wrong. Dr. Jerome Van Crowninshield Smith, a well-known physician from Boston and a former professor of anatomy and physiology, had reviewed the skeleton. He identified the remains as a male native, but not a "powerful one," possibly of mixed heritage.[22] Whether the parentage of the body included an early colonist or a Norseman, Smith could not ascertain. Instead, he made arrangements for samples of the brass to be shipped to the Ethnographical Museum of Copenhagen for study, apparently assuming that a Scandinavian museum would easily discern whether or not the armor was Nordic in origin. The metal was analyzed and found to be brass, not bronze, as was conventionally thought.[23] This made the plate and bandoleer unquestionably European in origin, probably from a brass kettle obtained in exchange with an early trader.

In 1965, during a Pemaquid, Maine, excavation, archaeologist Helen Camp uncovered the remains of a female native, buried with metal decorations similar to the Fall River skeleton.[24] It was not the first such find—Warren K. Moorehead reported in 1922 that a copper-clad corpse had been found in the Penobscot Bay town of Sedgewick (about 100 miles north of Pemaquid). An analysis of the copper proved it to be European.[25] A later article by Moorehead includes an account by Captain A.W. McFarland, who said a body was discovered in a shell midden at Robinson Cove (two miles south of Pemaquid) around 1854 that had so many pieces of metal nearby that it was assumed to be armor. Moorehead goes on to say that as of the article's writing in 1924, the location of that body was unknown.

Archaeologists refer to the reuse of a kettle in the burial process as the "Copper Kettle Burial Tradition." Dating from the 1500s to the late 1600s, this tradition seems to primarily be of the proto-historic period Mi'kmaq tribes, who were heavily involved in the fur trade. Not surprisingly, many of these burials have come to light in Canada's Maritime Provinces.[26]

Although the skeleton was destroyed in 1843, the notoriety Longfellow gave it enabled the skeleton to live past its destruction. If the local Indian tribe had buried their companion with garb and supplies needed for a continued existence in an afterlife, they succeeded beyond their wildest expectations.

Leif Eriksson Statue, Boston, Massachusetts

In 1872, Rasmus Anderson arranged for the renowned Norwegian violin virtuoso Ole Bull to give a concert at Wisconsin's state capital in 1872. The proceeds from the performance allowed Anderson to purchase the first collection of books for his newly-formed Department of Scandinavian Studies at the University of Wisconsin. Anderson was completing his first book on the Norse discovery of America, in which he theorized that Columbus had sailed to Iceland in 1477, learned of Eriksson's discovery, and stolen credit for the discovery when he was merely retracing Leif's route. As was the norm at the time, Anderson believed this erroneous elevation of Columbus was endorsed and encouraged by papal authorities to promote Catholicism.

Anderson would recall in later books[27] how he mentioned that Leif Eriksson ought to be honored with a monument and that Bull was inspired by the suggestion and tried to bring it to fruition.[28] Anderson and Bull also felt that a statue on the campus of the University of Wisconsin would help the college become "the chief center of Scandinavian study in the United States. It would help make Madison the Mecca of Norwegiandom in America."[29]

Unfortunately, the fund drive goal of $25,000 was short by $22,000. Other than the $1000 each pledged by Bull, Anderson, and John A. Johnson, a wealthy Madison manufacturer and the third member of the committee formed to facilitate the statue, no contributions were received, even after coverage of the project in numerous Norwegian-American papers. Anderson, in his autobiography, would recount how Ole Bull was both humiliated and angry by the Norwegian-American community's lack of interest.

Carte de Visite of Ole Bull, ca. 1870.

Bull decided to do the fundraising himself. With Anderson's help, Bull embarked on a series of concerts to fund the monument fund. When Bull returned to Norway the following year, Anderson accompanied him, and the performances continued in that country. Money was raised, but not enough to commission a statue. The project stalled as the three men pursued other more pressing matters.

In 1876 Bull returned for his annual winter visit to the United States, residing in the Cambridge, Massachusetts, home of the poet James Russell Lowell. Bull was a frequent visitor with his friend and neighbor, Henry Wadsworth Longfellow. Longfellow had based "The Musician" in *Tales of a Wayside Inn* on Bull.[30] Bull and

Longfellow were not just friends; they were remotely related by marriage. Joseph Thorp, Jr., had married Longfellow's daughter, Anne. Thorp's sister, Sara, had married Ole Bull.[31] The stalled plan for erecting a statue was discussed one night by Bull, Longfellow, and Longfellow's brother-in-law, author and noted patron of the arts, Thomas Gold Appleton. The three decided on a course of action.

A reception for Ole Bull was held at the Boston Music Hall. Edward Everett Hale introduced Ole Bull and noted that Bull had "spent almost the whole of his active life in knitting those ties which connected his country with ours and that he hoped that there might be erected a physical memorial to the early Norse discoverers of this country."[32]

Bostonians answered the call. The Scandinavian Memorial Association of Boston became a veritable who's who in Bostonian society. Chaired by Appleton, the committee's distinguished members included Longfellow, James Russell Lowell, Oliver Wendell Holmes, Eben Norton Horsford, Harvard president Charles Eliot, publisher James Fields, Massachusetts Governor Alexander H. Rice, the mayors of Boston and Cambridge—over fifty prominent Bostonians, as well as Ole Bull and Rasmus Anderson.

Early in 1877, encouraged by the support of the Bostonians, Ole Bull made contact with Anne Whitney, a local sculptress with a growing reputation, and some notoriety from an 1875 competition to design a statue of Senator Charles Sumner. Whitney had won the national competition, but the commission was given to a male competitor because the judges thought it inappropriate for a woman to be sculpting a man's legs.[33, 34]

Meanwhile, Appleton, as the committee chairman, contacted John Quincy Adams Ward of New York, one of the most famous sculptors in America.[35] Appleton convinced Ward that although funding was not in place, it would be easy to raise funds once a model of the statue was available. By December, Appleton was advising Ward that the money was still not confirmed but that the committee (or at least Appleton) knew precisely what they wanted in a statue of Leif—a burly Norseman, draped in bearskin, depicting the moment Leif stepped foot in Vinland.[36] Appleton also sent Ward a copy of his book of poems, which coincidentally happened to have an image on the cover nearly identical to the statue's description.[37]

Appleton, through Boston mayor Edward Price, learned of a $30,000 stipend available for city beautification projects and was able to convince the Postmaster to approve another $10,000 for the proposed statue, which would stand in Post Office Square, newly built after the Great Boston Fire of 1872. Opposition from the Massachusetts Historical Society, which had previously suggested that the country be renamed Columbia in honor of Columbus,[38] stalled the project. A second location in front of the Museum of Fine Arts was also contested.[39] The statue would eventually be relegated to Commonwealth Avenue in a location that Richard John notes was then the city's "western fringe."[40]

The inability to use the $40,000 stipend quickly evolved in the press from a possible funding source to the city's refusal of an outright gift of the money from Appleton himself. This inaccurate version would be played out repeatedly in the press when the statue was finally unveiled[41] and long after.[42]

The statue continued to be delayed by opposition from various sources, such as the Massachusetts Historical Society[43] and Henry Cabot Lodge, who had recently ended a scathing review of Anderson's book[44] by suggesting it was merely propaganda for the statue's fundraising.[45] The death of Ole Bull in 1880 further slowed the project. Appleton finally wrote to Ward in 1881 and advised him to stop work on the project until the funds were actually secured.[46] Longfellow's death in 1882 and Appleton's in 1884 brought the project to another halt. Ward eventually finished the model on his own. Ward's *Leif the Norseman*, a 28-inch bronzed plaster maquette of the intended statue, exists in the collection of the American Academy of Arts and Letters, New York.[47]

As the project languished once again, Eben Horsford took command of the committee. Eben Norton Horsford (1818–1893) was a chemist who held Harvard's Rumford Chair of the Application of Science to the Useful Arts. An expert in food chemistry with a particular interest in bread,[48] Horsford patented a new formula for baking powder[49] in 1859, which he marketed through his company, Rumford Chemical Works. Between the success of the new baking powder and several other products, such as "Horsford's Self-Raising Bread Preparation" and "Horsford's Acid Phosphate" (a tonic for "tired brain, physical exhaustion, nervousness, indigestion, etc. etc."), Horsford found himself a man of sufficient means to leave his university position.

A neighbor of Longfellow's in Cambridge, Horsford met Ole Bull at the poet's house[50] and became interested in Rafn's proposed location of Vinland in Massachusetts Bay. He first looked at the issue of John Cabot's explorations and the debate whether he had first made landfall in Newfoundland or Labrador in 1497. Horsford concluded that Cabot's landfall was not in either location. Based on his interpretation of cartographic evidence and explorer reports, Horsford declared Cabot's landfall was actually near Salem, Massachusetts, on Cape Ann, which was also the site of the fabled lost city of Norumbega.[51]

Horsford decided to underwrite the statue and assure that Ole Bull's vision of a Leif monument would see fruition. One of Horsford's other projects was his endowments to Wellesley College.[52] Horsford and his family were on the board of trustees of the fledgling college and frequent and generous contributors of time, money, and support. These two projects came together in the guise of the new sculptor Horsford selected to create Leif's visage in bronze—Anne Whitney.

It is unknown how Eben Horsford first met Anne Whitney. It may have been that he wished to follow Bull's original plan instead of Appleton's, or it may have been his way of supporting the women's equality movement. The suggestion has also been made that it was simply that Whitney's fee was less than Ward's.[53] Whitney would also sculpt busts of Horsford in 1890 and Wellesley president Alice Palmer in 1892, both underwritten by Horsford and still among the Whitney pieces in the collections of Wellesley College. Whitney would later become an art instructor at Wellesley as well.

The statue was made in 1886 and unveiled on October 29, 1887. With Ole Bull's widow in the audience, Horsford was the keynote speaker at the ceremony at Faneuil Hall. It was his opportunity to review the facts and reaffirm the accuracy of the sagas. After discussing the similarities in American Indian place names and the Norse equivalents, he announced the name Norumbega obviously must be a Native American corruption of *Norvège,* the name of the country Norway in Old Norse.[54, 55] Therefore, Horsford decided, the legendary lost city of Norumbega and Vinland were one and the same. Horsford gave credit to Longfellow and Appleton and concluded that the statue was a fitting memorial to Ole Bull, who had first envisioned it.[56]

The nod to Appleton was appropriate but ironic—the Whitney statue had nothing in common with the version Appleton directed Ward to create. Where Appleton had wanted a burly warrior garbed in animal skins, Whitney's figure was a youthful, lithe explorer, a "delicate young man whose jaunty pose is reminiscent of Andrea del Verrocchio's *David,* but whose focused gaze recalls that of Michelangelo's Renaissance giant."[57] This Leif stands and scans the horizon with a hand blocking the sun.[58] He wears a short chain mail tunic, with a sheathed dagger on his belt over a cloth tunic that ends mid-thigh. Art historian Eleanor Tufts suggests that the comparatively short tunic was Whitney's response to the previous rift over the Sumner statue.[59]

The statue stands on a pedestal base with bas-reliefs on opposite sides, one showing Leif on a mountaintop in the same pose as the statue. The other bas-relief shows Leif in a great hall, telling his tale of the discovery. The front of the base has a runic inscription composed by Anderson that translates as "*Leif the Lucky, Son of Erik.*" The back panel reads in English, "Leif, the discoverer, son of Erik, who sailed from Iceland and landed on this continent, A.D. 1000." A dragon-head prow of a Norse longship extends from the base.[60] The statue rests in a basin that once served as a fountain but is now used as a flower planter.

Out in Wisconsin, Rasmus Anderson was not impressed with the new look for Leif, expecting "a long bearded and shaggy haired Norseman of the tenth century." Anderson's thought was that Whitney had "taken the splendid physique and features of Ole Bull for her model."[61]

Although the statue was raised in Boston, not on the University of Wisconsin campus as Bull and Anderson had originally planned, a second casting did end up in Milwaukee. Lucy Allis Gilbert, the widow of Joseph T. Gilbert, a family friend of Ole Bull, commissioned the statue in 1887.[62] This version of *Leif the Discoverer* still stands in Milwaukee's Juneau Park, fully restored in 1996, and illumination added in 2001.[63]

In 1893, the original plaster version of the statue was modified, bronzed, and sent to the Chicago World's Fair at the request of Mrs. Potter Palmer, the queen of Chicago high society and a patron of the arts. Bertha Palmer was also the president of the Board of Lady Managers of the Chicago World's Fair and Columbian Exposition. She secured a separate Woman's Building for works by and about women from all over the world. Anne Whitney's Leif Eriksson statue[64] stood in the Italian Renaissance–style building near such items as a manuscript of *Jane Eyre* in Bronte's handwriting and murals by Mary Cassatt.[65] After the exposition, this version of the statue was sent to the Smithsonian for exhibit. After years hidden away in storage at the Smithsonian's American Art Museum, it is now part of the permanent collection of the National Museum of Women.

Whether Anne Whitney considered her statue an anti-immigrant tribute to colonial Protestants or an actual commemoration of Leif's claimed landfall in Cambridge is not found among her archived correspondence at Wellesley College. What is known is that, like Eben Horsford, Whitney was politically active in support of women's equality and suffrage. Her rendering of Leif Eriksson may not be a memorial to his actual landfall, but it is a memorial of the march toward women's equality.

Leif Eriksson statue by Anne Whitney, along Commonwealth Ave. in Boston, Massachusetts (Terry Deveau photograph).

Norumbega Tower, Weston, Massachusetts

Although the press and the audience at the unveiling of Anne Whitney's Leif Eriksson statue devoured Eben Horsford's announcement that Vinland was

Norumbega and both were along the Charles River, the revelation was not so widely accepted by historians.

When historian Justin Winsor published his *Narrative and Critical History of America*,[66] he had no difficulty accepting claims of pre-Columbian exploration in America by various Europeans, admitting "there is no good reason why any one of them may not have done all that is claimed."[67] However, Winsor's opinion of Horsford's claims was less accepting, referring to Horsford's work as "most incautious linguistic inferences and the most uncritical cartographical perversions."[68]

Horsford's theories on Vinland would be relegated to the same obscurity as so many other Vinland locations, except for one difference: Professor Eben Norton Horsford had the money to make his work more prevalent. Not only did he publish lavishly oversized books on his theories,[69, 70, 71, 72] he built the monuments that he felt his discoveries obviously deserved. His response to Winsor was to publish a rebuttal.

Horsford, whose father served as a missionary among the Seneca Indians for several also considered himself somewhat of an American Indian language expert because of his father's work.[73] Among his sources, Horsford used the account of David Ingram, an English sailor who claimed to have visited visit Norumbega in the 1560s,[74] and a 1575 map by Franciscan priest André Thevet[75] as evidence of Norumbega's location. Both these sources seemed to indicate that Norumbega was not in Maine as was generally believed, but near Boston, specifically in the same area where Horsford believed Vinland to be located. Unfortunately for Horsford, his choice of source material was questionable.

Ingram was an English sailor who was put ashore on the Gulf Coast of Florida in 1567. Ingram followed Indian trails northward, arriving in New Brunswick several years later. He was able to hail a French ship and return to Europe, where his story was written down. Historian Samuel Eliot Morison's study of early voyages to America[76] notes the travels of Ingram with a grain of salt,[77] pointing out that the illiterate sailor had been making a living retelling his story for a decade before it was recorded, ample time to "embroider the tale" as needed to keep it marketable.

André Thevet's visit to Brazil is well-documented and considered a good account of a French colony in Brazil ca. 1555. Thevet's visit to New England is, at best, suspect.[78] His previous work does not mention the visit to New England even though it would have occurred on the same trip, and his conversations with the natives of Norumbega appear to be constructed from word lists compiled by Jacques Cartier.[79]

The Rev. B.F. DeCosta translated Thevet's account in the *Magazine of American History*.[80] DeCosta had previously published one of the earliest English translations of the Icelandic sagas in a book that he also used to promote his theory that Vinland was in Rhode Island.[81] Considered an expert on the Vinland and Norumbega historical material, DeCosta politely refers to Thevet as "fraudulent" and "mendacious" and casts serious doubts on any possibility that Thevet had actually visited the area, offering evidence that Thevet had plagiarized accounts from other explorers. DeCosta also has little use for Ingram in his studies of Norumbega,[82] reminding his readers that Ingram and other early explorers were "reckless in their descriptions and beliefs."[83]

Not heeding cautionary opinions on his source materials, Horsford conducted small excavations near his home in Cambridge in an attempt to locate Leif Eriksson's winter quarters. A convenient three blocks from his own home in Cambridge, Horsford found house foundations. The artifacts associated with the cellar holes were from the Colonial period, so Horsford assumed the artifacts were added to the Viking site in subsequent years. After several noted scholars, including DeCosta, refuted his results, Horsford published an additional defense of his Norumbega theory, devoting pages to justifying his use of Thevet and Ingram as sources, a significant point of the dispute.[84]

Undaunted by critics and inspired by his archaeological results, Horsford explored further up the Charles River. At the mouth of Stony Brook, separating the towns of Waltham and Weston, he found a bluff that provided a commanding view of the area and strategic proximity to the river. An excavation immediately found an extensive collection of loose stones and possible stonework. Horsford had (at least according to Horsford) found the site of Norumbega's fort and the city it once guarded.

By this point, Horsford's theory had evolved exponentially in scope: Norumbega was now a vast area, with multiple settlements totaling nearly 10,000 people, and a capital city of the same name along the Charles River. Ancient stone dams, canals, and wharves were found along the Charles and interpreted as Norse in origin, built to support a burgeoning *mösurr* or mazer wood[85] industry that spanned three centuries.

After he announced that he had found Leif's camp, Horsford had a granite plaque placed near the spot. Although moved a couple of times over the years, that plaque can still be found near its original location, along the sidewalk on the property of Mount Auburn Hospital.[86]

Another plaque was placed on the parapet of a stone bridge between Watertown and Newton.[87] It overlooked an ancient stone dam, which Horsford believed pre-dated the colonists in the area. It was supposedly used to collect the mösurr wood that was floated downriver from the various outposts. The juxtaposition of Horsford's dubious claim with a venerated colonial landmark, which also had a tablet commemorating the bridge as the site of the first bridge across the Charles River in 1641, was not well received in historical or archaeological circles.[88]

However, Horsford's coup de grace was where Stony Creek emptied into the Charles River. Where he alleged the site of Norumbega's fort was located, Horsford had a tower erected. The 35-foot tower was made of local fieldstones with a spiral stairway in dressed granite leading to the top, opening on an unobstructed view of the Charles River from 110 feet above sea level. A marker resembling a cornerstone was mounted on a stone wall extending from the left side of the tower. There, Horsford acknowledged his involvement. It is subtle and apart from the tower to avoid distracting from a massive bronze tablet embedded in the wall off the structure. Towering over 6 feet high, this marker sums up Horsford's theories far more efficiently than Horsford ever did in his books.

> A.D. 1000–A.D. 1889
> NORUMBEGA
>
> CITY • COUNTRY • FORT • RIVER
> NORUMBEGA = NOR MBEGA
> INDIAN UTTERANCE OF NORBEGA THE ANCIENT FORM
> OF NORVEGA • NORWAY • TO WHICH THE
> REGION OF VINLAND WAS SUBJECT
>
> CITY
> AT, AND NEAR WATERTOWN
> WHERE REMAIN TO-DAY
> DOCKS • WHARVES • WALLS • DAMS • BASINS •
>
> COUNTRY
> EXTENDING FROM RHODE ISLAND TO THE ST. LAWRENCE
> FIRST SEEN BY BJARNI HERJULFSON 985 A.D.
> LANDFALL OF LEIF ERIKSON ON CAPE COD 1000 A.D.
> NORSE CANALS • DAMS • WALLS • PAVEMENTS •
> FORTS • TERRACED PLACES OF ASSEMBLY REMAIN TO-DAY
>
> FORT
> AT BASE OF TOWER AND REGION ABOUT
> WAS OCCUPIED BY THE BRETON FRENCH IN THE
> 15TH 16TH AND 17TH CENTURIES
>
> RIVER
> THE CHARLES
> DISCOVERED BY LEIF ERIKSON • 1000 A.D.
> EXPLORED BY THORWALD LEIF'S BROTHER • 1003 A.D.
> COLONIZED BY THORFINN KARLSEFNI • 1007 A.D.
> FIRST BISHOP ERIK GNUPSON • 1121 A.D.
>
> INDUSTRIES FOR 350 YEARS
>
> MASUR • WOOD [BURRS] • FISH • FURS • AGRICULTURE •
>
> LATEST NORSE SHIP RETURNED TO ICELAND IN 1347.

Horsford received support from the media and the American Geographical Society, which published most of his work.[89] With such support, combined with the reaction to vitriolic attacks by Winsor and the Massachusetts Historical Society, Horsford's reputation continued to grow.[90]

Horsford's death in 1893 did not stop the popularity of his theories. Tour guides were regularly directing tourists to his sites.[91] Horsford's theories never produced artifacts. Had Winsor, DeCosta, and other scholars simply ignored his work instead of debunking it, Horsford probably would have stopped publishing after his first book on the topic. Instead, he continued, producing the additional volumes defending his work that perpetuated his theory and built the tower that outlived both Horsford and his opponents.

The "Fort Nurumbega" tower is now part of Weston's Norumbega Tower Park.[92] The stairway to the top of the tower has been blocked by an iron gate for safety reasons, and surrounding trees now partially camouflage the structure. More people come to the park to feed the ducks than to reflect on the permanent reminder of a temporary theory of Vikings sailing up the Charles.

The Weston Stone, Weston, Massachusetts

Eben Horsford's youngest daughter, Cornelia, continued his work and expanded his search area. She also began using her position in Boston high society to bring experts in to examine her father's (and her) discoveries, such as Gerard Fowke, an archaeologist with the Smithsonian Bureau of American Ethnology. Fowke visited the locations and concluded they were neither colonial nor American Indian.[93] His only concern was the lack of artifacts.[94] Fowke, as with other academics brought to the location, were being wisely noncommittal; they still relied on decidedly anti–Norse in New England sources for funding fieldwork.

Norumbega Tower, erected in 1889 by Eben Horsford (photograph by and courtesy J.W. Ocker).

Valtýr Guðmundsson, the father of Icelandic archaeology, agreed to supervise a survey of Norse sites in Iceland for Cornelia, who was working under the assumption that if she could prove the location of Erik the Red's home, it would support the possibility of the voyage to North America.[95]

In a story that reads more humorously than Cornelia probably intended, she chronicles how she was out for a Sunday ride in 1893 with her half-sister, Gertrude Fiske. On the outskirts of Weston, they passed a pile of stones a farmer had brought from his back fields to build new gateposts. Cornelia had picked up a belief from her father that the Norse used large flat rocks for runic messages. To her much more society-conscious sister's horror, she stopped the carriage and began digging in the rock pile. This time, she found a slab with deep cuts. Cornelia Horsford had discovered her first rune stone. She returned the next day and offered to buy the stone. The farmer refused; the stone was the perfect size for his gatepost project.

Cornelia returned to Cambridge and wrote her sister. Gertrude was coerced into returning to the farmer and trying to obtain the stone again. Poor Gertrude finally went traipsing through the farmer's fields to find a stone of similar size and shape as a replacement.[96]

Cornelia was elated. Because of the way the stone weathered, Cornelia concluded the stone had been placed in the ground upright, with the inscribed portion showing as a signpost, and then slowly sank vertically into the soil over time.[97]

A few weeks after the Weston Stone arrived in Cambridge, Cornelia saw a report of a rune stone recently found in New York City. Alexander C. Chenoweth, a civil engineer by trade, was an amateur archaeologist who had been hunting Native artifacts on the upper part of Manhattan Island. He came across a series of caves near Inwood Hill that contained Native artifacts and a stone that Chenoweth believed had runes on the edge.[98]

Cornelia sent a drawing of her new runestone to Chenoweth. He sent a photograph of the "Inwood Stone" to her in return. As soon as the weather improved in 1894, she went to see the Inwood Stone for herself. She agreed that both stones were Norse but were carved at different periods in the Northmen's occupation of the East Coast.[99]

Although some of the markings were too weathered to read, Horsford was able to decipher the words. With a bit of help from Rafn's work, she filled in the blanks and decided the phrase was "K[irkju]ss [ynir] akta" or "Sons of the Church tax," a record of a census among the Norse settlers.[100] Oddly, she never translates the Weston Stone. By the end of the year, Chenoweth had donated the stone with his Native artifacts to the American Museum of Natural History.[101]

Cornelia continued on. In addition to arranging for academic examination of the stone and her excavations, she published additional books[102] and articles in such high profile periodicals as *National Geographic*[103] and *Popular Science Monthly*.[104] Without physical proof, the public quickly lost interest. By this time, so had Cornelia.

Today, the Weston Stone is part of the landscape at Sylvester Manor, Cornelia Horsford's former residence on Long Island (Donnamarie Barnes/Sylvester Manor).

By 1900, Cornelia had moved on from searching for Norse evidence. By now, her father had been dead for seven years. Brian Regal of Kean University suspects that Cornelia, who had promised her father on his deathbed that she'd continue his quest to prove his theory, simply had moved on from mourning him.[105] Cornelia had moved to Sylvester Manor, her mother's ancestral family estate on Shelter Island, New York. She would spend the next 40 years expanding and renovating Sylvester Manor and leading local civic improvements such as creating a public library and a historical society.[106] But some habits die hard.

In 2006, Sylvester Manor became the 243-acre historic plantation and nonprofit Sylvester Manor Educational Farm.[107] Now open to the public, Sylvester Manor prominently features Eben and Cornelia Horsford. There is no mention of their search for the Norse in the Charles River Valley, but it exists on the property. On the side lawn of the Manor sits the Weston Stone. It sits upright, precisely as she had envisioned its original use as a runic signpost. It is covered in lichen and shows minor damage from frost spalls. The family knew the stone was there, but in the 80 years since Cornelia died, their memory grew less specific as the decades passed.

Today, Sylvester Manor knows the stone as a monument to the Norse studies of Eben Horsford and his daughter. Whether it is a rune stone or not, it is a fitting tribute to the devotion of the father and daughter to their research and each other.

Chapter Three

Dighton Rock

For over 350 years, controversy has reigned over the origins of markings on a 40-ton glacial erratic boulder that rested in the tidal waters of the Taunton River. Covered with petroglyphs and graffiti, the Dighton Rock now rests in a small protective building with an adjacent museum.

The Dighton Rock, at one time considered "the most famous object of archaeological interest in America,"[1] is located on the eastern bank of the Taunton River in Berkley, Massachusetts, on the opposite shore from Dighton. Originally part of Dighton, Berkley was incorporated in 1735. The town was named for theologian, philosopher, and scientist George Berkeley, who had visited the Dighton Rock during a stay in Newport, Rhode Island.[2] He had come to Newport in 1729 to await the arrival of funds to create a seminary in Bermuda. When it became evident the funds were not coming, he returned to London in October 1731. Berkeley was made Bishop of the Diocese of Cloyne, Ireland, in 1734. The following year, the town of Berkley was incorporated from Dighton and was named after the Bishop.[3] The territory of Assonet Neck, where the Dighton Rock rests, was annexed to the town of Berkley in 1799.[4] By that time, the Dighton Rock moniker had already been attached to the artifact for over a century and would prove enduring.

According to Edmund Burke Delabarre,[5] the 11-foot long, 5-foot-high rock originally sat above the waterline, based on its proximity to an Indian encampment he uncovered.[6] As water levels rose, the rock began to be progressively submerged during high tides. By the 1760s, the rock was completely covered at high tide. This caused increased erosion damage but also limited access for vandalism.

The Dighton Rock first appeared in print in 1690, courtesy of Cotton Mather, the prominent Boston theologian and scientist. In the published sermon, *The Wonderful Works of God Commemorated*,[7] there is a dedicatory letter to Sir Henry Ashurst, which includes a small, somewhat inaccurate rendering of a sample of the markings. As far as can be determined, Mather never actually visited the site and based his sketch on a slightly less inaccurate rendering made in 1680 by John Danforth of the First Parish Church in Dorchester, Massachusetts.[8] Mather took the reproductions of the images as accurate and believed that the inscriptions were undecipherable because they were unintelligible, i.e., produced by the local natives in an illiterate attempt to emulate writing. Mather included notes about the rock in a series of letters about New England's natural history to the Royal Society of London in 1712. When the society first published some of those notes on local curiosities in 1714,[9] a steady stream of clergy and scholars visited the site.

One of the esteemed tourists was Ezra Stiles, who later became president of Yale University. Stiles was pastor of the Second Congregational Church of Newport, Rhode Island, from 1755 to 1777. Stiles occasionally preached in Dighton, where he had relocated his family after the British occupation of Newport (1776–1777). Dr. Stiles visited Dighton on several occasions, making his own copy of the markings during some of those trips.[10]

One of Stiles' numerous correspondents, the French philologist Antoine Court de Gébelin, used a drawing by Stephen Sewall to theorize a Phoenician origin for the inscriptions.[11] Court de Gébelin included his belief in the Phoenician theory in volume 8 of *Monde Primitif*,[12] a massive multi-volume attempt to document the existence of a prehistoric, commonly shared language. Court de Gébelin, known for an encyclopedic grasp of ancient linguistics and mythology,[13] interpreted the carvings as three distinct tableaus with symbolism representing the past, present, and future.

Stiles was so convinced by Court de Gébelin's translations that he declared Dighton Rock and similar stones were Phoenician in a sermon before Connecticut governor Jonathan Trumbull in 1783.[14]

A contemporary of Stiles, the Rev. Michael Lort, Regius Professor of Greek at Trinity College, learned of the Dighton Rock from Stiles' published sermons and discovered the previous renderings of the inscriptions sent to England. His 1786 report on his work is effectively the first bibliography of research on the site.[15] Lort admits that the first drawing of the carvings he saw, the Court de Gébelin illustration in *Monde Primitif*, had convinced him that the rock was nothing more than crude Indian scratchings, but after reviewing the other versions extant in London, he was not sure what to believe. Lort also puts Stiles' concept of Phoenicians into perspective. Stiles, Lort begins, is so enthused by the creation of the United States that he sees the rise of a vast new empire in North America, bringing to fruition the prophecy of Genesis 9:25–27.[16]

To Stiles, it was preordained that the United States allowed the Japhetites (i.e., the Indo-Europeans) dwelling in the tent of Shem (i.e., Christians) to expand across a new continent. The Indians, being the degenerate descendants of the Phoenicians, are Canaanites. Moreover, like those other Canaanites, the enslaved Africans, the Indians are to be pitied but are doomed to be subjugated and eventually vanish. The Punic carvings on Dighton Rock were just proof that the Indians had continued their decline after their Phoenician ancestors sought refuge in North America.[17]

The opinion of Ezra Stiles, considered one of the most learned men in New England, carried weight in the fledgling United States, but a Phoenician origin was far from unanimous, particularly in Europe.

By Stiles' death in 1795, just about every possible origin of the stone was being discussed. Irish antiquarian Charles Vallancey, who "inaugurated the Phoenician

Earliest known photograph of the Dighton Rock, a daguerreotype of Seth Eastman atop on Dighton Rock, circa 1853. Illustration from Henry Rowe Schoolcraft's *Indian Tribes of the United States*, Book IV.

Scytho-Celtic school of Irish philology based on a supposed kinship of Irish with Punic [i.e., Carthaginian] and Kabmuck (the language of the Algonquin Indians),"[18] felt that Dighton Rock exhibited similarities to published renderings of petroglyphs found in Siberia by Philip Johan von Strahlenberg.[19] Therefore, Vallancey concluded, any similarity of the Dighton Rock's inscriptions to Phoenician script was actually evidence of a Scythian presence in North America. These Scythians arrived via Siberia and were followed and subsequently wiped out by the Tartars, who evolved into the Native American tribes.[20]

John Finch, a prominent geologist,[21] also believed that Scythians were involved, but only as the ancestors of the Celts. In his opinion, Dighton Rock was a Druidic monument, one of many scattered throughout North America that should be preserved.[22]

Edward Kendall, an English observer, published his observations of the new nation while touring New England in 1807–8.[23] He considered the "Writing Rock" to be "a monument as rude as it is intelligible, yet it deserves attention, as well for what it really is, as for what various observers have supposed it to be: it is not a monument of the Phoenicians, nor of the Carthaginians, nor of the lost tribe of Israel, nor Prince Madoc, nor of Captain Blackbeard, nor of Captain Kyd[24]; but is a monument of the sculpture of the ancient inhabitants of America, whether Narragansetts or others."[25]

Kendall's general observation of the Rock's place in history was that there were two schools of thought about the origin of the carvings, divided between the "learned" and "unlearned" populace.[26] The "learned," Kendall observed, preferred a

Phoenician origin to the Dighton Rock, while the "unlearned" believed the rock to be a map to pirate treasure.

Kendall is not alone in his observation of the pirate treasure legend. Folklorist Charles Skinner[27] reports that 90 years later, Captain Kidd's treasure continued to bring the shore around the Dighton Rock under close scrutiny. Delabarre, with a summer residence near the rock, was well aware of the pirate tale,[28] and recorded a neighbor's story of a local boy who dreamt of the treasure by the Dighton Rock on three concurrent nights, then went to dig it up at low tide, only to encounter a fog-shrouded devil instead.[29]

Delabarre takes great delight in dredging up some of the more obscure theories on the Dighton Rock's creators, such as Ira Hill's 1831 use of the Dighton Rock as proof of the Indians being the descendants of ancient Jewish and Tyrian sailors,[30] or the 1838 theory by Moreau de Dammartin that the Dighton Rock is an ancient Egyptian celestial map of the constellations.[31]

In 1829, Carl Christian Rafn was preparing *Antiquitates Americanae*[32] for publication. In association with that work, he relied on the various historians and antiquarians in North America to provide evidence of Norse ruins in North America. Rafn, who, like far too many of the Dighton Rock theorists, never visited the Dighton Rock, proposed a Norse or Viking origin to the carvings, based solely on a drawing of the inscriptions provided by the Rhode Island Historical Society in 1835.

Not surprisingly, Professor Rafn interpreted the markings as proof of the authenticity of the Icelandic sagas—specifically, the tales of Thorfinn Karlsefni. He reads "Thorfinn and his 151 companions took possession of this land" by carefully selecting which carvings to include. The section in the book on the North American monuments prominently featured the Dighton Rock. When the first English translations were published,[33] the Dighton Rock reached the public consciousness as a Norse relic.

Norwegian violin virtuoso Ole Bull visited New England's "Norse relics" such as the Newport Tower and the Dighton Rock during his tour of the United States. Bull became convinced of the rock's significance to Norway's national heritage[34] and made arrangements to purchase the Dighton Rock in 1860 and transfer ownership to the Royal Society of Northern Antiquaries in Copenhagen. Delabarre implies the purchase was made not to preserve the rock, but to relocate it to Copenhagen.[35] However, these plans to move the rock fell through when Bull lost a significant portion of his personal fortune trying to establish a Norwegian utopian community in Pennsylvania.[36] By 1877, the society had decided that the inscriptions were not Norse runes[37] and tried to transfer ownership to the Scandinavian Memorial Club of Boston, the group formed to raise funds for the statue of Leif Eriksson that stands in Boston. However, it was discovered that the Memorial Club had never officially incorporated and could not legally own property.[38] Consequently, the Royal Society of Northern Antiquaries transferred ownership to the Old Colony Historical Society in Taunton, Massachusetts. The return of the Dighton Rock to American control was considered a triumph of sufficient merit to be mentioned in newspapers across the U.S., including a page 2 article in the *New York Times*.[39]

The Norse origin theory was similar to the proposed Phoenician visit in that it received a great deal of press, was repeated in various articles and books, and was far from universally accepted. Just as Cotton Mather had declared the rock aboriginal in origin in 1690, so did other visitors. George Washington viewed a drawing of the inscriptions during a 1789 visit to Harvard University and declared the carvings similar to those he had seen in his youth in Virginia.[40]

In his six-volume study of Indian tribes[41] prepared for the Bureau of Indian Affairs, Henry Schoolcraft states his belief that the stone was carved by the nearby Wampanoag Nation. Schoolcraft had an Algonquin shaman translate the stone. The translation came back as an Algonquin pictographic record of an epic ancient military victory, replete with limbless victims.[42]

Garrick Mallery of the Smithsonian Bureau of American Ethnology, one of the leading scholars and authors on Indian pictographs and sign languages,[43] was also of the opinion that the inscriptions were Indian but was less impressed with Schoolcraft's translation. He believed Schoolcraft was too preoccupied with associating concepts with simple symbols.[44]

Schoolcraft also had the earliest known photograph taken of the stone for his book. In the photo, an 1853 daguerreotype by Seth Eastman, the inscriptions have been chalked in to enhance visibility. Schoolcraft's chalking of the inscriptions illustrates, literally and figuratively, the problem with the images on the stone. Not all the markings are chalked in, only those he considered to be pictographs, just as Rafn's translation required him to add three "missing" lines to prove the rock was runic. All theorists of the Dighton Rock's origin agree that there are layers of later inscriptions and graffiti over the original markings, all of which have suffered erosion damage. Mallery also recorded an 1886 report of damage to the stone as a result of the stream of visitors. Locals were apparently scrubbing the inscription surface with a broom to remove silt from the daily tidal immersions to improve visibility for tourists.[45] All these factors combine to make it subjective at best as to which lines should be designated original and makes finding "proof" easier to identify for any theory you are looking to support.

At the beginning of the 20th century, psychology professor Edmund Burke Delabarre discovered that his summer home was a few miles away from Dighton Rock. As an amateur archaeologist, he was intrigued and began to research the topic. With the resources of Brown University[46] at his disposal, he started to compile a collection of the various theories offered for the stone. Six hundred citations and 13 years later, he began to publish articles about the rock from a historical perspective,[47] combining them into *Dighton Rock: A Study of the Written Rocks of New England*. The book is predominantly a historical overview of the various theories of the origin of the Dighton Rock and other inscribed stones, culminating with his own theory as to the origin of Dighton Rock.

Delabarre, as a psychologist, felt that the Dighton Rock, with all of its varying layers of carvings, was a study in purposive motivation. He felt there were very few carved rocks in New England of any antiquity and assigned most of them to modern origins or incomprehensible native scribbling. By Delabarre's reasoning, these modern carvings were not necessarily deliberate frauds but carved for many different reasons. In a 1935 article,[48] he lists 15 different motives for carving rocks with ancient letters, including a message from a shipwrecked crew, which was Delabarre's personal theory of the origin of the Dighton Rock.

In 1918, Delabarre had begun photographing the rock at night, using a new technology—flash photography. Theorizing that different carvings with different angles and depths would be more easily discernable by the shadows they cast in the flash, Delabarre took hundreds of photographs at different angles and from various distances. One new carving that immediately became visible with the flash was the number "1511." Assuming that 1511 was a date, Delabarre found only two people who could have been there in 1511 to carve the date: the brothers Corte Real, Gaspar and Miguel. Looking again at the various photographs, Delabarre soon discovered "MIGUEL CORTEREAL" written above the date. Additional scrutiny revealed the letters "V DEI hIC DVX IND," which, according to Delabarre, was abbreviated Latin for *Voluntate Dei hic Dux Indorum* or "Chief of the Indians here by grace of God." Beneath this, he also discovered a V-shaped heraldic symbol of Portugal.[49] Due to overlaying carvings and erosion, Delabarre was unable to discern any bezants traditionally associated with the Portuguese symbol, but points out that only Portugal used such an escutcheon.[50]

Miguel Corte Real was the son of João Vaz Corte Real (who himself may have visited Newfoundland before John Cabot). If Miguel indeed was in the Dighton area, it was because of his brother Gaspar.

Gaspar Corte Real received a royal charter on May 12, 1500, to discover a Northwest Passage and claim jurisdiction over lands in the New World. That summer, he left Lisbon for the shores of North America, probably reaching and exploring the coast of Newfoundland. Heavy ice conditions impeded Gaspar's northern advance, and he returned to Portugal.

The following year, with three ships, Gaspar again set out on an expedition of exploration. After traveling along what was probably the coast of Labrador and Newfoundland, the expedition captured a number of natives. Soon after, the ships somehow became separated. Two ships with several of the captives returned to Portugal. Gaspar Corte Real is said to have headed in a southerly direction and was never heard from again.

The Fortress of Louisbourg National Historic Site of Nova Scotia has a sixteenth- or seventeenth-century cannon in its collections. Although an 1891 article in the *Proceedings and Transactions of the Royal Society of Canada*[51] readily accepts a tentative identification of the cannon as a sixteenth-century Portuguese peterero,[52] it may well have been left by one of several other European nationalities known to have used Louisbourg Harbor during that period.

Although it would be tempting to extend this identification to suggest the cannon could be from the ship of Gaspar Corte Real, Canadian ethnologist and historian R.G. Haliburton noted that from 1500 to 1570, commissions were regularly issued to the Corte Real family as well as to subsequent adventurers for colonization attempts. Samuel de Champlain notes the ruins of a failed Portuguese colony on Cape Breton Island as he sailed past, referring to it as over 60 years old.[53]

Attempts to locate these lost colonies have been fruitless, but Haliburton hypothesized that Cape Breton was colonized by 1521, making the Portuguese the earliest European settlers in North America[54] and another potential source of the cannon.

On May 10, 1502, Miguel Corte Real sailed from Lisbon with three ships to locate and rescue Gaspar. Upon reaching Newfoundland, the vessels separated to search a wider area. The ships were to reunite on August 20, 1502, but Miguel's ship failed to make the rendezvous. Like his brother before him, Miguel Corte Real was never heard from again.

Delabarre also makes note of a local Indian oral tradition recorded briefly by Danforth in 1680[55] and a second, longer version reported by Kendall in 1807.[56] This folklore records that white men came up the river in a bird, took Indians into the bird as hostages, that the white men left the bird to look for water, and were ambushed at a spring. There was a counterattack, led by thunder and lightning emanating from the bird. Delabarre uses this tradition in support of his theory that this area was where Miguel Corte Real wintered, and may have died.[57]

Delabarre suggests that the abbreviated Latin inscription on the rock, *Voluntate Dei hic Dux Indorum* or "Chief of the Indians here by the grace of God," is evidence that during the battle, the local shaman was slain, and Corte Real assumed leadership of the tribe.[58] He also points out that within a few yards of the Dighton Rock, White Man's Brook empties into the river.

Perhaps the ship was in too poor condition to set sail in the spring, or too few of Corte Real's crew survived to man the ship, but this is where Delabarre places the intrepid Portuguese explorer. Either way, the carving of his name into the Dighton Rock then becomes a way to attract the attention of any would-be rescuers. The inscription underneath would advise where to find him and stake his claim to the land on behalf of Portugal.

Delabarre's theory was immediately embraced by both the local community (the population of nearby Fall River, Massachusetts, was 58 percent Portuguese by nationality) and Portugal. Professor Delabarre was awarded the Cross of the Order of Christ in 1926, one of the highest honors bestowed by the Portuguese government. Delabarre began using his acclaim to lobby for the protection of the Dighton Rock. Throughout the 1930s, various committees were formed, but little progress was made.

In 1939, Olaf Strandwold published his *Norse Runic Inscriptions Along the Atlantic Seaboard*,[59] including the Dighton Rock. He applauded Delabarre's work on the stone while carefully overlooking Delabarre's opinion that there were no ancient Norse inscriptions in North America. Strandwold looked at the Dighton Rock and ignored the material Delabarre identified as later graffiti. Instead, Strandwold concentrated on a series of lines that William Babcock had originally referred to as "tally marks" located in the center of the stone.[60] Delabarre considered them part of the layers of Indian carvings and graffiti that obscured Corte Real's message and also failed to be recognized by Schoolcraft's translator. Strandwold translated the four runes as Norse date marks and read them as "50." His theory was that the Norse settlers of North America implemented a new calendar system, so the "50" on the rock would be year 50 of the Norse American calendar, or roughly AD 1052. Strandwold's work concentrated on the actual translation process, not placing the stone in a historical context, so his translation does little to explain the various scripts on the rock. Privately published, his work did not achieve widespread recognition.

Nine years later, Strandwold published a second book, *Norse Inscriptions on American Stones*.[61] Based on a Malcolm Pearson photograph, this time Strandwold finds additional runes to translate (there is some question as to whether Strandwold was aware he had already translated this stone in his previous book). He remarks that there are 19 runes, easily readable. The only unusual variation was the cross-bar of rune 18, which had a lower oblique than usual but is similar to the Nybble Stone,[62] a runestone found in East Gotland, Sweden. His translation of the Dighton Rock is "Thygstri owns the ring of tideflat in Jesus' 50th Year," or in idiomatic English, "Thygstri is buried on the shore—Year 50 (1049 AD)." Strandwold's work on the Dighton Rock received little notice; Delabarre's Portuguese theory was unchallenged and no other view would attract similar devotion. Although Professor Delabarre died in 1945,[63] the Corte Real theory continued to strengthen and evolve.

Herbert Pell, the U.S. Ambassador to Portugal, theorized that, in addition to the Dighton inscription, Miguel Corte Real and his surviving crew also built the Newport Tower.[64] According to Pell, Corte Real erected the stone structure as a watchtower in the mistaken belief that the third and oldest Corte Real brother, Vasco Añes Corte Real, would come searching for him just as Miguel had done for Gaspar.[65] Unfortunately for Miguel, it appears that Vasco Añes was refused a charter by King Manuel I.[66] Pell's theory was published in the aftermath of an excavation in Newport that claimed a colonial origin for the tower, so Pell received little notice.

Obscurity was not the case with another theory evolving at the same time. Joseph Fragoso had been president of the Vasco da Gama Club in New York City when Edmund Delabarre was a guest speaker in 1930. Fragoso, a Portuguese language instructor at New York University, began his own investigations and looked into ways to preserve Dighton Rock. Shortly after Delabarre's death, Fragoso began to discern another Portuguese symbol on the rock.

He published a small article in *O Mundo Lusíada* (The Portuguese World), a small Portuguese language quarterly based in New York. Fragoso described three crosses of the Order of Christ engraved on the face of Dighton Rock. The Portuguese cross of the Order of Christ is distinctive; each of the four extensions ends with a flange angled at 45°. Fragoso also identified a second Portuguese heraldic symbol—a round point style shield, with the bezants intact.[67]

In 1951, Fragoso spearheaded the founding of the Miguel Corte Real Memorial Society to raise funds to purchase the property surrounding Dighton Rock and create a park to encompass and protect the rock.[68] In November of 1952, the society purchased 50 acres to create the park. Unfortunately for Fragoso, his attempts to generate interest in the park and protect the rock were so successful that the State of Massachusetts finally took notice.

On March 16, 1953, Massachusetts state senator Edmund Dinis introduced a bill that would create, by eminent domain, the Dighton Rock State Park. The bill was approved by the legislature in 1954 and signed into law in 1955 by Governor Christian Hearter.[69] The society's land was included in the state's seizure. Fragoso immediately sued the state and lost. Over the ensuing years, Fragoso waged a losing battle against everyone associated with the park, alienating his former allies as a result.[70] His complaint was not with attempts to protect the rock but with the attempts to move it out of the river. He argued location was just as significant to the historical context as the carving. The battle raged as the inscriptions continued to take damage from ice and erosion. The carvings were viewable at low tide, but only if the sewage dumped upstream that often covered the rock was scraped away first.

Even as Fragoso waged a losing war against the state, an attempt was made to hoist the rock out of the river and onto the shore as part of the development of the new park. The initial attempt failed to move the rock. The chains left considerable damage, significant enough to generate a scathing editorial in the *Boston Globe*.[71] A court order temporarily stopped any further attempts. Fragoso and the Miguel Corte Real Memorial Society leapt into action, petitioning the courts for a permanent injunction against the Massachusetts Department of Natural Resources. Although the suit was eventually dismissed in superior court in October 1956, the mounting bad publicity finally forced state attorney general George Fingold to decide that further attempts would be stopped until the Massachusetts State Supreme Court considered the case.[72]

The Dighton Rock remained in place, even after another act passed the legislature in 1958, once again authorizing the Department of Natural Resources to move the rock out of the Taunton River. By this time, Fragoso's discovery of the Portuguese crosses on the Rock was overshadowed by his personal war. He was alienated from the legislature, scorned by the Portuguese community, and abandoned by the media. His work would have been completely ignored if it had not been embraced and built upon by a scholar who continued to be the moving force behind protecting the Dighton Rock until his death—Manuel Luciano da Silva, MD.[73]

Da Silva had been a founding director of the Miguel Corte Real Memorial Society but had returned to Portugal to attend medical school. As a result, da Silva missed most of the uproar caused by Fragoso. By 1958, when Dr. da Silva returned, the clamor had died down, the Rock remained in the river, and Dighton Rock State Park was an 85-acre local attraction. Dr. da Silva also began looking at ways to preserve the rock.

Finally, in the spring of 1963, da Silva and his allies persuaded the Department of Natural Resources to give up moving the rock to the shore and instead, construct a cofferdam around Dighton Rock. The 40-ton glacial erratic boulder was then hoisted by crane 11 feet in the air, and a permanent foundation was built beneath it. Instead of helping, this turned out to be a problem—the rock was now exposed to the elements and vandals 24 hours a day, protected only by a chain-link fence.

A decade later, the state of Massachusetts finally budgeted the money to enclose the Dighton Rock in a sturdy octagonal pavilion. Dr. da Silva spent that decade visiting and cajoling legislators for funding. Through his efforts that, five years later, a small museum was constructed adjacent to the pavilion. The Dighton Rock Museum highlights the major four origin theories of the Dighton Rock petroglyphs theorized through the centuries: Native American, Viking, Phoenician and Portuguese. The museum also contains models of famous Portuguese sailing ships: the Nau São Gabriel, the flagship of Vasco da Gama in 1497 (a gift of Portuguese Prime Minister Pinheiro de Azevedo); the caravel Victoria, Fernão de Magellan's flagship on his circumnavigation (a gift from the King of Spain, Don Juan Carlos); as well as a white marble *Padrão*, or Portuguese discovery monument, donated by the Calouste Gulbenkian Foundation of Lisbon. Not only museum exhibits, the models are testimony to the depth and scope of the Portuguese community's devotion to the Miguel Corte Real theory.[74]

Currently, only the Native American and Portuguese theories remain popular. Most recently, archaeologist Edward Lenik[75] interprets the carvings as similar to various anthropomorphic and zoomorphic symbols found elsewhere in New England. What Fragoso and da Silva see as Portuguese crosses of the Order of Christ, Lenik views as styled human forms, vaguely similar to an "hourglass-like figure" found among Native petroglyphs in Maine. Lenik discusses correspondence with an elder of the Wampanoag Nation about the Dighton Rock. The Wampanoags believe the rock to have been carved by their ancestors, and records an oral tradition that explains the Dighton Rock as a visual aid for prophecies of visitors from the East with destructive ways.[76]

As with Delabarre's use of oral traditions, there is an inherent flaw with Lenik's view—there is no way to determine how ancient a handed-down tradition actually is. It remains one explanation for the Dighton Rock, but it does not determine if its carvings were inspired by the tale or if the tale was inspired by the carvings.

Dr. da Silva's Portuguese origin of the Dighton Rock remains the most prominent of current theories. He elaborated on Fragoso's work by finding a fourth cross on the face of the stone, and disagrees with Delabarre on a key point. Delabarre's inscriptions include "V DEI hIC DVX IND," a Latin phrase that da Silva believes Delabarre willed himself to see the term by connecting unrelated carvings, and is

Today, the Dighton Rock is protected in a climate-controlled museum along the Taunton River in Massachusetts.

nonexistent as a separate entity. Da Silva's reasoning is that of all of the various Portuguese explorers who left monuments and markers across the globe, no one used Latin. Additionally, the abbreviations are not standard, and they include a combination of upper and lower case letters of varying sizes. In addition, as far as da Silva is concerned, the final proof that the Latin inscription is erroneous is that the lines Delabarre attributes to the letters "X" and "N" are actually lines that form parts of one of the crosses.[77]

After reviewing all of the drawings of the Dighton Rock from Danforth (1680) through Seth Eastman's daguerreotype (1853), da Silva believed that, in retrospect, the historical documents all show fragments of the Corte Real inscription, particularly the distinctive angles that make up the Portuguese crosses.[78] They may be distorted and misinterpreted, but by showing that they are extant even on Danforth's original sketch, da Silva believed there is more than enough evidence to eliminate any claims of later modifications in support of the Portuguese theory.

The Dighton Rock remains a vibrant part of the community, three centuries after Cotton Mather. On Christmas Eve, 2004, the spotlights shined once again on the steeple at St. Bernard's Church in Assonet Village. The lights illuminated a newly installed gold and silver cross, constructed and installed by local Knights of Columbus. The design of the cross was specifically a Portuguese cross of the Order of Christ, which appears in the heraldic shield of the church as well as the emblem of the Knights of Columbus. The Dighton Rock is within the parish of St. Bernard—the crosses found by Fragoso and da Silva served as the basis for the parish's new spire cross.[79]

As a physician, da Silva knew the warning signs when his own health began to falter. His final goal was to convince the state of Massachusetts to hire a full-time curator for the museum, a goal he never achieved. In 2010, he wrote a letter to the Friends of the Dighton Rock, symbolically passing the torch of guardianship of the site to the group.

Manuel Luciano da Silva died on October 25, 2012, an ardent and vocal supporter of the Portuguese community, especially the Dighton Rock, to the very end. A decade after his passing, the museum is no closer to having a curator. But if the Friends group has half the determination and passion of Dr. da Silva, it is just a matter of time.

Chapter Four

The Newport Tower

Toward the end of the American Revolution, British forces occupying Newport, Rhode Island, decided to evacuate the city. As local legend would have it, upon their departure, the British attempted to destroy the structure they had been using as a munitions dump. The damage was minimal—the loss of the roof and 2 to 3 feet of stonework off the upper wall. An interesting sidebar to the America Revolution, it is also one of many undocumented stories attached to the mortared stone structure now known as the Newport Tower.[1]

The Newport Tower stands in Touro Park,[2] a cylindrical tower of local stone, rising approximately 26 feet on eight columns. The structure is located on one of the highest points on Aquidneck Island. It is roughly a half-mile from the ocean to the east (Narragansett Bay) and west (the Atlantic Ocean at the Sakonnet River). Without trees or other buildings blocking the horizon, the tower would offer a view of the Rhode Island Sound to the south as well.

The stonework is mortared, and there are sufficient remnants of the mortar remaining in spots to suggest that at one time, the entire surface of the structure was covered, giving the tower a finished surface. Arches connect the eight columns, with the height of the columns ranging from 7 feet, 2 inches to 7 feet, 10 inches. The arches are made of flat stones set on edge and are more decorative than functional. The capstone of each arch extends outward slightly.

Sockets on the inside face of the columns supported beams that held up the floor on the first of two stories. There are three windows in the tower and seven niches on the inner wall that do not go through to the exterior. A fireplace is also built over a pillar with two flues to the outside. Both flues curve up and outward away from the firebox and come out on the exterior.

The controversy with the Newport Tower, or Old Stone Mill, began when a windstorm destroyed Peter Easton's windmill. Easton jotted down notes about events of interest in a copy of Nathaniel Morton's *New-Englands Memoriall*.[3] In 1663, he added a note that "This year we bvilt the first windmill," and later notes a "storme blew dovne ovr windmill," on 23 August 1675.[4] Easton's record of the windmill's destruction is considered the benchmark for calculating the earliest the stone tower might have been erected. Less than two years after that unfortunate event is the earliest record of the tower.

In a deed transferring property for the creation of a Jewish cemetery[5] dated 28 February 1677, the boundaries of the property include a reference to "ye Stone Mill."[6] This is followed by two records that are claimed to prove a colonial origin for the structure; both documents were associated with an early governor of the Rhode Island colony—Benedict Arnold.[7] The first of these claims is a reference in a record of the death of Arnold's granddaughter, Damaris Golding, which refers to her burial place as "between my dwelling house and stone wind mill."[8] However, the best known and most widely cited evidence of the structure in colonial times is in the addendum to Governor Arnold's will, dated 24 December 1677. In this document, Arnold refers to "my Stone Built Wind-miln."[9] After this series of references, there is no mention of the tower until the 1740 will of Arnold's son-in-law, Edward Pelham.[10]

Earlier records that might mention the tower were destroyed. When the British evacuated Newport in 1779, they took the town's records in a vessel that subsequently sank. In 1782, the town requested the return of these records, and water-soaked bundles of papers were returned. The data was stored without attempts to restore them until 1857. By then, half of the documents were irretrievably damaged—thirty volumes of real estate and probate records effectively gone.

Archaeologist Philip Ainsworth Means studied the tower for a number of years and listed several other uses for the tower following the Arnold family ownership. Means includes a reproduction of a Gilbert Stuart painting as the frontispiece of his book. Painting it between 1770 and 1775, Stuart created a landscape of men cutting hay with the tower in the background. This painting reveals at least two feet of additional stonework above the current height, presumably the difference caused by the British retreat. Aside from Means' primary declaration that the tower predates the colonial settlement of Newport and that Arnold merely modified it for use as a windmill, he also cites local usage of the tower as a powder magazine ca. 1755[11] and as a hayloft from the mid–1760s.[12] One of these subsequent uses resulted in the windows being bricked up. They would remain so until a restoration attempt in the 1890s.

After the Revolutionary War, the property containing the tower changed hands several times, eventually ending up as part of the estate of Governor William Gibbs.[13] In 1848, historian Benson Lossing was a houseguest of Gibbs. The two discussed the tower and Gibbs' research on the structure. These conversations became the source of several unsubstantiated pieces of information, including the attempted British demolition and the amount of mortar on the exterior walls.[14]

Six years later, the city of Newport purchased the tower as part of Touro Park. Walkways were graded, a fence was placed around the tower, and ivy planted along the tower walls. The ivy rapidly covered the structure entirely, accelerating and obscuring the deterioration of the landmark. By 1885, the ivy was gone, but an architect's report warned that the ivy had pulled out the mortar and loosened the stonework—the tower was unstable and dangerous.[15] The city made repairs, rebuilding the entire top two feet by removing each stone and carefully placing it back in place, using Portland cement that was then textured to blend in with the older mortar. Any missing stones were replaced with ocean-worn stones from local beaches. Cracks and joints were repaired, and the windows were opened again. Finally, the top of the tower was rounded over to direct water away from the stonework.

Since then, the walking paths have shifted, and the fence has been replaced, but the tower itself has more or less remained unchanged since the 1885 facelift. It is a deceptive picture, for although the stone tower has remained unchanged, the controversy over who built it and its original purpose continues to rage unabated.

The first thoughts that the Newport Tower might not be a colonial artifact started to appear when the "skeleton in armor" was found in Fall River, Massachusetts, in 1831. A media sensation, the grave's proximity to the Dighton Rock was not overlooked. By 1836, both were considered Phoenician.[16] This was immediately subject to change when C.C. Rafn's work on Norse antiquities in America was published in 1837.[17] Although the Newport Tower is not included in the original publication, it does appear in a supplementary volume.[18] Correspondence about the tower between Rafn and Dr. Thomas Webb of the Rhode Island Historical Society also appears in various volumes of the journal of the Royal Society of Northern Antiquaries in Copenhagen.[19] Based on the data supplied by Webb, Rafn suggests that the tower was built in the 12th century as a Norse baptistery under the leadership of Eric Gnupsson, a.k.a. Bishop Henrikus, a papal legate to Greenland, and by extension, Vinland. Although Rafn never visited any of the sites he identified as Norse in North America, he does point out several circular stone ruins in Greenland also suspected of being round baptisteries.

In 1841, Longfellow published his poem "The Skeleton in Armor," which transformed the Fall River skeleton into a Viking who built the Newport Tower as a funeral bower for his beloved.[20] The poem became the catalyst that firmly attached Norse origins to the tower.

The Benedict Arnold association with the Newport Tower did not appear in print until 1851 when Newport clergyman Charles Brooks published a small but decidedly pro–Arnold book, apparently in response to the growing popularity of the Norse origins of the tower. Besides being the first published reference to Arnold's will, Brooks also quotes Newport resident David Melville, who explains that Arnold was born and raised in the town of Leamington in Warwickshire, England, near the Chesterton Windmill. The Chesterton Windmill is also a circular, mortared stone structure built on six, not eight, columns. Melville's conclusion was that since Arnold needed a new windmill for Newport, he obviously constructed a replica of the Chesterton Windmill as a nostalgic look back at his boyhood.

This theory first appears in print in Brooks' book,[21] in the form of an undated letter reprinted from an earlier battle between Norse and Arnold proponents in the pages of the Newport newspapers between 1846 and 1847.[22] This might have been the extent of the distribution of the Chesterton Windmill theory, except that the Brooks' book came to the attention of the Rev. John Gorham Palfrey. A leading historian of

Four. The Newport Tower

The Newport Tower in Touro Park, Newport, Rhode Island (Malcolm Pearson photograph).

the time, Palfrey was preparing a multi-volume history of New England.[23] In volume 1, Palfrey addressed the Norse exploration of New England, placing Vinland on Nantucket.[24] He also includes an extensive footnote on the "Old Stone Mill," noting Arnold had never actually said that he built it, but also mentioning that Arnold was born and raised near the Chesterton Windmill, making it logical he would copy it in his later years.[25] At the same time, James Fenimore Cooper's *The Red Rover* was being re-released by Putnam.[26] Originally written in 1827, the tale of revolutionary Newport includes pirates having clandestine meetings in the ruined tower. Having such prominent authors as Cooper and Palfrey as proponents of a colonially constructed tower mill brought that theory to the forefront, where it remains, particularly in the Newport area.[27]

The earliest recorded tower windmill in England was at Dover Castle, dating to 1295. This type of mill was developed from the earlier post mill,[28] but had a fixed body with a wooden roof or cap that housed the sail and windshaft. The miller would rotate the entire cap on a circular track to face the wind.

Cylindrical mills were usually made of stone or brick, with the outer walls plastered to keep out moisture. The mill needed to be cylindrical so that the cap could be rotated on the tower as required to face the wind. Early mills were short enough that the miller could repair/ adjust the cloth on the sails from the ground. It did not take much of a leap of faith to see the Newport Tower as a windmill, but not everyone was convinced.

In 1942, archaeologist Philip Ainsworth Means published his findings after eight years of research. Means was a former director of the National Museum of Archaeology at Lima, Peru; an associate in anthropology at the Peabody Museum, Harvard; and a widely published expert on the Spanish Conquest of the Incas and the cultures of the Andes. He was intrigued by the controversy after reading an article comparing the Newport structure to the church of the Holy Sepulchre in Cambridge, England.[29]

Means concentrated on two specific points—disproving the validity of the Arnold theory and supporting a Norse construction theory. Means' weakness was that he tried too hard, mentioning minor references to the tower, both pro and con, and citing sources that he felt should have included the tower but didn't. His implication was that the "Arnoldites" managed to perpetuate their myth so pervasively that the tower was being ignored in standard historical texts.

Means honed in on the key point that Governor Arnold ordered the structure built between 1675 and 1677 as a replacement windmill for Newport and, as Brooks and Palfrey suggested, built it as a replica of the Chesterton structure that was near his childhood home of Leamington in Warwickshire.

At first glance, the Chesterton Windmill does resemble the Newport Tower. Both are circular structures built of local stone resting on arched columns. Although Chesterton has six square columns as opposed to Newport's eight circular ones, Means points out two additional problems beyond the number of columns. First, the Chesterton structure was not built as a windmill. The Chesterton Windmill was built in 1632 for Sir Edward Peyto, owner of Chesterton Manor. The unusual design may have come from Peyto himself or John Stone, a pupil of architect Inigo Jones. Stone was at Chesterton at the time, but the structure, according to Means, was not built as a windmill. Sir Edward Peyto was a mathematician and astronomer, and the structure was built as an observatory.[30] A watermill was built in the same period. Means hypothesized that the observatory was converted for use as a windmill during a subsequent drought. Had Arnold seen the structure in the three years between its construction and his departure for America in 1635, it would have been an observatory, not a windmill.

Means' second point was that Arnold was not familiar with the British structure, regardless if it was used as an observatory or a windmill. Genealogical research showed that, contrary to prevalent theory, Arnold was not from Leamington or any other location in Warwickshire. The future Rhode Island governor was born in Ilchester in Somerset County. In 1635, the 20-year-old Arnold accompanied his family to Dartmouth in Devonshire County and off to America with no indication he left Somerset County, let alone traveled to Warwickshire.[31] Means concluded that Arnold could not have built the Newport structure to resemble the Chesterton structure since he had never seen it.

Means effectively raised questions about the Arnold theory but didn't present a strong case for the Norse. Although he initially believed that Rafn was correct in identifying the tower as a twelfth-century Norse baptistery, Means was swayed from that stance by one of his correspondents, Hjalmar Holand. Means had favorably reviewed Holand's 1940 book, *Westward from Vinland*,[32] for the *New York Times*.[33] Holand, in his monomaniacal pursuit of authenticating the Kensington Rune Stone, had begun work on a book of new evidence he had uncovered. Half of this new book would be devoted to the Newport Tower as the headquarters of a Viking expedition in 1355 that headed inland, resulting in the 1362 massacre documented on the Kensington Stone.[34]

Means adopted Holand's position that the only way to determine the age and origin of the Newport structure was by comparing its features to similar features extant on stone structures in Europe. Means focused on three points that he felt distinguished the tower from any other building in the western hemisphere—the columns, the windows, and the fireplace.

Means compared the Newport features to round churches across Europe, eventually focusing on Scandinavia. He found similarities at Newport to those in Scandinavian structures, finding two additional design features they share with the Newport Tower: a second floor above the arches and the structure's capability to be used as a defensive position. He found a window in the ruins of the Oephir Church apse in the Orkney Islands to be double-splayed, similar to the windows in the Newport Tower,[35] as opposed to the Chesterton Mill windows, which splay inward as is typical for the mill's seventeenth-century construction. Means found so many examples of double-splayed windows in twelfth- and thirteenth-century structures that he had no difficulty concluding that this must also be the era of the Newport structure's construction.[36]

Another anomaly in the tower's construction is the fireplace. F.J. Allen, comparing the Newport structure to the Church of the Holy Sepulchre in Cambridge, England, had no doubts that the Newport construction was not a mill—a fireplace in an area used for milling would be an extraordinarily combustible combination.[37] This was not a frivolous concern—written reports of mill explosions date back to a 1785 flour mill in Turin, Italy.[38] Means picked up upon Dr. Allen's concerns about mill-dust explosions and corresponded with author and engineer Rex Wailes, a leading molinologist in England. Wailes insisted that windmills did occasionally have fireplaces but did not specify where in the building they would be located.[39] F. Stokhuyzen's study of Dutch windmills may explain the confusion.[40] His discussion of tower windmills includes a profile of an eight-story tower mill where the first two stories are the living quarters of the miller, comparatively safe for an open flame.[41]

The other problem with the arrangement of the flue and chimney was pointed out by civil engineer Edward Adams Richardson.[42] With the chimney flue venting out of the wall only seven feet above the fireplace, flames, sparks, and gases will escape. In order for the tower to function as a windmill, the cap containing the sails must overhang the tower and freely turn. When the prevailing wind mandates positioning the sails near the chimney vent, the sails and turning arm are vulnerable to any sparks and flames emitted from the flue. Richardson's conclusion was that the tower's builder constructed an ordinary fireplace if built prior to AD 1400, but a date of AD 1675 or later indicated a "very inferior design and concept."[43]

Architect Suzanne Carlson pointed out that as late as the 16th century, rural buildings in England lacked chimneys.[44] Carlson, who studied the Newport Tower extensively, was only able to locate two other small fireplaces with a flue exiting on the face of the exterior wall similar to Newport Tower: Cormac's Chapel in the Rock of Cashel[45] and a post–1840 building of the Sulpician Fathers of the Grand Seminaire de Montreal. Means had previously lamented the fact that he was unable to find any extant twelfth-century wall fireplaces in Scandinavia.[46]

Although it does not have a chimney, an octagonal church in Store Hedinge, Denmark, is what Means found most closely resembles the Newport Tower. This church, with windows splayed in both directions, has eight columns and is surrounded by an ambulatory with the columns supporting a clerestory—exactly what Philip Means envisioned as the original form of the Newport Tower. The clerestory of the structure functioned both for ecclesiastical and defensive matters. In the case of the Newport Tower, Means suggests that Skraelings, not feuding jarldoms, would be the reason for a stronghold.

Means' weakest point in comparing the Newport structure to Scandinavian churches was his attempts at comparing features that should be on the tower but are missing, most notably the ambulatory. Based on European churches, Means felt that a roofed enclosure would completely surround the tower and extend out another 10 to 20 feet to create the ground floor of the church. His only proof was the setback at the junction of the tower wall and columns, which he believed was adequate to support a horizontal roof beam. To prove that the ambulatory once existed, Means sought permission from the Newport Park Commission to open test pits 10 to 25 feet away from the structure, far enough away not to further weaken the unknown condition of the structure's foundation, but close enough to uncover the ambulatory.[47] Newport was not interested in authorizing an excavation, whether or not it was funded by Means. Means stated he was no longer young enough to conduct the excavation himself and drew up a rough blueprint of what he thought should be done and recommended the dig be conducted by the Excavators' Club at Harvard University, a group of graduate students in archaeology of which Means was an alumnus.

Means ended his book complaining about the lack of cooperation from Newport officials and made one last plea for an excavation. Means died in 1944 at the age of 52. His obituary in the *New York Times* called him an "Inca lore expert."[48] The obituary lists a number of his earlier books, including a 1942 children's book,[49] but does not mention his last published book from that same year, *The Newport Tower*.

Means' wish for the Excavators' Club's involvement would be granted four years later, under the guise of William S. Godfrey, Jr., a graduate student from Harvard. However, the results were very different from what Means expected would be found.

A committee of the Society for American Archaeology planned the excavation.

The committee members included Hugh Hencken of Harvard University and Junius Bird of the American Museum of Natural History, both of whom had past dealings with claims of pre–Columbian settlements.[50] The excavations were carried out over two seasons by a team of students from Harvard led by Godfrey.

In the first year, a meter-wide trench was dug that ran south of the tower, through one of the *arches,* and out the opposite side. In the second year, the entire interior and the surrounding perimeter were excavated. The first discovery was that more than one foot of soil had accumulated in the area. They also discovered cylindrical bases for the pillars. They further found evidence of a circular construction trench, or ring ditch, about 7 feet wide, varying in depth from 9 to 24 inches. A pile of stones was dumped for a foundation where the columns were placed. It was upon these bases that the columns rested. Colonial-era artifacts were scarce in the ring ditch—a gunflint fragment, a potsherd, two pieces of a clay pipe, and surprisingly, a footprint left by a shoe with a flat toe and square heel. Inside the tower, fragments of a millstone were excavated, along with thousands of pieces of debris dated to the 18th and 19th centuries.

The result, published as Godfrey's Ph.D. dissertation,[51] concluded that since all of the artifacts excavated in the ring ditch were from the 17th century, the tower was probably built before 1675 by Benedict Arnold as a retreat or private study—the building was the folly of a rich, old man. When the 1675 windstorm destroyed the only windmill in Newport, Arnold allowed the structure to be converted into a windmill.

Johannes Hertz, a medieval archaeologist and head of the Danish State Antiquaries Archaeological Secretariat, offered an interesting alternative in a widely cited article on the Newport Tower.[52] He points out that it seems odd that if Easton's windmill was the first in Newport, the colony had been without a mill for nearly 24 years. He also suggests that Easton's use of "we" and "our" did not mean Newport as a whole, merely the community of the Religious Society of Friends (Quakers), of which Easton was a member.[53]

In the quest to determine a date of construction for the windmill, no one mentions that there were several watermills in Newport prior to the Easton windmill,[54] including one owned by Peter Easton's father, Nicholas.[55] Unless there was an unrecorded drought severe enough to affect the ability of watermills to operate, there was no particular urgency to replace the windmill. In light of Peter Easton's being a Quaker, there is also no motivation for Arnold to donate the tower specifically to help a religious community of which Arnold was not a member. This eliminates the 1675 date for conversion to a windmill due to urgency, but does not offer an alternative date.

Godfrey published his findings in *American Antiquity*[56] and *Archaeology.*[57] His conclusions were questioned immediately. Frederick Pohl honed in on the ring ditch.[58] Godfrey had discovered mortar fragments in the trench, but had also stated that the trench was filled prior to mortar being applied to the columns.[59] Pohl called this a contradiction and questioned the accuracy of Godfrey's age of the structure. Pohl suggested that since mortar fragments are associated with all of the colonial artifacts found, the only thing Godfrey established was that the artifacts were dropped during colonial era excavations by treasure hunters[60] and researchers when mortar was beginning to drop off the tower.

Godfrey replied that he never stated that the mortar work was begun exclusively after the ditch had been refilled, and perhaps some masonry work had started prior to the ditching being completely filled.[61] Even advocates of a colonial origin of the tower had issues with this explanation. Even Johannes Hertz, a self-admitted proponent of Godfrey's theories, who firmly believed the tower to be colonial,[62] questioned Godfrey's interpretation. Hertz suggested that the mortar in the ring ditch was not from the construction but debris from prior land use scattered across the area. He pointed to an anomaly on aerial photographs of Touro Park southeast of the tower, suggesting the outline of a house as a possible source of the debris.[63]

Unsurprisingly, Hjalmar Holand also disputed Godfrey's conclusions.[64] He pointed out that Godfrey's findings of a colonial origin for the tower was based on excavated artifacts, which would be definitive if the soil had remained undisturbed since the tower's construction. Godfrey himself, Holand continued, admitted that this was not the case, having documented a minimum of five previous excavations and acknowledging difficulty discerning the edges of these excavations. Holand also pointed out Godfrey's inability to find a construction level. As Godfrey explained in a letter to the Preservation Society of Newport County,[65] there should be a layer of debris left behind from the construction, but he could not identify it. Holand suggested that this implied that the debris was dispersed by subsequent disturbances around the tower, such as early farming, earlier excavations by William Gibbs, potholes by treasure hunters, or maintenance performed by groundskeepers.

Holand then discussed the unit of measurement used in construction, noting that although the dimensions of the tower had evidently been planned well enough that the columns were equidistant from a common center, the various dimensions were not in whole numbers or standard fractions. Converting the measurements to the Rhenish-Danish-Norwegian foot,[66] Holand's measurements equaled whole numbers. It did not prove who built the tower, but it did suggest a construction using non–English standards, i.e., before the British colonies.[67]

With his results being questioned in the media[68] even as he submitted the results as his doctoral thesis, Godfrey's comments grew progressively terse and defensive. After accusing Holand of nineteen epistemological solecisms in his response,[69] Godfrey discounted the measurements used by Holand as insignificant.

The work at Newport Tower continued to overshadow Godfrey's academic career. His last salvo would be a 1955 article in *American Anthropologist*,[70] summarizing all evidence of Norse explorations and taking one last shot at discrediting all pre–Columbian evidence, taking particular aim at the Newport Tower. This time, engineer Arlington Mallery answered the challenge and published an 11-page reply.[71] Mallery pointed out Godfrey had not addressed ancient maps and nautical charts from Scandinavia, citing two maps that predate the settlement of Newport yet indicate a structure already standing. Mallery also touched on similarities between Iroquois longhouses and iron smelting in Ohio[72] before settling into the Newport Tower, reiterating Pohl's questions about artifacts and plaster. Then Mallery went after a point that he and Godfrey had clashed over before—underpinnings on the eight columns.

In 1954, Mallery had received permission to reopen and examine some of Godfrey's excavations.[73] Mallery engaged two local engineers to assist: John Howieson, the city's chief engineer, and Gardner Easton. In a 1955 interim report to the Newport city council,[74] Mallery claimed that Godfrey's report stated that the foundations beneath the columns were loose piles of rock. Mallery found the foundations to be expertly dressed and fitted stonework. He also added an ominous note. In reviewing Godfrey's report, it appeared that the back wall facing the inside had been removed from all eight columns and that stones had been removed from at least half of the foundations.[75] He recommended that the public works department excavate immediately to see the extent of the foundation damage before winter set in. Godfrey, now on the faculty at Beloit College in Wisconsin,[76] was warned of the report and obtained a copy as it was submitted to the council. He fired back a letter claiming that Mallery's report was so riddled with errors that he could not attempt to address them all. Godfrey denied removing any stones and stated there was definite archaeological proof that the tower could not have been underpinned in the colonial era. Johannes Hertz would later concur with Godfrey, believing the "unbroken, precise course" of the ring ditch precluded later intrusions, such as underpinning.[77]

Despite Godfrey's admonishments that Mallery was unqualified to interpret archaeological data, Mallery's work continued. In 1956, the foundations of two of the columns were re-excavated.[78] Joined in the examination by Easton and Howieson, he concluded that the building was originally constructed with the pillars resting on soil and that the columns were underpinned in 1675 to bear the added weight of milling machinery and the windmill. Mallery also concluded that the amount of mortar found in the excavation pits demonstrated the disintegration of the plaster started centuries before the underpinning.

According to Mallery's report to the Newport city council,[79] the original structure had not needed foundations below the frost line because of the wooden structure surrounding the tower. Mallery proposed that the ambulatory suggested by Means[80] and others, such as French architectural historian Camille Enlart,[81] had been extant in some form until the modifications were started for the windmill conversion. This was so important to Mallery that within days of receiving permission to investigate the tower from the city manager in 1954, he was back in the park, measuring tower heights and showing an 8.4-inch setback created where the columns met the outside wall. Mallery claimed to local media[82] that this provided a shelf for a horizontal roof timber.[83] Mallery also pointed out that the archways undercut the wall by about 6 inches, providing a niche to anchor the rafters.[84]

Mallery's associate, Gardner Easton, was a direct descendant of Peter Easton, whose mill started the controversy in 1675. Easton had gone through family papers and found a 1714 map laying out the original Easton land grants, including a tiny sketch of the tower converted to a windmill with a surrounding lean-to.[85] Mallery used this map to suggest that the structure was actually located on Easton property when the windmill conversion took place, with Arnold purchasing the property at a later date, by implication quantifying Arnold's "my stone built windmill" quote as meaning, "the mill I bought," not "the mill I built."

The 1714 map is not one of the maps Mallery had initially referred to in his reply to Godfrey.[86] The two maps mentioned in that article were a 1614 map by Dutch explorer Cornelius Hendrick[87] and a map in William Wood's *New England's Prospect*.[88] Both, according to Mallery, showed that the mapmaker saw some evidence that was taken to be an English settlement before Newport's settlement in 1639.

Mallery noted that the Hendrick map[89] showed a small section of Narragansett Bay marked English, while the rest was Dutch. The Hendrick map is similar to numerous other maps of the time, with conflicting boundaries between New Netherlands and New England. As such, there is no way to assess its accuracy or relevance.

The William Wood map is more prevalent among advocates of a non-colonial origin for the tower and is usually discussed in conjunction with a document known as the Plowden Petition.[90] Both documents were introduced to Newport research in 1945 by Frederick Pohl.[91] In 1632, Sir Edmund Plowden petitioned to settle a colony by the name of New Albion on Long Island and adjacent lands. The document then lists 29 commodities or benefits that made this project feasible, such as the quantities of deer and turkey, good lumber, good fishing, optimal locations for drying fish, and excellent water. Commodity number 27 refers to keeping 30 men "resident in a rownd stone towre"[92] where they could trade with the Indians and keep their weaponry at the ready.

Pohl points out there are no recorded towers on Long Island in this period, nor were there towers in Virginia, New Jersey, or the Plymouth colonies. The English and Dutch were still at odds over boundaries, so New Albion could not be within the Dutch territories. References to approaching the settlement by pinnace and housing residents suggest significant travel required to reach the location. Pohl concludes that the only place where a colony could meet the criteria laid out in the petition was southern New England, where a round stone tower may have already been standing.[93]

Pohl then points out that the other commodities listed were pre-existing conditions—why wouldn't that include the round stone tower? He also considers a round stone tower a peculiar specification. If this stone tower were merely a recommendation that a defensive structure would be built, why would Plowden specify a round stone tower instead of a typical square wooden building? In support of the Plowden reference as a significant reference to the Newport Tower being extant 45 years before the 1677 documents, Pohl points to the William Wood map. Wood's map of

"The South Part of New England, as it is Planted this yeare, 1634" was published in his *New England's Prospect*,[94] a book that Wood admits is basically a promotional piece,[95] not a travelogue. It consists of 98 pages of text, dedicatory messages, a poem about Wood by his friend "S.W.," a *Nomenclator*, or table of Indian words, and the map. Wood places a settlement on the east side of Narragansett Bay labeled "Old Plymouth" as opposed to the settlement on Cape Cod labeled "New Plymouth." Pohl suggests that Wood placed a settlement near modern-day Newport because there was evidence of a prior English settlement, such as a stone tower. Why the tower had not been reported by prior explorations[96] may lie in the ethnoecological history of the region.

William Cronon[97] notes that forest fires were commonly mentioned from the time of the very earliest explorers, as well as areas stripped clear of wood, such as a 75-mile stretch of denuded land in Narragansett Bay noted by Verrazzano.[98] The treeless zones resulted from winter camps burning all of the nearby fuel. Forest fires served a purpose as well. Thomas Morton mentioned how "[t]he Savages are accustomed to set fire of the Country in all places where they come, and to burne it twize a yeare, viz: at the Spring, and the fall of the leafe."[99] If Wood had arrived either after a winter camp or after a fire had cleared the underbrush to facilitate hunting, he might have found a stone tower that had previously been obscured by undergrowth.

Paul Chapman, a former Naval Air Ferry Command navigator, located this notation on another map. Chapman applied his navigational background to interpret historical journeys in actual sailing terms. After applying his sailing background to St. Brendan's voyage, as told in the *Navigatio Sancti Brendani Abbatis*,[100] he began researching the Norse sagas.[101] During that research, he reviewed Gerald Mercator's map of 1569. On this map, published over 60 years before the settlement of Newport, Chapman claimed that Mercator had marked the location of Norumbega with a tower at the approximate location of Newport.[102]

It is interesting to note that most interpretations of this map associate the location of Norumbega with modern-day Bangor, Maine. The Mercator map also shows numerous other towers at locations further south along the East Coast and more along the Gulf of Mexico coastline. With this consideration, it appears that the walled city and tower marked at Norumbega on Mercator's map was merely an icon used to designate a Native American village, not an actual indicator of a walled city with towers.[103]

Chapman lauded the previously mentioned study by civil engineer Edward Adams Richardson. Richardson approaches the tower from an engineer's perspective. He points out a precise north-south alignment of the tower and how it could have been accomplished using the North Star.[104] Richardson concurred with theories that suggest an ambulatory or some sort of round structure surrounded the lower level and calculated the size of the enclosure as potentially extending 24 feet, based on the weight-bearing capacity of the structure.[105]

Based strictly on its design, Richardson contends there are absolutely no suggestions that the tower was built for a milling operation—the floors are not the correct strength, the fireplace is in the wrong place, there was no way to get the equipment into the structure, and the surrounding structure would interfere with the turning sails. Richardson does believe that the tower could have been converted to a windmill later at slightly less cost than constructing a new windmill from scratch.[106]

Richardson believed the structure was built for one purpose—a signal tower. He analyzed the window placement and concluded that the upper story with three small windows was built for observation, where the horizon could be scanned at night without the light from the lower floor affecting vision. The lower floor would be bright with light from the fireplace reflecting off the plastered walls and out the larger windows into the night sky. The varying sizes of the larger windows would affect intensity and distance of the light projection. Depending on the window, Richardson calculated the candlepower emanating to be visible at sea upwards of 6 to 8 nautical miles offshore.[107] Calculating the azimuths from the windows, Richardson explained how using the lights from the windows could easily be used as course correction beacons to navigate the route from Vineland Sound into Rhode Island Sound and finally into Narragansett Bay. Richardson did not know who would have had the technical background to construct the tower to such exacting specifications.

His best guess was based on an article published the previous year by Hjalmar Holand.[108] Holand wrote in support of the Kensington Rune Stone, suggesting that Nicholas of Lynn, an English friar who once published a now-lost book about his voyages, voyages that Holand believed could only have been in Hudson Bay. Friar Nicholas was mentioned by geographer/historian Richard Hakluyt as being an explorer and an astronomer who possessed the expertise to build and use an astrolabe. Holand believed that Nicholas had accompanied Paul Knutson to North America, into Hudson Bay, and eventually to Kensington, Minnesota. Holand himself did not suggest that Nicholas was the architect of the Newport Tower.[109]

Richardson's belief that the windows were specifically oriented was echoed in 1994. William Penhallow, an astronomer at the University of Rhode Island, published his findings on possible archaeoastronomical significance to the windows at a conference sponsored by New England Antiquities Research Society in 1992,[110] using measurements from Philip Means' book.[111]

Soon after, the Institute for Surveying and Photogrammetry of the Technical University of Denmark conducted a new study of the tower. This report gave precise measurements for windows and columns. Penhallow now had data specific enough to suggest a functional astronomical calendar. Taking lines of sight through windows from both inside the tower and from outside, using two windows, Penhallow found he could mark the position of the sun, moon, and the stars Polaris and Dubhe. He also reports that archaeologist James Whittall had reported cup-shaped depressions on the sill of one of the windows. Penhallow suggested these cup marks or cupules were sighting guides for an astrolabe.[112]

All of these alignments, Penhallow concluded, provided the determinations needed for religious observances by Europeans intent on colonization. He further hypothesized that the construction came after the development of the astrolabe in 1300 and prior to 1500 when the availability of printed almanacs eliminated the need for a calendar of this type.[113]

Hertz derisively suggests that a similar perpetual calendar could be used to validate a runic message on the outside of the tower, which Hertz believes to be nothing more than "5 or 6 scratches visible there bearing a certain resemblance to runes."[114]

The runes in question first appeared in print in Strandwold's *Norse Inscriptions on American Stones*.[115] On a 1946 visit to the Newport tower, Magnus Bjorndal, a Norwegian-born electrical engineer and inventor, spotted markings on a small reddish stone about 14 feet above the ground, 2½ feet above a column on the west-southwest section of the tower's exterior. Bjorndal, an active participant in the Norwegian-American Historical Association, often traveled from his laboratories in New Jersey to Newport to show fellow Norwegians the tower that could have been made by their Viking ancestors.

Strandwold, working from a Malcolm Pearson photograph, translated the markings as "Øn," Year 11 (1010 AD).[116] He identified the first rune in the name "Øn" as a "secret rune," a sentiment that would be echoed 20 years later when O.G. Landsverk and Alf Mongé retranslated the same markings using their runic cryptogram theories.[117] Mongé took the marks to be a five-rune cryptogram built around the letters "HENRIKS" for the name "Henrikus," arranged to provide key numerals that referred back to the Catholic Perpetual Calendar calculation for the date of the second Sunday of Advent in 1116.[118] Erik Gnupsson, or Henricus, was the Bishop of Greenland whom Rafn had initially offered as the possible originator of the tower.[119] Landsverk and Mongé believed Henricus had traveled extensively in North America, leaving runic puzzles behind him in such locations as Maine, Minnesota, and Oklahoma.[120]

Epigrapher Barry Fell offered a third variant translation in 1980.[121] Fell, working from the same photograph as Strandwold, found five consonants, "HNKRS," which he interpreted as a dedicatory plaque designating the tower as "of the Bishop's stool," the base of his episcopal operations.

A second inscription was found by geneticist Clyde Keeler[122] during a 1974 visit to Newport. Keeler was photographing Fell's "dedication stone" from ground level, aiming upward, compensating for the distance by blowing up the image in the lab. When examining the photos, he discovered a second stone with incised marks about 1½ feet from the original. Through a fluke of timing and angles, this inscription was visible because the sun was angled to cast shadows in the inscription.[123]

Keeler's interpretation of the inscription was that it was composed of the Latin letters "IHC," which he believed to be an abbreviation of the Constantinian motto *In Hoc Signo Crucis Vinces*, rather than the more common use of "IHC" as a sacred Greek monogram for Jesus.

Associating the tower with religious functions was not limited to runic evidence and Means' comparisons to Scandinavian churches. Herbert Pell, former U.S. ambassador to Portugal, suggested that the tower was similar to the charola located in Castelo Templário and Convento da Ordem de Cristo in Tomar, Portugal, a combination castle and convent built by the Knights Templar.[124]

The charola, an octagonal altar painted and carved in the Byzantine style, still stands, as do many other round and octagonal altars throughout Portugal.[125] After the suppression of the Knights Templar in 1314, Portugal's King Dinis founded a new order, the Knights of the Order of Christ, which assumed the functions, properties, and members of the banned Templars, including the castle at Tomar. This new order would provide the funding and fervor that culminated in Prince Henry the Navigator and the significant presence of the Portuguese in colonization attempts in the 15th and 16th centuries.

Pell theorized that the Newport Tower was built in the style of the Portuguese charola by shipwrecked Portuguese explorer Miguel Corte Real, the same Portuguese explorer credited with the Dighton Rock inscription.[126] According to Pell, the Corte Real crew built the Newport Tower as both a chapel and a watchtower, fully expecting that Miguel's oldest brother, Vasco Añes Corte Real, would come searching for him, as Miguel had gone looking for his missing brother Gaspar. Corte Real chose to build a stone tower instead of a wooden one, Pell continues, because fewer tools were required for a stone tower. If he had the tools to build a wooden tower, Corte Real would have built a replacement boat instead.[127] Hjalmar Holand, needless to say, had no use for the Portuguese origins of the Newport Tower or the Dighton Rock.[128]

Dr. Luciano da Silva, the most ardent of the contemporary scholars of the Dighton Rock, agreed with Pell.[129] Dr. da Silva went further, stating that the actual use of the Newport Tower could be a watchtower, a Catholic chapel, or even a windmill—any one of those origins would still suggest a Portuguese builder, since, contrary to American perceptions of the Netherlands, Portugal had many more windmills than even the Dutch.[130] Stokhuyzen also notes that windmills comparative to the Dutch windmills could be found in other European countries, including England and Scandinavia.[131] So, even if the Newport structure were to be conclusively identified as a windmill, it does not pinpoint colonial, Portuguese, Scandinavian, or English builders without a specific age for the tower.

The age question was addressed in 1991 by the Committee for Research on Norse Activities in North America AD 1000–1500, a multi-national attempt to study the Vikings in North America issue as a whole. The Newport Tower was one of the proposed sites to be examined. After a thorough photogrammetric survey,[132] an attempt to date the tower was made by carbon-14 (C-14) testing the lime mortar. The use of C-14 dating on inorganic material is a new testing tool. The process was successfully used to date medieval churches in Scandinavia,[133] which in turn brought the process to the attention of Johannes Hertz.

While mortar is setting, carbon dioxide (CO_2) is bound as calcium carbonate by reaction with calcium hydroxide (the slake lime in the mortar). The absorbed CO_2 will include C-14, which can be measured to determine the age.

The Norse Committee obtained permission from the Newport city council to attempt C-14 testing on the mortar in January 1993. Samples were taken from ten points on the tower using a 12 mm drill, drilling into the mortar to a depth where contaminants such as mortar from the 1885 repairs could be avoided. Samples were chosen for C-14 testing, along with a sample of surface plaster and an ox bone excavated by Godfrey in 1949.[134] Mortar samples from the Wanton-Lyman-Hazard house were tested as a control group.[135] All the samples were brought to Denmark and tested by Jan Heinemeier, director of the AMS C-14 Dating Laboratory at the University of Aarhus, and by Högne Jungner, director of the Dating Laboratory, Finnish Museum of Natural History, University of Helsinki, Finland.

Nine months later, Norse committee chair Jørgen Siemonson held a press conference announcing that the test results showed that the tower was probably built in the mid–17th century and possibly as early as the 16th century.[136] This, according to Siemonson, made the Arnold construction questionable but did offer support to the Plowden Petition. He also suggested that another miller in town, George Lawton, might be a possible candidate, something Lawton family genealogists[137] had been declaring for years.[138] Siemonson closed the press conference jokingly suggesting that if anyone could disprove the dating of the tower, it would be James P. Whittall II and his Early Sites Research Society.

Siemonson was aware of Whittall's interest in the tower, which Whittall believed was constructed by Henry Sinclair and his knights[139] in the style of Norman Romanisk architecture, which had been inspired by the Holy Sepulchre in Jerusalem, as were many Templar churches in Europe.[140] Whittall homed in on the photogrammetric results of the unit of measurement used to build the tower. The Norse committee's report was detailed enough to determine the standard unit, something numerous previous attempts had tried with significant variation in final results. Helge Nielsen, a Danish pioneer in calculating measurements using module analysis, considered by Hertz to be one of the best in the field,[141] used a new software program to detect modules (hidden divisors) in the numerical data and determine the standard unit of measurement used by the builders. This standard of measure would, in theory, determine the nationality and time period of construction. The measurement unit came back as 23.3 centimeters. When compared to the English foot at 30.48 cm and the Danish-Norwegian foot at 31.5 cm, it posed a problem for pre–Columbian and colonial construction advocates alike. Nielsen had no explanation, suggesting that the standard of 23.3 cm was similar to half of an "alen," or "ell," used in Norway and Iceland in the transitional period between the Viking Age and the Middle Ages.[142]

This measurement matched Whittall's theory of fourteenth-century Norse-Scots from the Shetland and Orkney Islands,[143] when 23.3 cm was roughly one-quarter of the Scottish ell, also tying the tower back to Means' suggestion of the Oephir Church apse in the Orkneys,[144] and reaffirming the theory of the Knights Templar association of the Sinclair expedition.[145]

Whittall also initiated a series of ground-penetrating radar surveys in Touro Park.[146] His work in 1994 and 1995 was overlaid with a later study sponsored by the New England Antiquities Research Association.[147] The tests confirmed the paths of original walkways, as well as Godfrey's screened dirt piles. They failed to show any evidence of another structure associated with the tower, such as Means' ambulatory. However, they did indicate a 10 by 10 meter circular disruption southwest of the tower near an intersection of modern sidewalks at the 3-foot deep level. Without excavation, it is difficult to say what this disturbance is—it could be an old public utilities work trench or the workspace where the mortar was mixed.

The mortar dating continued to raise more questions than it answered as other researchers questioned the C-14 results. Several issues were raised, questioning the committee's resulting dates.

Andre J. de Bethune[148] pointed out that thick walls impaired the diffusion of CO_2—the thicker the wall, the slower the absorption of CO_2. Slower CO_2 absorption could result in C-14 dates that shaved centuries off the actual age.

James L. Guthrie[149] noted that in a damp climate such as New England, modern CO_2 can replace the original CO_2 bound in the mortar at construction. Because calcium carbonate is water-soluble, exposure to rain could allow the C-14 lost by radioactive decay to be replaced by modern C-14, making the test results more recent.

J. Huston McCulloch[150] raised concerns that there was still the possibility colonial repairs contaminated the results. Although Hertz asserted that the samples were removed from deep enough within the material to remove any trace contamination from repairs or rain, he also mentioned they took surface samples.[151] Using the full Heinemeier and Jungner report, McCulloch noted that a surface sample from above the flue was used in the composite date.[152] This could bias the results with post-colonial mortar repairs or effects of rain-borne carbonates.

Guthrie also compared the tower results to the dates from the Wanton-Lyman-Hazard house. He noted that the samples were divided into two portions before testing and that there was a 200-year difference between the two sets of results. Heinemeier and Jungner assumed that the first portion, consisting of the finest of the mortar particles, would produce more accurate results than the second set because the more coarse particles of the second set would include any residual fossil carbonate from the shells used to create the lime. Based on the results from the Wanton-Lyman-Hazard house, the second set was actually more accurate. Guthrie's conclusion was that, based on the Heinemeier and Jungner date, the tower was unquestionably several hundred years older than the house.[153]

The debate remains unabated but seems to have coalesced, at least temporarily, into three theories. James Egan, a professional photographer and the operator of the Newport Tower Museum, has built upon Penhallow's work on astronomical alignments. He believes it is the only English Renaissance building in America. Designed in 1582 by John Dee to be the center of the first Elizabethan colony in the new world, he claims it is a replica of the Church of the Holy Sepulcher. Egan further claims the structure functions as a horologium using cameras obscura to track Christian holidays.[154]

Scott F. Wolter is a Minnesota geologist hired initially by the (Kensington) Runestone Museum to determine the age of the "Norse runes" carved on the face. Wolter found alternative history more alluring than geology and began espousing increasingly complex theories of ancient explorations, usually by Knights Templar. He visited the Newport Tower in 2007, looking specifically for alignments at the tower associated with the planet Venus, based on his enthusiasm for the Knight and Lomas book *The Book of Hiram: Freemasonry, Venus, and the Secret Key to the Life of Jesus.Jesus.*[155] These alignments would "prove" the medieval Cistercian monks and Knights Templars that carved the Kensington Rune Stone also built the Newport Tower. Wolter's theory was that the monks and knights revered the "sacred feminine" represented by Venus, using the Virgin Mary as a metaphor for the Goddess.

There are also other alleged alignments. As one example, the winter solstice shines through a window. The sunbeam angle changes as the sun rises until the sunbeam strikes an "egg-shaped keystone" in an archway.[156] This, Wolter explains, represents the Greek Orphic tradition of the cosmic egg. The sunbeam "impregnates" the egg, which symbolically hatches in the spring.[157] Knight and Lomas have no shortage of critics by themselves. However, there are further issues with Wolter's theory, not the least of which is the original second-story floor that would have blocked any sunbeams from the windows striking the archways.

Dr. Steven R. Pendery, at the time with Peabody Museum at Harvard University, offered a more prosaic theory. Governor Benedict Arnold's political ascendancy required certain social expectations, including formal gardens on his 16-acre estate. As Strong notes in his study of English Renaissance gardens, since the time of Henry VIII, the palace garden was a symbol of royal power and prestige that had evolved into a "sequence of interconnecting spaces whose vital link is the vista and point de vue."[158]

Pendery suggests the structure is a "prospect tower," a garden building that visually connected the walkways through the various plots of the formal garden and could be ascended for an overview of the gardens. Arnold's 1677 will, which mentions a path connecting the structure to the house, may support the theory.[159]

He notes that modern unfamiliarity with these early gardens, and architectural features such as prospect towers, is not surprising. Gardens, by their nature, are at best temporary, prone to remodeling to reflect more contemporary styles. In the 1720s, a "gardenless" form of landscaping popularized designed by English landscape architect Lancelot "Capability" Brown all but eliminated previous formal garden styles.

Pendery believes that a century of scholars debunking the tower's Norse origins prevented research that would have identified it as an architectural component of Governor Arnold's formal gardens. It is Pendery's opinion that it is more than likely that the Newport Tower is one of New England's earliest masonry structures and an example of a seventeenth-century prospect tower, one of the few surviving examples in the Western Hemisphere.

The most recent theory about the Newport Tower came in 2004 with the book *1421—The Year China Discovered America*.[160] Author Gavin Menzies announced that the tower had been built by early Chinese explorers during the 15th century to serve as a lighthouse. This identification is based on similarities between the Newport Tower and a lighthouse in the port of Zaiton in the Fujian province of southern China. Menzies noted that although the Zaiton is twice as large as Newport and five stories high, both were built on eight columns and covered in plaster.[161] Unfortunately for Menzies, that's about all the Newport Tower has in common with the Zaiton structure.

The tower at Zaiton, or Quanzhou, is not a lighthouse. It is a pagoda. Liusheng Pagoda (Pagoda of Six Victories) was an important navigational aid at the mouth of the Han River, particularly when lit at night, but it was primarily a pagoda. The exterior of each of the five stories has a veranda and alternating doors and niches to hold Buddhist statues on the eight sides. The closest the Newport Tower has to verandas, doors, and niches are the niches in the interior wall.

Not surprisingly, archaeologists and historians universally condemned Menzies' book,[162] and diffusionism advocates had little use for him either. The New England Antiquities Research Association, a staunch proponent of pre–Columbian visitations (including the possibility of the Chinese in North America), posted a page on their website that referred to his work as rife with "faulty research and ill-conceived premises...."[163]

The question of who built the tower remains a point of debate, but Menzies may have managed to do the impossible—get some sort of a consensus on the Newport Tower.

CHAPTER FIVE

America's Stonehenge on Mystery Hill

For over 50 years, the Mystery Hill site in North Salem, New Hampshire, has been open to interpretation, open to criticism, and most importantly, open to the public. In that time, theories have evolved, changed, and disappeared—only the stone structures and underlying mystery remain the same.

Regardless of who actually built the stone calendar site, it's a fascinating record of the changing perceptions about the hill. As an insight into the mindset of America, "America's Stonehenge" is an invaluable time capsule. The Pattee family owned the property from the 1700s into the 1920s. During that time, the hilltop was a homestead, a poorhouse, and purportedly an Underground Railroad station. Antiquarian William Goodwin purchased the acre of stone structures in 1937 as part of his research into the location of Vinland.[1] However, he soon decided that the stone ruins weren't Norse—this must be Great Ireland of the Norse sagas.[2] Goodwin died in 1950 and left the site to his associate and protégé, Malcolm Pearson. Pearson sold the site to Robert Stone, an electronic engineer. The latter, and his son Dennis, ushered in the current age of research with C-14 dating, astronomy, and epigraphy. The site has been theorized as the creation of Vikings, Irish Monks, Phoenicians, Celts, charlatans, Freemasons, and Native Americans. However, there may not be enough pieces of the puzzle left to ever determine conclusively why and by whom this site was constructed.

When Robert Stone acquired the site in 1965, he made a significant change in perspective—he also purchased over 100 additional acres surrounding the "main site," the acre purchased by Goodwin. In this way, when 12 acres of stone walls with astronomical significance were found surrounding the main site, it was already on his property. More importantly, minimal damage took place on this stone calendar because no one was looking for it. Until Gerald Hawkins' *Stonehenge Decodede*[3] was published in 1965, no one was cognizant of megalithic sites having astronomical implications. This is indicative of the problem with Mystery Hill—in addition to the rudimentary questions of "Who built the site?" and "What is its function?"—there is also the issue of "What are we looking for?" and "Where should we be looking?"

The main site is an acre of stone structures and stone walls surrounded by an arrangement of stone walls. The Sacrificial Table discussed in Chapter One is in the

Entrance to the "Oracle Chamber," the largest of the structures at America's Stonehenge.

geographic center of the acre, associated with the largest of the chambers, known as the "Y-Chamber" or "Oracle Chamber." The structure is a Y-shaped chamber with channeled bedrock drains. The north passage ends with a small opening in the roof that functioned as a vent with stone louvers to regulate airflow.[4] This passageway also contains a "speaking tube," a 6-foot, stone-lined passageway that carries sound from within the chamber out to beneath the Sacrificial Table, creating the oracle for which the chamber is named. The sound bounces off the stone walls of the recessed enclosure surrounding the table, disguising the direction that the sound comes from.

The east passageway is made up of two sections of bedrock. The right side is a block weighing about 40 tons that was split into two pieces and separated about 5 feet apart to form the main corridor. Accidentally or by design, an irregularity in the split forms a ledge that functions as a seat. Seated on this stone bench, you are in direct line of vision with a square recess in the opposite wall.

Goodwin believed this recess was the private altar of the abbot of the monastery.[5] Others have suggested that the niche housed a flame, used as a focus in a vision quest. Carved on the wall is a simply rendered zoomorphic carving, usually identified as a running deer or ibex. First noticed in the 1930s by Malcolm Pearson, it was the first carving found on the site. Goodwin compared the carving to native pictographs of the Southwest and Irish carvings and decided it was less dissimilar to the

Irish tradition.[6] However, because of the simplicity of the carving, there's no way of telling if Native Americans, pot-hunting neighbors, or the unknown builders of the site carved it.

The Pattee family house was built in the southeast corner of the ruins, incorporating the remains of several small stone huts as part of the foundation.[7] One of the small huts shows evidence of mortar being applied at a later date, the first indication that the chamber predates the Pattee house. The cellar hole of the house has several features of note, including a stone wall bisecting the cellar hole. This wall is of a different style of construction and abuts the outer wall instead of being incorporated into it. Assumed to be a later addition by Pattee to support the floor beams, it would also illustrate how poor a choice it was for a house lot. Drainage for a significant section of the site slopes toward the cellar hole. Prior to the bisecting wall, the drainage would continue through the recessed area and into one of the stone-lined drains that channel the water away from the site. The wall blocks the water flow, leaving half of the Pattee cellar prone to standing water.[8]

Other significant chambers on the main site included "The Lilac Chamber," named for the lilac bushes growing atop it. It is too small to be living quarters, and its limited space also makes it ineffective for storage. It is the only structure with an entrance oriented to the south. It is adjacent to a small stone wall that ends at a boulder, which is on the north-south alignment that bisects the site.

Another chamber with directional orientation is the "East-West Chamber." In the 1950s, this structure acquired the nickname "Tomb of Lost Souls." Noting the structure's similarity to European megalithic structures, archaeologist Frank Glynn hypothesized that ashes were placed in the larger part of the structure, sealed with a slab, and offerings placed in the smaller opening. It is now believed the chamber was a secondary entryway into the Y-chamber, and that the back wall of the chamber is actually a roof slab that has dropped down from a horizontal position into a vertical one. The East-West Chamber, had it continued, would have emptied into what is now the lower component of a two-tiered structure, known as the "Sundeck Chamber," adjacent to the Sacrificial Table.

Although the primary interest remains the acre of stone chambers that comprise the main site, comparatively undisturbed features outside the main site holistically augment research, such as the stone walls and standing stones.

Two parallel stone walls mark a path that starts at the southwestern side of the base of the hill, near a small structure known as the "Watch House."[9] This double-walled path serves a dual purpose—it leads up to the main site, and it supports some of the stones that comprise components of the astronomical calendar. Of particular note are stones that mark the sunrises of the winter solstice, as well as November 1 (Samhain) and February 1 (Imbolc).

A second double-walled path leads to the main site from the northeast. This path includes markers for the summer solstice and August 1 (Lammas) sunsets, and an alignment in the lunar cycle.

These two paths converge in an area where the worst damage was done in the 19th century. Any structures or features in this area are gone—the metal drill marks left by quarrymen are the only remaining clue. Quarrymen carried away large quantities of stone during the site's ownership by Seth Jonathan Mallon Pattee.[10] The extent of the stone removal can only be estimated, but the work was of a scope and duration to justify the erecting of a boom post to hoist and move rock. A socket was cut into the bedrock for the butt end of this post, and drill holes for the accompanying guy wires are still evident.

The area shows additional damage indirectly caused by the quarrymen. When William Goodwin arrived on the site, he found a pile of stone lining the edge of the stone ledge. This pile, especially in light of its proximity to the boom post socket, was probably part of a platform built by the quarrymen. However, Goodwin interpreted the stone pile as the remains of the pulpit of the early Irish monks that he believed was constructed at the site and had his work crew assemble all nearby loose stone into a wall along the edge of the ledge.

If this "pulpit" were removed, the original entryway would lead into the area where most of the stone was removed, an area that has carried such names as the "Megaron Area" and "The Compound." This area has a notch cut out of the bedrock, suggesting a support column once sat there, which held a roof too large to cantilever—indicating a comparatively large structure. The entire area is crisscrossed with drainage grooves cut into the bedrock, which still efficiently channel water out of the area.

Beyond the main site and the surrounding calendar, well beyond the public tour area, are cliffs with a sheer jagged face, created by glacial action. These cliffs became shelters for wandering Native Americans. Middle Woodland era[11] Native Americans stored clay vessels in the sheltering crevices, possibly as a winter hoard. One of these shallow caves beneath the cliffs collapsed, smashing the pottery into shards and covering them with protective rubble. Fifteen hundred years later, in 1959,[12] Robert Stone recovered two of these ancient bowls and part of a stone blade. Soon after, Stone discovered that the most likely source of the clay used in these bowls was located just south of the main site in a wet swale bordering the lower well. William Goodwin noted this area during his work on the site in the 1940s, but he did not pursue the matter.

Had he done so, Goodwin would have discovered what Stone did—part of the reason for the swamp's existence was the deep layer of glacial clay just beneath the surface that prevented water seepage. The proximity of a stone-lined well to the swale suggests it may have been an attempt by one of the various site occupants to draw water out of it. In 1969, researchers discovered a large fire pit southwest of the clay deposits that suggests pottery was made in the immediate vicinity. In 1995, during a series of test pits between the parking area and the visitors' lodge, fire pits and postholes were uncovered, indicating a lodge site that, based on radiocarbon dating of a hearth found there,[13] was occupied ca. AD 310 to ca. 755.

The Pattee family acquired the land in 1734, and it stayed in the family into the 20th century. Although several members of the family lived on the site, Jonathan Pattee is the most well-known. To this day, the Pattee family is divided into those who vow that Jonathan Pattee couldn't and didn't build the site and those who will tell you he was an insane mail robber who built the site with his seven burly sons. This is a particularly curious theory since Jonathan Pattee only had two sons, only one of whom lived to adulthood.[14]

Jonathan Pattee acquired the property from his mother in 1801 and raised a family there in a house he built.[15] As previously mentioned, the cellar hole of this house remains on the site. Sometime after Pattee's death in 1849, the house disappeared. There is a lack of debris to suggest the house collapsed and insufficient charcoal to suggest it was destroyed in a fire. The lack of brick and nails suggests that the house was dismantled. Based on the size and architecture of a house at the base of the hill, it appears that either Jonathan Pattee's son, Seth Jonathan Mallon Pattee, or grandson, Seth Mallon Pattee, had the house reconstructed along adjacent Haverhill Road. According to the local history,[16] the Seth Mallon Pattee house was destroyed in a fire, and a new one was built about 1902. However, that same history also includes a photograph of the Seth Mallon Pattee homestead[17] showing a house constructed in the Federal style, which was popular in the region ca. 1800–1830,[18] the time period that Jonathan would have been building the house atop the hill. In 1974, a survey of the Pattee house on Haverhill Road indicated that the dimensions of the structure were compatible with the cellar hole atop the hill.[19]

When antiquarian William Goodwin purchased the main site in 1937, he was purchasing property that had been a family farmstead, grown over, clear cut for a neighboring lumber mill, a popular picnic destination, and once again grown over. So popular was the denuded hilltop as a picnic destination that, to this day, a rainstorm will uncover shards of a variety of porcelain cups and plates, an indication of the traffic on the hilltop. Aside from damage caused by the traffic in and out of the structures, the surface was picked clean of artifact material. Goodwin was well aware of the traffic that continued through his acquisition. His solution was to hire a local caretaker and enclose the main site in a 6-foot chain-link fence topped with barbwire.

William Brownell Goodwin's fascination with his North Salem village would overshadow a successful career both in business and in antiquarian pursuits. An avid collector, his interests ranged from antique maps to colonial chests.[20] His initial thought was that the site was Norse:

> I have just been to visit the most amazing ruins of a stone village in New Hampshire that I have ever seen anywhere.... I am wondering if I have found the village site of the lost Norwegian Colony in Western Greenland that we know came from there in 1344 and amalgamated with the Indians, or as the papal records say "went native." I can't begin to describe it; I haven't the time in the first place; it is the most amazing thing I have ever seen.[21]

Goodwin ostensibly bought the site as part of his pursuit of Vinland. However, it took very little time to convince him of his error. Leaving Vinland centered at

Portsmouth, New Hampshire, where his original hypothesis placed it, he decided instead that this must be Great Ireland of the Norse sagas.

Goodwin then launched a full-fledged investigation, drawing together a vast amount of obscure information about the *Céli-Dé* or Culdee monks whose monastery he believed he now owned. Goodwin's theory was that these Irish monks, who, according to in historical records, abandoned their settlements as the Norse raiders encroached, were driven westward from Ireland to Iceland to Greenland. At this point the Culdee disappeared from historical records and were assumed to have assimilated into the mainstream Roman Catholic Church. Goodwin believed that a few Culdee continued westward and settled in North America. His argument was built on circumstantial evidence: beehive huts along Indian trails far from the shore, stone chambers, and oral traditions from the Norse sagas. These were his "proof" that the Culdee had set up a vast network to convert the Algonquins to Christianity, dwelling near the pagan Native Americans but always far enough inland to avoid the marauding Norse.

The only thing missing was artifact evidence. Goodwin had his protégé, Malcolm Pearson, assemble a team of workmen and begin cleaning up the site. Although his book would suggest otherwise, Goodwin spent very little time at his stone village.

Within a year, his "Irish Monastery" was receiving national coverage, thanks to a writer named Clay Perry, who mentioned the site in a book on New England caves.[22] Perry used Goodwin's monastery theory to get himself published in magazines and newspapers across the country (with varying degrees of accuracy). He also devoted an entire chapter to the site in a subsequent volume on caves.[23] Goodwin himself actively participated in one article, a Sunday supplement piece in his hometown newspaper, *The Hartford Courant*.[24] Goodwin was encouraged by the response and submitted a report on his "stone village site" to the *New England Quarterly*.

Instead of using Goodwin's article, Harvard University's Samuel Eliot Morison, on the journal's editorial board, sent a colleague to North Salem to write a new article. Hugh O'Neill Hencken was the curator of European Archaeology at Harvard's Peabody Museum. Hencken visited the site several times. He reviewed Goodwin's material and then wrote a very polite and very thorough dissection of the Irish monastery theory.[25]

Hencken's article addressed the possibility of the site being a medieval Irish construction. Goodwin's use of Norse sagas to establish the existence of a North American Irish presence was also examined. An example of how the article went is Hencken's assessment of the use of *Landnámabók*, which Hencken refers to as "an ancient and on the whole reliable text," except for the section utilized by Goodwin, which was "not on par with the rest."[26] Hencken then points out that the site had no characteristics in common with monastery sites in Ireland other than the use of corbelled vaulting in the roof of the Y-chamber, which was not conclusive since corbelling appears across the globe.

The question was then, having eliminated the Culdee, who could have constructed the site? Although Hencken notes a white pine stump whose roots had grown into the stone wall of a structure built well before Jonathan's birth, he nonetheless decided in favor of the local tradition that eccentric farmer Jonathan Pattee constructed the site with his large family and teams of oxen. A footnote on the final page of the article thanks Dr. George Woodbury for his assistance. Woodbury was a distant relation of the Pattee family, so the eccentric theory came from within the family. Woodbury was also later responsible for a 1958 newspaper article that remains one of the nastiest diatribes against the Pattees to date.[27] Although several more articles would run featuring the Irish monk theory, Goodwin's credibility was gone, and Goodwin's Irish monastery theory quickly lost the interest of the media. Goodwin blamed Morison for the decline in interest and his inability to gain research funding.

By 1946, Goodwin's progress on a book about his research at the North Salem site had stalled. Between his failing health and lingering post–World War II paper shortages, it appeared that the book was not going to be completed or published. Unexpectedly, a paper supply became available, and there was a rushed attempt to compile Godwin's notes. Ready or not, *The Ruins of Great Ireland in New England* was going to press.

Even a cursory glance through *Ruins* shows the haste with which the material was prepared for publication. What should be the most important record of early work on the Mystery Hill site is all but useless because of poor organization and unedited text. Materials on the same points are scattered, photographs are published upside down, and text from other books is included without credit or notation.[28]

Morison and Goodwin had clashed over the North Salem site, the type of ship used by Norse explorers, and the landing sites of Columbus.[29] Goodwin complained about Morison's interference in all of these topics in a lengthy statement that should never have been printed.[30] Goodwin also took the opportunity to remind his readers that Morison had verified the authenticity of the "Virginia Dare Stones"[31] in 1937, only to have the *Saturday Evening Post* uncover them as a blatant hoax in 1941.[32] Goodwin's reminder of Morison's humiliation undoubtedly did not help improve the situation. Historian Frederick Pohl theorized that Morison's high-profile embarrassment almost certainly tainted his opinion of any future encounter with inscriptions.[33]

The animosity between Goodwin and Morison was so deep that years after Goodwin's death, Morison, in his *European Discovery of America*,[34] was still taking shots at his rival.[35] Morison now admitted to the possibility of the Irish in North America, citing the same references in the Vinland Sagas as did Goodwin.[36] This places Hencken's refutation in a difficult position since his primary argument was the unreliability of the sagas. In fact, Morison's and Goodwin's primary point of contention turns out not to be whether or not Culdee monks came to America but whether Mystery Hill was a Culdee site.

After his death in 1950, Goodwin became academia's whipping boy, blamed for everything from incompetence to building the site with a team of oxen.[37] The question of how much of the site was rebuilt by Goodwin's team remains a point of discussion, but stylistic differences clearly identify wall sections modified by Goodwin[38] and the amount of unidentified modification appears to be minimal.[39] Yet, the explanation of the site as a product of Pattee and Goodwin continued. Archaeologist and historian Glyn Daniel of Cambridge University was adamantly opposed to diffusionists and any associated sites, such as Mystery Hill.[40] In his 1964 book on New Grange,[41] he places North Salem in Connecticut and insists the site was an eighteenth-century folly built by Pattee.

Goodwin's will left the North Salem site to Malcolm Pearson. To underwrite research, Pearson helped found the Early Sites Foundation. One of the first projects chosen was an excavation done by a qualified field archaeologist. On the recommendation of Junius Bird of the American Museum of Natural History, grad student archaeologist Gary Vescelius was hired to conduct the excavation. Vescelius had been an assistant to Junius Bird in a 1945 excavation for William Goodwin.

Vescelius and a three-man team completed a six-week series of excavations in the summer of 1955.[42] Bird was fascinated by the site back in 1945 but could find no evidence to support Goodwin's claims of a European culture. Now, a decade later, with the Early Sites Foundation, he mapped out a new plan for Vescelius.

Vescelius' conclusion was that the site was less than 200 years old. Bird, however, remained unconvinced, as did others in the Early Sites Foundation. However, the damage was done. Momentum was once again lost.

Vescelius' work at Mystery Hill mirrored similar work done five years previously by William Godfrey at the Newport Tower. Bird also had a part in planning the Newport dig, and the same difficulties arose at both sites. Both had a graduate student supervising an excavation at a possible pre-colonial site even though the student's specialty was South American cultures. Both excavations were purported to be hurried along, and extensive follow-up was required but not done.[43] Thousands of artifacts were recovered, identified as colonial, and ignored. Significant numbers of them are now missing.

There are numerous problems with the final excavation report submitted by Vescelius, not the least of which was Vescelius' use of erroneous genealogical data on the Pattee family:

> "Though in respects the Caves resemble certain Old World megalithic ruins, the similarities are not in themselves great enough to warrant belief in an historical relationship.... It is, perhaps, worth noting in this connection that the Pattees are said to have come from Brittany, and that at least one branch of the family resided for a time on the Isle of Jersey, in the English Channel. Megalithic ruins abound, of course, both in Brittany and on the Channel Isles, and it is conceivable that the eccentric Jonathan embarked upon his cave-building venture under the influence of some tale about huge stone monuments—a tale passed on from one generation of Pattees to the next."[44]

It appears that Vescelius' research into the Pattee genealogy consisted only of reading Ezra Stearns' *Genealogical and Family History of the State of New Hamp-*

shire.⁴⁵ Stearns' history not only borrows heavily from an earlier Pattee profile from a history of Warner, New Hampshire,⁴⁶ but also inexplicably combines it with the French Huguenot Pettee family (whose ancestry was from the Isle of Jersey). The first Pattee in New England was Peter Patee, who first appears in Haverhill, Massachusetts, records in 1677.⁴⁷ Court records in Haverhill indicate Peter came to Haverhill from Virginia before 1677.⁴⁸ Few pieces of documented evidence have surfaced as to the European origins of Peter Patee, resulting in different theories as to the origin of the family.⁴⁹

Vescelius' report states that he found more than 8,000 artifacts, all of which he identified as colonial or post-colonial. This means that, in a period of six weeks, Vescelius and three assistants found, sorted, examined, and identified 8,000 items. His excavations took place within the one-acre area known to have had a colonial/post-colonial occupation (Pattee) and prior excavations (Goodwin). At least two of his digs took place in the area known to have had the Pattee house on it.

Whether or not Vescelius overlooked artifacts of prehistoric age, there is no way to reexamine the artifacts. In the ensuing 50 years, the artifacts have been lost. This leaves Vescelius' report as the sole source of information on the excavation, and that report is not helpful. Even peers had problems with Vescelius' documentation, or more specifically, lack of documentation; it was significant to the point where it is actually mentioned in his obituary.⁵⁰ Vescelius majored in South American archaeology and apparently accepted the project as a favor to Bird.

Vescelius' rush to complete the assignment and his lack of familiarity with colonial American (and possible Megalithic European) artifacts surfaces in a report by Frank Glynn.⁵¹ Glynn had examined the Vescelius artifacts in 1959 and retrieved a metal fragment that the Vescelius excavation had identified as a potsherd. Glynn had the metal tested at Bowdoin College and found it was bronze, old enough to indicate possible colonial or European origin.

There is no doubt that in addition to centuries of New England weather and seismic activity, the site has also taken extensive damage from quarrymen, pothunters, picnickers, and overzealous researchers. But this activity has all focused around the acre of stone ruins—the surrounding stone walls and astronomical alignments remained comparatively unscathed.

In 1975, archaeologist James Whittall brought Barry Fell to Mystery Hill. Fell was compiling numerous instances of carvings in stone throughout New Hampshire and Vermont that he suspected of being proof of pre–Columbian contact between the old and new worlds. These suspicions would become the bestseller *America BC*.⁵²

Fell arrived at Mystery Hill and was shown one of several flat stones that site owner Robert Stone and Whittall had found previously. Fell immediately recognized the stone as written in Iberian Punic. After a week of study, Fell pronounced that the stone was a broken piece of a larger tablet. The remaining eight characters were a form of Iberian Punic used ca. 600–700 BC in the southwestern part of Spain during the early part of the Carthaginian occupation. The fragment read, "*walaya bi ... nahata-hu....*" It translated to, "Embellished by ... hewed this stonework...."[53]

The stone was the equivalent of an artist's signature. Fell translated a second tablet as a dedicatory tablet to the god Baal in Iberian Punic. Fell advised Stone that he suspected that various structures would have been dedicated to other divinities and that other tablets were out there to be discovered.

On a subsequent visit to the site with Whittall and Dr. George Carter of Texas A&M University, Fell was examining the area where the first tablet had been found when Robert Stone found another tablet, this time "dedicated to Bel" in Ogham. Fell considered this a significant find. He had long hypothesized that the Phoenician god Baal was the same deity as the Celtic sun god Bel—these two New World votive tablets offered proof of the Baal-Bel connection in the Old World.[54]

Ogham, or Ogam, is a script of 15 consonants and five vowels that use sets of parallel vertical lines to designate the positions of sounds. Visually, it looks like tally marks balanced above, below, and through a horizontal guideline that may or may not be supplied. Ogham can also run as parallel horizontal lines on a vertical stem-line. The variant found in North America is vowel-less, or consaine. Ogham is an alphabet, as opposed to a language. This means, in addition to variable orientation and no vowels, Ogham can also represent a variety of languages.

Fell felt that this variation of Ogham with Phoenician elements had to have originated on the Iberian Peninsula of Spain and Portugal. The Iberian Peninsula is virtually cut off from mainland Europe by the barrier of the Pyrenees. These mountains can be crossed only at their coastal edges, either west along the Atlantic or east along the Mediterranean. The Celtic population occupied about half of the Iberian Peninsula, with centuries of contact with Iberians in the east and Carthaginians in the south. A culture developed distinctly different from the *primary* Celtic identity, a hybrid of the Iberian and Celt cultures with Carthaginian influence.

Barry Fell considered this the most important inscription found at the America's Stonehenge site, translating it as a dedicatory tablet "to Baal of the Canaanites" (Robert Stone photograph).

There were actually numerous small tribes of Celtic origin, as opposed to one unified nation, but there was a unifying language spoken by all the Celt tribes, cleverly called "Old Celtic." The language seems to have come from the original Ur language and originated with the Indo-European language tradition. In fact, the form of Old Celtic was the closest cousin to Italic, the precursor of Latin.

The original waves of Celtic immigrants to the British Isles were called the *q–Celts* and spoke Goidelic. It is not known precisely when this immigration occurred, but it may be placed sometime in the window of 2000 to 1200 BC. The label *q–Celtic* stems from the differences between this early Celtic tongue and Italic. Some of the differences between Italic and Celtic include a lack of a "p" in Celtic and an "a" in place of the Italic "o." A second, later wave of Celtic immigrants to the British Isles is referred to as the *p–Celts*, speaking Brythonic. Goidelic led to the formation of the three Gaelic languages spoken in Ireland, the Isle of Man, and later Scotland. Brythonic gave us two British Isles languages, Welsh and Cornish, as well as Breton, spoken in Brittany.

Ogham was only used by q–Celts and the 2000 BC date of their exodus from the European mainland also coincides with the C-14 dates at Mystery Hill.

Before 1975 had ended, another stone was uncovered—an inscribed stele that Fell believed indicated the length of time the builders remained in the region. This inscribed stele, now known as "The Beltane Stone," is also written in Ogham but also has Roman numerals. It is edge-inscribed, in a style similar to that of Ogham steles found in Britain, but without vowels. Fell translated the stele as "Day 39." Fell felt this was a significant find because there was a very small window of time in which the phrase "39 days" was significant. The Celtic calendar began on the vernal equinox. When Julius Caesar introduced the reformed calendar in 45 BC, the vernal equinox was set at March 25 and the start of summer as May 8. However, in the Celtic regions, the traditional festival of Beltane on May 1 was considered the beginning of summer. By the Julian calendar, 39 days elapse between the start of the year and Beltane, which appears on the Latin Celtic calendar as Day 39. Because of precession of the equinox, the number of days between the vernal equinox and Beltane has increased, meaning the Beltane Stone would have to have been inscribed around the time of Julius Caesar and the early Roman emperors. Any later, the number of days would be wrong. It could not have been inscribed earlier because Roman numerals weren't used by the Celts until after Caesar conquered them.[55]

Combining the estimated age of the Iberian Punic with the age of the Ogham, Fell hypothesized that the site was occupied by 800 BC and remained in contact with Europe for seven centuries until the era of Julius Caesar.

Other stones were uncovered: a Celtic sun symbol, followed by a stone that appeared to be a zoomorphic image of a bird with the heart outlined and an arrow aimed at the heart. It is interesting to note that Fell paid little interest to this stone. Had he turned this bird/arrow pictograph upside down, it has a striking resemblance to an eye of Horus, which also appears in Phoenician symbolism as a sky god motif.

Both the running deer carving in the Y-chamber and Celtic sun symbol show some characteristics associated with entoptic phenomena in vision quests as discussed by anthropologists Haviland and Power[56] at the Bellows Falls petroglyphs site.[57]

The last petroglyph discovered on Mystery Hill was a badly weathered eye, found on a boulder with theorized astronomical significance. Based on Fell's previous interpretation, it soon became known as an "Eye of Baal," although on site records,[58] it is still simply, the "Eye Stone." An Eye of Baal on the boulder of a lunar standstill alignment is interesting since Baal is a sky god. With the other references to Baal found, as well as the sun symbol and the Eye of Horus, it would appear to be petroglyphic support of the astronomical calendar.

In the late 1960s, Gerald Hawkins found himself defending *Stonehenge Decoded* in the media.[59] With Stonehenge's proposed astronomical alignments in the public eye, Robert Stone decided to take a closer look at the standing stones in the stone walls ringing the main site at Mystery Hill. Stone reasoned that the stone situated farthest west along the horizon would mark the winter solstice since that was the point farthest west that the sun set. If the stone was astronomically aligned, then anyone standing in alignment with the center of the site on that date would see the sun set directly behind the stone.

Stone focused on four primary solar alignments: summer and winter solstices and fall and spring equinoxes. He had assumed that the geographic center of the site, the Sacrificial Table, was also the astronomical center. A large monolith was discovered pointing due north. Putting this "North Stone" in alignment with the stone ruins, Stone found that the marker bisected the acre of stone ruins, passed over the Sacrificial Table, and connected to a stone wall running due south from the main site. With a north-to-south line to work from, Stone hypothesized that the solstice and equinox alignments should intercept along the north-south line at the altar stone. Stone cleared away a swath of 50-year-old forest behind the suspected winter solstice monolith and attempted to validate his theory.

In 1970, Stone was able to photographically verify the sun setting behind the winter solstice sunset monolith. With proof that there were astronomical alignments, an investigation was launched to search for other possible alignments. Additional alignments followed, including sunrise and sunset on equinoxes and solstices, North Star, and several suspected lunar alignments. Not all the calendar stones were still standing. However, upright or not, they were still recognizable—calendar stones all have a distinctive design similar to that of the Sacrificial Table: two straight sides, two curved sides, or shoulders, that end in a rounded tip. The left shoulder is higher than the right one. The tip has been deliberately shaped to match features on the horizon with which it is aligned, and percussive flaking has expertly shaped the entire stone.[60] Quarry sites have been located and excavated,[61] and it appears that the stone was hewn to the proper shape and then transported to the final location where it was erected and then the tip shaped to match the horizon features.

Five. America's Stonehenge on Mystery Hill

Former owner Robert Stone at the summer solstice sunset alignment stone.

The megaliths do not appear to have been cut with metal tools. The shallow scalloping along the edges is indicative of the stones being shaped using percussive flaking. Metal drill marks,[62] such as those left by quarrymen who carried away large quantities of stone at the behest of Seth Jonathan Mallon Pattee,[63] are distinctive. Although the extent of the stone removal can only be estimated, the drill holes remain as a stark reminder.[64]

Stone's initial work on the astronomical alignments quickly discovered that the center of the main site was not the Sacrificial Table but a point located near it. The intersection point at which all the horizon sightings converged was just north of the Sacrificial Table along the north-south line and appeared to be located where the Sacrificial Table had been quarried from the bedrock. Research discovered that Goodwin had removed the remains of two small mounds from that point while searching for the source of the Sacrificial Table.[65]

In 1977, a local survey firm was contracted to survey site features. The survey confirmed that there were numerous stone walls that did not align with any boundary line, current or historical, nor did these walls conform to colonial stone wall construction techniques.[66] This survey placed objects in relationship with each other, but it did not explain the alignment of every stone or the rationale behind every feature. As such, new data creates new theories and occasionally returns to older ones.

The survey's positioning of the north line was considered the most critical work accomplished. This permitted the identification of two small stones symmetrically placed on either side of the North Stone. It was thought that these two small stones could have marked the horizontal limits of motion of the pole star around the celestial North Pole. The age of the site can then be calculated by determining at what date, with the earth's precession,[67] these stones aligned with some pole star. The smaller stones were placed as if to mark a 5-degree radius of diurnal motion. This suggests a pole star that was not stationary on the precise celestial pole but revolved around in a circle in the night sky.

The stars Thuban, between 3600 and 1700 BC, and Polaris, after AD 1450, both matched the data of a pole star with a 5-degree radius of revolution.[68] So, based on pole star alignment alone, it was inferred that the site was built between 3600 and 1700 BC or after AD 1450. The later date is not supported by carbon-dating data on the site.

Radiocarbon dating has been used with varying degrees of success on the site. Between 1967 and 1971, nine test samples were submitted for dating. One was unusable due to insufficient carbon. Of the remaining eight, seven predated Jonathan Pattee's occupation of the site, the oldest showing a date 3475 BP ± 210 years.[69]

This date[70] was significant for several reasons. First, it was the first carbon date retrieved between stones in a wall of a small chamber on the path to the Y-chamber. Even if the charcoal was from a natural source such as a brush fire, the chamber had to predate the fire to trap the charcoal. Second, it validated a previous date of 2995 BP ± 180 years found by archeologist James P. Whittall II.[71] Whittall had excavated along the pine stump that Hencken had pointed out as predating Jonathan Pattee[72] to discover whether the structure was built on bedrock.[73] The excavation found three distinct layers of soil. The first 5 inches were topsoil, leading to a second level of reddish soil, 11 inches deep. In these first two levels, Whittall found colonial and post-colonial artifacts—buttons, hooks, eyeglass frames, and pottery. This was expected and merely confirmed use by the Pattee family over time.

The third level was yellow soil 10 inches deep, which sat on bedrock. The color matched the glacial clays surrounding the hill, suggesting that this was windblown accumulation over a significant period of time. The first 3 inches were sterile soil—no evidence of disturbance. However, in the next 3 inches, Whittall uncovered a hammerstone, a scraper, and quarrying spalls—evidence of someone working with stone beside this structure. Whittall continued down a fraction of an inch and uncovered flakes of charcoal.

The carbon dating report came back with a 2995 BP ± 180 years date—around 1045 BC, someone was on Mystery Hill using stone tools. Whittall would continue through another 3 inches of sterile yellow soil before reaching bedrock. It proved the structure had been built upon bedrock. And since there were roughly 24 inches of soil between the surface and 3000-year-old charcoal, soil accumulated in that vicinity at the rate of approximately one inch per 125 years, allowing calculations for other parts of the site.

Later carbon dating would bolster the occupation dates. An excavation in 1995 in the vicinity of the North Stone gave a date of 5440 BC,[74] and a fire pit near the same monolith came back with a 1748 BC date.[75]

Penn State University astronomy professor Louis Winkler revitalized astronomical research in the late 1990s by building on and reinterpreting the previous alignment work, with the addition of stellar alignments involving zenith stars and grazing-circumpolar stars.[76]

Winkler's work encompasses the various walls that cross the 14 acres of the astronomical area, and he believes that the walls indicate a large variety of alignments—solar, lunar, and stellar. Winkler's interpretation included stellar alignments and notes two distinct types: zenith stars and grazing-circumpolar stars.[77] Both types of stars disappear as they near the horizon because of the extinction effect of the atmosphere, and the point of extinction is what alignment stones are marking.

When the site was being built, Arcturus, Alphecca, and Vega were three distinctly bright zenith stars—stars with an apparent magnitude brighter than 3.[78] Winkler hypothesizes that Arcturus was the focal point not only because it was the brightest but also because it was in the same constellation as the only grazing circumpolar star with a magnitude brighter than 3–Izar. Both Arcturus and Izar are part of the constellation Boötes, one of the constellations most widely recognized by ancient cultures, depicting a herdsman driving a bear (Ursa Major) around the sky (some cultures see a plow or a wagon instead of a bear).

Winkler's alignment work suggests construction ca. 2000–1500 BC, corresponding with the carbon dating but not suggesting who may have built the calendar. He notes striking similarities between the site and Callanish, a Scottish astronomical site on the Isle of Lewis, with both locations having an equinox alignment of four collinear stones, a north-south line of stones, and a ceremonial path of parallel stones.

In Germany, a Bronze Age artifact was recovered from looters in 2002. Now known as the Sky Disk of Nebra,[79] it is a bronze disk that functions as an astronomical calculator. From the Mittelberg hill near the town of Nebra in Germany's Saxony-Anhalt, the disk appears to determine solstices *and* lunar and stellar phenomena by orienting markings on the disk with horizon features. The 3,600-year-old artifact was buried under a stone mound surrounded by a low circular rampart or ring-ditch. The recognition of a Bronze Age culture with astronomical alignments in Germany offers new interpretations in New England.

A Bronze Age culture is what Frank Glynn had initially hypothesized in the 1960s. Glynn focused on Malta, but his framework was utilized by James Whittall in Portugal. There Whittall found sacrificial tables and astronomical knowledge that supported Barry Fell's Celt Iberian inscriptions.[80] Each field of research builds on the prior work, but still, no definitive answers come from Mystery Hill.

Robert Stone died in December 2009 after a long illness. He lived long enough to see that daily operations at America's Stonehenge were in the capable hands of his son Dennis and grandson Kelsey. The personnel had changed, but not the search for answers. Ironically, even as the future direction of research was being mapped out, the subsequent discovery came about by accident.

A brush fire roared through 15 acres on the southwestern slope of the hill in 2010. Extinguished by the Salem Fire Department in short order, it exposed additional quarry sites hidden beneath layers of plant matter. Those sites were far more than appear to have been needed by the structures and monoliths on the site. Soon after, Kelsey was clearing brush from the paths cut through the woods to allow views of the horizons behind the monoliths. He found even more quarry sites. Based on the scope of stone quarrying suggested by these additional sites, either far more stone was removed from the hilltop by the Pattees than had been previously estimated, or a habitation site was in the vicinity.

It had long been hypothesized that the culture that built and used the hilltop stonework lived below the hill, and the location of these new quarry sites suggests the village was along the Spicket River, now beneath the Arlington Mill Reservoir. When the reservoir was drained in 1983 for repairs to the dam, there were reports that unusual stone piles were found, visually different from the cellar hole from Wheeler's Mill. Debris was removed while the dam was repaired, and the lake bed was dredged. There is no record of what was removed in terms of lithic material, so it is possible some of the potentially ancient stone ruins still rest beneath millions of gallons of water.

Like his father before him, Dennis Stone personally maintained the sightlines for the astronomical alignments and walkways for visitors. In the course of clearing brush, Stone began paying attention to the unexplained stonewalls that seemingly started and stopped for no apparent reason. He discovered some of the walls started with a roughly triangular boulder with the wall undulating for about 100 feet before tapering to a stop. They appear to be deliberate attempts to create giant serpents out of stone.[81]

These zoomorphic serpentine walls open new avenues of research, none of which suggest European diffusionism. Among Native Americans, there is a widespread belief in a horned water-beast, usually a serpent of enormous size. Ethnohistorian George Lankford refers to it as "the Great Serpent," a "universally known figure in the Eastern Woodlands for many centuries" in the cultural cosmology.[82]

Archaeologist Edward Lenik also notes serpentine images carved into rock surfaces with ideological significance appear throughout the Northeast. These images occur predominantly on outcroppings located along shorelines. These serpents were portrayed as fish-tailed or horned monsters representing, for Algonquian peoples, creatures of evil and darkness and as symbols of power. They were viewed as powerful manitous, the guardian spirit of many Indians whose horns signified its great power.[83]

When William Goodwin acquired the North Salem property, the first carving found on the site was a simply rendered zoomorphic carving, usually identified as a running deer or ibex in the so-called "Oracle Chamber." It could also be interpreted as a horned serpent, which would, in turn, support suggestions the chamber was used for vision quests.[84]

Hedden notes that such rock art in the Northeast, historically associated with Algonquin-language speakers, seems to have been the work of spiritual leaders who obtained special powers through visionary experiences.[85] Anthropologist Kathleen Bragdon similarly believes most of these petroglyph sites are shamanic in origin.[86] The widespread occurrence of similar images, especially in southern New England, suggests a symbolic meaning that a meaning shared regionally that extends beyond different languages.

And the serpent appears in other locations, mislabeled as pre–Columbian European. On private property off Old Tyng Road in Tyngsboro, Massachusetts, is a boulder with a carving on it. Located in the river's floodplain, it is roughly 10 foot by 8-foot and has split apart. On the surface is a carved groove, weathered with age but consistently ½-inch in depth. It is claimed that when viewed from its southwest corner looking northwest, the carving resembles the path of the Merrimack River as viewed from a high altitude. The "Tyngsboro Map Stone" makes no sense as a map. It is located where the Merrimack River shifts direction from north-south to west-east. It is 42 miles from the Atlantic, following the river's twisting course, and 75 miles from its headwaters. None of the major tributaries are marked, and there is no indication of the significant number of waterfalls along the way.

A theoretical European explorer heading upriver would reach Bodwell Falls in Lawrence, now the site of the Great Stone Dam. With a 9-foot drop blocking the route, it would be necessary to anchor in the vicinity, portage shallow draft boats around it, and continue upriver another 10 miles until they reached the 32-foot Pawtucket Falls in modern-day Lowell. Neither obstacle nor the Concord River confluence is in the Map Stone.

If it is Native, such a pre-contact cartographic petroglyph, explains Mark Warhus, must be examined from a non–Eurocentric perspective.

> It is necessary to suspend western preconceptions of what makes a map. Unlike western cartography, where the primary document is the physical map and the conventions of scale, longitude, latitude, direction, and relative location are believed to "scientifically" depict a static landscape, Native American maps are pictures of experience. They are formed in the human interaction with the land and are a record of the events that give it meaning.[87]

Native American maps represent encounters or relay messages in a given location. Garrick Mallery includes Mikmaq, Penobscot, and Passamaquoddy examples in *Picture-writing of the American Indians*.[88] The three are stylistically similar, relaying hunting information or the appearance of strangers, but they are not worked on stone. Such maps were ephemeral in nature. The Tyngsboro carving can't be interpreted as a map of the river because there is no associated iconography; it relays no message.

However, just because the Native population didn't carve a map does not mean they did not create a petroglyph that happened to be mistaken for a map. Assume the fork at the top of the Map Stone's carving does not represent the Merrimack's headwaters at the confluence of the Pemigewasset and Winnipesaukee rivers. It could then be considered an eroded representation of horns or antlers on a serpent's head, turning a useless map into a petroglyph of the Horned Water Serpent, a widely distributed figure found in the beliefs of almost all indigenous peoples in the Eastern part of North America.[89]

Placing the Tyngsboro stone in such a context, the serpent petroglyph is on a boulder within sight of Wickasee Island, the principal residence of Wannalancet, the last sachem of the Pennacooks, and a former home of his father Passaconaway, one of the most prominent New England shaman or pow-wows.

In his study "The Great Serpent in Eastern North America," ethnohistorian George Lankford notes that among the various Native American groups in the Eastern Woodlands and the Plains, the cosmos is a series of layers, each of which is identified with particular powers. The bottom layer is primeval water, and the world was created specifically to float upon the waters. The mythological creatures that rule these waters are horned and aquatic. Even today, these residents can come to this world and occasionally be seen by humans, but only if they choose to be seen.

Lankford argues that although it is referred to as a single creature, a careful reading of the folklore suggests the Horned Water Serpent is a race of beings with individual members dwelling in water. If Dennis Stone's interpretation of the walls as serpentine is correct, it changes the understanding of America's Stonehenge from pre–Columbian European colonists to a Native American origin as a sachem's residence. The site had a Native presence in the vicinity, as evidenced by clay pits and pottery sherds. The site is on an Indian trail that became a colonial post road. But it may be the site's stellar alignments that support a Native origin.

Lankford's earlier work focused on the ancient Natives and how they used the stars in their oral traditions. Lankford devoted an entire chapter to "The Serpent in the Stars," which we still know as the Draco constellation.[90] Draco is quite near the stars Winkler had been focused on in the constellation Boötes. But Winkler is basing his calculations on a fallen monolith that could just as easily point to the serpentine Draco. A Native culture constructing stone structures and calculating astronomical alignments is feasible. Dix and Mavor connected astronomically-oriented stonework.

It is but the latest theory at America's Stonehenge. Advocates of Phoenician, Norse, and Irish colonization all still claim "America's Stonehenge" as proof of their pet theories. Whether or not the secret of Mystery Hill's origin is ever solved, its mark on the American landscape is indelible.

Chapter Six

Celtic New England

There are carvings and messages written in ancient scripts across New England. Some are unquestionably Native American in origin, while others, such as Mystery Hill's inscriptions, continue to be debated back and forth. A good rule of thumb is that if the interpretation involves an ancient script that originated on another continent, there is controversy about accuracy and authenticity. For every claim of a Norse or Phoenician inscription, there is a counterclaim of glacial marks, plow strikes, or erosion.

The Celts were occasionally suggested as an alternative to the usual Pre-Columbian suspects, but the theory never gained popularity. Ogham was not identified as a translatable alphabet[1] until well after the famine influx of Irish immigration had created an anti-Irish/pro-Norse movement in the United States.[2]

In 1976, Barry Fell's *America B.C.*[3] was published and immediately became a bestseller. The premise was simple many ancient civilizations routinely made visits to North America; the proof was the carved inscriptions they left behind. This book, and Fell's subsequent volumes,[4] immediately galvanized the academic world against Fell and his work and anything remotely attached to him. Although his degree was in Marine Biology, Dr. Fell was also an accomplished linguist with a working knowledge of Russian, Gaelic, Sanskrit, Egyptian hieroglyphics, and more than a dozen other languages.[5] This knowledge allowed Fell to recognize, if not immediately translate, a variety of obscure alphabets.

As *America B.C.* climbed the bestseller lists, Fell continued to receive new reports of epigraphic finds. Unable to keep up with the influx, Fell made more translations off the cuff, often from poor copies of reproduced images. Each time he made an error in translation or translated a fraudulent tablet, his critics jumped upon it as proof of Fell's facetiousness. Although Fell continued to publish and translate until his death, the forward momentum of his epigraphic movement could not to sustain the initial popularity of *America B.C.* against the criticism from archaeologists and linguists.

Philologist David H. Kelley, author of *Deciphering the Maya Script*,[6] a 1976 text instrumental in establishing the phonetic character of the Mayan glyphs, wrote a 1990 article for *Review of Archaeology*[7] discussing the occurrence of Tifinagh and Ogham in North America. Tifinagh, the alphabet used by the Berbers of northern

Africa, is generally assumed to be Phoenician in origin. The Punic sources of Tifinagh combined with Ogham was one of Fell's postulates for identifying Celtiberians as colonists in New England. Kelley, a noted linguist and archaeologist, made no excuses for Fell, but pointed out a basic fact—Barry Fell, flaws and all, brought North American examples of these ancient written languages to the attention of scholars. Kelley points out that regardless of anyone's opinion of Fell and his work, there is Ogham in North America. And that equates to the possibility of ancient Celts in North America.

Calendar One, South Royalton, Vermont

The "Ancient Vermont" Conference was held in October of 1977 on the campus of Castleton State College in the lakes region of western Vermont, chaired by Castleton professor of history and anthropology Warren Cook. It was a gathering to discuss a large number of stone chambers and root cellars that had gained some notoriety both before and after Barry Fell's *America B.C.* had brought the limelight to the structures and their associated inscriptions, fertility symbols, and astronomical alignments.

The published proceedings[8] show the conference strived to show both sides of the controversy, with topics ranging from Barry Fell's discussion of "Vermont's Ancient Sites and the Larger Picture of Trans-Atlantic Visitations"[9] to cultural geographer Stewart McHenry's "Colonial Field Patterns in Vermont."[10] No issues were resolved, but the conference demonstrated the scope and variety of questions surrounding the structures in Vermont.

In the summer of 1974, an optical systems designer named Byron Dix was searching the hills of central Vermont for a rumored stone chamber. He did not find the chamber but instead found himself in a natural bowl or amphitheater with variously marked stones and standing stones in rows along the ridge. The east, west, and north sides were surrounded by hills. Dix returned to the site in February 1975, and by the time he snowshoed in to photograph the stones, it was late afternoon. Dix realized that the photographs would not show the markings because of the angle and position of the sun in relation to the stones and that this perhaps indicated that the rocks were placed to observe the sunset over the ridge. Dix suspected that he had found an ancient solar calendar marking the rising and setting of the sun over specific peaks, depressions, and stone markers around the edge of the bowl. With the snow compressing foliage, Dix located a small stone chamber first reported by William Goodwin in 1946.[11]

In the area around South Royalton, Vermont, William Goodwin had noted six stone chambers discovered in the fall of 1945. Malcolm Pearson took photographs which was the extent of Goodwin's research. Between Goodwin's failing health and the publication of *Ruins of Great Ireland in New England*, the sites were never explored further until Dix rediscovered the area.[12]

Dix's initial findings indicated a central observation point in the bowl that appeared to be the ideal location to observe alignments behind the major horizon features. Dix found all eight major solar events—equinox and solstice sunrises and sunsets aligned with features on the horizon. On the summer solstice, the sun rose over the northern peak of the eastern ridge wall and set at a depression in a western ridge wall. At equinox, the sun rose through a notch in the east and set along a point on the western horizon marked by a stone row. For obvious reasons, Dix named the site "Calendar One."

Dix's preliminary report raised interest.[13] Possible alignments had recently come to light at Mystery Hill,[14] and Gerald Hawkins had released a follow-up book to expand his astronomical research at Stonehenge.[15]

Entrance to Calendar One chamber in South Royalton, Vermont (Terry Deveau photograph).

At a subsequent conference, Dix met James Mavor, and the two began a research partnership that would continue until Dix's death in 1993. James Mavor, who died in 2006, was a retired oceanographic engineer affiliated with the Woods Hole Oceanographic Institute. He was one of the designers of the Deep Submergence Vehicle *Alvin*, best known for surveying the remains of the *Titanic*. Mavor suggested that the volcanic destruction of a Minoan settlement on the Aegean island of Thera (also known as Santorini) was the basis of Plato's tale of Atlantis.[16] He had done some work on European astronomical sites, but Vermont was new territory for him.[17]

After a decade of excavation and astronomical observation, Mavor and Dix published their findings in book form. Although the original hypothesis had been to find evidence of European diffusion on the site, when *Manitou: the Sacred Landscape of New England's Native Civilization*,[18] was published, it emphasized the possibility of Native American origin for the various features at various sites, particularly Calendar One.

The scope of the site had changed as work continued.[19] The focal point remained the bowl but included features 20 square kilometers around it. This area consists of eight chambers, three of which appear to be oriented with solar events. There are at least 10 astronomically aligned standing stones one meter in height. There are cairns across the research area. One cairn field on the eastern slope alone has over 70 cairns.[20] Altogether, 18 possible solar and lunar alignments were identified, using man-made and natural features as sighting points.[21]

Mavor and Dix hypothesized a New England-wide shamanistic society that focused on the relationship between earth and sky, with the alignments and structures having a ceremonial function within this Native American geomantic sacred landscape.

Throughout the book, Mavor and Dix acknowledged the possibility of European influence but did not embrace it. They also found evidence that the site is significantly older than initially believed. During an excavation of the "Dairy Hill monolith," a small pile of chocking stones was found to support the standing stone, as well as a stone tool. A geologist examined the layer of dark, gray-green soil surrounding the artifacts and felt that it had been deposited directly after the glacial recession, about 10,000 BP.[22] The authors began to hypothesize a different symbolic origin to some of the stones, coining the term "Manitou stone." As used by Mavor and Dix, *Manitou* is a standing stone with a human head and shoulder effigy, usually found in a row of stones. They believed this to be an anthropomorphic icon representing a spiritual presence that was found worldwide, possibly pre-dating the last ice age.[23]

Vermont State Archaeologist Giovanna Neudorfer also spoke at the Castleton Conference, interpreting the chambers as unquestionably colonial in their origin.[24] Because of the increased traffic and reports of trespass, theft, and vandalism after Barry Fell's *America B.C.* became a bestseller, Neudorfer and the Vermont Division for Historic Preservation began a study of the chamber.

Neudorfer noted the cultural context of the structures, including proximity to cellar holes and cisterns. She cautioned that years of additional work would be required before a final report would be filed. That final report would appear in 1980 as the book *Vermont's Stone Chambers*.[25]

According to this survey, there were 52 stone chambers located in 21 towns across five counties in the state.[26] The chambers are divided into two categories: Type A and Type B.[27]

Neudorfer defined 14 chambers as Type A, identified by the structure's integration into the stonework of an existing structure or foundation hole, or its location as part of another structure or cellar hole.

The Type B chambers are built into hillsides or freestanding structures that may or may not be covered with earth. From the perspective of the study, their location merely indicated the chambers were no longer associated with a structure that would identify original use, not that they were pre-colonial. Neudorfer notes that

Calendar II site in South Woodstock, Vermont (Terry Deveau photograph).

ten of the chambers exhibited vent holes comparable to those described in documented root cellars. The vent in the Calendar II chamber, which Dix had initially suggested as evidence of the European "megalithic yard"[28] in use at the Vermont sites,[29] was the same dimension of root cellar vents recommended in an 1825 issue of *New England Farmer and Horticultural Journal*.[30]

Neudorfer also traced the property deeds and interviewed descendants of property owners. In several instances, the interviewees identified ancestors as the builders of the chambers during the 19th century for use as root cellars.[31]

Robert Stone at America's Stonehenge recalls cautioning about using oral history for determining site provenience, noting a similar problem at his North Salem, New Hampshire, site.[32] In 1934, the *Haverhill Evening Gazette* ran an article on the "caves" in which Susie Bendel unequivocally stated her grandfather built the structures on the site.[33] In researching the history of his property,[34] Stone found that Bendel incorrectly identified the country of origin for her family; missed the family's date of immigration by a century; and, based upon her timeline, her grandfather would have built the structures a decade or more after her great-grandfather was already living in a house he had built on top of several of the structures.[35]

Another Vermont site uncovered by Dix,[36] Calendar II in South Woodstock, was classified as Type A by Neudorfer, but Cook considered it even more important than Calendar One,[37] and Fell viewed it as the finest example of a chamber in the Western hemisphere.[38] The site is centered on a large chamber with nine large lintel stones, the heaviest weighing approximately 6000 lbs. It is within a stone wall enclosure which Neudorfer notes is located near cellar holes and a colonial cistern.

Manitou also recorded that Mavor and Dix found "many hundreds" of stones with grooved markings on them, both in Vermont and at other sites they investigated.[39] They noted a concentration of these marked stones at Calendar One, which they felt was indicative of a ritual site. Most of the grooves were straight, often in groupings parallel to each or occasionally intersecting each other. Some were in patterns resembling a grid. They also noted that similar markings in the British Isles are unquestionably prehistoric and usually associated with megalithic tombs and stone circles. However, Mavor and Dix were not convinced that such marks were evidence of diffusion. Although they also stated support for Barry Fell, they questioned the validity of translating such badly eroded marks.[40] They noted that at the Vermont sites, the marks were found only between 250 and 500 meters above sea level. Excavations in similar strata levels are associated with Paleo and Archaic Indian tools. Their conclusion was that the marks were a form of notation by early Native Americans. Any similarity to European sites was coincidental—parallel development of basic numerical notation.[41]

Barry Fell's interpretation of the structures was published as *America B.C.* Because his work pre-dated the development of the Dix and Mavor theory of a prehistoric shamanistic society, Fell never addressed the specific points. However, Fell had his own distinct view of the Vermont chambers. He found three characteristics that occurred regularly at the Vermont sites: references to Bel, both as inscriptions on the chamber entryways and as a carving Fell named an "Eye of Bel"; large numbers of phallic monuments representing the genitalia of both genders; and a small grid-like pattern on specific stones that he referred to as a "sun grid."[42] The chamber at Calendar II, according to Fell, has dedications to the sun god Bel on the lintel and so many additional inscriptions to various gods that Fell named the chamber "The Pantheon."[43]

Francisco Marco Simón of the University of Zaragoza notes that prior to the arrival of the Romans, there was little known of the Celtiberian pantheon and that the Roman influence led to a refinement of deity identity reminiscent of Graeco-Roman pantheons, including the introduction of the ritual of dedicating altars to the gods, specifying the name of the divinity.[44]

Bel, a cognate of the Celtic solar god Belenos, was found on numerous other Vermont chambers, with three distinct parallel lines spelling the letters "B-L" in the Ogham alphabet. One of the small chambers at Calendar One contains both the Bel dedication and a sun grid.

In addition to the name Bel, some of the chambers were found to have a stylized "Eye of Bel," with or without additional Ogham. Fell hypothesized that the eye was an inscription reading "B M-H-G," representing the Celtic term *Bi amharg*, or "observation stone," with the Ogham letter "G" stylized to resemble an eye.[45] Fell suggests it was either a visual representation of the eye of the god or a way of identifying the stone's purpose to the illiterate. Literacy rates in the Celtiberi region were low,[46] as writing was a privileged form of communication for centuries; visual images were the primary means of communication.[47]

Fell's earliest explorations at Calendar II uncovered evidence of fertility rituals in the guise of stones with phallic connotations.[48] A nearby hill has so many representations of genitalia that it was named "Phallus Hill."[49] In addition to these anthropomorphic stones, along a mile-long line between the Calendar II chamber and Phallic Hill, Warren Dexter identified stones shaped to resemble animals, or "animated stones."[50] These stones, Dexter hypothesized, were modified to resemble such shapes of fish, mushrooms, and turtles.[51]

The sun grids, first spotted by Dix on his original discovery of Calendar One,[52] were located on stone slabs with astronomical alignments. Fell identified them as solar symbols, similar to those found in Europe, most notably on the walls of the Bronze Age Cachão da Rapa rock shelter in northern Portugal.[53]

Fell's conclusion was that the combination indicated Bronze Age Celtiberians had sailed up the Connecticut River 25 centuries ago, leaving behind their pagan monuments with symbols that had not survived in Europe because of the introduction of Christianity.

There are other numerous small sites scattered through Vermont and even more unanswered questions. The sites themselves are part of the problem, but equally at fault is the research. Giovanna Neudorfer's work raises serious questions, but she does not address the pre-Columbian issue.[54] Her name doesn't appear in any of Fell's books. Mavor and Dix do not mention the Neudorfer work either and make only two passing mentions of Barry Fell. Trento mentions Neudorfer's report (but not her name) in passing in his 1997 book. Neudorfer briefly addresses the phallic aspects of the sites in the closing paragraphs of her work as a byproduct of geology and erosion.[55]

Anne Ross of the archaeology department of the University of Southampton, UK, and Peter Reynolds, director of the Butser Ancient Farm Project, were the British members of a team assembled by Vermont's Goddard College to investigate Calendar One.[56] Their report was submitted at the Castleton conference[57] and later reproduced in *Antiquity*.[58] Their conclusion was that the "B-L" inscriptions were combinations of plows scoring the rock and the effect of erosion, a conclusion with which, not surprisingly, Neudorfer concurred[59] and Cook disagreed.[60]

James Whittall also cautioned against assuming that every series of lines is an ancient text. In a series of studies on the work of Fell and other epigraphers,[61] Whittall coined the term *petromanteia* for natural rock surfaces that appeared readable as scripts.[62] Whittall and his fellow authors took both the epigraphers and their critics to task for lack of dialogue and poor research. They included an appendix devoted to examples of uncritical interpretations.[63] The subjects range from Barry Fell and his critics to one amateur archaeology group that had identified and translated an Iberian Punic inscription on a boulder in the America's Stonehenge parking lot. Several weeks before their "discovery," these marks had been made when a bulldozer spreading gravel had accidentally backed into the rock.[64]

The legacy of Warren Cook's "Ancient Vermont" conference remains at Castleton State College. On the second floor of the Coolidge Memorial Library is a permanent exhibit of various stone monuments rescued from vandals. They remain mute and unyielding, much like the scholars on both sides of the issue who refuse to address opposing perspectives.

Phaeton Rock, Lynn, Massachusetts

In 1824, Scottish geologist John Finch suggested there was ample evidence for the Celts in North America in the form of Druidic monuments, such as the Dighton Rock and the various standing stones, balanced rocks, and stone circles across the country.[65] Finch was particularly enamored of a large boulder resting on three smaller stones in North Salem, New York, which he considered a "magnificent cromlech."[66] He also noted an unconfirmed report of rocking stones[67] in Massachusetts, somewhere between Lynn and Salem.[68] Finch, and subsequent researchers, did not always differentiate between rocking or balanced stones, perched rocks, and dolmens as proof of ancient visitors. Of the three types, only a dolmen, by definition, is always man-made.

The North Salem, New York, dolmen that Finch had admired may have been a megalithic monument,[69] or simply a large piece of glacial debris, carried by the ice and left behind in a terminal moraine when the glacier retreated. A dropped erratic would be deposited in a large mass of rocky till, and as the clays, soil, and smaller particles were washed away by erosion, the boulder would come to rest atop other rocks too big to wash away. Since all of New England was glaciated, any perched boulder or balanced rock can easily be identified as either a fluke of geology or a man-made structure.

However, as Mavor and Dix point out in *Manitou*, boulders feature prominently in both native and Colonial folklore.[70] Mavor and Dix are more interested in the occurrence of other stone structures in conjunction with these sites but note that some of the rocking stones appear to have man-made modifications, either to augment the stone or, in later cases, to prevent use as an Indian signaling device by colonists.[71]

Mavor and Dix noted that dolmens (or, as they preferred, "pedestaled boulders") are found in New England, and although they believe them to be used for prehistoric Indian rituals, they would not eliminate the possibility of "an intercontinental influence." They noted similar pedestaled boulders are found in Great Britain and Korea,[72] and compared one located in Sullivan County, New Hampshire, to one in Dunkeld, Scotland, adding that the Scottish dolmen is called a "rocking stone," even though it is up on pedestals and immobile.[73]

Such references to a stationary dolmen as a rocking stone in Scottish texts suggest that Scotsman John Finch's 1824 reference to a rocking stone in the Lynn area may be the first reference to what is now known as "Phaeton Rock" or the "Lynn Dolmen."

Phaeton Rock was named by Joseph Mason Rowell, a member of a local society

Phaeton Rock in Lynn, Massachusetts. Note the proximity to encroaching residential development (Richard Lynch photograph).

called the Exploring Circle, a group of local men interested in the arts and sciences. Led by botanist Cyrus Mason Tracy,[74] this group was also the core membership of the Lynn Free Public Forest, a group responsible for the preservation of a large undeveloped parcel of woods now known as Lynn Woods.[75]

Founded in 1881, Lynn Woods is a 2,200-acre municipal forest/park, the second largest municipal park in the United States. Aside from numerous local folklore landmarks, such as Dungeon Rock,[76] a tunnel associated with pirates, spiritualists, and treasure seekers, some researchers feel that the assorted boulders and walls are part of a possible astronomical alignment site in the park.[77] The proximity of Phaeton Rock to Lynn Woods has been noted as part of that research.

The forest was so littered with boulders and geologic oddities that the Exploring Circle actually formed a "Committee on Bowlders and Erratic Rocks" in 1858.[78] Joseph Rowell's original report on finding the "curious boulder" is on file at the Lynn Museum.[79] Rowell noted that the boulder rested on the edge of a granite outcropping 20 feet in the air with the boulder projecting beyond the cliff edge, raised on four smaller boulders. Rowell also mentioned taking the liberty of naming the boulder "Phaeton Rock."[80]

Joseph Rowell either miscounted, or the boulder has lost a base stone—today, the 70-ton granite capstone rests on three stones. By 1866, the venerable Essex Institute was looking into how to best preserve the "very remarkable erratic rock," including possibly purchasing the rock and moving it to Essex Institute property.[81] Nothing came of these plans to move the rock, possibly because of the weight of the boulder, or because the dolmen had recently been identified as a glacial erratic boulder moved to Lynn during the ice age.

This identification was by Joseph Henry, the first director of the Smithsonian Institution. In an 1859 letter to his wife,[82] Henry reports a visit to Lynn to see the *"huge boulder as a large as a one story house which remains poised in the edge of an elevated ridge apparently threatning* [sic] *the inhabitants below with destruction...."*[83]

Phaeton Rock became a popular destination for tourists and picnickers, as evidenced by an iron ladder attached to the boulder to allow easier access to the top and the panoramic view of the area.[84] This popularity did not continue into the 20th century; Hurd's *History of Essex County, Massachusetts*,[85] lists Phaeton Rock as one of several "curious drift boulders" that, if located more conveniently near summer resorts, would be internationally acclaimed instead of the infrequently visited sites that they were. Even William B. Goodwin, the owner of the Mystery Hill site, with his well-publicized theory that all the stone structures in New England were created by 9th century Irish monks,[86] did not list the Phaeton Rock among the dolmens he cited as evidence.

It was not until 1983 that the dolmen label was firmly affixed to Phaeton Rock by James Whittall, director of the Early Sites Research Society. Whittall had researched various sites, inscriptions, and artifacts with Yankee skepticism and an adamant belief in pre-Columbian contact. His insistence on objective scientific research was just as likely to discredit a discovery as endorse it.

In a story that has been repeated to the point of legend,[87] Whittall was visiting the Peabody Essex Museum in Salem, Massachusetts, on a research project. He noticed a large painting of a dolmen on the wall. After asking the docent if the dolmen was in Ireland, France, or England, he was astonished to discover it was four miles away. After traveling the world to examine stone structures and compare them to the American ones, Whittall had found a dolmen practically in his own backyard.[88] Whittall left the museum and proceeded to the top of Prospect Hill, where he found Phaeton Rock, now known as "Cannon Rock," after a dubious claim that it looked like a military cannon.

Whittall's discovery of the dolmen was fortuitous. The area around the structure was in the middle of a construction boom. Within a few years, Whittall was in the midst of a controversy to save the site.[89] After convincing the city council not to sell the parcel including the boulder, he continued his research on the site. Whittall found two additional dolmen-like structures on hills around Lynn, including one that he felt was aligned with Phaeton Rock, or as he preferred, "Lynn Dolmen."[90]

Whittall's research indicated that the three support stones under Phaeton Rock were set at a 75-60-45-degree triangle, mathematical precision that made it "extremely difficult to consider this monument a glacial erratic."[91]

Today, Phaeton Rock still rests on its three support stones. However, the three support stones are held in place in a bed of bentonite cement poured into a frame around them. This was done in response to construction in the area and the fear that blasting for cellars in nearby new housing would topple the boulder and send it down the slope and into one of the houses that now surround the tiny city-owned parcel.[92]

Dolmen or geologic quirk, the community felt the rock deserved to be preserved. Phaeton Rock is firmly anchored, both in place on Prospect Hill and in the local consciousness.

Bellows Falls Petroglyphs, Bellows Falls, Vermont

William B. Goodwin, compiling evidence that all the stone structures in New England were created by 9th-century Irish Culdee monks, noted the Bellows Falls carvings in conjunction with a discussion of a site in Acworth, New Hampshire.[93] Goodwin wondered if the "so-called Indian pictograph" at that location was actually an Indian record of the Culdee outpost ten miles northeast in Acworth.

Irish monks notwithstanding, most researchers agree that these carvings are Native American in origin. Possibly anywhere from 300 to 1,000 years old, the meaning of the figures is unknown and probably always will be a mystery—the original appearance of the carvings was irreparably altered 75 years ago, thanks to a local chapter of the Daughters of the American Revolution (DAR) who had a professional stone carver deepen the carvings with metal tools to make them more visible. In 1961, the local chamber of commerce had the carvings outlined in yellow paint to increase visibility.[94]

Situated on the west bank of the Connecticut River at the base of the Great Falls, there are two groupings of petroglyphs. Located 35 and 55 feet south of the Vilas Bridge, they are immediately visible south of the bridge along a road that parallels the river. The west-facing petroglyphs are carved into the steeply angled, water-worn granite bedrock that makes up the river bank. The petroglyphs depict life-sized, circular "heads" with eyes and mouths. Some of the heads have horns (or antennae). The first grouping consists of eight heads in a 5-foot area. The second group has 16 heads across a 10-foot section of rock. The number of heads visible at any given time seems to fluctuate from observer to observer, partially because of water levels and weather, and partially because of the weathered stone.

Bellow Falls is where the Connecticut River narrows at the base of a mountain. Native tribes gathered at the falls to harvest shad and Atlantic salmon migrating up the river to the spawning areas in the north. This annual fishing ended abruptly with the arrival of the colonists. A covered bridge spanned the gorge in 1785, and a dam in 1798 eliminated of the fish runs. By this point, the carvings were already a local landmark, with a print record of them dating back to 1794, when Samuel Williams described them in his *History of Vermont*.[95] Interpretations ranged from Benjamin Hall's commemoration of a great chief and his followers[96] to Henry Schoolcraft's theory of a battle memorial.[97]

The most recent entry is by anthropologists Haviland and Power. They believe that the faces carved on the bank are depictions of supernatural spirits encountered by shamans during the trance state known as a vision quest.[98] The visions, they believe, are a physiological reaction to the altered states of consciousness during the vision quest. The interpretation of these visions varies from person to person, depending on the cultural background and emotional state.

Neuropsychological research has shown that there are many features common to all participants despite these differences. During the first stage of altered consciousness, people experience geometric shapes called entoptic phenomena. These include such shapes as zigzags, parallel lines, dots, and grids. Haviland notes six common entoptic phenomena and compares them to imagery in South African and European Paleolithic rock art.[99] As the subject passes deeper into a trance, these entoptics evolve into people and creatures based on the cultural perceptions of the

Close-up of "faces" at Bellows Falls, Vermont (Malcolm Pearson photograph).

person, known as iconic imagery. Haviland and Power believe the basis of the Bellows Falls petroglyphs are iconic images (faces) surrounded by entoptics (small holes) from numerous shamanistic vision quests in this particularly sacred spot. The holes that Haviland identifies as entoptics are barely visible because of the cumulative erosion damage done to the carvings. So instead of relying on the modified extant carvings, Haviland uses an engraving of the petroglyphs found in Schoolcraft's book,[100] believing it to be a more accurate rendering than the current, modified carvings. The accuracy of Hamlin's reproduction of the images can be contested. Besides Hamlin's rendering of the circular "faces," giving them a much more anthropomorphic appearance than other images, Lenik's study of the site[101] discovered that Hamlin's image in Schoolcraft's book is reversed.

Although many petroglyph sites show the passage of time, the Bellows Falls site is a particularly dramatic case of how the appearance of carvings has drastically changed in the last hundred years.[102] In the early 20th century, a riprap, or jumble of loose rock, was dumped to the west of the carvings to shore up the railroad bed. This riprap may have actually helped preserve the site—it may have covered up more of the carvings, sparing more of them from erosion, the DAR, and multiple yellow paint baths.

By 1927, the carvings were obscured to the point that Delabarre considered them lost when compiling his book on New England carved rocks.[103] Goodwin, in 1946, also considered the Bellows Falls pictograms destroyed, but he faulted the construction of an electric light plant, not erosion.[104] This lack of visibility apparently prompted the DAR to "restore" the carvings for future generations of tourists. As late as 1968, warnings were issued that the carvings were being destroyed by the city dumping snow and debris into the river.[105]

However, the riprap's effect on the water flow around the carvings may have merely exacerbated an existing problem—there are some indications that the carvings periodically disappeared prior to the construction. Historian Zadock Thompson, in his 1842 history,[106] states that the only petroglyphs in the state are a few unimpressive scratched lines near Brattleboro[107]; a 1907 article picked up by national newspapers reported the carvings were obliterated by river action.[108]

Archaeologist Edward Lenik, who has studied the Bellows Falls carvings, theorizes that these carvings are not all original.[109] Based on the images and descriptions through the last four centuries, Lenik believes that the DAR's stone carver not only "improved" the carvings but also may have added a few more for good measure. Lenik also has little use for Haviland's entoptic phenomena, believing that the holes near the faces are the eroded remnants of additional faces.

In 2022, the town of Rockingham and the Elnu-Abenaki Tribe received a National Park Service grant to study the petroglyphs[110] and the historical context of the carvings and the surrounding land from the Abenaki perspective.

Celtics, vision quests, or simple carvings, Bellow Falls petroglyphs reveal more about the mindset of the researchers than the original carvers.

Pearson Chamber, Upton, Massachusetts

In 1928, machinist Charles Pearson moved his family to Upton, Massachusetts. The papers were signed in the house, and as the previous owner John Thiel was preparing to depart, he suddenly remembered he had not shown the Pearsons the "cave" in the back of the property. In the back half of the property, there was a large domed stone hut buried in the hillside. Entered through a 14-foot passage barely 4½ feet high, the chamber itself had a ceiling over 10-feet high and was circular with a diameter between 10 and 12 feet. The walls average 2 feet thick and are topped by a massive capstone, weighing upwards of 1200 pounds. The exterior is covered with glacial gravel on which topsoil has formed, effectively camouflaging the structure. Seventeen-year-old Malcolm Pearson was entranced by the structure. He began investigating the chamber, seeking who could have built such a chamber and for what purpose. Pearson found an article in an 1893 *Milford Journal*[111] that concluded the structure was a refuge for attacks by warriors that pre-dated the Indians (i.e., the Vikings). The reporter had also queried the oldest members of the town. As Pearson later recounted in the town's bicentennial history,[112] even those with ancestors dating back before the incorporation of Upton in 1735, had no clue as to the origin or purpose of the structure. As early as 1743, records indicate questions and speculation about the chamber's origins,[113] but no evidence ever made an identification conclusive.

Pearson would later recall writing to the Smithsonian Institution to ask its opinion. After sending photographs and measurements, the Smithsonian wrote back, suggesting it was a colonial root cellar. Pearson was not impressed. "It's too damp and there's no ventilation for the preservation of perishables in the chamber. The entrance is too narrow to fit a wheelbarrow through, or even a bushel basket. It just wasn't a food storage chamber. Their reply got me so agitated that I boldly entered the field of archaelogy."[114]

Pearson began writing to other researchers, including Olaf Strandwold, who was attempting to translate runic inscriptions on the Atlantic seaboard as a way to prove a Viking presence in North America. It was the start of a correspondence that would continue until Strandwold's death in 1949. Pearson also began researching and photographing possible rune stones for Strandwold. Strandwold would publish two books,[115] both relying heavily on Pearson's fieldwork and photography.

While Pearson continued searching for answers, Strandwold was entertaining an old acquaintance, William B. Goodwin of Hartford, Connecticut. Goodwin, formerly of Seattle, had returned to Washington for a visit.[116] While there, he looked up Strandwold for his opinions on aspects of the Norse sagas. Like so many before him, Goodwin was attempting to locate Vinland by comparing geography to the physical descriptions in the sagas.[117] In the course of their discussions, Strandwold asked Goodwin if he was familiar with the unmortared beehive hut in Upton, Massachusetts.[118] When Goodwin admitted he wasn't, Strandwold made arrangements

Entrance to the Pearson Chamber, Upton, Massachusetts (Malcolm Pearson photograph).

for Pearson to show Goodwin the Upton chamber. When Goodwin arrived, Pearson also mentioned an article that had recently run in the *Boston Globe* about another site in Salem, New Hampshire.[119] In 1936, Pearson and Goodwin visited the Mystery Hill site in North Salem, New Hampshire, a site he would subsequently purchase.[120]

The partnership between Pearson and Goodwin was invaluable and continues to impact archaeology. Pearson has photographed the stone chambers and ruins of New England for over 75 years. In numerous cases, his photography is the only record remaining of these structures. His photography has appeared in the seminal books of Olaf Strandwold, William Goodwin, Barry Fell, and innumerable others.

Before Goodwin had completed his research on Vinland, the Pearson chamber and his North Salem hill had convinced him that another group was involved—the Irish.[121] As far as Goodwin was concerned, the "Great Stone Beehive" in Upton was one of the three most important sites in New England, along with the North Salem site and the Turtle Mound in Andover, Massachusetts.[122] All three were ceremonial centers for the vast network of Irish missionaries he envisioned across New England. Unlike Mystery Hill, there are no altars, fireplaces, or hidden niches in the Pearson chamber. In the back is a section of stones partially collapsed, where a lintel stone cracked and allowed the stonework above it to shift downward. As late as 1946,[123] Malcolm suspected the lintel was the sealed opening to an inner chamber, but Pearson's subsequent excavations outside the chamber opposite this door found it to be simply a recessed shelf, not a passageway to another room.[124]

Goodwin's death in 1950 found Malcolm Pearson the heir to the North Salem site. Pearson simply did not have the resources to underwrite research as Goodwin had done for years.[125] Rather than try to underwrite research himself, he helped found the Early Sites Foundation research organization with Frank Glynn (then recently elected president of the Connecticut Archaeological Society), Dr. Junius Bird (at that time a curator of the American Museum of Natural History), Arctic explorer Vilhjalmur Stefansson (director of Polar Studies at Dartmouth College), and other interested parties, to investigate both the Mystery Hill site and other related sites.

Early Sites Foundation launched with excavations at North Salem and Upton in 1955. The six-week excavation at North Salem remains controversial and showed no definitive results. The Upton excavation, however, yielded a few surprises.[126] Besides the top level of expected contemporary debris, the remnants of a wooden floor were discovered in the passageway. There was no indication if the floor was contemporary with the chamber's construction or if it was a later addition. Kelley and Glass[127] feel the wood flooring is contemporary with the chamber construction. Salvatore Trento[128] disagrees, interpreting the report as giving proof that the wood was laid at a later date.[129]

There were also large stones placed adjacent to the wooden floor, and the excavation team's best guess was that the stone and wood were used as a crude path at a time when the groundwater flooded into the chamber, as it still occasionally does. When removing one of these stones, Glass found a small artifact, a 9/32-inch fragment that would later be identified as composed of silver. It was curved both vertically and horizontally, leading Glass and Kelley to hypothesize it was a piece of the rim of some sort of container. Examination of the artifact suggested it was wheel-turned. On the fragment are three lines that parallel each other in a chevron pattern.[130]

In the fall of 1979, James Whittall was returning from an Early Sites Research Society expedition to map a site threatened by highway construction. Since one of his team members had not visited the nearby Upton chamber, Whittall made arrangements for Malcolm Pearson to meet them at the site. The team member who had never seen the Upton chamber was James Mavor. Mavor and Byron Dix had already discovered the astronomical alignments at the Calendar One site in Vermont and were beginning to expand their search for sites with alignments as sacred geometry from Native Americans.

With the Vermont alignments fresh in his mind, Mavor immediately noticed that the entrance passageway appeared to be aligned with the summer solstice. With the help of Pearson, Mavor and Dix decided to investigate further. While Mavor and Dix measured angles at the chamber, Pearson went to the top of nearby Pratt Hill. If there were alignments, there should be some sort of marker or mound on the hill in line with the chamber.

Instead of a marker, Pearson found three stone cairns. Further investigation determined that the first and third mounds marked the edges of the field of vision of someone in the chamber looking out to Pratt Hill. The third mound also was situated to mark the summer solstice sunset. It seemed apparent that the chamber was some sort of observatory.[131] Using the solstice alignment as a benchmark, Mavor and Dix determined that the period 370 to AD 970 would be when the alignment over the mound would mark the summer solstice sunset.[132] With a tentative date, they were able to calculate what celestial events would align with the first and second mounds.

They found the answer was not a solar alignment but a stellar event. In that same AD 370 to 970 time period, the Pleiades set over the first two mounds.

With two major celestial events, Mavor and Dix continued to examine the top of Pratt Hill. Seven large mounds were found, as well as seven other features, such as marker stones and rows of stone. Assuming a treeless hilltop, all 14 features were visible from the chamber as horizon features. In addition to the sun and the Pleiades, the seven brightest stars in the sky set precisely at one of the various horizon markers.[133] Mavor and Dix also point out that in 1524, Giovanni da Verrazzano[134] noted that the Narragansett tribe of modern Rhode Island timed their plantings by celestial observations, including lunar cycles and the rising of the Pleiades.[135] This was the seed that developed into Mavor and Dix's theory of a Native American geomantic culture.

The directionally of the chamber, Meagher argues,[136] is significant, but not because of solar alignments. He maintains the structure is a late eighteenth-century ice house. He quotes a letter to George Washington from Robert Morris with advice on building an ice house: mortarless stone walls, northern entrance, buried in the hillside.

It seems fitting that in 2004, Malcolm Pearson returned to Upton to lead the battle to preserve the chamber. After the 1973 death of his father, Charles Pearson, the property left the Pearson family. After passing owners, it ended up on the auction block at a foreclosure sale in 2004. Two Rhode Island speculators bought the property, intending to sell the property to a developer. They had not anticipated the local reaction to the potential loss of the landmark.

When word reached the Upton Historical Commission, it immediately began discussions with the new owners to obtain the small parcel surrounding the chamber. A year later, Upton Historical Commission worked with the Board of Selectmen to explore options. After the Associated Press carried the story of the chamber and an interview with Pearson,[137] support for saving the structure poured in from across the country.[138] Using this momentum, the Upton Historical Commission started a "Save the Cave" project. Upton residents voted to preserve the historic stone structure and purchase the seven-acre property for a community park using Community Preservation Act funds. By the end of 2006, Upton owned the parcel. Instead of being destroyed and replaced with nine new houses, the newly renamed Pearson Chamber became part of Upton Heritage Park, formally dedicated in April 2012.

Under municipal control, the Historical Commission could utilize a grant to treat the champer as a cultural resource instead of a local curiosity. It allowed the Historical Commission to complete an archaeological survey, deal with drainage issues, and repair the entranceway of the chamber, which was becoming unstable from centuries of visitors and caused the capstone to slump dangerously.[139] In addition to repairs, the area was searched with ground-penetrating radar to look for future avenues to pursue.

The GPR detected an anomaly that has been flagged for investigation. There is something buried 5 feet underground with a 16½ foot square shape. It could be a buried wall or another structure, but time will tell.[140]

With rock being temporarily removed during the masonry rehabilitation, it was decided to use the opportunity to take samples of the soil behind the stonework to test using Optically Stimulated Luminescence (OSL) dating, a method that calculates the last time the quartz crystals had been exposed to sunlight.

Three samples were tested. The test results returned ages are between AD 1350 to AD 1625, dates.[141] These dates mean the Pearson Chamber was constructed before the English settlement of the area; the nearest settlement was Mendon, founded in 1660. Suddenly, much as is happening at America's Stonehenge, the Pearson Chamber becomes a possible Native site, with stone structures and astronomical alignments.

The origin of Malcolm Pearson's beehive chamber remains a mystery, but it will remain a strong and lasting legacy to his contribution to New England's history.

Chapter Seven

The Westford Knight

In 1998, the Scottish clans of Sinclair and Gunn celebrated the 600th anniversary of their ancestors' explorations in North America. The focus of this sexcentenary gathering was a carving discovered in 1954 on a granite outcropping in the Massachusetts community of Westford. Known as the "Westford Knight," this carving is believed to be an effigy of a fallen knight of the Clan Gunn, a member of the party of fourteenth-century explorer Henry Sinclair.

The town of Westford was aware of the carving on the exposed bedrock, but it was attributed to local natives. In his 1883 history of the town, the Rev. Edwin Hodgman briefly mentioned the ledge and that "rude outlines of the human face have been traced upon it, and the figure is said to be the work of Indians." Hodgman's referring specifically to a face, as opposed to an entire figure on the ledge, raises the question of how familiar Hodgman actually was with the carving. Hodgman liberally borrowed geology notes from the 1874 *Gazetteer of the State of Massachusetts* by Elias Nason but seemed to have misread the earlier reference to the carving being upon the "face of the ledge" as being a "face on the ledge."[1]

In some ways, it is surprising that neither Nason nor Hodgman had previously attempted to interpret the Westford carving as evidence of Vikings in their histories of the area. When they were writing their books, an obsession with Norse exploration was sweeping New England. Malcolm Pearson, the photographer who introduced William B. Goodwin to the Mystery Hill site, had heard of this carving during his reconnaissance work for Goodwin and dutifully photographed it and filed a report to antiquarian Goodwin and runologist Olaf Strandwold. Strandwold was compiling sites that would appear in his books[2] and had no use for a Native American pictograph. Goodwin, searching for proof that Great Ireland and Vinland were in New England,[3] saw something in the photograph that was not Indian—he saw the hilt and a piece of a sword. A simple line rendering from the Pearson photograph, drawn by Notre Dame professor of architecture Vincent F. Fagan, appears in Goodwin's 1946 *Ruins of Great Ireland in New England*.[4] Fagan illustrated the carving as Goodwin saw it, but the book doesn't identify where the carving was located.[5] Goodwin doesn't elaborate on the illustration elsewhere in the book, except for two uncaptioned photographs of the sword that appear later in the book.[6] A simple note on the drawing mentions that a broken blade is an ancient symbol of a warrior's death. Although not stated, the implication is that the sword is Norse.

As *Ruins of Great Ireland in New England* was being published, so was a book by spelunker Clay Perry, *New England's Buried Treaures*.[7] Perry had included Goodwin's "man-made caves" in his previous book, *Underground New England*[8] and subsequently kept current with Goodwin's research. Perry refers to the Westford site as depicting a "cross with a human face atop of it, typical of Irish carvings of sacred significance in the old country."[9] Considering the haste in which *Ruins of Great Ireland in New England* was compiled for publication, it is quite possible that Perry is echoing Goodwin's most recent interpretation, an interpretation omitted from his own book.[10]

In 1948, Dr. T.C. Lethbridge published a collection of essays on Britain in the Dark Ages entitled *Merlin's Island*.[11] Lethbridge was the director of excavations for the Cambridge Antiquarian Society and the University Museum of Archaeology and Ethnology. One of the essays in *Merlin's Island* was Lethbridge's opinion that long before the Vikings, and possibly as early as the Roman occupation, the Celt inhabitants of Britain, Ireland, and Scotland had crossed the Atlantic to Iceland and possibly Greenland and America.[12] This was a fairly controversial opinion by 1948 standards, and Lethbridge felt the need to elaborate on his theory in 1950's *Herdsmen and Hermits*.[13]

To Malcolm Pearson and his research associates (William Goodwin had died in May of 1950 and left the Mystery Hill site to Pearson), this initially appeared as vindication of Goodwin's theory of Irish Culdee monks being the architects of the stone structures found in New England. Lethbridge's statement was that he wouldn't be surprised if Irish relics were found in North America,[14] not that any relics had actually been found.

Lethbridge's theories caught the attention of Frank Glynn, a well-respected amateur archaeologist, and president of the Archaeological Society of Connecticut. Glynn was conducting his own research at Mystery Hill and was a staunch supporter of the theory that there was a connection between the New England sites and European megalithic cultures. In the course of the subsequent correspondence between Lethbridge and Glynn,[15] Glynn began sending Lethbridge copies of books with data that might support his research. One such book was Goodwin's *Ruins of Great Ireland in New England*.

Lethbridge immediately focused on the broken sword illustration, identifying it not as Viking but as a hand-and-a-half wheeled pommel sword used in Britain in the 13th and 14th centuries.[16] A hand-and-a-half, or "bastard," sword is a form of a long sword with a shaped grip and a longer handle, which allows use by one or both hands. The pommel, at the end of the hilt, acts as a counterbalance against the weight of the sword's blade. Pommels came in various forms as swords evolved; the "wheel pommel" was popular among knights and is a simple, unadorned, round disc. It was more than decorative—in certain feinting moves, the sword was used in reverse, and an opponent struck in the face with the metal pommel.

Lethbridge urged Glynn to investigate the site immediately. He suspected that it would be part of a larger carving. Unfortunately for Glynn, although Goodwin did include a map of southern New England in the book (with Westford marked as a community of note), there is no key to the map. Nor is there any mention of the sword's location other than "in Massachusetts." Goodwin and Fagan had both died recently, and Pearson, struggling to reinvigorate research at the Mystery Hill site, incorrectly recalled the carving as being in Byfield, Massachusetts, and that it had been destroyed during road construction.[17] Glynn queried the local historians, who did confirm the destruction of several runic inscriptions during road widening but did not specifically recall a carving of a sword being among the casualties.

Glynn, not convinced that the destroyed carvings included the sword, worried that the location of the broken sword had died with Goodwin or if it even still existed. So Glynn began a systematic search of Massachusetts. Using Goodwin's notes, Strandwold's book, and several listings of sites compiled by research organizations, he began visiting locations as weather and time permitted. For three years, Frank Glynn searched for the elusive sword.

Then, in the spring of 1954, Frank Glynn and Malcolm Pearson were returning from a trip to the America's Stonehenge site. Traveling along Route 110, Pearson suddenly pointed to a turn-off leading to Westford and casually remarked that the sword carving was about two miles beyond Westford on that road.

On May 30, 1954, Glynn and his daughter Cindy headed back to Westford. Passing through Westford, they found themselves in Graniteville. He was directed to a local historian who had never heard of any local carvings of a sword. The historian made some phone calls to no avail—none of the locals knew of a sword. Several did suggest that since he was in the area, perhaps he should stop and see an old Indian carving. Glynn had no interest in the "Old Indian Chief," but his daughter insisted that they should investigate. So, begrudgingly, he got directions and drove to the site.

In a later interview, Frank Glynn remembered that the sword "jumped right out at us."[18] Goodwin's broken sword and Westford's old Indian were one and the same. It was too dark to take photographs, so an elated Glynn returned the next day. By then, word had gotten out that an archaeologist was looking at the Indian carving, and locals began stopping by to chat. Eighty-four-year-old Lila Fisher recalled that the carving had been there when she was a child,[19] and that it was always known as "The Old Indian." She also recalled the time her brother Edward decided to "improve" the Indian by adding a carving of a peace pipe.[20] Glynn actually was pleased with young Edward's attempt—the three crude V-shaped cuts into the rock were easily identifiable and showed that the carving was not done by local children, a popular explanation of the New England carvings.

Glynn cleared the sword, chalked in the pecked holes, and connected them. He then sent a copy of this to Lethbridge. Lethbridge felt the sword was reminiscent of effigies common in Ireland and the Hebrides and suggested to Glynn that there almost certainly had to be more to the carving.[21]

Glynn spent several weekends clearing away the moss, lichen, and soil built up on the rock. Then, when he was done, he began chalking in any marks that he didn't think were natural. When he was finished, there was a life-sized image of a knight in full regalia, just as Lethbridge had predicted.

Glynn's discovery received widespread press coverage, but not everyone was prepared to cede the Westford carving to the Sinclair expedition. Although archaeologist William Fowler published his own theory that the site was a memorial on the site of a battle between the local colonists and the native population,[22] Westford was divided into two camps—those who believed the knight was a military effigy and those who thought Edward Fisher and his brothers had too much time on their hands.[23]

Wielding a 39-inch sword, the knight in his greatcoat and visored helmet is outlined on the ledge using a combination of the striations in the rock and man-made punch holes. The holes vary in size and depth but appear to have been punched into the stone by a sharp tool, such as a metal punch or awl, standard tools in an armorer's repair kit.[24] The varying depth and size of the punch holes, according to Frederick J Pohl,[25] is an indication of the legitimacy of the image. As the punch tool was struck repeatedly into the resisting New England stone, it dulled and flattened the tip; a prankster would have had the time and means to sharpen the tool as needed.

Most telling was the great shield with images of a crescent, a star, a buckle, and a ship. While Glynn continued to examine and reinterpret the lines that made up the image, Lethbridge sent the rendering of the shield to a leading Scottish heraldry expert, Sir Iain Moncrieffe. Sir Iain identified the imagery on the shield as the coat of arms from a chieftain knight of the Clan Gunn from Caithness, the northeastern county of the

Frank Glynn's original 1954 chalking of the Westford Knight in Massachusetts. His daughter Cindy adds scale (Frank Glynn photograph, courtesy of Cindy Glynn).

Scottish Highlands. More importantly, it was an early version of the crest, so early that Sir Iain felt there were no more than four or five heraldry experts in the world who would have known of it. And none of whom would have been in North America, let alone carving the image into a ledge. Sir Iain was so confident in the legitimacy of this shield that in his book, *The Highland Clans*,[26] he referred to the Westford Knight's shield as "the earliest surviving example of the Gunn chief's coat-of-arms...."[27]

The Gunn Clan territory neighbored territories controlled by the Clan Sinclair. And the Clan Sinclair had a member who was legendary for his explorations— Henry Sinclair (1345–1400).

Frederick J. Pohl had published a book in 1950 chronicling the voyage of Henry Sinclair to Nova Scotia.[28] The Westford Knight seemed to indicate that the Sinclair expedition went further south along the coast. Frank Glynn corresponded with Pohl, who immediately visited the site.[29] Pohl also believed the carving to be authentic and began to study his previous research to see if there was data to support or disprove a continuation of the Sinclair voyage.

Burke's Peerage lists Henry Sinclair as Baron of Roslin, Earl of Orkney, and Lord of Shetland, "who on 2 August 1379, was formally invested by Haakon, King of Norway, as Jarl of the Orkneys."[30] According to Pohl, this made Henry the first Sinclair to be the crowned Jarl (or Earl, in English) of Orkney. Though given his title by the King of Norway, Sinclair was descended from leading Scottish nobles. This political base and the sheer size of his jarldom (200 islands and 5,000 square miles of the main sea lanes between Norway and Scotland) made him a political force.

The story of how Sinclair ended up in New England is a complicated tale of translation and interpretation, based on a small book and map published in Venice by Nicolò Zeno in 1558, now known as the *Zeno Narrative*.[31] The book was published by a descendant of the Zeno family, also named Nicolò, and is based on the correspondence of Nicolò Zeno and his brother Antonio. These brothers were Venetian navigators of the second half of the 14th century, lesser-known siblings of the military hero Carlo Zeno.[32]

Nicolò, according to the narrative,[33] was shipwrecked during a journey and rescued by a prince named Zichmni. Nicolò was hired as a pilot by Prince Zichmni and was soon joined by his brother Antonio.[34] Antonio was made captain, as Nicolò, returning from an exploration of a neighboring island, succumbed to the cold. Zichmni soon heard of a fisherman who had returned from unknown lands after 25 years. The remaining text includes the search for these lands by Antonio and Zichmni.

Shetland archivist Brian Smith, a noted critic of the Sinclair voyage,[35] refers to several problems in the Zeno Narrative that he feels undermine the journey's validity, such as geographic errors. Venetian records suggest Nicolò Zeno was a political prisoner in Venice at the time he would have been with Prince Zichmni,[36] and there is a dearth of records of Earl Henry Sinclair's exploits in the biographies and genealogies of the Sinclair family in subsequent centuries.

It wasn't until 1784 that a writer suggested that Prince Zichmni was actually Henry Sinclair. Johann Reinhold Forster, a German naturalist who accompanied James Cook on his second expedition, published a book in German on the voyages of such North American explorers as Baffin, Bering, Cabot, Cook, etc. An English edition followed two years later.[37]

The suggestion that Sinclair was Zichmni did nothing to abate the ongoing debate on the *Zeno Narratives*; it merely added another facet to the discussions. Zahrtmann[38] and Lucas[39] are the two most commonly cited foes of the *Zeno Narrative*. Both concentrate on the errors in the placement of islands and routes. Samuel Eliot Morison also briefly weighs in on the topic,[40] dismissing Forster in favor of Lucas and reiterates Lucas' suggestion that Zichmni is a mispronunciation of the name "Wichmannus," a member of the Vitalian Brotherhood. Lucas is basically insinuating that the Zeno brothers were pirates, not explorers.[41]

Pohl concurs with Forster's assessment and, in two of his books on the topic, presents two different scenarios in which the name Sinclair could have evolved into Zichmni. His first book shows how Sinclair in fourteenth-century script could be misread,[42] and his later book presents graphics of the cursive style of the time, which show how easily the translation of Orkney into Italian could have resulted in the garbled Zichmni.[43]

Geologist William Herbert Hobbs, a contemporary of Pohl, believed that the map inaccuracies were caused by the younger Nicolò's attempt to superimpose a contemporary longitude and latitude grid on his ancestor's map.[44] Hobbs believed that allowing for the confusion between magnetic and true north and estimated mileage of distances, the map becomes surprisingly accurate.[45] Alternately, Arlington Mallery argues that the Zeno Map rendering of Greenland, although inaccurate at first glance, is an accurate outline of the coasts beneath the ice cover.[46]

Hobbs gave a lecture in 1950 that Pohl attended.[47] Hobbs announced he had located the Zeno landfall based on a description in the narrative of a spring of pitch running into the sea. Hobbs believed this was a reference to a mineral tar pit in Stellarton, Nova Scotia.[48] Pohl used Stellarton to match descriptions in the *Zeno Narrative* to geographic features and calculated that Sinclair's fleet sailed into Nova Scotia's Chedabucto Bay and made landfall at Guysborough Harbor. A striking memorial stands in Boylston Provincial Park overlooking the harbor, erected by Clan Sinclair of Nova Scotia, that relates the tale of the *Zeno Narrative* in English, French, and Mi'kmaq.[49]

One of Jarl Henry's descendants, Andrew Sinclair, also researched his ancestor's voyage, using clues in the *Zeno Narrative* to identify Guysborough Harbor. Andrew Sinclair's 1992 book[50] suggests that the Newport Tower, usually identified as a Norse or colonial structure, is actually a Sinclair relict—a church/lighthouse/watchtower from Prince Henry's attempts at colonization.[51] Philip Means, in his study of the Newport Tower,[52] notes the similarities between the Newport Tower and the ruins of the Oephir Church apse in Jarl Henry's Orkney Islands.

Herbert Pell[53] and Manuel Luciano da Silva[54] also assign a Templar origin to the Newport Tower, based on their work on the Dighton Rock. However instead of assigning it to Sinclair, they credited it to Miguel Corte Real, claiming he built a watchtower to spot a rescue mission, using the rotunda of the Castle of Tomar, Portugal, built by the Knights Templar, as its design.

Andrew Sinclair also mentions a cannon found in the collection of the Fortress of Louisbourg National Historic Site in Canada.[55] It was snagged on an anchor and pulled out of Louisbourg Harbor in the 1840s.[56] Sinclair identifies it as a *peterero*, a type of cannon similar to those developed for naval warfare by Carlo Zeno. Although an 1891 article in the *Proceedings and Transactions of the Royal Society of Canada*[57] tries to establish an evidence trail for locating a lost Portuguese colony in the vicinity, the same material can suggest Sinclair lost or scuttled one of his ships at this stopover. The *Zeno Narrative* does not specify how many ships were in the expedition, but Johann Forster's inventory of Sinclair's military strength in the Orkneys[58] suggests that several vessels could make the trip and still leave a strong navy to guard the Orkneys.

After landfalls at Louisbourg and Guysborough, Jarl Henry would have traveled southward down the New England coast, exploring navigable rivers, eventually ending up at the mouth of the Merrimack River in Newburyport, Massachusetts. The Merrimack River would have been an ideal route for exploration; the river's channel was more than adequate to allow the ships' progress inland. Haverhill, Massachusetts, 15 miles upriver, was among several river communities building ships in the colonial era. In an 1861 history of Haverhill, the author mentions that ships were regularly built that sailed down the river and out to the British ports.[59] Sinclair's ships, most likely a variation of the cog used throughout northern Europe,[60] would weigh in fully laden at 50–150 tons.[61] Compared to the 340-ton *Ulysses* built in a Haverhill shipyard in 1798,[62] Sinclair would have no difficulty sailing his fleet up the Merrimack.

Their first obstacle in the river would have been Bodwell Falls in Lawrence, Massachusetts, now the site of the Great Stone Dam. With a 9-foot drop blocking the route, it would have been possible to anchor in the vicinity, portage shallow draft boats around it, and continue another 10 miles until they reached the 32-foot Pawtucket Falls in modern-day Lowell, Massachusetts. Ten miles to the west, they could see a hilltop from which the Indians frequently sent smoke signals. The explorers could have made the trip overland or portaged their vessels around the falls and continued to Stony Brook and followed that to within a few miles of the hill in Westford.

Pawtucket Falls may have been enough of an obstacle that Sinclair reversed direction and sailed down the Concord River, which empties into the Merrimack River less than five miles downstream from the falls.[63] The area south of Westford is low, with numerous swamps and the remnants of glacial ponds that dotted the area after the last ice age.[64] It is possible that some of these glacial ponds were still extant and adequate for Sinclair to approach Westford from the south.

Regardless of his approach, Sinclair and his crew proceeded to the summit of what is now called Prospect Hill in Westford, Massachusetts. Its 465-foot height afforded a good view in all directions. It was there that tragedy struck. A member of Sinclair's scouting party died.

Based on the shield's heraldic symbols, the fallen knight was Sir James Gunn of Clyth, Crowner of Caithness and Chief of Clan Gunn.[65] An effigy to the fallen knight was carved where he fell, as was the custom. The lines of the sword have a decided break in them, indicating the blade was broken, i.e., he died in battle.

A battle on a hilltop in 1399 in Westford requires an opponent, and by inference, that indicates Indians. Hodgman notes a local tradition of a pre-settlement battle between the Nashoba and Wamesit tribes on Frances Hill, about three miles northeast of the knight effigy.[66] The logic was that it is possible that the Sinclair expedition stumbled into a long-disputed territory and was attacked by one side or the other.

In his interpretation, Frederick J. Pohl paints Henry Sinclair as an early explorer. Andrew Sinclair also portrays Henry Sinclair as an explorer, but in the context of a prominent Knight Templar. Andrew Sinclair's text on his ancestor draws heavily from the history and lore of this order from the Crusades, whose influence spread throughout Europe until it was perceived as a threat to national sovereignty. First in France, and then in other countries, Knights Templar were arrested and their assets seized, until the order was dissolved. Andrew Sinclair has the surviving knights escaping to Scotland, where they found a safe haven at Balantradoch near Rosslyn Castle of the Sinclair family and the birthplace of Henry Sinclair. The specious connections between Rosslyn and the Knights Templar are carved in stone at the nearby Rosslyn Chapel; to this day, the chapel's symbolic carvings and architecture are considered by Scottish Rite Masons as relics of their founding.[67]

Andrew Sinclair hypothesizes that the regrouping Knights could have provided the impetus for Earl Henry Sinclair's expedition to the New World, with an eye toward founding a new base of operations. Not every researcher who believes Sinclair made the journey embraces the Knights Templar involvement. Tim Wallace-Murphy, in his book *Templars in America*,[68] declares the thought of the defunct Knights accompanying Sinclair as a "bizarre speculation."[69] Wallace-Murphy cites several other titles that take the Knights Templar involvement to the extreme, having the knights hiding lost treasures and the Holy Grail in America. With the subsequent success of the book *The Da Vinci Code* and the ensuing film version,[70] an avalanche of poorly researched, speculative "nonfiction" appeared, with more convoluted reasoning and increasingly conspiratorial in nature.[71]

The historical Henry Sinclair disappears from the records very quickly. Theories of his final days range from his death in 1400 in defense of his kingdom against an English attack to an unrecorded return to North America. Between Sinclair's death or disappearance and the ongoing struggle against the invasion of Scotland by England's Henry IV, the voyage to the west never received widespread coverage. It would take Antonio Zeno's great-great-grandson over a century to find and publish the correspondence that would become the *Zeno Narrative*. By that time, Columbus was firmly established as the discoverer of the New World, even though European fishing vessels and Norse explorers had all come and gone from the land for centuries.

A second stone was found in Westford, roughly 2½ miles from the knight.[72] Considered an Indian carving by local residents, it was rescued from oblivion in 1932 by Westford resident William Wyman, who moved the rock into his barn during road construction. Glynn interviewed Wyman and Edwin Gould, a direct descendant of one of Westford's original settlers. Both recalled the rock being located along the road when they were teenagers, some 60 to 70 years earlier.[73] In 1963, the stone was deeded to the Westford library, and it is now safely located in Westford's J.V. Fletcher Library as part of a growing collection of Knight material. This oval stone, interchangeably called the Ship Stone or Boat Stone, measuring about 18 inches in diameter, is inscribed with the image of a ship, an arrow, and the number 184.

Lethbridge suggested to Glynn that the Ship Stone's inscription was a navigational aid; 184 paces away would be Sinclair's base of operations. Glynn divided the area into quadrants and began a systematic search in a radius of 184 paces around the stone's original location, at the junction of two Indian trails. In 1966, Glynn found a 32-foot by 40-foot stone enclosure, about 3 feet high, with a spring nearby, now dried up. The low walls and proximity to water suggest a colonial springhouse, not a twelfth-century campsite.[74]

Frank Glynn's locating a stone structure 184 paces away is tentative proof at best. Between stonewalls, cellar holes, and glacial debris, you're likely to find something that could be interpreted as significant in any search of the New England countryside. Additionally, Glynn appears to have used U.S. units of distance. In the United States, a pace is 30 inches. In England, however, since at least the 12th century, one pace is 60 inches, further increasing both the search area and the odds of finding something.

Without knowing the unit of measure, there is ample room for interpretation. As an example, 184 furlongs is roughly 23 miles, a fair estimation of the 22½ mile distance from a ship anchored at Bodwell Falls to Prospect Hill via Stony Brook and the Merrimack River. There is no evidence to support this or any other interpretation of the number on the rock; without the key, the "184" is at best permutable in the various theories.

As it turned out, all of the interpretations are because of cultural amnesia. The mystery number is not 184. Former president of NEARA Terry Deveau examined the Boat Stone using a high-intensity, narrow beam light. Shone at extreme angles, there seems to indicate a theorized fourth number, a suggestion that Glynn had originally scoffed at. Badly worn, it is all but impossible to determine what the fourth digit reads, but a fair guess would be 1845. The Boat Stone does appear to be a directional marker, just not a medieval one.

A stone gatepost at the Meadowbrook farm on Gould Road, just west of Wyman's corner where the stone was found, shows an arrow done in the style of the Boat Stone arrow, a tree, an apple, and the year 1845.[75]

The eight is similarly open at the top, suggesting not age or zodiacal importance but difficulty carving arcs on stone. And if the Boat Stone was located less than 1,000 feet away from the "Apple Post," making it part of the same property as the farm on Gould Road. This makes the Boat Stone one of a series of markers that appear on the farm property associated with the Wright and Gould families, now known as Meadowbrook Farm but known locally as the old Gould Farm.[76]

In 2007, the Boat Stone was sent to Minnesota for petrographic analysis to see if the age of the carvings could be determined using microscopic examinations of the carving. The tests were conducted under the supervision of Scott F. Wolter. Wolter was the Minnesota geologist who had published a book on the Kensington Rune Stone declaring that geology proved the carving was too old to be a modern hoax. Wolter's results in Westford were less than impressive, restating the obvious. The rock was a glacial boulder and the carvings were man-made, created by a dull pointed tool to peck out the lines. He also noted the carved area "has a dark gray to black colored organic-like material" of unknown origin, apparently unaware that 45 years of contact with hands that touch and trace the carvings on the rock will leave oils and grime. The Boat Stone was returned safely to its home in Westford's Fletcher Library, no worse for wear other than a 1¾-inch diameter hole on the underside where Wolter drilled in the stone to take a core sample.[77]

Also found in Westford, the "Ship Stone" is now on display in the local library (Frank Glynn photograph, courtesy of Cindy Glynn).

In his subsequent book, Wolter gives his opinion on the stone's carvings. He suggests that the open end number 8 might actually be ♉, the zodiac symbol of Taurus, and the numeral 4 might actually be ♃, the astrological symbol for the planet Jupiter, making the Boat Stone a directional map for astronomical navigation.[78]

The Boat Stone remains on display at the Fletcher Library in Westford. Whether the directional marker is medieval or Victorian, it remains a fascinating part of Westford's past. And like the Knight carving, it has begun to develop its own body of pseudoscientific folklore.

The knight carving has finally been encased in a protective case of Plexiglas, but it may be too late. The elements and amateur attempts to clean the carving have rendered all but the sword indiscernible. In fact, it appears the protective case doesn't cover the entire image, as illustrated by Frank Glynn. Instead, it cuts the knight image off at the knees. A new plaque explains the various theories, leaning heavily on the Sinclair expedition.

There is also a new statue adjacent to the knight. It is a stunning life-size bronze representation of the knight created by local artist David Christiana. The stunning sculpture is as if he was interred in a medieval church. The custom of carving such a recumbent effigial monument in full relief did not become fashionable in the Scottish lowlands until the 13th century.[79]

There is no indication of when the style reached Caithness or the Orkneys, but Brydall notes the incised slab was still used after its introduction. This was the earliest form of the effigy, a treatment of the figure in flat relief, which the Westford Knight is.

To a casual visitor, it appears that the sculpture is the knight. To someone driving past, it appears more like a roadside yard sale. The only thing missing is a

The Westford Knight ledge today (courtesy William C. Darmon).

tattered string of pennants and a collection of mismatched cutlery to complete the impression.

Whether you believe the carving to be a military effigy from a pre-Columbian expedition, a fortuitous collection of erosion and glacier damage, or a Templar artifact, one thing is sure, the Westford Knight is a local landmark. It has brought Westford itself on a journey Henry Sinclair never envisioned. It is a tragedy that the Westford Knight is being allowed to simply disappear into the ages without an attempt to preserve it for future generations. Erosion has been replaced by a new threat. The carving is being overwhelmed by fake science advocated by its own supporters, effectively driving off the scientist and historians needed to debate, ponder, and perhaps resolve the mystery of the Westford Knight.

CHAPTER EIGHT

Runic Relicts

Although Vikings were popular in England as part of Victorian historical musings, the fascination with physical proof of a Norse expedition was primarily a New England phenomenon. Not until the 1898 discovery of the Kensington Rune Stone would the possibility that the Norse had been throughout North America in their first sweep of the entire country. The effects of this turn of the century craze remain with us today: the Minnesota Vikings play football, Boston's Longfellow Bridge's four central piers are decorated with the prows of Viking ships, and the Kensington Rune Stone's authenticity continues to be hotly debated. The Vikings may or may not have colonized New England, but their presence has thrived in the American collective consciousness.

Even the Smithsonian Institution gave tacit approval to the Norse theory with its 1913 publication of William H. Babcock's *Early Norse Visits to North America*.[1] A Washington, D.C., lawyer by trade, Babcock had no use for any runic inscription site in North America but was still a staunch advocate of Norse visitation. He approached the question of Norse explorations as Rafn had 80 years before—by a literal application of the description of voyages and landfalls. Babcock believed that the Norse had unquestionably visited North America (with Narragansett Bay being the site of Vinland) but that there was not a single legitimate Norse inscription stone on the continent.

An antiquarian specializing in myth, Babcock's strength was interpreting medieval texts.[2] His subsequent publications addressed various topics: mythical islands in the Atlantic Ocean as found on medieval maps, St. Brendan's voyage, and pre–Columbian references to natives. Babcock's work was ignored by a public so intrigued that intrepid Norse explorers had been in North America that the radiator caps on their cars were stylized Viking designs,[3] architectural features on buildings included Norse ship motifs, and Leif Eriksson had a statue in Boston.

Sites such as L'Anse aux Meadows in Newfoundland and Tanfield Valley on Baffin Island may or may not validate the existence of Vinland in the Norse sagas, but they do confirm that the Norse made it to North America. Excavations suggest the Vikings did travel farther south.[4] The question is, did they make it to New England?

Hanging Rock (The Whittier Runestone), West Newbury, Massachusetts

In 1830, a meeting of the Bradford Lyceum featured what the local paper referred to as "a piece of Aboriginal Statuary."[5] The artifact, found on the neighboring bank of the Merrimack River, was made of weathered gray stone. It was not an entire statue, merely the foot and lower leg. Within a decade, thanks to C.C. Rafn's book and Longfellow's poem, "The Skeleton in Armor," the stone was indelibly marked as a fragment of a Viking relic.

John Greenleaf Whittier used the rock as inspiration for "The Norsemen,"[6] one in a series of his works using Norse inspiration.[7] Whittier briefly exposits the topic of the poem before launching into images of Viking longboats sailing up the Merrimack River:

> In the early part of the present century, a fragment of a statue, rudely chiselled from dark gray stone, was found in the town of Bradford, on the Merrimac. Its origin must be left entirely to conjecture. The fact that the ancient Northmen visited the northeast coast of North America and probably New England, some centuries before the discovery of the western world by Columbus, is now very generally admitted.[8]

In 1859, *Atlantic Monthly* published another of Whittier's works, "The Double-Headed Snake of Newbury."[9] This was a satire of Cotton Mather's tendency to believe all reports of oddities and anomalies were sent to him as true accounts of God-given wonders. One of these reports told of the amphisbaena, a mythical snake with heads at both ends of its body. When the Rev. Christopher Toppan of Newbury wrote Mather in 1724 that some locals had killed a double-headed snake,[10] Toppan refers to the snake as an amphisbæna. Mather took this literally when Toppan was being figurative. This was the rare but documented abnormality of bicephaly, meaning the snake did have two heads but conjoined at the neck.

One of the places in Newbury that this amphisbaena dwelled, according to the poem, was "coiled by the Northman's Written Rock." The name appears to be an invention of Whittier; the local name for the area was "Old Hanging Rock," after an overhang formed by the top of a ledge.[11] The ledge is an outcropping of granite 12 to 15 feet high, currently located in the 2,123-acre Crane Pond Wildlife Management Area under the jurisdiction of the Massachusetts Division of Fisheries & Wildlife. At the time of the rock's first published report in 1854,[12] the ledge was in the pasture of a local farm.

The 1854 report was by George I. Pool, a Newburyport resident who visited the carving while hunting in a nearby field. Pool reported two parallel lines of carvings. Neither line showed recognizable characters except for the middle character in the lower line, which appeared to be a stick figure with a spear. The lower line extended beyond the protection of the overhang, and the end showed weathering damage as a result. Pool made a sketch of the carvings, noting that he had a poor copy of the Dighton Rock inscriptions and felt the two had some similarities.[13]

George I. Poole's inscription on Hanging Rock in West Newbury, Massachusetts, as originally published in *New England Historical and Genealogical Register*, 1854.

Edmund Burke Delabarre included the ledge in his 1928 study of New England "written" rocks.[14] Delabarre could find no earlier reports than Pool's and noted he could find no further discussions of the inscription's authenticity in the ensuing 75 years.[15] Delabarre asked renowned antiquarian and author George Francis Dow[16] to visit the carving and make an assessment. Dow's report was not encouraging. Dow and William Merrill, a local historian, examined the ledge, only to discover the markings were nothing more than natural cracking in the rock face. Dow also told of a discussion between Merrill and an elderly West Newbury resident named Follansbee, who was part of the hunting party the day Pool saw the inscriptions. According to Merrill, Follansbee recalled that Pool sketched the rock,[17] but there was no mention of an inscription. He also recalled that Pool "was much intoxicated" at the time.[18] Delabarre had heard enough and relegated the site to a chapter in the back of his book devoted to frauds and rumors.

William Goodwin was able to track down a copy of Pool's transcription for Olaf Strandwold to use in his book.[19] Strandwold considered it "one of the most remarkable of all runic inscriptions."[20] He interpreted the first line as a message in a Christian context and the second line as a heathen context. Strandwold translated the first line to read, "On the ice are 34 men, on an island. God, on dry land is Yule-tide." The second line was an appeal to Thor to use the great magic of the runic alphabet to save the men from a cruel fate. Combining the two lines, Strandwold found a record of 34 men stranded on an island in the winter and a supplication to the gods to intervene and return the men safely to shore to celebrate Yule with their comrades.

The same year Strandwold published his translation, Johannes Brøndsted, director of the National Museum of Denmark, was touring New England's "Viking" sites.[21] The West Newbury inscription was discussed as a possible site for Brøndsted to visit, except that no one could find it. Instead, Brøndsted included a copy of the Pool image with a collection of possible inscriptions that he was sending to runologist Erik Moltke at Denmark's national museum in Copenhagen. Moltke's report was succinct—the only inscriptions he reviewed that were even remotely runic in nature were the Kensington Rune Stone in Minnesota and Noman's Land Island in Massachusetts.[22] Neither one was ancient or Scandinavian in origin. Moltke's opinion of the lost carving was that it was simply an Indian pictograph.[23]

Whether or not the inscription was actually lost was a matter of opinion. To the local residents, its whereabouts were known if you knew who and what to ask. When Milo and Laurie Williams moved to Groveland, Massachusetts, in 1962, they set about finding "the Whittier Runestone." After a decade of searching and researching, they discovered that they had been asking the wrong question. "Whittier Runestone" was known locally as "Old Hanging Rock" and was well known by the older members of the community as a perennial favorite picnic spot. Once that connection was made, the Williamses were easily led to the site by a local resident.

The local media covered the rediscovery of Old Hanging Rock, repeating Strandwold's woeful translated tale. In one of the articles about the inscription, the *Newburyport Daily News* included a reprint of a 1944 unnamed local newspaper's interpretation of the markings, significantly different from the Pool version but equally non-runic.[24]

Laurie Williams filed a report with the New England Antiquities Research Association.[25] The Williamses found that "old Hanging Rock" hung no longer—sometime after Pool's visit and before an 1892 photograph,[26] the top had broken away from the ledge. The only part of the original inscription they could find was the stick figure holding a spear. The rest was either eroded or scraped away when the overhang came down. The report ends with a summation of Strandwold's translation work and plans to excavate the area, pending permission of the Fish & Game Commission and the state archaeologist.

Whether the commission did not want such a disruption in a woodland setting or the state archaeologist chose not to get involved in the matter, the excavation never took place.

The Byfield Viking Graves, Byfield, Massachusetts

In 1870, Mrs. Anna Rogers of Byfield was out gathering wild berries when she was caught in a sudden storm. She took shelter under an overhanging rock, where she noticed strange markings. She later mentioned her discovery to her son Lawrence.[27] They searched for the rock again, but searches were sporadic with a farm to maintain. They never found the location again, but not for lack of trying. Anna Rogers had likely sheltered under the Hanging Rock (The Whittier Runestone), which had collapsed by 1879, possibly making Mrs. Rogers the last person to see the stone before its demise.

Lawrence did eventually notice a carved boulder on the family property. It was not the rock described by his mother, who had died in 1917. Still, it was odd enough to write a letter to archaeologist Warren K. Moorehead at the Peabody Museum in nearby Andover. Moorehead came to look at Rogers's find in Byfield and several other purported sites in the area, including the Whittier Rune Stone.

Moorehead was accompanied by game warden Orrin Arlin and Wallace Ordway, a farmer who knew the rivers and marshes of the area better than anyone, but the Whittier Stone still evaded rediscovery. Moorehead was not impressed by the rock of the Rogers farm but realized that a survey of surviving Native sites needed to be done. Moorehead's study took place in 1930, assisted by Ordway in the Newburyport leg of a canoe trip up the Merrimack River. There was no mention of Byfield or the marked stone of Lawrence Rogers.[28]

In 1938, Olaf Strandwold released his translation of "Thorvald's gravestone" in Hampton, New Hampshire.[29] The article appeared in the *Boston Globe*[30] and was carried nationally by Hearst's INS newswire. Lawrence Rogers' local newspaper, *Newburyport Daily News,* also ran the story.[31] The article gave Rogers two new correspondents: William B. Goodwin and Olaf Strandwold. Goodwin's health had begun to deteriorate, but in 1943, on one of his infrequent visits to his Irish monastery site in New Hampshire (now America's Stonehenge), he stopped in Byfield to see Rogers's find. By then, Rogers had a collection of additional smaller stones that he had found scattered across the woods and wetlands of the region. Goodwin politely examined the rocks while his assistant Malcolm Pearson took a photograph or two as a sampling for their files. Goodwin and Pearson dismissed the markings as grooves randomly created when struck by farming implements, particularly plows and harrows.

Strandwold, on the other hand, was thrilled to be contacted. When Rogers sent photographs to him, he immediately began his translations. His translation of the Byfield stones was that they were gravestones marking a series of Christian Norsemen buried in the first half of the 11th century. Strandwold considered this to be a significant discovery, so much so that he decided to make it a focus of his next book. He wrote to Malcolm Pearson and asked him to return to Byfield and take better photographs of the rune stones.

Pearson, working full-time, raising a family, and conducting his own research, was already overwhelmed. Strandwold had become increasingly difficult to work with as he grew more defensive about his translations. Unanswered questions about his interpretations and feuds over his translations with such high-profile figures as the Kensington Rune Stone's Hjalmar Holand made Strandwold a pariah among researchers and publishers of Scandinavian topics.

This was the final straw for Pearson. He reminded Strandwold that he and Goodwin had examined those stones firsthand, which were unquestionably plow strikes. Strandwold, translating them from photographs, was risking his reputation by translating stones out of context again. When it became apparent Strandwold would ignore his warning, Pearson simply became unavailable to do further photography for Strandwold's book.

Lawrence Rogers died in April 1945. Rogers's two adult daughters and his wife had no interest in operating a farm. Strandwold was concerned enough about his Viking graves to make a rare trip east to discuss the farm's future with Lawrence Rogers's widow, Charlotte, and Wallace Ordway, who had helped Rogers collect the stones. To Strandwold's relief, Charlotte had decided that if they sold the property, it would be the actual farmland, keeping the house (and the runestones) as their residence. Ordway released Strandwold's translation to the Newburyport newspaper as the front page story.[32]

William Goodwin had his *Ruins of Great Ireland in New England* published at his own expense in 1946. That expenditure meant that Goodwin had no interest in underwriting Strandwold's next book. Strandwold's insistence on the legitimacy of the Byfield Norse graves had effectively cut him off from Goodwin, his primary sources of support, funding, and information.

Strandwold died in December 1948 at his home in Washington. His last book, *Norse Inscriptions on American Stones*, was published in June 1949. It was not the magnum opus he had envisioned. The 70-page pamphlet had 32 pages on American translations, over half of which was his work on the Byfield runes. It was underwritten by Magnus Björndal, who had replaced Goodwin as Strandwold's benefactor. Björndal had the book postdated 1948, so it would not appear to be a posthumous publication.

Björndal was such a staunch advocate of Strandwold that he may have accidentally sabotaged Strandwold's legacy. Before Strandwold's death, Björndal had managed to alienate such figures as Malcolm Pearson and Hjalmar Holand. NEARA archives only have Björndal's replies, but it appears Björndal took overreacted to minor slights and would threaten to withhold future funding for research that had not been solicited.

As a result, the book and the Byfield stones languished in relative obscurity until 1961, when Charles Michael Boland released *They All Discovered America*.[33] The first successful mainstream book on pre-Columbian visitors, Boland claimed 19 separate waves of exploration from Europe. The number would be higher, but Boland tended to combine local claims, regardless of chronology. Boland proposed the Icelandic survivors of the shipwreck on the Whittier Rune Stone were captured by William B. Goodwin's Irish Culdee monks from the America's Stonehenge site. The monks kept the Icelanders subjugated around West Newbury and Byfield. As they died, the converted Norsemen were given Christian burials, per Strandwold's translation. His sole rationale is the proximity of the three sites.

With no reliable source material available, Boland gives the impression that the collection of stones he saw was organized as if in a cemetery. Strandwold had only seen the stones after Rogers had started relocating them in his yard. In truth, the runic rocks had been collected over a wide area ranging from the 6000-acre Crane Pond Wildlife area to the shore of the Merrimack River to the salt marsh grasslands along the Newbury coast. Boland also notes that Charlotte Rogers had sold the house lot, the last of the Rogers farm parcels, by his book's release. New construction had bulldozed the stones into oblivion.[34]

This should also have been the end of the Byfield rune stones. But Landsverk and Mongé then published their theory that runic carvings were a complicated cryptography system, using the Spirit Pond Stones as an example.[35] In the wake of the contentious debate over their results with the Spirit Pond Stones, Landsverk had started looking for more evidence of Henricus cryptograms. He found Strandwold. Landsverk disdainfully suggested that Strandwold's sole contribution to runology was getting Pearson to photograph sites for future use. Landsverk used those photos, culling the "gravestones" down to three.[36] Two of the stones fit nicely into his coded name and date evidence of Henricus, but one did not. The newly named "Byfield 1," the first marked boulder that Rogers found on his property, did not conform to Landsverk's Henricus theory. So, he decided that Byfield 1 predated Henricus by a century and was carved by the same runic puzzle master that inscribed the Heavener Rune Stone in Oklahoma.

Olaf Strandwold on a research trip to New England, ca. 1936 (Malcolm Pearson photograph).

Despite saying he used Pearson's photographs, Landsverk also claimed to have inspected the Byfield in 1969 and 1972. This is a decade after Boland declared them destroyed and at least five years after Charlotte Rogers had finalized the sale of the house parcel to a developer.

At least one stone from Strandwold's book appears to remain in the neighborhood,[37] possibly salvaged by a concerned neighbor, or just construction debris. So the lost Byfield runestones, which are not runestones, and were not all found in Byfield, may also not be lost.

Monhegan Island Inscription, Manana Island, Maine

William Jenks was the pastor of the First Congregational Church in Bath, Maine, from 1805 to 1818. In addition to his pastoral duties, he was a professor of Oriental

A Byfield "Viking grave" found by Rogers in what is now the Crane Pond Wilderness Management Area. Strandwold's translation—"Resurrect the Men on Sea Island, Jesus"—reinforces his translation of the Hanging Rock (The Whittier Runestone) (Malcolm Pearson photograph from Strandwold's *Norse Inscriptions on American Stones* [1948]).

languages and English literature at Bowdoin College. In 1818, Jenks returned to Boston, founding a mission for seamen and becoming an active member of Boston's various reform movements. He continued preaching and writing on a variety of historical topics. By the time his multi-volume *Comprehensive Commentary on the Holy Bible*[38] was published, he was renowned as a Biblical and Oriental scholar in antiquarian circles. So, in 1851, when he spoke at a meeting of the American Academy of Arts and Sciences about his 1808 investigation of Norse inscriptions on Manana Island off the coast of Maine, there was no question that Dr. Jenks had found Norse inscriptions.[39]

Maine is noted for several spectacular native petroglyphs such as those in Machias Bay or Embden.[40] But the earliest documented petroglyph site in Maine may not be Native American, and it may not even be petroglyphs. Jenks admitted to his esteemed colleagues that he had not impressed with the inscriptions at first, believing them to be unimportant tally marks from some early crude inventory.[41]

The inscription on Manana Island is also known as the "Monhegan Inscription," because Manana is a small island, less than a half-mile in length, located off Monhegan Island. Both islands are ten miles southwest of the mainland at Port Clyde, Maine, but Monhegan shows up more often on maps and is a better-known landmark for the adventurous few looking for the inscription.

There is a U.S. Coast Guard fog signal station on Manana. The fog signal building, the former keeper's quarters, and associated structures are located on the top of the island near the western edge. A path leads from a boat landing on the east side of the island to the station. It is fully automated now and activated by radio signal from the lighthouse station on Monhegan, with an electronic horn that emits two blasts every 60 seconds—there is no longer a keeper for the Manana station,[42] and the island is uninhabited.[43]

Along an overgrown path leading from the abandoned boat landing to the Coast Guard station, there is a faded yellow "X" painted on the rocks, marking the site of the reputed Norse inscription. The inscriptions are on a smooth vertical plane distinctive from the surrounding rock. This "inscription tablet" runs diagonally from left to right. On this smooth face are the alleged runic characters, each 6 inches in length and ranging from ¼ inch to ½ inch in depth.

Ida Proper in *Monhegan, the Cradle of New England*[44] lists all the documented and probable possible explorers who visited the area, such as Giovanni da Verrazzano in 1524 and Samuel de Champlain in 1604. But she also lists pre–Columbian explorers that may have visited Monhegan Island, such as the Norse, the Phoenicians, St. Brendan, Nicolò Zeno, and Culdee monks. More important to Proper were the annual visits by fishermen—Basque, Spanish, Portuguese, and Breton.

By the 16th century, French and Basque fishing vessels were regular visitors to the waters of Maine and the Maritime Provinces. By the early 17th century, the Dutch and English were also fishing on the Grand Banks. Some of these fishing vessels established settlements near the fishing banks to dry and salt the cod.[45] Even Captain John Smith was dabbling in the dried fish trade with stages and fish-flakes on Monhegan in 1614 while exploring the coast, according to Samuel Eliot Morison.[46]

There is a spring near the base of the inscription, and on top of the ledge above the inscriptions are a series of drilled holes which Proper suggests might have been "made to fit rounded ends of poles or timbers, used to hold upright some structure to carry a cross, or other symbol of possession, or a signal, either of distress, or to attract the attention of passing craft to the fine spring, or good harbor, or both. These holes or depressions are arranged [in a cross] so that the end one was evidently used as a brace. Placed in this location on Manana such a signal could not have been overlooked by any passing craft."[47] One possible explanation overlooked by Proper was that in the ensuing years after the inscription was first identified as Norse, someone had tried to remove the inscription by drilling into the stone and attempting to break off the face of the inscription.

A. C. Hamlin, a physician by trade and a noted avocational geologist, visited the island and made a plaster cast of the carvings to illustrate remarks he made at a meeting of the American Association for the Advancement of Science in 1856.[48] Hamlin felt the inscription was proof of his theory that the Kennebec River was the site of Vinland. His theory on the origin of the inscription was that the stone contained natural fissures augmented by the Norse to create the line of runes.[49] A drawing from that casting appears in Schoolcraft's *History of Indian Tribes*[50] the following year. This drawing has been reproduced continually by subsequent authors in discussions of the site. Schoolcraft himself felt the carving was Norse, placing it in a chapter on European and Asian "intrusive elements." He conceded that Hamlin could be correct in locating Vinland in Maine.[51] Daniel Wilson[52] recounts Hamlin's work, pointing out that Hamlin had sent a copy of the casting to Copenhagen for examination. Wilson finds it amusing to note that while Hamlin hypothesizes the runes were carved by a semi-literate Norseman, the Royal Society of Northern Antiquities in Copenhagen suggested the same marks were made by a literate Indian, educated by the Norse in runic letters.[53]

William Jenks had the opportunity to review Schoolcraft's text before publication. He was impressed with Schoolcraft's work on the Dighton Rock inscriptions, identifying parts of the stone as native and other parts as Norse or Phoenician.[54] With Schoolcraft considering the possibility of Norse markings on rocks, and in light of Rafn's declaration of Norse origins for the various stone structures and inscriptions, Jenks reconsidered the Manana inscriptions.[55] He reviewed Rafn's work and consulted a Norse thesaurus.[56] Now, when Jenks looked at the marks on the rock face, he saw at least 18 runes. He suggested that one of the other members might visit the island and make a plaster casting of the inscription to send to the Royal Society of Northern Antiquaries for translation, unaware that Hamlin's casting had been Schoolcraft's source.[57]

Two geologists examined Monhegan and Manana: George Stone, a professor of geology at Colorado College, and Edwin Chesley Estes Lord, a petrographer with the U.S. Office of Public Roads. Neither was convinced the marks on Manana were manmade.

Stone investigated the site in 1885.[58] Stone, who had done extensive work in Maine for the U.S. Geological Survey, went to Manana specifically to investigate the inscriptions. He found both Monhegan and Manana were composed of an uncommon form of gabbro.[59] Gabbro is a coarse-grained igneous rock, similar to basalt. Stone found the rock was covered with thin fractures filled with other types of rock, such as quartz, white granite, and a fine-grained black rock. He noted that different minerals, particularly those of different grains, weathered at different rates. The diagonal plane which contained the inscriptions was a finer grain vein intruding into the coarse-grained gabbro surrounding it. The letters were furrows, intersecting obliquely, caused by a different erosion pattern in the intrusion vein. Stone's assessment was that the Manana Inscription did, at first glance, look like runes on a section of the rock specifically smoothed and prepared as a writing surface. However, examining the stone closely, it was apparent that the "inscription" was a "freak of surface erosion."[60] To further illustrate his point, he located a smaller example of the furrows a few yards away and a third example on Monhegan Island itself.

In 1900, E.C.E. Lord published his study on the geology and petrology of Monhegan Island. Although not explicitly specifically addressing the inscriptions, his work verified Stone's previous study. Lord discovered that Manana Island and most of Monhegan were composed of olivine-norite gabbro, a rock common in New Hampshire and New York but rare in Maine. Lord also determined that Manana was part of a pluton formed in the Precambrian Eon, 2,500 million years ago, and was actually part of Monhegan until glaciers gouged out the channel that created Monhegan Harbor.[61] The diagonal plane that includes the runes is one of numerous dikes or segregation masses found on the island and common in gabbric rock. Lord found two types of dikes: bytownite, common and plentiful on the island, and dikes made of pyroxene with some bytownite, magnetite, and apatite. These two different types of dikes are from two distinct periods of eruption. Of particular note are the dikes of gabbro aplite,[62] which Lord notes have a feature specific to rocks of the area—a frequent occurrence of veins and seams of green hornblende. Hornblende, on the Mohs' Scale of Hardness,[63] is softer than the gabbro, meaning it would erode faster, leaving grooves in the relatively unscathed gabbro.

B. F. DeCosta, in one of the earliest English language compilations of the Icelandic sagas,[64] had previously suggested a similar origin for the Manana inscription as George Stone. DeCosta compared Monhegan to the Hoby Stone as recorded by Saxo Grammaticus, the thirteenth-century Danish historian. According to DeCosta, the Hoby inscription was transcribed and sent to scholars who translated it as a record of battle. It was subsequently found to be merely the impressions left when veins of a softer rock eroded away.[65] Other experts joined in the dismissal of the site; Garrick Mallery's study of Indian pictographs,[66] citing Stone's report, mentions the Manana inscription as a natural and inadvertent example of a fraudulent inscription.[67]

The opinions of DeCosta, Mallery, and Stone were not sufficient to counteract the growing legend of Norse explorers on the island. Historian and folklorist Samuel Adams Drake's mention of the inscription,[68] and the belief that it was either the work of the "Northmen or the Devil," showed the scope of the inscription's presence.[69]

John Campbell, a professor at Presbyterian College in Montreal, Canada, translated the inscription as a grave marker for a Huron chieftain.[70] Campbell did not elaborate on why an Indian tribe on the shores of Lake Michigan would commemorate their leader with a marker 1100 miles to the east. However, Campbell had previously translated the Davenport Tablets[71] as Indian phonetic transliterations of Hittite text,[72] so the Monhegan inscription supported his phonetic Indian/Hittite theory. Aside from the fact that Hittite would not be translated by recognized linguists until 1915, over 40 years after Campbell's initial publication on the Davenport Tablets, his Monhegan work was based on a rendering from the copy of Hamlin's casting that had been shipped to Copenhagen.[73] The casting had been damaged in transit and reconstructed, "bearing a very remote resemblance"[74] to the original.

By the time Edmund Delabarre discussed the runes, calling them "the most famous inscription in Maine,"[75] the Phoenicians, the Vikings, and Native Americans had been discussed as possible inscribers. There was also a new candidate: Proto-Nordics.

According to author Herman Wirth,[76] Proto-Nordics were the ancient ancestors of the Nordic peoples. These ancestors settled North America, Atlantis, and

Asia, becoming the ancestors of, among others, the Sumerians, the Mongols, the North American Indians, and the paleolithic Magdalenian culture. Wirth identified the Monhegan carvings as the oldest inscription in the world, 25,000 years old. Wirth's work on quantifying a Nordic-Atlantean culture was not an isolated case. Various "scientific" writings appeared in Germany at that time, connecting Nordic ancestry with a superior, blond, blue-eyed "master race," the precursor to the National Socialist movement that would culminate in World War II.[77]

In *Norse Runic Inscriptions along the Atlantic Seaboard,* Strandwold concentrates on nine inscriptions found in North America, unfortunately including the two inscriptions found on Manana and Monhegan Islands.[78] Unfortunately, Strandwold was working from images in other sources. He failed to recognize that the runic inscription found on Manana Island in 1808, as illustrated in Wilson's *Prehistoric Man,* was the same inscription he identified as the Monhegan Inscription, illustrated in the 1859 *Mémoires de la Société Royale des Antiquaires du Nord.*[79] The latter rendering used the fallacious inscription from Hamlin's broken casting. Strandwold devotes 16 pages of his 107-page book to two entirely different translations of the same inscription. Strandwold translated the Wilson inscription, based on the drawing made for Schoolcraft as "Aunir Hewed Runes—Year 36" (1041 AD). The Royal Society version, with two rune rows, he translated as "Asur's Property—Thor's Blessing," on the first line and the second line reading, "Aunr owns property on the estuary, Year 56" (1058 AD).

To further complicate the matter, Strandwold translates the inscription a third time in his next book.[80] It is unclear if Strandwold believed the "inscription on a cliff, Manana Island, Maine" was a third inscription or if he simply was ignoring the previous confusion and starting from scratch. This time, working from a Malcolm Pearson photograph, Strandwold found a record of a shipwrecked Norseman: "I, Veigle, remained 7 years, year of Jesus 32" (1031 AD).

Historian Frederick J. Pohl, wary after his adventures on Cape Cod searching for Vinland,[81] remained noncommittal as to the origins of the markings.[82] He summarized the positions of Stone and Proper before moving on to Strandwold.[83] He scolds Strandwold for changing his translation because of his reliance on other people's accuracy in copying the inscription. Pohl was always an advocate of firsthand observations. Pohl concludes by agreeing with Proper, who suggested a new plaster cast be taken of the runes and compared to Hamlin's. If the inscription was natural erosion, the grooves should show additional deterioration from weathering.

Whether he was following up on the suggestion or not, in the early 1970s, archaeologist James Whittall took another casting from the rock face, using latex instead of plaster.[84] The two castings, although done over a century apart, are similar—a testament to Hamlin's accuracy, even if it does not clarify the origin of the markings.

Whittall's casting was for epigrapher Barry Fell, who was compiling petroglyphs as proofs of his theory of sustained pre-Columbian contact between the old and new worlds by numerous cultures. This theory would become the bestseller *America BC*.[85] Fell's analysis of these inscriptions concluded that the North American inscriptions were inscribed using an unknown variant form of a Celtic script. Hinge-Ogham, a consaine, or consonantal Ogham, did not use vowels.

Fell felt that the language represented by this variation of Ogham showed a Phoenician element, suggesting the carvers originated on the Iberian peninsula of Spain and Portugal. Fell theorized the language on the New England carvings was a merging of the Iberian and Celt cultures with a Carthaginian influence. His critics contended that this allowed Fell enough latitude to drop vowels into the text wherever he chose, to get a preconceived result.[86]

Reading from right to left, Fell translated the Monhegan inscription into idiomatic English as, "Ships from Phoenicia, cargo platform."[87] Whittall reproduced a more literal version of Fell's translation: "Long-ships from Phoenicia: Cargo-lots (and) landing-quay."[88] Fell believed this was evidence of Phoenician ships of the late Bronze Age using Manana Island as a centralized trade station. The flat-topped island was used for loading/unloading vessels as the mainland Celts ferried goods to/from and from the island.[89] Fell predicted that because of the treacherous currents around Monhegan, he would not be surprised if ancient shipwrecks were discovered. Several years later, United Press International ran a story about a Castine, Maine, diver who had found two amphorae in the waters off the mainland coast near Monhegan.[90] Fell was interviewed, delighted to see his claim come true.

When New England Antiquities Research Association member Suzanne Carlson visited Manana,[91] she found that, like Campbell and Strandwold before him, Fell's work suffered from working in a vacuum. Fell's inscription designating the site of a Phoenician wharf would require unloading "any cargo nearly 150 feet up a rocky cliff."[92] Carlson also notes that the Monhegan side of the island has a sloping beach, making that side of the coast a better location for loading ships.

Carlson concluded that the markings were natural, with no signs of chisel marks enhancing them. She also found that many of the vertical rune lines appeared to continue beyond the dike and into the gabbro. Her conclusion, as a non-geologist, was that the grooves of the inscription were reminiscent of natural cracking caused by conflicting rates of expansion and contraction between two different types of rock.[93] Considering the conflict generated by this inscription, it seems only fitting that conflict also caused the inscription itself.

The Ellsworth Runestone, Ellsworth, Maine

An ancient Native burial ground was found in 1892 in a gravel pit along the Union River about a mile south of Ellsworth, Maine. When it became apparent there were undisturbed graves, Harvard was contacted. Excavations found the graves were so old that the bone had been reduced to dust. The remains and grave goods had

The misnamed Monhegan Inscription is on neighboring Manana Island, Maine (Malcolm Pearson photograph).

been interred ceremonially within layers of red ochre. The Red Paint People had been rediscovered.

According to the report by Charles C. Willoughby, in what was designated "Grave L," among the powdered dust of decomposed bone of one or possibly two bodies were found interred ceremonially within layers of red ochre. Within the red ochre were artifacts: a scraper, a stone flake, and an engraved object. Willoughby identifies it as a broken semi-lunar blade, similar to the ulus of the Inuits. The cutting edge broke off long before being placed in the grave, and the stone was covered with a design of lines. The reverse had been used to sharpen knives, and the whetting had all but obliterated the decoration.[94]

Edward J. Lenik, an authority on rock art in the Northeast, disagreed with Willoughby's assessment and considered the artifact a slate tablet. The shape and damaged edge made it the wrong shape for an ulus.[95] Archaeologist Bruce L. Bourque of the Maine State Museum concurred. Bourque found the entire gravesite filled with "unparalleled workmanship and fanciful design that were probably intended for ceremonial purposes."[96]

In fact, there was only one person who has ever suggested the decorated slate stone was something other than Native American—Olaf Strandwold. Strandwold

Line art of the Ellsworth artifact from Willoughby's 1898 report on the excavation. Strandwold's "runes" were only in the upper left region, disregarding the other markings.

was sent a copy of the rendering in Willoughby's report, but not the entire article. So once again, working in a vacuum, he translated the "Ellsworth Rune Stone." The results were not unexpected, considering Strandwold's track record: it was a Norse grave marker. Typical of the lack of context, the copy of the image of his book is over 4 inches long and presumed to be a reduced image from a larger rock. In truth, the stone is barely 3½ inches long. Strandwold focused on just a part of the carvings, ignoring two incised parallel lines across the stone with perpendicular lines connected to the bands. He also ignored chevrons with short perpendicular lines below the bands. He does, as an afterthought, associate the chevrons with gables of Norse houses, and the short lines were posts to tie cattle. He doesn't address why a grave marker would be in the grave rather than above it.[97]

Considering the Ellsworth burial site dates back to between 2,000 to 6,000 years ago, the bodies were interred millennia before Norse visits to the New World. The rock survives, but the Norse claim lost.

The Magunco Stone, Upton, Massachusetts

Harry A. Cheney of Hopkinton, Massachusetts, was a farmer and local historian, highly regarded for his encyclopedic knowledge of the local area's history and his interests in botany, mineralogy, and archaeology. Cheney's collection was as diverse as his interests. It included an array of town histories, Indian artifacts, and newspaper clippings on reported Viking sites.

As it would turn out, Cheney's Norse interests would be pivotal in introducing the significant figures in New England pre-Columbian research to each other. Teenager Malcolm Pearson approached Cheney about the structure on the Pearson farm, now known as the Upton Beehive or Pearson Chamber. The two, responding to a newspaper query from Olaf Strandwolf, relocated the purported site of Thorvald's

Gravestone in Hampton, New Hampshire. Strandwold introduced them to William B. Goodwin. Goodwin, Cheney, and Pearson would then identify dozens of man-made stone structures and markings across New England, most notably the Westford Knight. Goodwin would buy the "artificial caves" in Salem, New Hampshire, as proof of 9th-century Irish Catholic monks, leaving the site now called America's Stonehenge to Pearson in his will.

Cheney asked Strandwold about a small stone he had found as a teen 50 years earlier. He found the 3½-inch by 2-inch-wide stone while digging for Indian artifacts on the shore of a lake near Bear Hill in Upton. This deliberately vague location obscured the fact Cheney was searching at Whitehall Reservoir, then still part of the region's water supply, with restricted access.

Strandwold saw three runes and agreed with Cheney's assessment that there was fire damage on the reverse side, and the stone was a fragment of a more extensive inscription. He translated the marking as the Old Norse spelling of the English word "son" in the objective case. The missing part minimally contained the subject and verb needed to complete the sentence.[98]

Cheney had initially assumed it was Native American in origin. The name "Magunco Stone" is a nod to Magunkaquog in neighboring Ashland, Massachusetts. Magunkaquog was the seventh of the fourteen "Praying Indian" settlements created by Puritan missionary John Eliot between 1651 and 1674 as part of the Massachusetts Bay Colony's attempts to convert local Native American populations to Christianity.

Cheney also noted he had found other artifacts near the stone, a brass boss and a colonial buckle. Both Strandwold and Cheney apparently missed the significance of Cheney finding the "Magunco Stone" in the same layer of silt as a colonial shoe buckle. Goodwin, an expert on colonial metal items, refers to the brass boss as a bronze disc he was willing to consider from a Norseman's shield. Interestingly, Goodwin doesn't mention the shoe buckle when discussing what he refers to as the "Cheney Stone."[99] This omission may suggest that the one item that would immediately allow him to identify and date the artifacts as colonial was deliberately kept from him. The only possible reason to avoid mentioning the shoe buckle would be last-minute issues with Goodwin's financing Strandwold's book.

Harry Cheney died in 1954. The family broke up his collection of books, and his collection of Indian artifacts is now part of the Hopkinton Historical Society. This is no record of what happened to the Magunco Stone after its mention by Goodwin.

The Chatfield Stone, Sebec Lake, Maine

Greeley's Landing is in the Town of Dover-Foxcroft, a steamboat stop where Bog Creek empties into Sebec Lake at the lake's southernmost point, sixty miles northwest of Bangor. It was a small town that served as a resort for nature lovers and sportsmen who wanted to get away from it all. In 1940, Charles T. Chatfield, a New

Eight. Runic Relicts 127

The Sebec or Chatsfield Stone is a 100-pound rock found in the sand of Sebec Lake in Maine, rescued, and brought to New York City by Charles Chatfield as a vacation souvenir (Malcolm Pearson photograph from Goodwin's *Truth About Leif Ericsson* [1941]).

York City civil engineer, was one of those who heard the call of nature and vacationed at Sebec Lake.

Chatfield returned from Maine with a souvenir that didn't require a taxidermist. It was a 100-pound granite rock, white from the amount of quartz in its composition. It was found in the sand while caretakers prepared a beach for swimming. The flat face had carvings on it. While William B. Goodwin was elated that another runic inscription had been found, this one also bothered him.[100]

As Goodwin interpreted the sagas, there was no evidence that the Northmen went up the Maine coast further than Camden, never mind inland as far as Sebec, which would entail sailing over 60 miles up the Penobscot River, then another 30 up the Piscataquis River into the Sebec Lake. So, Goodwin continued, it was either a Norse expedition that was undocumented in the sagas or that Indians carried the rock inland as a sacred totem of the strange visitors.

Goodwin may have been on the right track by considering the stone as being transported to Sebec. A surficial geology study of Lake Sebec[101] shows no naturally occurring sand at the lake. So, the stone may have been carried by the lake with a shipment of beach sand dredged elsewhere, which means the carvings may only have been damage by metal tools during the dredge.

Copies of the markings were sent to Olaf Strandwold. He identified the same rare rune types found on the Dighton Rock and Monhegan Island. He believes it was a stone memorializing a woman of the Thorfinn Karlsefne expedition from the Icelandic Sagas. Goodwin was not entirely convinced. He had underwritten Strandwold's first booklet of translation work in 1939, but by the publication of his *Truth About Leif Ericsson* in 1941, Goodwin advised caution in using Strandwold as a sole source, despite having used Strandwold to translate most of the suspected inscriptions discussed in the book.[102] When Strandwold's second booklet was released, it included the Chatfield Stone with a completely different translation. Now, Strandwold believed it was an evocation for successful fishing.[103]

Charles Chatfield returned to his position as a topographic draftsman for the borough of Queens. He never sought publicity or credit for the find. He continued to work quietly for the borough and occasionally published local history research before retiring. He died in 1965 while visiting his son in Connecticut. The photograph of the Sebec stone he sent to Strandwold is the last record of the rock, presumably lost in Queens.

CHAPTER NINE

The Spirit Pond Runestones

Popham Beach Stone, Phippsburg, Maine

In 1939, a suspected rune stone was reported to William B. Goodwin by Mrs. Etta Hall Taylor, a former neighbor in Hartford, Connecticut. She and her husband had relocated to Popham Beach, where she now covered Phippsburg for the *Portland Press Herald*. Her letter to Goodwin asked for suggestions. A carved stone had been found nearby on the Kennebec River. Malcolm Pearson flew to Maine and documented the stone. Meeting Mrs. Taylor, she led him to Sabino Head. The rock was partially buried in the grass on the side of a field on a small farm. Pearson photographed it and noted the grooves were severely eroded. Part of the surface was covered in lichen, suggesting long-term exposure. He could not determine the size or weight of the rock. Goodwin sent the Pearson photograph to Strandwold, who did a quick translation, declaring that it simply reads "In the Year 19." Goodwin interpolated this as referring to 19 years after the settlement of the Greenland colony, or AD 1005.[1]

Strandwold used the Pearson photograph in his 1948 book. Strandwold was already dead, and Goodwin and Pearson had given up on his work after Byfield. So no one could point out that although Strandwold's publisher used the same photograph as Goodwin, it was printed sideways with the image compressed, changing the appearance of the marks. Strandwold now translated the stone literally as "Year 19 is an ill year," which he offered colloquially as "Year 1018 is a year of famine."[2] The Strandwold book faded into obscurity, as did most of the stones he translated

When Malcolm Pearson went to photograph the Spirit Pond Stones in 1972, he paused to return to the nearby Popham Beach Stone that he had photographed in 1939. He found the inscriptions had eroded to the point of being indistinguishable.[3] Today, when Popham Beach Stone is mentioned at all, it is due to its proximity to more famous alleged runes. The stone sits ⅔ of a mile across Atkins Bay from the Spirit Pond Runestones.

Spirit Pond Runestones, Phippsburg, Maine

In his search for the location of Leif Eriksson's Vinland, William Goodwin placed Streamfiord as being near Portsmouth, New Hampshire, in a shallow channel

Thirty-three years later, the Popham Beach stone was only recognizable because Pearson recalled the rock's shape. The inscription had eroded away (courtesy NEARA Archives).

of the Piscataqua River called Broad Cove.[4] Of this placement, Goodwin was adamant, devoting extensive text in his book to the location. Goodwin was a little more flexible early in his research about the various other place names associated with the sagas. He seemed to associate the saga locations deliberately with inscription stones found by Olaf Strandwold (this was before their falling out). Goodwin places Leif's landfall at Hampton, New Hampshire—coinciding with Strandwold's work on the Hampton runestone.[5] Hóp was placed in the vicinity of the Bourne Stone on Cape Cod, also discussed by Strandwold.[6] Keelness, where Thorvald repaired his ship before meeting his doom, is south of the mouth of the Kennebec River on Popham Beach.

Twenty-six years later, Walter Elliot, a carpenter from Quincy, Massachusetts, was exploring the very same area. Elliot, a Maine expatriate who spent his spare time returning to Maine to search for Indian artifacts near his family's hometown, was on one of his expeditions along Maine's Morse River in May of 1971. He had beached his rubber raft near Spirit Pond and was exploring the vicinity of an ancient shell heap. Instead of the expected arrowheads, he came across three small stones—a 5 by 6-inch stone of diorite, a second diorite stone measuring 6 by 7 inches, and a slate sized 8 by 10 inches. All appeared to have markings on them.

Elliot's immediate thought was of buried treasure—one of the stones appeared to have a map of the area on it. He brought them to the Bath Marine Museum to show the curator, Harold Brown. Brown, a retired math teacher, recognized them as runes and tried to impress upon Elliot the importance of his find as proof that the Vikings had traveled farther south than Newfoundland. Elliot brought the stones to Bowdoin College, futilely seeking an archaeologist. He spent the next year trying to find someone to translate his find. He wrote letters to colleges and language experts asking if someone would look at the stones. Elliot brought the stones to Harvard and waited five hours for someone to assist him before leaving in frustration.

One of the few people who had shown interest in his stones was O.G. Landsverk. Landsverk had been working with Alf Mongé, a former cryptologist with the U.S. Signal Corps during World War II. Landsverk and Mongé claimed to have discovered secretly dated cryptograms hidden in runic inscriptions. Applying this theory to American runic stones, the authors believed they could differentiate between legitimate ancient inscriptions and modern hoaxes. Since no one remembered these Norse dated puzzles for over 500 years, the forgeries would not have them.[7]

Landsverk's disdain for other rune translators seems to have prevented his inclusion of the original Popham Beach stone in his work. He is aware of Strandwold's books but never mentions the previous inscription. This disdain was mutual.

Elliot originally sent a partial transcription of the marks with his letter to Landsverk. Landsverk convinced Elliot to send the actual stones. Landsverk transcribed the marks and forwarded the copy to Mongé. Mongé recognized cryptographic runic markings but had difficulty deciphering the puzzle. Elliot, growing impatient, asked for the stones back when months passed without a translation. In his 1974 book[8] on runes, Landsverk admits that he missed several "short and inconspicuous cuts which later turned out to be cryptographically significant."[9] These other lines were found on subsequent photographs and pointed out to Mongé, allowing him to finalize his decipherment.[10]

Landsverk and Mongé claimed that the Spirit Pond stones were part of a series of runic puzzles left behind by their creator, Erik Gnupsson, known as Henricus, who was made Bishop of Greenland in 1112. Henricus was believed to have made several trips to Vinland. Apparently, Henricus went further inland than legend suggested since some of the other runic puzzle evidence includes the Kensington Rune Stone in Minnesota and several runic inscriptions in Oklahoma.

The obverse of the first stone is a map with a modern rendering of the area and the word "HOOP," which Landsverk and Mongé equate with Thorfinn Karlsefni's settlement at Hóp. Also on the obverse of the stone are sailing directions that say to sail in the direction of an arrow for 2 days, which Landsverk suggests would bring you to Vinland on Cape Cod. Also on the face of the map is a cryptogram that gives the date October 6, 1123, a recurring date.

The reverse of the stone contains pictographs depicting flora and fauna found in Vinland: grapes, wheat, a fish, a deer, a bird, a serpent, and local native symbols: a native's head, a canoe, a bow and arrow, and an animal hide. Also on the reverse is a combination of eight runes that even Cyrus Gordon,[11] the most ardent supporter

Spirit Pond "Map Stone," obverse and reverse. Photograph is computer-enhanced for visibility (Malcolm Pearson photograph).

of Mongé's work, admits is nonsense but assumes that any untranslatable combination of runes must be an unsolved cipher for the name Henricus.[12] Gordon also suggests that the pictograms, a total of eight, may also be a second cryptogram for Henricus.[13]

The second stone contains two lines of runes, which Mongé claims are an anagram for the word "sailed," the date, October 6, 1123, and another unsolved cipher for the name Henricus.

The third stone is the longest of the texts, with 374 runes crowded onto both sides of the stone. It was carved in a style sufficiently different from the previous two that it is assumed it was created by a second runemaster. Mongé and Landsverk believe that this stone was intentionally untranslatable. The text was strictly a vehicle to convey the extensive cryptography associated with the stone.[14]

By the time Landsverk returned the stones to Elliot, Maine had realized that the stones had been found on state property. Unbeknownst to Elliot, the area along the Morse River where he had uncovered the stones was part of the newly opened Popham Beach State Park. Since the artifacts had been found on state-owned land, they legally belonged to the state of Maine, regardless of who carved them.

Elliot later said he had always intended to donate the rocks to the museum at Bath, but when he received a letter from the Maine Park and Recreation Commission threatening legal action, Elliot's frustration boiled over. He sent the commission a telegram advising them that he had driven back to Maine and reburied the stones where he found them and to "let some other damn fool dig them up." Several attempts to relocate the stones netted a few native artifacts but no rune stones.

By late October 1971, the national newswires had picked up the story of the ancient stones and their subsequent reburial. Maine had no choice but to follow through. In December, Maine filed a civil complaint in Sagadahoc County Superior Court for the return of the Spirit Pond Stones. The papers were never served to Walter Elliot; he simply went to Florida with no forwarding address.

Meanwhile, Harold Brown, knowing Elliot would never relinquish the stones now, had been quietly working on their return through other means. Brown and a local banker, William T. Webster, managed to find a private donor to lend money to buy the stones from Elliot. The benefactors were Mr. and Mrs. Lawrence M.C. Smith of Philadelphia, the couple who had donated the majority of the land that had become Popham Beach State Park.

In late January 1972, Walter Elliot quietly returned to Maine, dug up the rocks, carried them back to Brown, and walked away with a check for $4500. With the stones safely in its possession, the state of Maine went looking for an expert to interpret the find.

They found Einar Haugen, professor of Scandinavian and Linguistics at Harvard University and the country's leading scholar of Norwegian and Scandinavian culture. Prior to his arrival at Harvard in 1964, Haugen had chaired the Department of Scandinavian Studies at the University of Wisconsin. Unlike the Wisconsin department's founder Rasmus B. Anderson, Haugen discounted all the Norse artifacts and carvings in New England.[15]

Haugen had no use for the Spirit Pond Stones. In an article in the anthropology journal *Man in the Northeast*,[16] Haugen declared the stones unquestionably frauds, based on four points in his studies. First, the runes were inconsistent with those used in the 11th century. Second, the spelling and numerals were inconsistent with runic usage. Third, the grammar was not Old Norse. Finally, Haugen felt that the peculiarities in the runes were similar to the problems with the runic inscription on the Kensington Rune. Mongé and Landsverk also noted the similarity between the rune usage on the third Spirit Pond inscription and the Kensington Rune Stone, offering it as proof of the authenticity of the stone.[17]

Haugen concluded that the stones had been created by someone with minimal knowledge of runes, using a book by Hjalmar Holand on the Kensington Stone[18] as a guide to carve them. Therefore, the earliest that the Spirit Pond Stones could have been carved was 1932.[19] Hagen's identification of a specific title by Holand may have been overly optimistic. Holand had included a chart of the Kensington runes, including his transliteration, in his book as early as a 1919 booklet.[20]

Haugen also questions the qualifications of both Landsverk and Mongé, referring to them as amateurs. He cites Norwegian runologist Aslak Liestøl, who, in a review of Landsverk and Mongé's 1967 book, had pointed out that Landsverk's formal training was in physics and mathematics, not linguistics, and went on the record as declaring there was no such thing as a runic cryptogram.[21]

Landsverk was not amused by Haugen's dismissal of the stones and his credentials and fired off a reply to Haugen that was printed in a subsequent issue of *Man in the Northeast*.[22] In a lengthy, rambling rebuttal, Landsverk reiterates his position that Haugen and Liestøl are not qualified to translate ancient runic cryptograms—Haugen because he is an expert in modern linguistics, and Liestøl because he had consistently ignored ciphers in Norwegian inscriptions he had documented. Landsverk then proceeds to decipher a cryptogram from Norway that Liestøl had obviously missed.

Landsverk then summed up Mongé's work on the runic cipher on the Spirit Pond stones, using an unknown rune that "Henricus apparently created deliberately" to be part of the puzzle and the machinations behind the combination of numbers that arrive with the date October 6, 1123. Landsverk then defends his and Mongé's credentials. He claims that Mongé's work on World War II code-breaking, as well as Landsverk's work as a public school administrator, his Ph.D. in physics, and his work as a metallurgical physicist, made them more qualified to decode runic puzzles than Haugen, who was obviously too busy with outside projects[23] to grasp even the fundamental concepts of their work.

Haugen was asked to comment on Landsverk's rebuttal. In a brief, five-paragraph reply, he chose to ignore most of Landsverk's text since Landsverk and Mongé were claiming to be the sole authorities in a non-existent field of study.

He reiterated that Landsverk's claims about the Old Norse language and runes are marked by "gross errors in knowledge and understanding."[24] Haugen points out that all competent reviewers dismissed their claims, citing reviews by leading rune scholars such as Hans Karlgren,[25] a Swedish mathematician and linguist who devoted five pages in his review of *Norse Medieval Cryptology* to discrediting its linguistic, etymologic, statistical, and historical data.

Erik Wahlgren later affirmed Haugen's dismissal of the Spirit Pond runes, primarily as a more recent derivative of the modern Kensington Runestone.[26] He further suggested that the hoax was a deliberate satire of the Vinland voyages, the Vinland Map, the Kensington Rune Stone, and runic cryptograms.[27] Wahlgren also points out a "staggering [...] disproportion between demographic factors and the runological production,"[28] noting that several thousand Norse Icelanders lived on Greenland for several centuries, but only 40 runic inscriptions exist there; Iceland has 53 inscriptions all dated after 1200. Yet Landsverk and Mongé have a handful of Norse explorers creating a dozen or more inscriptions older than the Icelandic runes, interpreting them based on "numerous historical and cultural assumptions for which one can find no support, either in early sources or in modern scholarly commentary."[29]

Wahlgren also makes a passing note of a booklet produced by the New England Antiquities Research Association.[30] It was composed of a reprint of a Calvin Trillin *New Yorker* column on the discovery of the stones,[31] archaeologist James Whittall's overview of the area, and a preliminary translation by Donal Buchanan. Wahlgren's opinion was not favorable. Buchanan's work, notes Wahlgren, was "not based on a knowledge of the Scandinavian languages."[32]

Wahlgren offers an alternative translation of the third stone that includes a report of Skraelings releasing a sea serpent against a ship, sailing directions to Canada, and a signature by "Norse Folk's Jak,"[33] all of which led Wahlgren to believe that the stones were carved in the recent past. Wahlgren thought whoever he was, Norse Folk's Jak had a passing knowledge of Scandinavian languages and knew runic form but pretended to know less than he actually did. Wahlgren also notes the similarity between the Spirit Pond inscriptions and Hjalmar Holand's work on the Kensington Rune Stone, noting Holand's 1940 book includes a chart of the Kensington artifact's variant alphabet.[34]

The discovery of a fourth rune stone in 1974[35] could not reinvigorate the fading interest in the Spirit Pond Stones. The fourth stone, a diorite oval with a well-worn hole drilled through one end, has a carving of a cross on one side and the runes for "Vinland 1010" and the letter "J" on the reverse. Wahlgren remained unimpressed.[36] He found that the stones used modern dating and mathematics and anachronistic terms,[37] and anyone who considered the stones legitimate to be "rather far removed from real life."[38]

Paul Chapman had just completed a study of the sagas from a navigator's perspective[39] when he was shown a copy of the map stone by Donal Buchanan. Chapman

Spirit Pond "Inscription Stone." The inscription continues for an additional six lines on the reverse, including multiple "hooked X" runes (courtesy NEARA Archives).

was shocked to discover that the map stone, which most researchers considered a map of the area around Spirit Pond, was actually a map of the northern promontory of Newfoundland, the same location that Chapman had just recently identified as Leif Eriksson's Vinland. Chapman began his own study of the stones, concluding that they were authentic Norse artifacts.[40] He concluded that the map stone was indeed a record of Thorfinn Karlsefni's explorations. Although Karlsefni was first associated with the map stone by Landsverk and Mongé, Chapman's version had no hidden messages or puzzles. He identified it as a map on one side with runes that noted it was a 12-day trip to Iceland. The reverse was a pictographic list of the resources, a brief runic note on the arable land, and a small Ogham script, which was translated into Old Norse as "KI"—the abbreviation of Kalsefni, which Chapman felt validated the Karlsefni association because Karlsefni's family had moved from Ireland to Iceland.[41]

Chapman started translating the 364 runes on the largest of the stones. He found that the runes were in the Danish short futhork alphabet, but the language was a combination of Old Icelandic and Danish. The use of Danish and the absence of Norwegian suggested to Chapman that the runemaster was a Dane, which again pointed to Thorfinn Karlsefni. His final conclusion was that it was a memorial stone addressed to Odin, memorializing 17 men who drowned when their worm-infested ship sank. This paralleled a similar account in the sagas.

This version was similar to one proposed by architect and amateur runologist Suzanne Carlson. Her translation is also a memorial to 17 drowned Norsemen, but her more literary interpretation tells of a sudden storm and Vikings trying to save their ship from "the foamy arms of Aegir, angry god of the sea."[42]

Despite a number of articles in the early 1990s on the stones,[43] interest did not regain momentum. Currently, aside from an occasional exhibit,[44] the stones remained out of sight in the custody of the Maine State Museum. Then in 2006, Richard Nielsen and Scott Wolter published a book on the Kensington Rune Stone.[45]

Wolter was hired by the Minnesota Historical Society in 2000 to conduct an analysis of the Kensington Rune Stone and determine the age of the carvings. To Wolter, it was obvious the stone had been carved at least two centuries before it was uncovered in 1898. Nielsen, a petrochemical engineer, had been actively researching the Kensington runes since 1985. Although self-taught, he was considered a meticulous researcher. Nielsen was unwavering in his belief that various North American rune stones were authentic and proof of Norse pre-Columbian exploration. The Kensington inscription, based on Nielsen's comparisons to rune sets used across Europe at the date stated on the rune stone, is written in Old Swedish in a dialect used by Cistercian monks, particularly in East Gotland.

His work on the runes and Wolter's weathering seem to dovetail, so a book was planned. That book was *The Kensington Rune Stone: Compelling New Evidence.* The 573-page book only includes 249 pages of research and supporting evidence. Another 138 pages are Scott Wolter's rambling thoughts on his personal experiences with the Kensington artifact. The rest is a mishmash of timelines and biographic sketches of previous researchers, none of which is "new" evidence, let alone "compelling." Nielsen's work, arguably the more important part of the book, is relegated to a discussion of fewer than 50 pages and an appendix of his comparisons with European runes and Nielsen's rune by rune interpretation.[46]

The book, self-published by Wolter, is a precursor of the direction Wolter's future research would take. The "Knights Templar secret conspiracy" fad was gaining popularity, and Wolter went along for the ride, introducing the Templars and hidden codes to his interpretation.[47] Wolter also maintained that the "hooked X" rune used as an "A" on the Kensington Rune Stone connected it to the three "medieval" Spirit Pond inscriptions and the Narragansett Inscription.[48] Nielsen had been publishing on the Spirit Pond hooked X over a decade and felt it was valuable, but only in identifying the rune carvers at Spirit Pond and Kensington as an early fifteenth-century Swede using the distinctive Gotland dialect.[49]

Wolter's next book, *The Hooked X*,[50] repeats much of his first Spirit Pond visit from the previous book. He attempts to build a case for the symbol as evidence of secret missions to the New World by a select group of medieval monastic and military orders associated with the Templars. He also gives a few details of interest. The Spirit Pond stones are soft and easily carved, compared to the Kensington Rune Stone. As such, Wolter cannot perform comparative dating by examining the weathering. He admits that identification of the stones must be made through the language and runes.[51] Considering the visit took place in the months before *The Kensington*

Rune Stone: Compelling New Evidence was released, all the work on the Spirit Ponds stones is from Nielsen's earlier work on the runes.

Nielsen was apparently unamused by being used as proof of medieval transatlantic secret societies in the later book. He published a cautionary article stating that either or both the Spirit Pond and Narragansett runes could have obtained their hooked X from a prankster using modern-day books on the Kensington Rune Stone.[52] The author of the Spirit Pond runic texts, Nielsen continued, would have known Swedish and had at least an Icelandic-English Dictionary. The mystery carver did not know Old Icelandic well. The fact that two different Swedish rune-rows were mixed with an Icelandic language was enough for Nielsen to doubt the medieval origin of the Spirit Pond Rune Stone.

By Wolter's third book, Nielsen was only referenced passingly as a past co-author. Wolter has accumulated additional examples of his hooked X, dating back to an AD 600 Anglo-Saxon medallion. This date, obviously predating Gottlanders, Cistercians, and Knights Templar, is evidence because Wolter's theory has changed. The hooked X is now a symbol of "Venus Families," an ancient order of secret Goddess worshipers dating back four millennia to the 18th Dynasty Pharaoh Akhenaten. The Spirit Pond stones had become "proof" of a Templar base.[53]

Most historians believe the Knight Templar theory is unadulterated fiction. Combined with the runic scholars who similarly believe the Spirit Pond Rune Stones are a hoax, Wolter may have been better off staying with his geology roots. His *Akhenaten* book is so far outside the norms, even by pseudoscience standards, that the book includes a legal disclaimer that it is not associated with the A&E Television Networks, which also happened to be home to a television program he was currently hosting.

CHAPTER TEN

Thorvald's Grave

Thorvald's Stone, Hampton, New Hampshire

Thorvald's Stone is a glacial erratic boulder with a series of incised lines; the markings are said to be three Christian crosses and Norse runes. Vandals and artifact-seekers have chipped off pieces of the stone as mementos; to protect the rock, the local historical society moved it to the grounds of Tuck Museum. It now rests on the museum grounds, enclosed in a mortared cobblestone well with iron bars across the mouth to prevent further damage.

According to *Eiríks Saga Rauda* (*The Saga of Erik the Red*), Thorvald Eriksson found a shallow cape that he called "Keelness." On a headland to the east of Keelness, Thorvald stopped at a wooded promontory. It also says that he was so taken with the beauty of the area that he said he wanted to colonize it. Unfortunately, Thorvald was shot through the heart by an arrow during a massive retaliatory strike by the Skraelings (a word used in Old Norse sagas to describe natives that the explorers encountered). Before he died, he asked to be buried at the spot where he wished to build his home. He also requested that his grave be marked with a cross. The promontory being unsuited for a burial, Thorvald was buried in a nearby glen. Making the huge assumption that Keelness is indeed Hampton, the saga places Thorvald's gravesite roughly on the glacial promontory known as Great Boar's Head, where the stone was originally found.

The stone didn't gain notoriety as a Norse artifact until a local judge, Charles Lamprey, mentioned the stone in a 1902 newspaper article,[1] the culmination of a series of events orchestrated by Lamprey.

Lamprey was an attendee at an April 1888 meeting of the New Hampshire Historical Society where the guest speaker was author Edmund Slafter, who spoke on "The Discovery of America by the Northmen," based on his book. The talk was popular and reprinted in the *Proceedings of the New Hampshire Historical Society*.[2] Slafter offered a cautionary tale that the sagas are too vague to pinpoint locations, not that such sage advice stopped anyone from trying. Reprinting the talk, if anything, spread awareness of such sites as Hampton. By 1889, it was on the "Ober Broadside," line drawings and inscriptions of Norse inscriptions compiled by Andrew K. Ober, a reporter for the *Beverly* [MA] *Citizen*[3] who had gone looking for the Vikings on his own. The broadside was widely disseminated and became a standard reference as the earliest renderings of runic objects, referenced by figures like Goodwin and Delabarre.

In 1890, the Annual Field Day of the New Hampshire Historical Society was held in Hampton, hosted by Charles Lamprey. President Samuel C. Eastman delivered an address on the Northmen in America. Lamprey began discussions with Howard Abel of Boston, who was convinced Thorvald's grave was legitimate. Abel was also on the Board of Directors of several trolley companies north of Boston.

The Lamprey family had originally owned the land that included the stone as part of the original land grants dating to 1672, giving Judge Lamprey's claims some gravitas. Lamprey believed the stone lay unnoticed until about 1875. This date may be an early sign something is amiss; there is no mention of the rock in Dow's 1893 *History of the Town of Hampton*.[4]

Soon after the Lamprey article ran in the local newspapers, the property with the rock was sold to Wallace D. Lovell for $1. Lovell ran the Exeter, Hampton & Amesbury Street Railway, which was, to put it delicately, not a financial success. He envisioned a "Norse Park," replete with a monument and Thorvald's gravestone as the centerpiece to attract passengers for the trolley. Electric companies charged a flat monthly usage fee to the streetcar operators, regardless of actual passengers. The trolley was used to commute to work, so ridership dropped on the weekends. Streetcar operators across the region devised a plan to defray the cost of electricity on weekends when ridership was low. They would provide the workers a place to go on their days off and make the trolley the easiest way to get there. Thus was born the "pleasure resorts."[5] The pleasure resorts or trolley parks were created by the streetcar companies and constructed near the end of streetcar lines.[6] Hampton's would be built around the Norse Grave.

The trolley was in receivership within five years, and the grand plans fell through. There had been two significant flaws in the plan. First and foremost, the financial viability of the trolley line had never been good. Second, the interest in Norse visitations had moved beyond novelty and into the mainstream. A rock on the New Hampshire coast could not compete with Viking longboats at the World's Fair or aerodynamic Norse profiles on the radiator caps on Chryslers and Pontiacs.

Lamprey's original article was reprinted in the *Boston Journal* (undoubtedly nudged by Howard Abel) and picked up by the *Philadelphia Times*.[7] William Babcock mentioned the carving in his 1913 book for the Smithsonian,[8] it was already forgotten. Babcock cited the *Philadelphia Times* article in his book, considering Hampton a more likely runic site than some of the better-known sites of the time, such as Newport Tower and Dighton Rock.

In 1934, Olaf Strandwold released his first booklet, *The Yarmouth Stone, Mystic Characters on Yarmouth Stone Yield Startling Evidence of Norse Discoveries*.[9] The booklet was released in October, two months after William B. Goodwin had been to examine the stone while vacationing in Nova Scotia. As always, he was still searching for Norse settlements. It did not take long for word of the book to reach Goodwin in Connecticut. Goodwin began corresponding with Strandwold and planned to visit on his 1935 visit to Seattle.

The booklet received mixed reviews, but there was sufficient positive feedback that he decided to expand his research to the entire Eastern Seaboard.[10] Strandwold, the superintendent of schools in Prosser, Washington, had a significant obstacle. The runes he was interested in were on the East Coast, and he was in the Pacific Northwest. Goodwin was amassing a list of stone sites. A collaboration came to be.

Strandwold was already corresponding with Malcolm Pearson after Pearson had contacted him, trying to discover who had built the stone chamber on his father's Upton, Massachusetts, property. Pearson began tracking down and photographing sites for Strandwold, one of which was the Hampton stone, which Strandwold had seen mentioned in Babcock's book. Babcock's book was not particularly helpful if one was searching for the actual location.

> A certain field on the narrow marsh and beach on the main road up town [Hampton] contains the rock on which are cut the three crosses designating the grave where was buried Thorvald Ericsson 1004. The rock is a large granite stone lying in the earth, its face near the top of the ground with the crosses cut thereon and other marks cut by the hand of man with a stone chisel and not by any owner. That field came into possession of the author's ancestors 250 years ago.[11]

In 1936, Pearson and Harry Cheney rediscovered the stone for Strandwold by doing the one thing that would plague Strandwold's research. The two physically traveled to Hampstead. After hours of searching and interviews, they were directed to Fred R. Batchelder. Batchelder knew the location well. His family had lived on Great Boar's Head since colonial times. They were led down State Road 101E (Winnacunnet Road) to a neighborhood called alternately called "Surfside Park" and "Norseman's Rest." They took Viking Street to Thorvald Street. They arrived at an abandoned lot where the rock had begun to sink into the sandy soil and was all but obscured by trash and debris. The toponyms and the rock were the vestiges of the original trolley park plans.

The visit reinvigorated local interest. The dumping stopped, and the town began investigating how to seize the abandoned property through eminent domain. The owner stepped up, the lot was cleaned up, and directional signage was added for the town's 1938 tercentenary. William Cram, a local newspaper columnist that had published several stories on the rock, wrote up an article for the anniversary booklet.[12] The article barely discusses the stone, spending more time on the original saga. An earlier article in his "Little Stories of Old New England" column in the *Hampton Union & Rockingham County Gazette* is more Thorvald-centric and included an interview with Pearson.[13]

As the tercentenary festivities were starting, Olaf Strandwold finished his translation of Thorvald's Gravestone. The *Newburyport Daily News* debuted the work in a front-page story.[14] While Strandwold confirmed it was a Norse grave marker, it was not

Thorvald's grave, ca. 1938 (Malcolm Pearson photograph).

Leif Ericsson's brother Thorvald. Instead, it was a man named Bui, a common Norse name. Strandwold translated the runic markings as *"Bui reis stein"* or "Bui raised stone." Based on what Strandwold chalked in, he had disregarded the description of the crosses and integrated them into his runes. Hampton Historical Society had made Thorvald a feature of the events and was justifiably unamused by Strandwold's timing.

The historical society was not the only one underwhelmed by Strandwold. Goodwin, illustrating the growing rift with Strandwold, was reconsidering whether the Hampton stone was Norse. Hampton had always been a bit of an issue for him. Goodwin had identified nearby Portsmouth Harbor as Vinland and, in his 1941 book, had identified Hampton Beach as Leif's landfall. So Strandwold's identification of the Hampton rock as Bui's grave, not Thorvald's, actually was helpful. But now, Strandwold was becoming a liability with his translations, particularly in Byfield, where Goodwin and Pearson had warned him the stones he was translating were plow strikes.

Goodwin began distancing himself by noting that Ober's articles in 1899 include a reference not found on the broadside, a small silver cross found in 1742 near the beach about 200 yards from "the so-called runic stone."[15] The cross was melted down and made into spoons. He also notes metal fragments found nearby.

Goodwin's opinion was that the silver cross was evidence of a French Jesuit mission at the time of the French and Indian Wars but didn't follow through by connecting the proximity to the three crosses on Hampton's rune stone.[16] Because of the haste in which *Ruins* was put together, there is no way to tell what Goodwin's final thoughts on Hampton were. Ostensibly earlier notes appear later in the book, eliminating any sort of chronology in his thinking. But, at various points, the text also suggests, at least initially, that he had thought it was Norse.

As Hampton debated the legitimacy of the stone and whether they should acquire it and move it to city lands, interest waned. In 1941, the lot was sold to Joseph Mantegani, who built a summer cottage on the lot, leaving the stone intact. Within a decade, that would change. When *Hampton Union* columnist James Tucker visited the stone in 1951, the rock had been moved off to a sloped side of the lot, all but buried in tall grass. A septic system had been installed where it originally stood.[17]

Tucker wasn't surprised and faulted the town for not protecting the stone. Tucker also interviewed Frank Glynn when he came to town in 1959 to examine the stone. Glynn was well read on the stone's history and was not impressed.[18]

Glynn pointed out to Tucker that the rock is very soft, almost to the point of being friable. He was able to scratch it with his fingernail. As a result, there were no traces of individual chisel or punch marks. After an admittedly brief inspection, he felt that the local farmers who thought these were plow strikes were probably correct. Unaware of the rock's recent relocation, Glynn suggested someone might have been buried at the foot of this rock. He also thought that the silver cross and metal found in the area should be tracked down for metallurgical dating.

The rock was moved again in 1967. Mantegani was building a cottage for his son on the other half of the lot, and it was in the way of equipment excavating the new cellar, so it was pulled to the side by a bulldozer. The plan was to put it back (presumably at the second location), but it was moved yet again when it was discovered it would block the bulkhead entrance into the new cellar. Local newspapers found it amusing that an Italian was moving a Norse stone, equating it to the Columbus versus Leif as America's discoverer debate. The newspaper also points out the rock continued to attract visitors and the occasional school field trip.[19]

The school trips were probably led by Harold Fernald, a history teacher at Winnacunnet High School, who also taught an anthropology class. In November 1973, his class conducted an excavation at the rock.[20] Nothing was found, but since the stone had been moved several times, there's no way to ascertain if the test pits were in the correct location (based on accompanying photographs, they were not). The article also notes that the Mantegani family was selling the cottage.

Virginia Fraser, a neighbor with a summer cottage on Thorvald Avenue, was concerned. She steadfastly believed Thorvald was buried under the stone and started the Historical Preservation Society to lobby Hampton to acquire and protect the stone. She and Fernald were both concerned about the continued damage from souvenirs being chipped off the rock. The rock was developing even more of a local legend, including a neighbor who insisted a helmeted and bearded ghost walked the neighborhood on foggy nights.

Fraser's real concern was the fate of the rock once the land was sold. Because it was located on private property, the rock's fate was at the whim of new owners who might not be sympathetic to random strangers wandering across their lawn or could deny access for continuing research.

It took until 1989 for the Hampton Historical Society to acquire rock. The increased interest in the supernatural and pre-Columbian explorers on Thorwald Ave had increased the stream of curiosity-seekers to the point where Thorvald's Grave was at serious risk of burial or destruction.

Today, Thorvald's Stone remains safely ensconced in its enclosure on the campus of the Tuck Museum, surrounded by other field stones dedicated to local figures, such as the original settlers of the town and Eunice Cole, a local victim of the colonial witchcraft hysteria that swept the region. Thorvald's Stone remains a local landmark, rarely visited, and occasionally used as a novelty piece in local newspapers around Columbus Day. Considering the translation is still listed as "Bui raised this Stone," Thorvald's Stone's most extraordinary claim may be as Olaf Strandwold's sole surviving claim at a legacy.

The Healey Stone, Hampton Falls, New Hampshire

One member of Hampton's tercentenary committee was Frances Healey, the undisputed doyenne of local history with a family tree that predated the creation of Hampton in 1638.

The day after the *Newburyport Daily News* article where Strandwold translated the "Norse Grave" as belonging to some Norseman named Bui, not Thorvald, Miss Healey wrote to Strandwold. She had found a carved stone a few years earlier while searching for stepping stones. Her family had owned the Nathaniel Hubbard Dodge House on Kensington Road in Hampton Falls since the 1780s, and this stone was unique. Could Strandwold offer some thoughts?

Thorvald's grave, now on the campus of Hampton's Tuck Museum (photograph by the author).

Strandwold notified William B. Goodwin. Goodwin was also intrigued. This stone was only six miles from Thorvald's gravestone. He sent Malcolm Pearson to examine and photograph the "Healey Stone." It was about 11 inches by 5 inches and weighed 33 pounds. The surface had five runes deeper than superficial scratches with an even deeper furrow above the runes. Strandwold translated the runes as "owns me," which he alleged was a standard inscription on Norse runic gravestones. It was usually preceded by the name of the deceased, which was missing on the Healey Stone. Healey then showed Pearson a second stone, circular, with a hole in it. Goodwin was more intrigued by the circular stone, which he thought could be a Norse anchor. By autumn, Goodwin had offered to purchase both artifacts for a small museum he was planning at his North Salem property.[21] The museum never came to fruition.

Although Goodwin and Pearson were not convinced Strandwold had read the first rune correctly, Healey was thrilled. Her "Norseman's Rock" would remain in a place of honor near one of the fireplaces. Locally, the Healey Stone became a fixture, but it gained no interest outside of Hampton. Strandwold published his translation in his 1939 booklet.[22] "Goodwin had so little faith in the interpretation that he simply took the pages from Strandwold and slapped them in the back of his 1941 book without comment."[23] (Goodwin paid for Strandwold's book and felt he owned it.) Other than an occasional passing reference in local newspapers, there was no serious interest in the stone. Then in 1952, Willard du Lue, a *Boston Globe* columnist, featured the stone in a series of columns on "New Hampshire Ramblings." When asked about a Norse relic so far from the coast, Miss Healey noted that before all the dams had been built for the mills by her ancestors, the Falls River was an unobstructed route to the ocean two miles away. High tide in the salt marshes was navigable by shallow-draft boats, which would be carried travelers within walking distance

Malcolm Pearson's original photograph of the Healey Stone for Goodwin and Strandwold (courtesy NEARA Archives).

of where the house was now. If someone died on a vessel in the river, he would be buried on the nearest high ground, the area near the house. None of these details came from Strandwold or Goodwin, so Healey had been doing some research on her own. Unfortunately, the *Globe* series was considered light entertainment, and the elderly spinster came across in the piece as quaint.[24]

In 1975, Early Sites Research Society member Gertrude Johnson was investigating lost and forgotten stones in Goodwin's books. Frances Healey had died in 1962, and the estate was divided among close friends, with most of her heirlooms given to the children of friends and the State Historical Society. The stone, however, remained with the house after its sale and was still available for Johnson to examine in 1975.[25]

James Whittall sent a copy of Johnson's 1975 report in *Early Sites Research Society Bulletin* on the Healey Stone to Barry Fell. Fell felt the brevity of the markings made any translation suspect.[26] It wasn't until 1977, when Fell was visiting Libya, that Fell realized the weight and shape were the clues needed to decipher the Healey Stone.

Fell explained that Arabic-speaking Libyans carved the stone circa the 4th century AD. The inscription translated to "certified to the Tunisian standard." This was an American example of a "kula," a standard of weight the measure of oils.[27] The weight of the kula varied regionally, but Fell noted the Tunisian kula weighed 15.155 kilograms or 33.41 lbs. The Healey Stone weighed 33 pounds. Although Fell's subsequent book *Saga America* discussed Libyan trade missions to North America,[28] Hampton Falls is omitted. Whether it is an oversight by Fell or he was having second thoughts about his interpretation, the Healey Stone is not mentioned.

The house has since changed hands and been remodeled often enough that the Healey Stone has gone missing in the 50 years since Gertrude Johnson last examined the stone.

CHAPTER ELEVEN

Byzantine Connecticut

The Gungywamp Complex, Groton, Connecticut

Anthropologist Frank Speck of the University of Pennsylvania was noted for his research and efforts to preserve the cultures of Native Americans. Among his projects, Speck recorded the folklore and ghost tales of the Pequot tribe.[1] Speck recounted folktales of encounters with mysterious lights and spectral animals.[2] Of particular note are encounters near a swamp on the road from New London, Connecticut[3]—the same area as the collection of stone ruins known as the Gungywamp Complex.

The Gungywamp, as a supernatural place,[4] first appears in print in *Holdfast Gaines*,[5] a historical novel set in the American Revolution. Written by Pulitzer Prize-winning author Odell Shepard[6] and his son Willard, the early part of the tale has Holdfast Gaines, a Mohegan Indian raised by English colonists, discussing the Gungywamp as a wild land, haunted by the ghosts of countless scores of Indians killed in King Philip's War. Willard Shepard, a charter member of the Gungywamp Society, confirmed that he and his father had based the descriptions on actual visits to the Gungywamp and its stone "caves" and that the Shepards believed the site features to be Indian in origin.[7]

The Gungywamp does not need fiction to supplement the mystery of the locale. Indian folklore of the Gungywamp region is well represented by mysterious lights and unusual apparitions.[8] One explanation for these lights relies heavily on the geology of the area. It also offers a possible theory as to why the location was selected. Michael A. Persinger of the Behavioral Neuroscience Laboratory at Laurentian University in Ontario, Canada, originally introduced his Tectonic Strain Theory (TST) as a terrestrial explanation of UFO sightings.[9] Although Persinger did not advance TST specifically for archaeological research, the basic concept remains applicable: Tectonic pressures along fault lines where quartz is prevalent in the local rock create conditions where piezoelectricity is generated. This is manifested by an electromagnetic discharge that produces "ghost lights" or "earthquake lights."[10]

Persinger coined the term "transient geophysical fields" for a sudden radical change in the local magnetic field caused by these tectonic electromagnetic discharges. The radical changes to the magnetic field create transient electrical displays in the brain's temporal lobe. These temporal lobe transients can impact hippocampal function, affecting memory reference—creating new memories that are remembered as if real, or the conviction that something meaningful and deeply personal has transpired.[11]

In other words, the observer has a vision,[12] sudden physical and emotional changes that, depending on the frame of reference and culture of the person, could be interpreted as a religious experience,[13] a UFO encounter, or a ghostly apparition. If it occurs once, it is a personal vision. If it happens on enough occasions to enough people, the site develops a reputation as haunted or sacred.

The Gungywamp Complex is located in the same area of southeastern Connecticut as the Pequot tales of specters, and it is positioned in a historically active seismic zone.[14] Research has discovered that negative magnetic anomalies register on a fluxgate magnetometer in the vicinity of several stone chambers and a site feature named the "Cliff of Tears." An electrostatic voltmeter also shows negative electrical charge peaks over the magnetic anomaly.[15]

The Cliff of Tears is part of the North Gungywamp Complex, as categorized by David Barron, founder and first president of the Gungywamp Society.[16] Combined with the Gungywamp Complex, Barron referred to several smaller sites that can be examined holistically or individually as "The Greater Gungywamp." In a heavily forested area of hills, 65-foot cliffs, and a swamp, the complex includes stone walls, inscriptions, stone structures, astronomical alignments, colonial ruins, an iron smelting kiln, and native evidence. The acreage encompassing the various features is secluded and privately owned, encouraging vandalism and complicating research and preservation attempts.[17]

With fluctuating perimeters, it is easy to include various sites as they are found.[18] Within the area under the Gungywamp banner are Native American sites with projectile points and pottery fragments dating to the Early to Middle Woodland Period (4000–1650 BP), a colonial homestead, a stone circular trough possibly used as a tan bark mill, and a slag iron production kiln site. There are also two large stone chambers and the ruins of several smaller ones that do not fit neatly into association with these other features.

Chamber One is located in the southwestern section of the Gungywamp Complex. The structure is built without mortar, in a method known as "drywall construction," and is partially underground. The roof is seven one-ton slabs of garnet-bearing rock. The entrance is built against an anchor stone that supports the lintel and is part of the wall for both the main chamber and a smaller, secondary room off the main structure. The smaller room is attached to the larger structure but uses a different construction technique; the larger chamber uses corbelled walling, while the smaller chamber uses beehive construction and was sealed when first discovered.[19] Excavations have uncovered nothing but contemporary trash.

In the fall of 1984, a team of volunteers led by master mason David Stewart-Smith was completing repairs to the vandalized entry to the chamber.[20] The crew was breaking camp when someone noticed a beam of light from the setting sun was entering the chamber through a narrow but long opening in the back of the chamber thought to be a vent. One of the volunteers had cleaned accumulated soil and debris from the vent as part of the restoration work.[21] As the volunteers watched, the beam gradually moved across the chamber, finally shining across the chamber's interior and into the smaller chamber.[22] Perceiving the beam of light as an attempt to mark the equinox, Barron concentrated the Gungywamp Society volunteers in research around the chamber's exterior.

They found that a stone wall running on a diagonal behind the chamber appeared to have a "break" in it, which was hypothesized as a deliberate attempt to avoid interfering with the angle of the sun. East of the chamber's entrance, they found a fallen standing stone, suspected to be a solar alignment associated with the entrance to the structure.

James Whittall examined the 9-inch stone and found that the base slab had been chiseled out to adjust the beam's path after the construction of the tube. To Whittall, this suggested a modification made specifically with the sunbeam and a target in mind, i.e., someone cognizant of the design for ceremonial usage.[23] Although the significance of having a beam of light strike the smaller chamber on the equinox is unknown, Whittall notes that this feature is "strange" to find in a colonial root cellar as some researchers identify the structure.[24] Whittall had previously hypothesized that the smaller chamber was a burial chamber[25]; the discovery of the equinox-oriented light could support his theory.

Nearby is a second intact chamber, also built using drywall masonry and dug into the hillside. It was first discovered in the 1950s when a hurricane toppled a nearby tree. The upheaval of the tree's root system and storm erosion exposed the entrance. The chamber was sealed when first found, and local legend has it that when the stone blocking the entrance was removed, a badly tarnished small metal pot was found inside. The story continues that the pot was brought to a local college for identification. When the man returned to claim it several weeks later, no record of it was found.[26]

Excavations have uncovered nothing but contemporary trash in these stone constructions and the smaller chamber ruins nearby. Connecticut state archaeologist Nicholas Bellantoni suggested that these smaller ruins could be the remains of livestock birthing shelters.[27] Placement of the ruins in relationship to the stone walls[28] makes the suggestion reasonable, particularly in light of the proximity to the foundations of the Adams homestead, a known colonial site.[29]

An alternative to construction by Nathaniel Adams was introduced in 1976 by Alfred M. Bingham.[30] Bingham, a lawyer, legislator, and historian,[31] proposed that the chambers were built by freed and escaped slaves, based on comparative studies of stone ruins from a colonial slave settlement on the border between Lyme and Salem, Connecticut. Bingham also notes that the Salem ruins are off Gungy Road, which suggests that both sets of stone ruins are related because of the location names, both

David Barron of the Gungywamp Society examines Chi Rho inscriptions on site (courtesy of David Barron).

derived from the Mohegan word *gungy*, the word for large rock.[32] Although Bingham's squatters could explain certain aspects of the site, such as the smaller chambers, it does not address the question of the equinoctial sunset light alignment.

The Gungywamp Complex also contains inscriptions, which, not surprisingly, are controversial.[33] Unlike other sites with symbols inscriptions that claim to be messages in ancient languages, Gungywamp has early Christian symbols known as Chi Rhos carved on a rock outcropping in the northeastern part of the complex.

Christianity has used monograms and initials as symbols since its early beginnings. Many examples are found in ancient catacombs and cemeteries, and their purpose was identification with secrecy amidst persecution. Chief among these monograms is the Chi Rho, composed of the first two Greek letters of the word "Christ" ("XPICTOC") superimposed on each other.

In 1979, David Barron and property owner Carl Vogt found the first inscription. While out examining a stone outcropping, Barron and Vogt found the letters "IC" carved on the face of the stone, followed by three hash marks. Barron sent a latex peeling of the carvings to epigrapher Barry Fell, who immediately flew to Connecticut from San Diego. Fell identified it as a Christogram and predicted that there would be Chi Rho symbols found on the site as well.[34]

Three years later, while excavating a collapsed chamber adjacent to the ledge, the first Chi Rho was discovered on the ledge, all but obscured beneath layers of lichen and moss.[35] At least seven Chi Rho symbols have been found to date. An excavation in the collapsed chamber recovered charcoal that was carbon dated to ca. AD 1740; a second excavation at the chamber's mouth was dated to ca. AD 1100,[36] and a third to AD 560.

Barry Fell determined the style of these Chi Rho symbols found in the Gungywamp was consistent with those of the fourth to seventh centuries found throughout Christendom. Despite this intriguing avenue of research, after David Barron's death in July 2000, the Gungywamp Society unilaterally reversed its original stance on the authenticity of the Chi Rho inscriptions, labeled them probable modern-day graffiti or survey markings,[37] and removed the Christogram logo from the organization's website and publications. In effect, 20 years of David Barron's work on the site quietly went away.[38]

The combination of sixth- to twelfth-century C-14 dates and the Chi Rhos could indicate that Irish Catholics were practicing their faith in the stone structures of the Gungywamp complex, as William Goodwin had proposed at his site in New Hampshire.

Suppose William Goodwin had been correct in his theory that the America's Stonehenge site was actually the stone vestiges of the center of an early Irish Catholic monastic network of an order known as *Ceilie De* or the Culdees. Goodwin felt that these ascetic monks had gone into voluntary exile rather than be absorbed into the Roman Catholic Church. Goodwin also postulated his monks used Indian trails to spread out and set up a vast project to convert the Algonquins to Christianity, dwelling near the pagan Native Americans but always far enough inland to avoid the marauding Norse. The Christogram could suggest the Culdees made it to Groton and established an outpost in the Gungywamp.

Goodwin does not explicitly mention the Gungywamp site in his *Ruins of Great Ireland in New England*,[39] but the two sites share enough features to make Goodwin's theory worth reexamining.[40] Both sites have astronomical alignments. Both have stone chambers that are partially subterranean and utilize large glacial boulders in construction. Both show evidence of Indians nearby. Both sites have inscriptions, rambling stone walls, and numerous other similarities. Mystery Hill's external sighting props are replaced by the more sophisticated internal equinox alignment, a logical change in a later construction. Goodwin also pointed out that the Celtic Church utilized pagan rites to aid in the transition to Christianity, which Goodwin believed included the Oracle Chamber and Sacrificial Table in North Salem.[41] Goodwin also identified a site in Andover, Massachusetts, as a clochan.[42] It has been suggested that Irish beehive huts evolved into the clochán, which was the early form of stone churches known as oratories.[43]

James Mavor echoed this sentiment 40 years later, noting he had examined 11 randomly selected oratories and found alignments to the horizon at all locations.[44] Mavor pointed out that the mainland oratories had equinox sunrise alignments while oratories situated on islands utilized stellar alignments. Mavor suggested this indicated that the island monasteries were not as concerned with the calendric festivals of the Church. Combined with Icelandic references to the Culdees[45] that Mavor believes show a shamanistic influence in Culdee lore, Mavor believed that the Culdee monastic tradition was similar to a Druidic star cult and remained so as late as AD 1200.[46]

The Chi Rho as a symbol suggests other possibilities beyond early Irish Christians.[47] Although few examples of the Chi Rho exist before Constantine's conversion on the night before the Battle of Milvian Bridge,[48] the Chi Rho had to have been familiar to the militia to raise it overnight as Constantine's standard. By AD 324, Constantine had control of the Roman Empire and set about consolidating the religion of the empire by excommunication and expulsion. The Arians were perceived as a faction threatening Constantine's interpretation of the orthodoxy,[49] as were the Donatists of North Africa.[50] Barry Fell indicated that the "IC" Christogram was primarily associated with the Byzantines. The Byzantine Empire began in AD 330 when Constantine moved the capital of his empire from Rome to Byzantium (Constantinople) five years after declaring the Arians heretics. The Muslim subjugation of Byzantine North Africa marks the end of the Donatist stronghold. Fell's connection of Gungywamp to the Byzantines is not a singular claim. Telepneff also argues that the ancient Celtic Church had extensive ties with the Byzantine Church, as evidenced by the similarities in ascetic literature and monasticism.[51] Father Gregory Telepneff notes that numerous Eastern texts, including Coptic literature, were found in the Celtic monasteries. In addition, he notes similarities between Celtic artwork and Eastern illuminated manuscripts, stories of monks traveling from the Eastern Mediterranean to Ireland, and Irish ascetics traveling to Egypt, Byzantium, and the Middle East. He concludes that the Celtic Church developed its distinctive identity from contact with Coptic theologians. Telepneff also notes that themes of voluntary exile and pilgrimage are part of both the Celtic and Eastern Church practices. Voluntary exile from their homeland was a form of asceticism.[52] But Telepneff's concern is the Byzantine influences in the Celtic Church, not whether this exile could have included journeys to North America.

Researchers have noted features of New England sites and compared them to European structures to see if this question can be resolved by identifying comparative features. When archaeoastronomer and educator Vance Tiede first watched the vernal equinox alignment at the Gungywamp chamber in 1988,[53] he formulated an alternative method of comparison and reversed the process. In a 1998 magazine interview,[54] Tiede explained his reasoning. If the vernal equinox chamber in Gungywamp was built by Irish monks, early Irish chapels or oratories should exhibit similar solar alignments. Irish monastic use of sundials and astronomical data to regulate hours of prayer was already well established.[55]

Tiede went to Ireland, the Hebrides, the Orkneys, and the Shetland Islands. He found that a small eastern window in Irish oratories, previously thought to be a design feature, invariably "framed the rising solar disk on the Feast Days of selected saints of the Celtic Early Christian Church."[56] Tiede also found that the most frequent alignments were sunrise on the Feast Days of St. Patrick (March 17) and St. Aidan, the Bishop of Lindisfarne (August 31).[57]

Returning to Gungywamp with this new revelation, Tiede returned to studying Chamber One. Relying on criteria developed by Gerald Hawkins, the astronomer who discovered and popularized ancient astronomical alignments at Stonehenge,[58] Tiede began surveying the site for additional alignments.

After being inundated with requests for assistance for other archaeology sites, Hawkins published an article, first in 1968,[59] and then again in 1973,[60] to serve as a guideline for future astroarchaeologists. Hawkins' primary goal was to see that any attempt to determine astronomical significance needed to be approached consistently. Hawkins' criteria were:

1. Construction dates should not be determined from astronomical alignments.
2. Alignments should be restricted to man-made markers.
3. Alignments should be postulated only for a homogenous group of markers.
4. All related celestial positions should be included in the analysis.
5. All possible alignments at a site must be considered.

Tiede was surprised to discover more alignments associated with Celtic solar festival dates than expected.[61] Aside from the vernal equinox sunset entering the larger chamber and striking the small chamber, the structure itself was oriented to the winter solstice and the two winter cross-quarter days. On December 22, sunrise was aligned in a diagonal from the southeast corner of the chamber to the entrance of the smaller chamber. So, light enters the small side chamber on the two most holy seasons of the Christian year, Christmas and Easter (the first Sunday after the first full moon after the vernal equinox). On February 1 (Candlemas) and November 1 (All Saints' Day), the sun rose over the southeast corner of the chamber in a diagonal line with the northwest corner.[62] Tree foliage prevents determining alignments with the summer solstice and the May 1 and August 1 cross quarters. His final conclusion was that the Gungywamp Chamber One demonstrated solar orientations consistent with the rectangular drywall chapels in Early Irish Christian oratories.[63]

Celtic monasteries were built on sacred ground, including locations that were holy to pre–Christian traditions. To the Celtic mind, if the Pequots considered the area sacred, as suggested by the supernatural legends of the area, what better place to build a monastery?

The site's reputation as "different" continued into colonial times. In 1654, Springfield, Massachusetts, colonist John Pynchon wrote to his friend and mentor, John Winthrop, Jr., of New Haven, Connecticut: "Sir, I heare a report of a stone wall, and strong fort in it, made all of stone, which is newly discovered at or neere Pequet. I should be glad to know the truth of it fro your selfe, here being many strange reports about it."[64]

The younger John Winthrop was a logical person to ask about oddities in the region—aside from his political connections and popularity,[65] he was a scientist involved in astronomy, metallurgy,[66] medicine, and chemistry. His reply is lost, but Winthrop was undoubtedly familiar with the Gungywamp area as the owner of a stone quarry north of the site.[67] The editor of the published Pynchon papers annotates the Winthrop letters as a reference to Pequot Stone Fort, the stronghold of Mohegan chief Uncas. Gungywamp historian Alicia Larson disagrees,[68] noting that Pequot Stone Fort had been captured by the English by the time the query was written, making it far from "newly discovered."

In the northeast corner of Gungywamp are two rows of standing stones. One row is oriented toward true north, the other toward magnetic north. Each stone stands in its own socket, holes packed with small rock and gravel to hold the standing stone upright. One of these standing stones is a bird effigy, with wings spread apart and the head looking to the side. In this case, the bird is facing east.[69] Iron Thunderhorse of the Quinnipiac Tribal Council believes this carving is a thunderbird Manitou, as found in the Algonquin cosmology.[70] Thunderhorse notes that several Quinnipiac legends deal with the thunderbird being summoned to battle Hobbomock, the stone giant said to dwell beneath Mount Tom, who creates the seismic activity known as "Moodus noises."[71]

Mavor and Dix[72] agree that the Gungywamp effigy is a manitou, noting that images of the sacred bird (*wakun-bird*) were placed in sacred places to appease Hobbomock.[73]

Manitou as a concept is difficult to explain in Western concepts. It is a manifestation of spirit and mystic presence that permeates the world in ways that are apparent but not readily understood. This also describes the Gungywamp quite nicely.

The Cockaponset Carvings

In 1952, historian Frederick J. Pohl published *The Lost Discovery: Uncovering the Track of the Vikings in America*. Although not his first book on pre–Columbian explorations, it was his first released through a mainstream publisher. As a result, he began receiving letters about additional potential Norse sites. One such report concerned a series of rock carvings in Connecticut, situated on a wooded hill in the Cockaponset State Forest of Connecticut. Pohl assembled a team to investigate that included Charles Michael Boland, future author of the seminal *They All Discovered America*, and Bernard Powell, who would become a significant figure in Connecticut and Massachusetts archaeological societies. Even with a map and detailed instructions, it was an arduous trek through the woods.

Pohl was perplexed by the site, but it was obviously not Viking. Instead, he saw carvings that had no relationship to each other—a stone throne, a four-petalled flower, a rectangular trough, an oval bowl, several groupings of cupules, and a collection of undecipherable symbols carved on a nearby ledge. Pohl was particularly intrigued by an outcropping with horizontal grooves that he considered similar to the plinth in the classical Greek style. Pohl uses the term "plinth" to describe the size and shape rather than suggesting it was the start of an actual column. The name would remain, inferring a column, despite Pohl's intent to use the term as an object such as a display pedestal in statuary for displays, such as rumored carved heads that had been taken from the site.

For lack of a better name, Pohl dubbed the site the "Cockaponset Carvings" after its location in the Cockaponset State Forest. Cockaponset State Forest contains over 16,000 acres with unconnected parcels in 11 towns. As intriguing as the site was, it was not Norse, and Pohl was focused on an imminent excavation by the Massachusetts Archaeology Society of his proposed Viking winter camp in Cape Cod. That excavation was inconclusive and ended prematurely because of interference from amateur archeologist and publicity hound Roland Robbins.[74] Pohl published several titles over the next decade defending his work. The Cockaponset site was forgotten.

In 1977, Frederick Pohl was 87 and had released his final book on Pre-Columbian explorations, devoted to the fourteenth-century Sinclair expedition to Canada, a topic he had also spent his life examining. *Prince Henry Sinclair: His Expedition to the New World in 1398* also included his most recent work on the Westford Knight in Massachusetts, which he believed was a funeral effigy from that expedition. Pohl had begun sorting and dividing his papers to donate to university archives when he

The Cockaponset Carvings are a series of rock carvings in Connecticut (first visited by Pohl in 1952). He was particularly intrigued by an outcropping with horizontal grooves that he considered to be similar to a plinth in the Grecian style (courtesy NEARA Archives).

came across his Cockaponset field notes. The notes and photographs still intrigued him, but as Pohl neared the nonagenarian threshold, his mobility would no longer permit traipsing through the woods to a site as remote as Cockaponset. Instead, he decided the location needed a fresh set of eyes. He knew an enthusiastic member of the Leif Erikson Society of New York, John D. Gallagher.

Gallagher found the trek far less of an ordeal than Pohl remembered. Since Pohl's visit, Guilford, Connecticut, had acquired additional lands and blazed trails. The forests were now known more commonly as "Westwoods," with a trail system containing 39 miles of trails on 1,200 acres, and although parts of Westwoods are part of the State Forest, Guilford Land Conservation Trust manages the entire property.

Gallagher visited the site several times, photographing features to compare to Pohl's photos and developing his own interpretation of the features. Gallagher was initially convinced the site was Celtic and sent his sketches to Barry Fell, whose *America B.C.* had just hit the bestseller lists. Pohl was neither impressed nor convinced by Gallagher's Celtic identification. Fearing his discovery was about to be handed over (and credited) to Fell, Pohl published in a 1978 issue of the *Anthropological Journal of Canada*.[75] The article is a brief overview of the site features, mentioning the reported theft of two sculpted heads.

Pohl revisited the topic in a longer piece in *Epigraphic Society Occasional Publications (ESOP)*[76] the following year. The tone of this article is a little defensive; the previous piece had generated mixed results. Pohl remained convinced he had a pre-Christian European settlement and noted similarities to Vermont sites in Barry Fell's *America B.C.,* specifically a "Druid Throne" and "libation bowls." In this article, Pohl was more concerned about the approach by sea with his explorers sailing up Long Island Sound into Joshua Bay. Passing Leetes Island, the small ship found a small landlocked harbor below the carvings.

In true historian fashion, Pohl bemoaned the progress that allowed a road and railroad track to block boat access and allowed silt to build up, turning his access route around Leetes Island into swamps. Unfortunately, Pohl's lack of familiarity with coastal ecosystems made his proposed marine approach problematic; his "swamps" were actually naturally-occurring salt marshes, coastal wetlands with soil composed of deep mud and peat. These marshes had been harvesting salt hay since the colonial settlements. Any ship sturdy enough to cross the Atlantic would draft too deep to approach the harbor without being mired in the waterlogged peat and mud.

Gallagher followed up in a similar length *ESOP* article.[77] While not overtly disagreeing with Pohl, it is evident from his careful wording that he had already decided the site was a religious site, again mentioning the rumor of the missing stone heads. He mentions sending the material to Fell, but there is no evidence that Fell examined the site or the data. However, Gallagher had found a series of articles in 1976 *ESOP* issues where Fell translated a series of rock carvings at El-Hadj-Mimoun, near Figuig, Morocco.[78] On the strength of Fell's translation, Norman Totten dated the inscription to AD 535 and referred to monks who had returned from exile in Asqa Shamal about AD 480.[79] Totten and Fell translated Asqa Shamal as a continent to the west, i.e., North America.

Gallagher decided that these Moroccan monks set up a friary at Cockaponset, using the Fell/Totten theory of Asqa Shamal as evidence. He would wait a decade to publish his findings in *On Site*, the newsletter of the American Institute for Archaeological Research,[80] a small, short-lived organization best remembered for "translating" bulldozer scrapes in the America's Stonehenge parking lot as Ogham.

Gallagher missed an opportunity to shore up his shaky theory. Thirty miles away, in the Gungywamp Complex, Barry Fell had already determined the style of the "IC III" Christogram was primarily associated with the Byzantines, and the Chi-Rho symbols throughout the site were consistent with those of the 4th to 7th centuries found throughout Christendom. This suggested the petroglyphs could indicate a Byzantine settlement in exile, which could fall into the time period of Fell's work in Morocco, although it is a connection Fell himself never suggests.

Telepneff notes that themes of voluntary exile and pilgrimage are part of both the Celtic and Eastern Church practices. Voluntary exile from their homeland was a form of asceticism that Telepneff notes dated back to the Old Testament edict to Abraham in Genesis 12:1–9.[81] As stated earlier, Telepneff's concern is the Byzantine influence on the Celtic Church, not if this exile included journeys to North America.

All three members of the original team that visited the Cockaponset site, Pohl, Boland, and Powell, had very different theories on the site. Pohl decided it was pre–Christian and was not enamored of Gallagher's Byzantine monastery theory. Gallagher would publish on his theorized fifth-century church one more time in the pages of *Ancient American* in 2003, reusing material from his previous *ESOP* pieces but now fully embracing the Moroccan origin theory.[82]

Boland briefly mentions the site in *They All Discovered America*, but his text appears to be based on a vague recollection of his visit combined with Pohl's notes, mentioning multiple florets and an unfinished Doric column.[83] Boland connects the "Guilford site" to a small carving on a rock at Assawompset Pond in southeastern Massachusetts, which he identifies as a Phoenician ship at anchor, carved 2000 years earlier.[84]

Bernard Powell was the one member of Pohl's original expedition who never wrote about the site. Powell was an ardent avocational archaeologist, but his interest was Native American, and he was aware his occasional forays into pre–Columbian research were frowned upon. He met Pohl after a brief article in the *Bulletin of the Massachusetts Archaeological Society* discussing possible mooring holes that correlated with mooring holes at Pohl's Viking winter site on Cape Cod. And Powell accompanied Boland on the boat when Boland attempted to recreate the Ericsson voyage from Pohl's notes, which resulted in Boland's discovery of the Rocky Nook

Norse axe, a sister blade to William Goodwin's Tor Bay "Norse Axe."[85] His lack of publishing on the Ericsson trip and the Rocky Nook axe may be due to the pushback he received for bringing Norse theories into a "mainstream" journal.

Boland may not have published on the Cockaponset site, but he did write about it. After retiring, he dabbled in various hobbies, including the pre-Internet computer Bulletin Board Systems. One BBS Powell dialed in to was the Bay Area Skeptics Board BBS in San Francisco. There, he posted his recollection of the Cockaponset visit and later reposted it on his own website in 2007.[86]

His recollection, justifiably fuzzy in spots, recalls one crucial detail. After several hours, Powell wandered off and ascended to the top of the neighboring hill. He discovered a large estate with a hedge maze around a rose garden. Powell realized the center of the rose garden had a weathered stone Doric-styled pedestal with a carved stone head of Medusa sitting on it. He asked the gardener, who explained the owner had him drag it up the hill from the camp where the tombstone makers used to practice. It seemed a large monument company up to New Haven would send their apprentices to the area to practice on the limestone outcrops similar to the nearby limestone quarry. The gardener noted several people had taken carved busts from the site. Powell returned to Pohl and Boland and repeated the story. Two decades later, Pohl would recall Powell's stolen heads, but not the associated stone carver origin.

Whether the Cockaponset site is pre-Christian, Phoenician, Moroccan, or just early 19th century carvers honing their skills in the popular Greek Revival style, the site itself has undergone a journey that was not anticipated when Frederick Pohl first assembled his team to investigate a Norse site in Connecticut.

CHAPTER TWELVE

Norse Cape Cod

Two types of evidence suggest Norse contacts with North America: written sagas and archaeological artifacts. The traditional method of deciding where to look for Vinland is to interpret the sagas and then go to that place and look for the archaeological proof. Unfortunately, the ambiguous descriptions of distance and geography have researchers considering Helluland and Markland locations in the Canadian Maritime Provinces even as other researchers locate Hóp in New York City.[1] There is ample room in such a large search area for the wide variety of interpretations of the sagas.

Cape Cod and the surrounding islands remain perennial favorites in the search for Vinland the Good. Perhaps it's because the progenitor of the theory of Norse ruins in America, C.C. Rafn, thought that the first settlement in America might have been somewhere on Cape Cod.[2] Perhaps the very name of Martha's Vineyard is evocative of Vinland. Even Vilhjalmur Stefansson, who proposed that the *Kitlinermiut* or "Copper Inuits," of Victoria Island in the Canadian Arctic had intermixed with early Norse explorers,[3] had no problem with the concept of Vinland extending into New England.[4] Perhaps it was actually part of the Norse settlement. And perhaps because of this scrutiny, there is a higher density of proposed Norse sites in this area than any other part of the North American east coast.

In 1966, British journalist J.R.L. Anderson and a small crew sailed a 44-foot cutter from England via Iceland and Greenland to Martha's Vineyard to duplicate Leif Eriksson's journey.[5] Using navigational evidence in the sagas and the then recently published, still controversial Yale University Vinland Map,[6] the trip was made to demonstrate Anderson's theory that the evidence fit Nantucket Sound and the Massachusetts seaboard very well.

Even today, interest remains high in the possibility of Cape Cod as a Norse landing spot.[7] In 2004, Neil Good believed Waquoit Bay was a logical location. Waquoit Bay is a public estuary entering Nantucket Sound. Good believed Nantucket Sound was the only place that matched descriptions of the Norse Viking excursions from Greenland. He obtained a permit to do subsurface electronic scanning of Waquoit Bay in 2004. Unfortunately for Good, Nantucket Sound was in the middle of a prolonged legal battle about constructing an offshore wind farm in the Sound's shallows. Good was concerned the construction would impact the search for a Norse ship the sagas said was scuttled.⁸ Good never found his Viking ship, but in 2000 did locate the wreck of a rumrunner lost in Waquoit Bay in 1942.⁹ The wind farm controversy would rage on until the project was canceled in 2017. The Norse on Cape Cod shows no such signs of ending.

Bourne Stone, Bourne, Massachusetts

It is almost miraculous that the Bourne Stone, located on historic Cape Cod, survived the turbulent colonial era of the Massachusetts Bay Colony. It remained unscathed through Indian wars, religious revivals, and anti–Indian/pagan backlash.

In the mid–1600s, Harvard's John Eliot attempted to convert natives to Christianity by translating the Bible into the Algonquin language and establishing "Indian Praying Towns" where the Christian Indians could live. Between 1650 and 1675, 14 Indian Praying Towns were built, each with a religious leader appointed by Eliot. Circa 1658, Captain Thomas Tupper, a resident of Sandwich, Massachusetts, built a church in modern-day Bournedale, known to the natives as Comassakumkanit.¹⁰ This church was the start of the Comassakumkanit Praying Town, and Captain Tupper spent a number of years visiting as a missionary.

Captain Tupper had the stone, believed sacred to the Wampanoag Manomets, built into the church as a stepping-stone. Local tradition reports that the stone was repositioned with the face down after the natives refused to step on or across the symbols. True or not, the front of the stone has been protected, and the two lines of carvings remain well defined.

The bloody King Philip's War in 1675–76 created a backlash of anti–Indian sentiment, dooming the Praying Town experiment to failure. Considered traitors, the Praying Indians were distrusted by the English as potential spies for Philip. With their loyalty suspect, the Praying Indians who survived attacks from both sides were relocated to Deer Island in Boston Harbor. They were released in 1677, but the damage was done, and by 1680, less than 300 Praying Indians remained alive. John Eliot's great mission ended by attrition.

Sometime after the end of Eliot's missions, the abandoned Comassakumkanit church burned down. The stone was retrieved from the burnt ruins and hidden in the home of a local Indian. The stone, possibly passed among local Wampanoags, disappeared for nearly 200 years. It was rediscovered (or a similarly carved stone believed to be the original was found) and then passed through several owners, finally ending up in the possession of the Bourne Historical Society. The stone was moved to the Aptucxet Trading Post museum when it opened to the public in 1930, where it remains today.

The origins of the markings are obscure. Local legend says Samuel Sewall, a judge at the Salem witch trials, brought the stone to the area as he built the church in atonement for his part in the proceedings. Although Sewall does refer to the church in his diary in 1687, unfortunately for local legend, the church was built and abandoned by the start of the trials in 1692.

The stone is a bit excessive as a stepping-stone—it is 4 feet long and 18 inches thick, weighing roughly 300 pounds. Based on marks along the top edge, the stone may have been quarried into a rectangle. The flat face of the stone has two lines of incised markings, with the first row consisting of four 4½-inch petroglyphs. The second line contains numerous 2-inch inscriptions. The number of runes varies by the translator (Barry Fell[11] and Olaf Strandwold[12] each show 15, and Edward Lenik[13] lists 20). Delabarre would not attempt to count the carvings. He believed the markings were Native petroglyphs, cut in 1658 to deliberately be on the threshold, where foot traffic had nearly obliterated them. The only markings Delabarre felt were still clear enough to interpret were a "number of angular marks near the lower left-hand corner suggest[ing] wigwams. Just to the right of them, a third of the distance across the stone, can be seen a fairly sure 'white man and Indian shaking hands.'"[14]

At some point since the museum opened, the marks have been filled with charcoal to enhance visibility. Various origins have been attributed to the Bourne Rock since the stone's rediscovery—Norse, Irish monks, and even local natives practicing their writings skills.

Olaf Strandwold struggled to read a Norse translation on the stone for his 1948 book. He eventually translated the stone using a complicated mishmash of Old Norse, Danish intrusions, and an older form of an Icelandic verb. He finally decided it read "Jesus amply provides for us here and in heaven." He also disregards the last three runes in the top row and inserts the first of them into the lower line. He also states that the name of Jesus (Jasui) has been inscribed as a contraction (Jui). His final paragraph on the topic admits that there is considerable room for interpretation in translation because of the encompassing use of several of the terms.[15]

A 1947 photograph of the Bourne Stone on Cape Cod, taken for Olaf Strandwold (Malcolm Pearson photograph).

Barry Fell was introduced to the Bourne Stone by archaeologist James Whittall[16] while Fell was researching *America B.C.* Fell immediately recognized the letters as Iberian Punic. According to his translation, the rock is a stele proclaiming the annexation of the surrounding territory on behalf of a Carthaginian: "A proclamation of annexation. By this Hanno takes possession."[17]

According to the fifth-century B.C. histories by Herodotus, there was a Phoenician explorer named Hanno, who sailed through the straits of Gibraltar and then part of the way around Africa in the first half of the fifth-century B.C. Fell does not equate the two in his translation.

Whittall published his own research notes on the stone in conjunction with Barry Fell's translation.[18] Whittall was more interested in narrowing down the exact location of the Comassakumkanit church. Conflicted oral traditions placed the building at either the Great Herring Pond or along the Herring River. The church, in either location, would have been situated approximately halfway between Cape Cod Bay and Buzzards Bay, roughly two miles from the ocean in either direction. Whittall hypothesized that Hanno and his early explorers could have navigated up the Manomet River to the Herring River and into Great Herring Pond, leaving the stone at the Manomet's headwaters or a neighboring Indian Village. Any evidence at the headwaters is gone: The Cape Cod Canal, completed in 1914, was dug along the bed of the Manomet River.

Fell suggested another alternative was the theory put forth by folklorist Elizabeth Raynard in her 1934 collection of Cape Cod tales.[19] Raynard suggested that when the Vikings visited Cape Cod, the Great Herring Pond was an inlet of Cape Cod Bay. It became a pond after the Viking visits, as the land continued to rebound from the last ice age. Fell has no use for the Viking theory but notes that the only thing separating the pond from the sea is a swamp and a few sand dunes.

Fell's work on the Bourne Stone consists of one page of text, a chart comparing the Bourne Stone's alphabet to that of the Iberian alphabet used in southern Spain, and a page with a letter-by-letter breakdown of his translation.[20] Yet, some of the most wildly inaccurate attacks against Fell by professional archaeologists (who apparently never actually read the book) are associated with the translation. As an example, Mesoamerican anthropologist Nigel Davies, in *Voyagers to the New World*,[21] discredits Fell's work while claiming that the stone had been found in 1653 by the English and had recently been discovered by Hindus embedded in a flight of stairs. Either Davies is unaware of the difference between a Native American Indian and a native of India, or discrediting Fell took priority over fact checking.

Edward Lenik's interpretation of the carvings on the stone is the most feasible but it is undoubtedly not the last. Lenik hypothesizes that the glyphs are native in origin and date to the last half of the 17th century. Lenik notes that American Indian sachems each had an identification mark used on treaties and other documents in lieu of a signature. This stone, according to Lenik, carries the marks of numerous tribal leaders.[22] Why a stone would be created with multiple signatures remains open to interpretation, but then again, that also describes the Bourne Rock itself.

Nomans Land Island, Chilmark, Massachusetts

Even if Nomans Land Island did not play host to a runic inscription, it would be a fascinating place. First named Martha's Vineyard in 1602 by Bartholomew Gosnold during his explorations of the New England coast,[23] in the subsequent 60 years, it was renamed "Hendrick Christiaensen's Eylandt" and "Ile de Hendrick," both references to a visiting Dutch explorer, as well as "Isle of Man" and "Dock Island." By 1666 the current name of Nomans Land Island was being used on deeds, although the etymology of the name is unknown, possibly an anglicized version of "Tequenomans Land," after a sachem from Martha's Vineyard who held jurisdiction over the island when English explorers arrived in the 1600s.[24]

The island, for all of the nomenclature, is barely a mile across at its widest point, and the circumference is less than three miles. It has always been a sparsely inhabited speck of land, rarely visited because of rough surf and treacherous currents limiting access for months at a time.

The earliest recorded attempt at a settlement on Nomans Land Island was sheep farming in 1715. By 1800 the island was noted for the high quality of its wool, and local fishermen used the island as a base of operations. The population peaked in 1860 and then declined sharply.[25]

In 1914, Joshua Crane bought the island. The former national court tennis champion, polo luminary, and general bon vivant planned to make the island into a private game reserve and build an artificial harbor for his friends and their yachts.

Before Crane's acquisition, the island's inaccessibility provided limited use to the small summer fishing community and as a rumrunner's rendezvous. Its primary claim to fame was the pre-radar/sonar ships and submarines constantly going aground on the shores.[26] It remained so desolate after Crane's purchase that one of the alleged kidnappers of Charles Lindbergh's son proposed the location for the ransom exchange.[27]

In 1923, Edward F. Gray of the British consulate in Boston approached Joshua Crane about his summer retreat. Gray, recently assigned to Boston after 25 years in Norway, was researching a book on the location of Vinland[28] and wanted to know if Crane had seen any evidence of runes or stone ruins to support his theory that Nomans Land Island was the winter quarters for Leif's expedition. Gray hypothesized Leif's route as also landing on Nantucket Island, Martha's Vineyard, and the nonexistent Nauset Island. According to DeCosta,[29] Nauset Island had been charted by Gosnold in 1602 but had been completely destroyed by storms and erosion before Champlain's 1606 exploration.[30] By the date of DeCosta's book (1868), the water was over six fathoms deep where Nauset Island had been.

In 1926, Crane reported to Gray that he had been exploring the southern beach of his island at low tide and came across a runic inscription carved on a black sloping rock. Only exposed during low tide, the rune rock was located at the base of 20-foot-high cliffs, near a 400-ton rock[31] that had fallen from the top of the cliffs in

The Nomans Land Island inscription, 1930. Runes are chalked in for visibility by island caretaker Cameron Wood (Cameron Wood photograph).

the previous century. The shallow runes form four lines of lettering. Each rune is about 4 inches high. The first line of runes reads "Leif Eriksson," and the second line reads "MI," the Roman numerals for the date 1001 (A.D.). The third and fourth lines are either unfinished or badly eroded—only the vertical lines are clearly discernable.

Gray was elated to find proof so readily. By the end of 1927, Gray sent copies of the runes out to several runic experts, asking for opinions. However, the feedback was not promising.

Edmund Delabarre, who felt few, if any, carved rocks in New England were of any antiquity (except, of course, the Dighton Rock[32]), corresponded with Gray on the topic and visited the runes himself, but only vaguely mentions it in his book.[33] Professors A.W. Brögger and Magnus Olsen of Oslo University also examined photographs of the runes.[34] Brögger questioned the "genuineness" of the inscription based on the runes carved in Leif's name and the omission of a nominative form. He also points out that the "Eriksson" should be "Eiriksson." He was also suspicious of the use of Roman numerals for the date because they were not a method of dating in Scandinavia until the 14th or 15th century.

Finnur Jónsson of Copenhagen University also questioned the date, noting that the custom of leaving runic records was unknown among Icelanders in 1000.[35] Sir William Craigie, the foremost lexicographer of the time, also pointed to the lack of nominative form on Leif and the incorrect spelling of Eiriksson. Craigie also believed he could read the third line of runes as "VINLAND," which would also be incorrect usage. He found the inscription to contain a mix of old runic alphabets and Roman letters, an odd mix for someone used to writing in the later runes.[36]

By the time Gray's book came out in 1930, he was convinced that the runes were of post–Viking in age but not a hoax. His revised conclusion was that the inscription was a tribute to Leif, carved by a later admirer exploring the area, such as Giovanni da Verrazzano or Bartholomew Gosnold.[37]

This was patently absurd, noted Harvard professors Frank Stanton Cawley and Samuel Eliot Morison in a scathing review of Gray's book for the *New England Quarterly*.[38] Cawley, a professor of Scandinavian languages and literature, points out grammatical lapses and errors in form that suggest to him that Gray "lacks the most rudimentary knowledge of Icelandic inflections."[39]

Morison notes the coincidence of the stone being found by Crane three years after Gray first mentioned he was investigating the topic and that Crane had a reputation for practical jokes.[40] The practical-joke theory was further advanced by photographer Malcolm Pearson when he met Joshua Crane's son Alexander in 1945. Alexander readily admitted his father carved the runes.[41]

Cawley and Morison ended their review by pointing out that seagoing types like Gosnold were hardly likely to carve a tribute to a Norse explorer when even scholars of the time were unfamiliar with the sagas. Annie Wood, the wife of Joshua Crane's caretaker, Cameron Wood, published a history of the island that included a chapter recapping Gray's work on the runes. She further muddied the waters by claiming that the Woodses had actually spotted the runes a full year before Crane.[42]

Edmund Delabarre and Brown University geology professor Charles W. Brown visited the site in 1931, publishing their findings in a 1935 issue of *New England Quarterly*.[43] Brown and Delabarre reviewed the rock, comparing it to photographs taken in the previous five years. In just those five years, they found pronounced erosion on the runes, suggesting a recent carving on a soft stone that, between sand scour and sea action, would return to oblivion quickly. Brown also noted that the lines were consistent with the types of marks made by a chisel being struck by a hammer and that the boulder had probably fallen from the eroding cliff in the past century, as had the rocks surrounding it.

As a psychologist, Delabarre found modern carvings just as enlightening as if they were legitimate antiquities. Prior to his assessment of the Nomans Land Island runes in *New England Quarterly*, he published an article in *Scientific Monthly* on the New England petroglyphs as a self-contained environment for studying human motivations.[44]

Delabarre felt that just as ancient inscriptions had been motivated by different reasons, not all recent petroglyphs were meant to be deliberate frauds. He uses

Nomans Land runes as an example of assigning different motives based on who carved the stone.[45]

Delabarre and Brown, having determined that the stone was recently carved, then considered the various theories as to who could have carved the runes.[46] Delabarre concluded that, minimally, it was carved after Rafn triggered the initial interest in 1837 and probably after 1904 when the *Encyclopedia Americana* first published a table of rune letters.

Delabarre's suspicion was that the culprit was Walton Ricketson of New Bedford, Massachusetts. As a noted sculptor, Ricketson knew how to handle a chisel. He was a local figure known to wander the coast in his sailboat. He was also the son of Daniel Ricketson, a scholar and historian whose history of New Bedford[47] includes references to possible Norse visits to the area. Delabarre stops short of saying Ricketson was the carver, probably out of deference to Ricketson's death in 1923. Olaf Strandwold, using Delabarre's photograph, suggested that the inscription was legitimate but mistranslated by people focusing on Roman numerals in the second line.[48] Strandwold interpreted these runes as "ey" or "island" in English. Strandwold builds from this correction, ending with a translation of "Leif Erikson's Island" and a year that converted to AD 1175.

Strandwold later modified his translation after receiving a better photograph from Gray.[49] Regarding the four rows of runes, Strandwold's new translation kept the first two lines as "Leif Erikson's Island" and changed the remaining lines to "Thirty Men." This new translation read that a ship crew of 30 men had raised the monument and dedicated the island to Leif. Strandwold also points out that Leif's brother Thorvald had a 30-man crew, according to the sagas. What Strandwold did not know was that the stone was missing and believed washed away by a hurricane that struck New England in 1938.

Any remaining debate as to whether the carving was a dedication to Leif Eriksson, Thorvald commemorating his brother, or a practical joke by Joshua Crane was made significantly more difficult to resolve when Crane abandoned his island sanctuary in 1941, leasing the island to the U.S. Navy for bombing practice by the South Weymouth Naval Air Station. Runic inscription or not, the island was now a military target range, and unauthorized visits were both illegal and dangerous.

In August of 1966, *Martha's Vineyard Gazette* reporter Peter McGhee accompanied Bertrand Wood, the son of island caretakers Annie and Cameron Wood, back to the island after 33 years. Apart from pointing out landmarks such as graveyards and identifying cellar holes, he also implied that the reason Crane allowed the Navy to lease the property was due to Crane's financial losses in the Great Crash of 1929.[50]

In September 1952, the Navy bought Nomans Land Island for $67,500 under eminent domain. Considering that live ordnance had been dropped on the island for 10 years, there probably was not much argument from the Crane family. This also reaffirmed that any researcher wishing to visit the island would need both the permission and the cooperation of the military to visit the island. Neither was readily obtainable, but this did not stop attempts. The stone was rediscovered in 1954[51] and 1985,[52] but little interest was generated and plans to rescue the stone never generated enough momentum or funds to warrant the attempt.

In 1975, a U.S. Fish & Wildlife Refuge was established on the northeastern third of the island. By 1987, although the navy had long since switched to dummy munitions, pressure was mounting for it to stop using Nomans Land Island, as complaints mounted from Martha's Vineyard residents.[53] Biologists sided with the Navy, grateful that the specter of unexploded shells kept the public off the island, allowing the wildlife to thrive without human interference.[54] The debate ended when the South Weymouth Naval Station was among the casualties in a wave of military base closures, ceasing operations in 1996. Two years later, the U.S. Navy transferred ownership to U.S. Fish & Wildlife following a $2.9 million cleanup by the Navy, the Department of the Interior, the Environmental Protection Agency, and the Commonwealth of Massachusetts. Today, Nomans Land Island National Wildlife Refuge provides a habitat for migrating birds and nesting for waterbirds. It is a resting and feeding area for migrating peregrine falcons. The island is closed to the public and strictly protected as a sanctuary for migratory birds.

In August 2003, a group of investigators led by James Mavor, a retired oceanographic engineer at the Woods Hole Oceanographic Institute,[55] obtained permission to search the shoreline of Nomans Land Island for the inscription stone. At a 2003 autumn meeting of the New England Antiquities Research Association in Norwich, Connecticut, Mavor reported that they had relocated the inscription stone, badly eroded and only accessible for a few minutes at the lowest point of the ebb tide.

Mavor did not publish a report, but some of his investigators did. Scott Wolter and epigrapher Richard Nielsen had flown in to join the expedition, and Wolter's account in his and Nielsen's book[56] paints a grimmer picture. After scraping seaweed and barnacles off the rock, Wolter could only confirm its identity by touch, finding the letter M on the second line.

Visiting the runestone remains complicated and expensive. Any visit needs a filming permit from the town of Chilmark and clearance from the Massachusetts Board of Underwater Archaeological Resources (MBUAR), which also clear such requests with the Wampanoag Tribe of Gay Head. In addition, there must be a qualified archaeologist and a representative of the Wildlife Commission. The Coast Guard must agree since potential unexploded ordnance off the coast makes the area prohibited to boats. Wolter's 2002 visit was under the auspices of James Mavor's credentials and included a documentary filmmaker, meaning a filming permit from Chilmark was also required. They also coordinated with a team hired by the federal government to find and remove any undetonated bombs.

In 2007, a treasure-hunting company, newly reminted as a non-profit marine archaeology salvage company, approached Chilmark for permission to remove the rock.[57] The town sent them to MBUAR and included an official letter adamantly opposed to the plan. MBUAR immediately denied the request, officially declaring the rock was under their jurisdiction and that any proposals to remove it would be tabled. The state archaeologist and the Wampanoag Tribe agreed, effectively eliminating any chance to salvage the stone as it continues to sink into the ocean.

When Wolter returned to Nomans Land Island for an episode of his *America Unearthed* series in 2013,[58] he was surprised at the change in the landscape. Two hurricanes in 2006 and 2007 had generated tidal surges of over 10 feet, accelerating the erosion that was pushing the rock into the water. Except for the lowest point of the tide, it was all but inaccessible.

In 2017, Josh Gates filmed an episode of his program *Expedition Unknown* at the rock.[59] Gates located the rock by risking a scuba dive. Scouring the plant life off the rock, Gates was able to identify several of the horizontal incised lines but was unable to continue, as the rising tide was making it too dangerous to continue. He left intrigued but unconvinced. At this point, six or more tropical storms have battered the coast of Nomans Land Island since the *Expedition Unknown* episode. It is probably safe to face what was inevitable; the rune stone is irretrievably lost.

Although the stone's current whereabouts and condition have again been assessed, the original question remains—is this a legitimate runic inscription or a practical joke by Joshua Crane that has exceeded his wildest expectations?

Priester Runestone, North Tisbury, Massachusetts

In 1949 Hjalmar Holand published a report of a short runic inscription discovered in 1922 on private property north of North Tisbury on Martha's Vineyard.[60] Holand received a letter from a Mr. Thoreson, who had spent part of the summer of 1946 as a guest of Godfrey Priester at Priester's summer home on his wooded estate two miles north of Tisbury. The letter reported that as Godfrey and Thoreson talked of local history and the possibility of Vikings on the island, Priester recalled that 24 years before, his hired hand had given him a scrap of paper with carvings copied from a rock he had come across while working in the woods. Priester found the paper in a box of loose paper in the attic.

The two men attempted without success to find the rock. Holand and historian Frederick Pohl also tried to locate the stone on several occasions but to no avail. In addition to two decades of new undergrowth and acres to search, Holand noted that rocks had been removed for pond embankments and stone walls.[61] Priester's 1962 obituary notes he had restored an ancient mill dam and pond during his ownership of the property, so Priester himself may have inadvertently thwarted Holand's attempts to find the stone.

Holand hoped the stone's disappearance was only temporary. Since it had been found ten years before Holand's first book on the Kensington Rune Stone,[62] it could not be claimed that the book's rune chart had been used to create the runes. This was important to Holand because the Tisbury stone included a runic character similar in shape to a capital "Y." Holand claimed that the only other known inscription containing this unusual variant form was the Kensington Stone. Ergo, the Tisbury stone validated the Kensington inscription.

Of course, for the Tisbury inscription to be translatable, Holand had to assume either weathering or an error in copying the runes. The five runes, as copied and translated, were a "jumble."[63] Fortunately, Holand felt the error was easy to correct. By extending the vertical line on the second rune and adding a dot to the fifth rune,[64] the Norwegian name "THOLIV" appears. Holand then devotes several pages to demonstrating how this nonstandard form of the name is actually proof of the age of the carving, tying it into both the Kensington Rune Stone and the Newport Tower, which Holand had recently announced was actually Paul Knutson's base of operations for the expedition that ended in Kensington.[65]

Holand never found the lost rune stone. A portion of Godfrey Priester's estate is now the Priester Pond Preserve, still heavily wooded but now a wildlife sanctuary open to the public for hiking, fishing, and picnicking. So perhaps someone may once again stumble upon the rune stone, just as it was found in 1922.

Three interpretations of the Priester runes of North Tisbury. Top: original version, as transcribed by Priester's hired hand. Middle: The runes as modified by Holand to make the runes translatable. Bottom: The 1867 runes from the book Old-Northern Runic Monuments of Scandinavia and England. Top two images after *Scandinavian Studies* 21.2 (1949), used with permission.

Quitsa Cromlech, Martha's Vineyard, Massachusetts

In 1938 William Goodwin wrote to William Inglis Morse about Norse visits to North America.[66] As far as Goodwin was concerned, there were only two pieces of evidence beyond reproach—an axe head found in Tor Bay, Nova Scotia[67] and a "small stone tomb still resting peacefully in a deep valley on the western end of the Island of Martha's Vineyard."[68] By the publication of his book on the location of Vinland,[69] Goodwin had changed his mind. Goodwin believed that the coast of New Hampshire was the heart of Vinland—Streamfiord at Portsmouth Harbor, Leif's Landfall at Hampton Beach. His theory was that the Norse never ventured south of the tip of Cape Cod and never saw Nantucket or Martha's Vineyard, so the cromlech did not fit with his theory. Goodwin would resurrect the cromlech for his book on Irish settlements in New England,[70] but even in that text, the cromlech was anomalous. Goodwin believed the stone ruins in New England were, in fact, built by Irish Culdee monks who were deliberately avoiding the coast and their enemy, the marauding Norse. The Martha's Vineyard site was his only Irish site near the ocean.[71]

Irish, Viking, or other,[72] Goodwin was mistaken in his assessment of the

William Goodwin examines the Quitsa Dolmen on Martha's Vineyard in a 1946 image from *The Ruins of Great Ireland in New England* (courtesy of Malcolm Pearson).

tranquility. The "little cromlech"[73]—known as the Quitsa Dolmen because of its proximity to Nashaquitsa or "Quitsa" Pond—had already been a topic of debate for many years.

Located on Martha's Vineyard near Menemsha Bight along the road to Gay Head,[74] the structure acquired its earliest identification as a cromlech in a 1927 photograph in the *Vineyard Gazette*,[75] a year after the discovery of the Nomans Land Island inscription. There is no elaboration in the caption beneath the photo, but it may have been Edward Gray who was responsible for identifying the structure as a cromlech. Gray felt that Menemsha Bight matched the sagas as the site of Leif Eriksson's ship running aground.[76] Gray does not specifically mention the cromlech in his book, suggesting that he was unaware of the cromlech or leery of conveniently placed evidence after the Nomans Land Island incident. It is certain that the publicity of the previous year about Gray's work on Nomans Land Island brought about the structure's Norse association.

This small stone chamber is set into the hillside, constructed of four boulders of about 3 feet in height. The walls are covered by a granite capstone with a slightly oval top. Smaller stones were inserted between the supporting stones, and the opening faces due south. Like many of the stone chambers in New England, it may have originally been covered in earth.

In 1934, Frederick Johnson, the curator at the Peabody Museum in Andover, Massachusetts, excavated the dolmen.[77] Removing the sod from the entrance, he discovered a 7-foot-long by 2-foot-wide pathway of handmade bricks, leading north to the entrance and then west away from the entrance. Johnson was not able to determine if the bricks had been laid on bare soil or pre-existing turf but felt they were probably placed over the sod. Post-colonial artifacts were found outside the structure, but nothing in a context that would help date the structure.[78] Inside the chamber, there was evidence of a fire with wood fragments and hand-cut nails. Fire damage to the wall and earth was minimal, suggesting a fire of short duration, not a long-term usage pattern. Excavations inside the structure indicated approximately one foot of accumulated soil and then hardpan, with no signs of human disturbance. He believed that to determine the chamber's age, a long-term study would be needed to calculate the rate of soil accumulation.

Johnson's conclusion was that the structure was post-colonial, based on the artifacts, the fact that the local Indian tribe did not work with stone, and the Vikings had stopped building megalithic structures long before the age of the Vinland explorations.

Johnson's report was published in 1945. Three years later, Johannes Brøndsted, director of the National Museum of Denmark, visited the site as part of a tour of New England's "Viking" sites.[79] He felt the structure was of so little significance that any additional time and money spent researching the site was not justified. He was confident it was not Native American in origin, and that it had no resemblance to any type of Nordic grave. In fact, Brøndsted doubted it was a grave at all, instead suggesting a "grotto" or child's playhouse.[80]

Archaeologist James Whittall revisited the site in 1970.[81] He found that a new origin had evolved in local tradition, and it was now known locally as the burial site of a Viking chieftain. He pointed out that the dolmen is comparable to Western European dolmens from 3000 to 1000 BC, not the era of Viking exploration. Whittall instead suggests that it marked the grave of an early European explorer too prominent for burial at sea, such as from the Gosnold or Champlain expeditions. Whittall attempted to ascertain the age of the capstone using carbon-dating, theorizing that if the capstone had been quarried by pre-colonial visitors, it would have been split off using the fire setting method[82] which would leave carbon residue. The suspected source of the capstone was a large boulder nearby, and Whittall excavated a test pit beneath the boulder's edge that matched the capstone.[83] No carbon was found, although Whittall reported quarry spallings were uncovered at a layer below two arrowheads. The *NEARA Journal* article contains significant differences from a subsequent one-page excavation report Whittall filed with the organization. References to the site being a possible European grave are gone, and the excavations at the boulder no longer mention the spalling. Now instead of two arrowheads, there is a reference to only one, which was identified as a Squibnocket triangle.[84]

In Barry Fell's third book on pre–Columbian visits to America,[85] he briefly mentions the structure in a discussion of dolmens in both the New World and Europe as evidence of a Bronze Age Norse trade route, ca. 1700 BC. Without elaborating on the statement, Fell also mentions that one of the wall stones contains a faint Ogham inscription.[86]

In Vermont, where Fell sees European structures, Mavor and Dix see native ritual landscape architecture.[87] Mavor and Dix consider the Quitsa dolmen architecturally associated with stone rows with embrasures[88] and manitou stones, giving the structure an origin and function within a Native American geomantric sacred landscape.[89]

The question as to whether these four stones with a capstone were built by the Norse, Irish, early European explorers, colonial Vineyarders, or Native Americans may not be answered. But this lonely little structure remains a microcosm of the entire New England megalithic environment.

Oak Bluffs Runes, Martha's Vineyard, Massachusetts

A story occasionally crops up about a second Norse location on Martha's Vineyard. Most versions say that internationally renowned Norwegian violin virtuoso Ole Bull visited Martha's Vineyard. There he saw a Norse inscription on Lover's Rock at the bathing beach in the town now called Oak Bluffs.

It is a fallacious connection of unrelated facts. Bull was an ardent Norwegian nationalist when Norway was still Swedish territory. He visited New England's "Norse relicts," such as the Newport Tower and Dighton Rock, as a tourist and to raise awareness of Norse accomplishments. He was convinced that Norse visited New England and, as did most Norsophiles, believed Vineland was on Cape Cod or Martha's Vineyard. In 1876–1879, Bull wintered in Cambridge next door to his relative by marriage, Henry Wadsworth Longfellow. In the wake of his Norse-themed poems, Longfellow often received fan mail with additional Norse sites he could visit or use in his poetry. So, Bull had motive, opportunity, and knowledge to explore any runes he wished. Unfortunately, it's theoretical at best.

Bull had died in 1880, the year Cottage City became a town, named after the proliferation of cottages from the beach's use for Methodist revival meetings. The rock in question was already a landmark. Ole Bull's every movement was tracked in the papers, and a visit to such a feature would appear in the newspapers.

A massive glacial erratic boulder that submerged at high tide, it was such a popular spot to pitch woo beneath the stars, at least at low tide. It was known locally as Lover's Rock. By the time Cottage City was renamed Oak Bluffs in 1907, it was a tourist destination with a ramp down from a boardwalk. It had been painted and carved with initials for decades and appeared in town histories, newspaper articles, postcards, and on souvenirs. Yet, no source mentions Vikings, Norse runes, or Ole Bull at Lover's Rock until the *Martha's Vineyard Gazette* passingly mentions it in 1954 coverage of the rediscovery of the Nomans Land Rock.[90] In his 1961 book, Gale Huntington, the leading resident historian and folklorist of Martha's Vineyard, mentions a possible runic boulder that eroded into the ocean off Oak Bluffs, an apparent confusion with Nomans Island.[91]

In this case, with or without runic inscription, the 100-ton Lover's Rock was buried in 1973 when the town undertook erosion control by dumping more than 85,000 cubic yards of sand onto the beach along Seaview Avenue. The Army Corps of Engineers could determine no way to move the massive but beloved landmark. So, despite public outcry, it was buried. A (comparatively) small gray granite boulder marks its burial location. Still, it is unlikely Lover's Rock will ever see the light of day again.

Leifsbudir, Follins Pond, Yarmouth, Massachusetts

Two of the Icelandic sagas tell the story of the initial Norse discovery of North America: *Grænlendinga Saga* (The Saga of the Greenlanders) and *Eiríks Saga Rauda* (The Saga of Erik the Red). *Grænlendinga Saga*,[92] considered more reliable, has Leif Eriksson learning of a new land from the earlier voyage of Bjarni Herjólfsson, who had sighted it when driven off course by a storm on his way from Iceland to Greenland.[93]

Frederick J. Pohl, in reviewing the various theories, came across the work of Harvard botany professor M.L. Fernald. Fernald believed that the southern side of Cape Cod was Vinland, based on the flora and fauna as mentioned in the sagas.[94] A quote from Fernald resonated with Pohl: "the matter-of-fact accounts of the voyages are so direct and without embellishment as to indicate that in the main they are trustworthy historical documents."[95] The quote impressed Pohl to the point that it reappears in many of his books on the topic.[96]

Although Fernald was comparing saga references to botanical data in order to place Vinland, Pohl reasoned that it should also be possible to use the descriptions in the *Flateyjarbók* to retrace the path of the Norse and determine the location of Vinland. Using the sailing directions of Bjarni Herjólfsson that Leif later used as they were recorded in the *Graenlendinga saga*, Pohl studied the maritime charts. Based on his calculations,[97] Cape Cod was a likely location. However, Pohl ran into trouble immediately; the *Flateyjarbók* says that after Leif named Markland, he sailed for two days and came upon an island north of the land. As far as Pohl could tell, such an island did not exist on the East Coast.

Pohl found his answer in the excerpt of a letter from a Nantucket lighthouse keeper reprinted by Edward Rowe Snow, a legendary, although not necessarily always accurate, old Yankee storyteller.[98] Pohl learned from this text that the Great Point of Nantucket Island was cut off from the main island under certain extreme conditions, such as a northeaster or an unusually high tide.[99] Pohl theorized that Leif's crew, coming from the northeast, spotted Great Point during a separation from Nantucket. Nantucket extended beyond the horizon, and it could have been assumed to be part of the mainland.

Having found an island north of the land, it was easy to spot the next feature in the sagas: a "cape that went to the north" was Cape Cod.[100] Pohl then rapidly found the features he needed to match up to the saga. Leif sailed into a sound west of the cape and was grounded in the shallows at the mouth of the Bass River during low tide. Leif sailed up the Bass River when the tides refloated his ship, sailing into Follins Pond, where he decided to make winter camp. His crew built huts that the sagas call *Leifsbudir* or "Leif's Booths" and settled in for the winter, returning to Greenland the following year.

Pohl found he was not the first to suggest the Bass River as the site of Leif's winter camp. The Rev. Abner Morse found stone hearths near South Dennis along the Bass River, which he felt were atypical of Native American construction.[101] William Hovgaard, a professor of Naval Design at the Massachusetts Institute of Technology, was one of the earliest researchers to move beyond the usual tools of comparative geography and linguistics.[102] Adding botany and ethnology and the technical limitations of Norse shipbuilding, Hovgaard concluded that the difficulty in finding Vinland was not in the saga description but in the forced attempts to reconcile the different accounts. Hovgaard hypothesized two separate Vinlands, depending on which saga was being interpreted. Leif Eriksson's Vinland was on Nantucket Sound, and Thorfinn Karlsefni's Vinland was in Newfoundland.

Other researchers assumed that Cape Cod was the heart of Vinland simply because it fit neatly in with their own projects, such as Bowdoin College's A.S. Packard, who was less concerned with Vinland's location than with proving Bjarni Herjólfsson was the first European to sight Labrador.[103] Edward Gray may be remembered primarily for the Nomans Land Island inscription, but his theory also placed Vinland on Cape Cod.[104]

Pohl realized that saga descriptions alone would not prove his theory. He needed physical evidence. If this was Leif Eriksson's winter camp, there should be archaeological artifacts to verify the campsite. In 1947 he went to Follins Pond to look for proof. Borrowing a rowboat, he focused on the south side of the pond, where large boulders could be used for mooring the ship. As he approached, Pohl found a rock islet near the shore that was so small that it did not appear on U.S. Geologic Survey maps. Realizing the water was too shallow to moor the ship at the shore, the islet was the perfect location to secure the ship. Almost immediately, Pohl spotted a "neat, inconspicuous inch-wide hole on the shore side of the crest of the rock"[105]—a mooring hole. Subsequent searching located another boulder at the eastern end of the pond and a third mooring hole along the shore of the Bass River.[106] Based on the angle and the triangular shape of the holes, Pohl could differentiate between these chiseled holes and drilled quarrying holes. However, Pohl knew there was no way to corroborate the age of holes in rocks.

He spent 1947 and 1948 searching for additional evidence that he ultimately did not find,[107] but nonetheless published a short article on the mooring holes in *American-Scandinavian Review*.[108] The article was picked up by the *Saturday Evening*

Post,[109] whose article was condensed for *Reader's Digest*.[110] Suddenly, Follins Pond was in the public eye. For several years, it was a major tourist destination with divers in the pond, boat tours in the river, and treasure seekers wandering the shore.

In addition to attracting tourists, the articles caught the eye of the Massachusetts Archaeology Society. By the spring of 1952, Pohl and the society had arranged to excavate at Follins Pond. On May 10–11, fifty members of the society met on the south shore of the pond. Thirty-two of the members,[111] led by the society's director of excavations, Dr. Maurice Robbins, would excavate in a spot selected by Pohl—a gully perpendicular to the shore that Pohl believed to be the only place on the south shore where the Norse could have brought their ship ashore for the winter.[112]

The trees were cleared out of the gully, and the first test pit uncovered a wooden post, 2 inches in diameter and 2 feet in length. It stood on a stone base with stones on each side holding it vertical, exactly what would be needed for a keel bearing. It was the first of a number of vertical posts. Soon nine vertical posts running in a line down the gully were exposed. Also found were eight slightly angled stakes, four on each side of the central keel bearing line, which were positioned to support a ship on an even keel.[113] Using the stakes as benchmarks, the dimensions of the ship were calculated at 18 feet wide and 65 to 69 feet long, the dimensions of an oceangoing Norse knorr such as Leif would have used. The initial findings made international news with such staid media as the *New York Times* proclaiming Vikings had been located.[114]

The media support lasted barely 24 hours. The second day of excavations started with a celebrity visit, Roland Wells Robbins. Robbins entered the gully, looked at the excavation for three minutes, and pronounced that since the wood was above the water table, the site could not be more than 200 years old. He decided it was a hiding place for a ship during the American Revolution. He neglected to mention to the media that the trees removed had held so much water that the wood was water-soaked when found or that ditches had been dug earlier that day to drain the water from the trenches.

Robbins, a house painter by trade and amateur archaeologist, had found the remains of Thoreau's cabin at Walden Pond in 1945, marking the start of a controversial but high-profile career in archaeology. Most archaeologists at the time had moved past Robbins' "pick and shovel" methods, regarding "his methods as deplorable and Robbins himself as a poseur and showman."[115] Robbins' fame outweighed his credentials,[116] and the same journalists quickly reported on the demise of Pohl's Viking theory.[117]

Even the Massachusetts Archaeological Society, whose final report was inconclusive, quoted Robbins.[118] Pohl continued to research the site and publish his condemnation of Robbins' Revolutionary War–era claims. Although Pohl would plead his case in additional books[119] and journals,[120] the momentum had been lost.

Pohl was unable to radiocarbon date the wood.[121] The groundwater that preserved the wood also contaminated the wood by allowing C-14 lost by radioactive decay to be replaced by modern C-14, invalidating any results. However, he was able to calculate the weight-bearing capacity of the posts as consistent with a knorr, not an American ship.[122] He was able to find corroborating evidence in the saga chronicles of Thorfinn Karlsefni and Thorvald Eriksson.[123] The one thing he could not find was a way out of the shadow of Roland Wells Robbins' pronouncement.

Pohl may have become a victim of his own success at the site of Leifsbudir, lamenting that in 1948 he predicted that, right or wrong, the legend he started would increase land values. When he returned to Follins Pond four years later to supervise the Massachusetts Archaeological Society excavations, he found that a local house owner had taken the remarks seriously and bought up all available land on the south side of the pond for new housing. With 14 new houses on the land, any chance of finding evidence of Leif's shelters had been bulldozed into oblivion.[124] Since then, development has continued. Ironically, aside from all possible cellar holes being destroyed, a boathouse now sits in the gully that was once excavated for evidence that Leif wintered his boat in that spot. Pohl ended the 1957 account of his work on Cape Cod by challenging archaeologists to continue searching the area. The attention brought to the site by Pohl made that impossible. Pohl's prediction came true, as predictions often tragically do in sagas.

Forty years after the excavation and ten years after his death at the age of 102, Pohl's theory remained popular. South Yarmouth's Robert "Capt'n Bob" Littlefield still believes Bass River and Follins Pond were the correct location and credits Pohl. An amateur treasure hunter, Littlefield scoured the Bass River with an underwater metal detector, recovering a silver ring and a small brass object.[125] Littlefield felt the ring was sand-cast raw silver, making it potentially Norse. He believes the found brass item might be "the foot of a common hand-held Norse statue." Hopefully, this was a misquote by the newspaper, mistaking brass for bronze. Capt'n Bob, as an old Cape Codder, must have been aware that the Bass River is the largest tidal river on the eastern seaboard, and nothing corrodes brass as quickly as submersion in salt water. A bronze artifact from the Norse age might survive, but a brass fragment would have corroded in years, never mind centuries.[126]

Josef Berger, writing as Jeremiah Digges, released *Cape Cod Pilot*, a travelogue unlike most WPA-funded travel books. This was an anecdotal tour of Cape Cod, filled with local stories.[127] One such tale is how Yarmouth is the burial site of Thorvald Ericsson, off Center Street near Bass Hole Beach. Berger could find no proof for the claim, nor was any offered. Berger is not surprised. He notes that "a half-dozen towns along the eastern seaboard make a similar claim," including Hampton, New Hampshire (see Chapter Ten). He equates Thorvald's grave to the plethora of Fountains of Youth in Florida. A more accurate comparison might be made that Cape Cod is a microcosm of the Norse mania that had swept New England, just with better longevity.

Chapter Thirteen

The Norse of Narragansett Bay

The Sakonnet Stones, Aquidneck Island, Rhode Island

Edmund Burke Delabarre's 1928 book on Dighton Rock[1] is actually two distinct books. One section is a history of the Dighton Rock, and the other investigates the various carved stones of New England. Although he discusses sites across the region, his focus is Rhode Island. Delabarre assigned them either a modern origin or Indian pictograms.

And if carvings were identified as Norse, he was relentless in debunking the claim. He was particularly interested in inscribed rocks that attracted C.C. Rafn's attention as Norse evidence in his 1837 book *Antiquitates Americanæ*.[2] Rafn had gathered and translated the Icelandic sagas in one volume, with the text in Old Icelandic, Modern Danish, and Latin. And since he also believed Vinland was in New England, he mentioned petrographic evidence of "Norse carvings" as proof. One area along the Sakonnet River, a narrow saltwater passage in Narragansett Bay that separates Aquidneck Island from the Rhode Island mainland, was of particular interest. He used these locations to place Leifsbudir in the Tiverton area in Narragansett Bay and Hop in the Mount Hope areas near Bristol, Rhode Island. The inscriptions were line drawings sent by the Rhode Island Historical Society, which was more than happy to upstage Boston.

The Tiverton and Portsmouth Stones included rocks that had shifted or vanished along the shore. The ones they could find were severely eroded, but the historical society did what it could. Rafn took the renderings to runologist Finn Magnusen who identified runic characters but could not find actual words. So Rafn claimed the single runic symbols were monograms for Leif Ericsson, his servant Tyrker, and other crew members.

So many inscriptions in comparatively small areas as Tiverton, Portsmouth, and Mount Hope were an obvious target for Delabarre, who did what Rafn couldn't—he examined the carvings himself. Many of the stones were illegible, and the Portsmouth stones were completely missing. The ones he studied were obviously Native pictographs, not Norse runes. He declared that a Norse origin was "an extreme example of solemn silliness posing as serious science."[3]

Detail from Edmund B. Delabarre's photograph of Northmen's Rock on the western shore of Rhode Island's Mount Hope Bay. By the 1920s, it was surrounded by modern graffiti. Delabarre was undecided whether the canoe shape above the Indian letters was original (Edmund Burke Delabarre photograph from *Dighton Rock: A Study of the Written Rocks of New England* [1928]).

"Northmen's Rock," a massive piece of greywacke rock on the western shore of Mount Hope Bay, particularly intrigued Delabarre. When Delabarre was examining the Mount Hope inscription, there was a movement afoot in nearby Bristol by the "Rhode Island Citizen's Historical Society" to officially change the name of Northmen's Rock to "Leif's Rock" for tourism purposes.[4] Delabarre devoted an entire chapter of his 1928 book to the rock, how and when it obtained its Norse nomenclature, and the various researchers who copied the inscription.[5] The glyphs vary from transcription to transcription. Most have two lines. The first line is a chevron surrounded by smaller chevrons, suggesting a village. Next to it is a stylized boat. The bottom line is 7–9 runes. In comparing the transcriptions to the original, Delabarre's final conclusion is that it reads "Great Metacomet, Chief Sachem" in the Wampanoag dialect, written in Cherokee letters. Delabarre discovered that a party of Penobscot Indians visited the area sporadically from the 1830s to 1860. One of their visitors was a Massachusetts mariner, Thomas Mitchell, a half–Cherokee who had married into the Wampanoag. Delabarre thought the location added credence to the information. Metacomet, better known as King Philip, had been ambushed and killed near Mount Hope, effectively ending King Philip's War.

Twenty years later, Olaf Strandwold would also translate "Northmen's Rock" based on a Malcolm Pearson photograph.[6] Pearson's shot was recent, but some of the more recent graffiti has interfered with Pearson's attempt to chalk in the runes for the picture. Strandwold had so much difficulty with the translation that he decided it was written in retrograde. Reading it right to left, he came up with, "There is a house over on the clearing." He doesn't address the boat next to the runes.

As usual, Strandwold translated it in a vacuum. Although it is quite possible there was a clearing with a house on the heavily wooded Bristol Neck, Strandwold defended his retrograde translation by noting it was acceptable as it had also been done on the Vånga stone of Västergötland, Sweden. The flaw in this defense is that the Vånga stone was carved c. AD 500, which means it was written in Older Futhark runes, the oldest form of the runic alphabet, used from c. AD 200 to c. AD 750.[7] Unfortunately for Strandwold, the Norse exploration of North America began in the late 10th century. His questionable translation uses a runic script that was no longer in use and hadn't been for at least a century.

Not to be outdone, Barry Fell also worked strictly from Malcolm Pearson's photos. Fell focused on the canoe, which he argued was a "Tartessian high-stemmed vessel."[8] The inscription was translated as "'Voyagers from Tarshish This Stone Proclaims" in a script used in the Tartessos area on the southwest Iberian Peninsula. Fell couldn't accurately date the text but was comfortable with circa 700–600 BC. He added the inscribers were "probably not explorers but rather merchants trading with the New England Celts,"[9] neatly tying into his theory that New England was extensively visited by Celts from the Iberian Peninsula.

The stone face has been so heavily vandalized over the decades that a new translation is impossible. Considering the range of attempts and claims of origin already being bandied about, perhaps that's for the best.

The Narragansett Rune Stone, Wickford, Rhode Island

Pojac Point is a stretch of land formed by the southern shore of the Hunt River emptying into western Narragansett Bay. In December 1984, a local quahogger, the local term for someone digging for clams, noticed a boulder in nearby mud flats with a small series of carved letters. He notified the Rhode Island chapter of the New England Antiquities Research Association. In April 1985, a team went to investigate.[10]

The boulder was about 8 feet by 6 and weighed 2 tons. One surface contained two rows of characters, clearly visible. The top row consisted of eight characters, with a second row of two characters below it. The boulder was located roughly 60 feet offshore and was only visible during extreme low tide. This inaccessibility would prove more valuable than expected.

Photographs of the inscription were sent to O.G. Landsverk. Landsverk felt the carvings were indeed runes. He concluded that since he couldn't find a cryptographic date hidden in the inscription, it must be a modern creation.[11] NEARA's "inscriptions consultant," Donal Buchanan, observed that no runic alphabet contained all

Originally discovered in 1984 off Pojac Point in North Kingston, two rows of runic characters are clearly visible. The top row consisted of eight characters, with the second row of two characters below it (photograph by Malcolm Pearson, courtesy NEARA Archives).

the runes in one single alphabet. On the other hand, he felt that the characters were from one of the variant Pan-Mediterranean alphabets, possibly a North Italic version, with a strong Latin influence. In a comment that foreshadowed the future direction of research, Buchanan notes one of the runes was a hooked X, although "apparently identical in form to a controversial Runic character found on the Kensington Stone and the Spirit Pond Stones, it is not in this instance Runic."[12] His opinion was that it was a property marker written in a type of Latin. Since it was not runic, Buchanan agreed with Landsverk that it did not contain a runic cryptogram.

The announcement of the stone's discovery was immediately dampened by two of the staunchest advocates of rune stones in North America dismissing the rock for two different reasons. Not surprisingly, the stone gained minimal interest outside of pre–Columbian Norse theorists trying to translate the runes.

Paul Chapman also believed it was Norse runes, but for one of the very reasons Buchanan dismissed a Norse origin. Chapman didn't think that any runic alphabet uniformly adhered to in usage.[13] Chapman had earlier published a translation of the Spirit Pond Stones that was similarly dependent on a mixture of Danish and Icelandic runes.[14] His final translation of the Narragansett boulder, in Old Icelandic, was idiomatically "Beware of the bears."

Even septuagenarian Malcolm Pearson, now a revered elder statesman of New England diffusionism, visited the boulder in 1987, using his experienced eye to capture the runes in a photograph that is still widely used today.

Suzanne O. Carlson attempted a translation in 1991.[15] In an article that suggests the Narragansett Stone was already mostly forgotten, the self-admitted amateur runologist walked the readers through her process of deciding the rock read *skraumli[gr], a cognate for the Skraumá River in Iceland. Carlson suggests the carving may be a possible nod to the nearby Hunt River.

In 1993, the site began to attract public interest. It was briefly mentioned at the end of *New England's Ancient Mysteries,* one of Robert Ellis Cahill's booklets aimed at the tourist trade around Cape Ann, Massachusetts.[16] Cahill doesn't mention specifically where the boulder is but does offer another translation of the runes as "four victorious near the river." He doesn't identify the translator, but *New England's Ancient Mysteries* relied heavily on James Whittall's insight and files, the translation may be part of Whittall and the Early Sites Research Society's investigation. Cahill's booklet was enough to draw attention.[17] David Barron of the Gungywamp Society accompanied Whittall to the rock, resulting in a front-page article in the Gungywamp Society's *Stonewatch* newsletter.[18]

Ian Kirby, professor of medieval English at the University of Lausanne, heard of the runes in Narragansett Bay. He examined the runes in 1993 and was intrigued enough to return in 1999. While others looked at the runes and tried to translate them in isolation, Kirby approached the runes holistically. He began exploring the context and the provenance of the boulder. Among others, he interviewed James McMahon, a former property owner near the stone. McMahon recalled the inscription already in place when he bought the land in 1947, back when the boulder was on dry land. Kirby discovered that the beach, remote and adjacent to private land, was rarely visited by anyone besides the occasional quahogger. The local service station owner only learned of the carving after people started asking him for directions in the mid–1980s after the first NEARA articles appeared.

Kirby presented his findings at the International Association of University Professors of English symposium at the University of Munich in 2001. His paper would be published in *Beowulf and Beyond,*[19] the collected papers of a symposium primarily focused on Old and Middle English language and literature. Released in 2007, his findings were not widely distributed because of the specialized, academic nature of the book.

Nielsen and Wolter's book on the Kensington Rune Stone[20] had been released the year before, directing interest from Rhode Island back to Minnesota. Although the book doesn't specifically mention the Narragansett Rock, much of the book focused on the hooked X rune, which both authors believed was the key to identifying the Kensington carver. It would be one of the few things the two authors agreed on. Nielsen continued to methodically compare European records for the hooked rune. Wolter went in a more esoteric direction, his next book with his theory that the hooked X was a secret symbol. The hooked X rune also appears on the Narragansett Stone, which Wolter connected to a similar rune on the Spirit Pond stones.[21]

Nielsen countered Wolter's "hooked X = secret Templar symbol" claim with a cautionary article with the Epigraphic Society. He noted that both the Spirit Pond

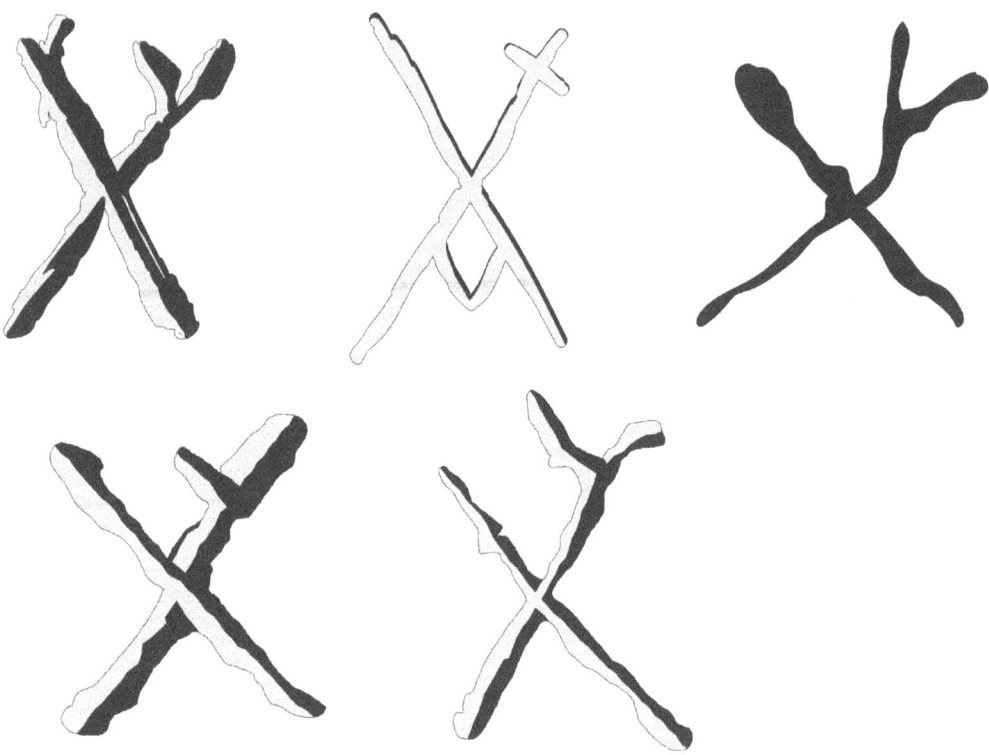

In comparing the hooked X on various stones, the American runes show similarity. Depending on your theory, this demonstrates a shared runic language or the use of a Hjalmar Holand chart to make hoaxes. The outlier is the pareidolic Westford scrape. *Top Row:* **Kensington Runestone (Minnesota), Rosslyn Chapel (Scotland), Westford Knight (Massachusetts).** *Bottom Row:* **Narragansett Stone (Rhode Island), Spirit Pond Inscription Stone (Maine)** (images scaled for comparison).

and Narragansett runes could have obtained their runes, including a hooked X, from modern-day books on the Kensington Rune Stone.[22] He lists several published sources that include a chart of the Kensington markings that could have been used as a guide to carve the runes. Nielsen's partial list assumes a window for the runes to be cut, dating after the discovery of the Kensington Runestone to before Spirit Pond discovery in 1971. His list of possible sources for runic alphabets included easily obtained titles such as those by Wahlgren (1958) and Pohl (1966).

Nielsen's logic was sound, but he had not seen Kirby's article with neighbors who recalled the inscription as far back as the 1940s. That date eliminates most of the books on Nielsen's list. This leaves one obvious choice, Hjalmar R. Holand. The prolific author and avid supporter of the Kensington Rune Stone had included a chart of the runes with his transliteration as early as 1919.

The Rhode Island Coastal Resources Management Council examined the rock and issued a report in 2012.[23] The report included shoreline changes over time at Pojac Point using orthophotography. A 1939 aerial photograph shows the approximate location of the boulder was 100 feet above the high tide line. The rock itself is not visible in earlier aerial photographs. This indicates it was buried in the sand until the erosion from the Great New England Hurricane of 1938 traveled straight up Narragansett Bay. Erosion from the storm exposed the rock. The hurricane damage also sped up beach erosion. The encroaching ocean ate at the shoreline, making the rock an intertidal landmark when the runes were discovered.

Assuming Kirby's witness is correct in his 1947 recollecting of the carving, the creation date is narrowed to after 1938 and before 1947. That suggests the carver's runic knowledge source was Holand's *Westward from Vinland* (1940). The book was Holand's first with a national publisher whose distribution made it more likely to be available in Rhode Island.

In July or August 2012, the Narragansett Stone disappeared. Since two-ton boulders do not vanish, the neighbors knew precisely what happened to the stone but could not prove it. A billionaire had bought two large parcels of land on the water's edge in 2008. This was just before Scott Wolter visited the stone for *Holy Grail in America*,[24] a two-hour documentary on The History Channel, undoubtedly bringing an increase in curiosity seekers.

The assumption was that the new neighbor had it removed because people were crossing his private beach to visit the runes. If privacy was his desire, he had made a significant miscalculation. As a new property owner from out of state, he mistakenly thought the rock belonged to him. Some states consider the property line to extend into the water. In Rhode Island, however, private property ends at the point of the median high tide.[25] The Narragansett Rune Stone, only visible at low tide, was obviously below the high tide mark. Therefore it fell under the jurisdiction of the Rhode Island Department of Environmental Management, which immediately launched an investigation jointly with the state Attorney General.

The stone's disappearance appeared to be on the verge of being forgotten when the theft received a new wave of media attention.[26] Scott Wolter now had a wildly popular television series looking at ancient sites. A March 2013 episode of *America Unearthed* aired[27] opens with Wolter at an airport as he prepared to leave for his next expedition. He received a phone call learning about the theft and raced into action.[28] The program was averaging 824,000 total viewers per episode. Suddenly the rock's theft was either a high-profile investigation or a national embarrassment.

Barely a month after the episode aired, the boulder was recovered. It had become a media circus and even more of an invasion of privacy. An anonymous informant had made contact with the investigators and offered to provide the location and assist with the return of the stone. The return of the rock was such a relief that the Rhode Island Attorney General and the Department of Environmental Management issued a joint press release to all state newspapers, heralding its return.[29]

Amy Kempe of the Attorney General's office was interviewed and asked why no charges had been filed. She skirted the issue by stating, "The state felt it was best to have the stone returned versus engaging in a potentially protracted legal battle with an unknown outcome."[30]

The Narragansett Stone today, in a protective gazebo in Wickford, Rhode Island (courtesy William C. Darmon).

The location was never disclosed, but Rhode Island had its rune stone back. Now, the state had no idea what to do with it. It was stored in a warehouse on the University of Rhode Island's Narragansett Bay campus for two years while state and town officials discussed its future. It was finally decided to keep it out of the water but near the bay. Since Pojac Point was part of the town of North Kingston, it would stay in town. The Wickford Economic Development Advisory Board successfully lobbied to have the stone placed in its small North Kingston village to augment revitalization of its downtown tourism.

Established in 1709, Wickford protects a remarkable collection of antiquities, including the largest collection of owner-occupied Colonial & Federal period homes in the nation, the oldest all-wooden lighthouse in America, and the oldest Anglican meeting house in the northeast. The stone was a good fit for the history-minded community.

On October 30, 2015, the rock was unveiled at its new home behind Old Library Park,[31] next to the Town Hall annex, on Brown Street. Adjacent to the town parking lot, the rune stone rests in a gazebo accompanied with interpretative signage. The signage is careful not to commit to an origin theory, but the display includes reference to NEARA and credits Scott Wolter for photography of the stone in the water, so there may be an inclination toward the original Norse tourists, if only for modern tourists following in their wake.

Chapter Notes

Introduction

1. Erik Wahlgren, "American Runes: from Kensington to Spirit Pond," *Journal of English and Germanic Philology* 81, 1982, p. 164.

2. Birgitta Linderoth Wallace, "Vikings in North America—New and Old," *Viking Heritage Magazine*, April 2003, p. 7. The New England grouping includes a subset in Oklahoma with a similar focus.

3. Salvatore Michael Trento, "A Bogus Inscription on Cape Cod, Massachusetts," *NEARA Journal* 14 (1), Summer 1979, p. 24.

4. Stuart J. Fleming, *Authenticity in Art: The Scientific Detection of Forgery* (London: Institute of Physics, 1975). The reference is in the foreword to the book by physicist Samuel A. Goudsmit.

Chapter One

1. A dolmen or chamber tomb is a burial chamber consisting of two or more upright stone slabs supporting a capstone. An altar stone is differentiated by the groove on the roof slab, suggesting a use other than in funerary rites. Only North Salem and Foxboro have been found on supports; both use smaller stones piled atop each other instead of the traditional large slabs set on edge.

2. Howe, "Good-by Columbus, says local archaeologist," *The Sunday Sun* [Lowell, MA], December 19, 1982.

3. James L. Swauger, "Petroglyphs, Tar Burner Rocks, and Lye Leaching Stones," *Pennsylvania Archaeologist* 51 (1–2), 1981, pp. 1–7.

4. For a pictorial essay on the process, see "Making Tar" in *Foxfire 4* (New York: Anchor Press, 1977).

5. James Burke, *Connections* (Boston: Little, Brown, 1978).

6. The smallest of these "sacrificial table" artifacts is the Leominster Table Stone, 6 feet × 5 feet.

7. Tilda Mims, "Turpentining: One of the South's Oldest Forest Industries," *Alabama's Treasured Forests* 18 (2), 1999, pp. 12–13.

8. Salem, NH, was founded in 1735, Leominster in 1740, and Foxboro in 1778. Pelham, MA, the origin of the Monroe slab and the most likely origin site of the Hadley stone, was founded in 1743. The Sturbridge and Foxboro stones have no provenance, so no origin is known.

9. North Carolina's governor Gabriel Johnston was particularly concerned by the depressed prices. In 1734 he wrote, "...there is more pitch and tarr made in the two Carolinas than in all the other provinces on the Continent and rather more in this than in South Carolina but their two Commodities (tarr especially) bear so low a price in London (1000 Barrels scarce clearing 20s sterling) that I find the Planters are generally resolved to make no more." Quoted in Elizabeth A. Fenn and Peter H. Wood, *The Way We Lived in North Carolina* (Chapel Hill: University of North Carolina Press, 2003).

10. Old Sturbridge Village in south central Massachusetts is the largest outdoor living history museum in the Northeast. The museum covers 20 acres with over 40 buildings that recreate an early 19th-century community.

11. Kent McCallum, *Old Sturbridge Village: A Visitor's Guide*, 2nd ed. (Sturbridge, MA: The Village, 1996).

12. Marietta Ellis, *Introduction to Soap Making* (Mount Rainier, MD: Volunteers in Technical Assistance, 1981).

13. Juliann Sivulka, *Stronger Than Dirt: A Cultural History of Advertising Personal Hygiene in America, 1875–1940* (Amherst, NY: Humanity Books, 2001).

14. Until the onset of Prohibition, the term *cider* meant almost exclusively "hard" cider, which ranged widely in alcohol content based on the quality of the apples, and the length and conditions of fermentation. Before fermentation, it was referred to as "sweet" cider.

15. Jonathan Pattee, the farmer who lived atop the Mystery Hill site, died of dysentery in 1849. On the farmstead were at least two stone-lined cisterns, neither capable of storing potable water.

16. Carole Shammas, "How Self-Sufficient Was Early America?" *Journal of Interdisciplinary Studies* 13 (2), 1982, pp. 247–72.

17. Shammas, p. 260.

18. *B. F. Clyde's Cider Mill, Established 1898, Old Mystic, Connecticut, National Mechanical Engineering Site Dedication, October 29, 1994* (Old Mystic, CT: American Society of Mechanical Engineers, 1994).

19. Dennis D. Picard, "A Short Note on Cider Making in 19th Century New England and the Lyford-Hutchins Mill" (Old Sturbridge Village, MA: Papers and Articles: OSV Research Paper, January 1905), Report No. 874.

20. The current viewing platform was built in 1975 as the alignments came to light. The height is estimated since all traces of the original structures are gone. William B. Goodwin, *The Ruins of Great Ireland in New England* (Boston: Meador Press, 1946), casually mentions removing two mounds of rock, rubble, and dirt while searching for the quarry site of the table.

21. David Goudsward and Robert Stone, *America's Stonehenge: The Mystery Hill Story* (Wellesley, MA: Branden Books, 2002), pp. 33–34.

22. See Goodwin (1946), pp. 7–13, for his rationale on Culdees as the colonists of his stone huts.

23. Goodwin (1946), pp. 95, 190.

24. Goodwin (1946), p. 343. Goodwin is adamant that these sacrificial rites would not have included human sacrifice.

25. Hugh Hencken, "The 'Irish Monastery' at North Salem, New Hampshire," *New England Quarterly*, 12:3 (September 1939).

26. Hencken, p. 431n3, "Information from Mr. Goodwin and from Mr. Douglas S. Byers, Director of the Department of Archaeology, Andover Academy."

27. Goodwin was actively involved with the Wadsworth Athenaeum in Hartford, CT, and was appointed to the honorary position of Curator of Colonial Arts for his work with the museum. He would buy colonial houses to strip of paneling and metalwork for the Athenaeum's collection. He saw colonial houses regularly, and had he even suspected the Sacrificial Table was a lye stone, he would have identified it as such.

28. Thomas G. Fessenden, editor, "Receipt for Cold Soap," *New England Farmer and Horticultural Journal, Containing Essays, Original and Selected, Relating to Agriculture and Domestic Economy; with Engravings, and the Prices of Country Produce* VIII (1829).

29. Edgar Gilbert, *History of Salem, N.H.* (Concord, NH: Rumford Printing, 1907).

30. Goudsward (2002), pp. 99–101.

31. Pascal A. Bright, "The Making of Tar in Hocking County," *Ohio Archaeological and Historical Quarterly* 41 (2), 1932, pp. 151–160.

32. Gary S. Vescelius, "Excavation at Pattee's Caves," *Eastern States Archeology Bulletin* 15, 1956, pp. 13–14.

33. Gary S. Vescelius, "North Salem, N.H., Site Excavations," 1955.

34. Optimal cider fermentation is at temperatures between 40° to 60° Fahrenheit. This low temperature leads to slower fermentation with a more robust taste and aroma.

35. Goodwin (1946), p. 95.

36. Goodwin (1946), p. 343.

37. Richard Pattee operated a tavern along the main road from Boston to Concord (now Route 28) on the Salem/Methuen, MA border and would have needed the additional cider production. This is not to infer cider from North Salem was being shipped to Richard's tavern on the far side of town.

38. Jonathan's grandfather, Seth Sr., lived on a 48-acre parcel he had purchased in 1734; this parcel included Goodwin's stone village. Seth built a house, a barn, and then a sawmill along the Spickett River on this property. The house and barn foundations still exist—the house is the Pattee cellar hole within the America's Stonehenge main site. The barn foundation is to the south side of a walking path leading to the winter solstice sunset stone. In 1765, the property was sold to Seth Sr.'s son Jerediah, who eventually sold it to his brother Seth Pattee, Jr., Jonathan Pattee's father.

39. Shammas, pp. 250–251.

40. Shammas' data is based on a theoretical nine-person colonial household in Pennsylvania. Between children and/or town paupers, nine people is also a reasonable estimate of the number of Pattee household members.

41. Gilbert, p. 417n616. There were also two additional cider mills in the center of North Salem, n543 and n545. Gilbert does not specify operation dates for the latter mills.

42. Lessard, Ryan. "Sacrificial stone at America's Stonehenge vandalized with power tool, cross left behind," *New Hampshire Union Leader*, October 2, 2019.

43. Feely, Paul. "NJ man accused of vandalism at America's Stonehenge," *New Hampshire Union Leader*, 3 March 2021.

44. Schreiber, Jason. "N.J. man indicted for Qanon defacement of America's Stonehenge in Salem," *New Hampshire Union Leader*, 20 April 2021. There have been some preliminary hearings, but as this book's publication, the case is still pending.

45. Benjamin Cole, "Mysterious Stone Finds New Home," *Sentinel and Enterprise*, 24 June 2002.

46. Mike Bassett, "Leominster Rock Ready to Roll," *Sentinel and Enterprise*, 6 February 2003.

47. Goodwin (1946), pp. 109, 200.

48. Goodwin (1946), p. 180.

49. Goodwin felt this rock was similar enough to Irish pictographs that he included a picture of an Irish stone for comparison. Goodwin (1946), pp. 59, 111–113. The stone's whereabouts are currently unknown.

50. Goodwin believed the monks utilized the Indian trails for both transportation and the location of the outposts. All of the outposts Goodwin identified in his book are located on or near a major Indian path.

51. J. R. Greene, *The Creation of Quabbin Reservoir: The Death of the Swift River Valley*, 2nd ed., 20th-anniversary ed. with a new introduction by the author (privately published, 2001).

52. In addition to the spalls or flakes, there has been more severe damage. Comparing the stone in 2004 to photographs taken in the 1960s, one corner shows impact damage, probably from a snowplow

clearing the nearby parking area shared by the museum and Hadley Town Hall. This has left that corner cracked and uneven. This exposed area will undoubtedly take additional weather-related damage, with or without snowplows.

53. The stone is not on public display.

54. R.W. Smith, "Memorandum No.16 Cider Mill" (Monroe, NY: Museum Village of Old Smith's Clove, 1960).

55. Greene, p. 83.

56. This stone slab is slightly larger than the Hadley Farm Museum stone, roughly 7 feet wide × 8½ feet long.

57. The Metropolitan District Water Supply Commission, created in 1926, was responsible for construction of the Quabbin Reservoir. By this point, most buildings in the valley had been dismantled and hauled away for the beginning of the flooding.

58. R.W. Smith, *correspondence*, 1953.

59. If standing on the slab, the "miller" would have insufficient leverage to screw the press downward without walking into the pooling cider, creating sanitary and safety issues. Postcard in the collection of The Museum Village at Old Smith's Clove, Monroe, NY.

60. Goodwin (1946), pp. 183, 216, 351–352, 410–412.

61. Robert Stone, the owner of the Mystery Hill site, points out that slabs of this size have been found at the North Salem site, propped up in this fashion. His research suggests that instead of an altar stone, it could just as easily be a quarry site with the slab being shaped for use elsewhere.

62. The author once had explained to him, in excruciating detail, how the table would be covered with a thin layer of mercury, which would channel the ley lines into a communications beam between the orbiting UFOs and the ones in the hollow earth.

63. Frank Glynn, *communication regarding Maltese sites*, 1967.

64. Evans, J. D., *The prehistoric antiquities of the Maltese Islands: a survey* (London: Athlone Press, University of London, 1971), p. 196.

65. Evans included details from archaeologist Napoleone Tagliaferro's initial report in the *Daily Malta Chronicle* (no date given, ca. 1909) that indicate the ground level under the table had been cut away to deepen the chamber.

66. Glynn died in 1968, but his parallels between Mystery Hill and Malta can be found in letters and manuscripts from as far back as 1955.

67. James P. Whittall II, *correspondence*, 1970.

68. The area west of the Quabbin is less developed than the eastern section of Massachusetts. As such, a number of items of note have survived. Shutesbury is less than 15 miles from the Hadley Farm Museum and less than 5 from Pelham, where the Monroe stone was originally found. In the woods between these communities are many small, stone-lined holes known locally as "Monks Holes."

69. Robert Stone, "The NEARA Symbol," *NEARA Newsletter* 2 (3), 1967, p. 36.

Chapter Two

1. Henry Wheaton, *History of the Northmen; or, Danes and Normans, From the Earliest Times to the Conquest of England by William of Normandy* (London: Murray, 1831).

2. Henry Wheaton, *Elements of International Law: with a Sketch of the History of the Science* (London: B. Fellowes, 1836).

3. Oscar J. Falnes, "New England Interest in Scandinavian Culture and the Norsemen," *New England Quarterly* 10 (2), 1937, pp. 211–242.

4. Carl Christian Rafn, *Antiquitates Americanæ sive scriptores septentrionales rerum antecolumbianarum in America* (Copenhagen: Hafniæ, typis officinæ Schultzianæ, 1837).

5. Charles Wingate Chase, *History of Haverhill, Massachusetts* (Haverhill, MA: George Wingate Chase, 1861).

6. J. M. Mancini, "Discovering Viking America," *Critical Inquiry* 28 (7), 2002.

7. Janet A. Headley, "Anne Whitney's Leif Eriksson: A Brahmin Response to Christopher Columbus," *American Art* 17 (2), 2003, pp. 40–59.

8. Robin Fleming, "Picturesque History and the Medieval in Nineteenth-Century America," *The American Historical Review* 100 (4), 1995, pp. 1061–1094.

9. Fleming, p. 1082.

10. Marie A. Shipley, *The Norse Colonization in America by the Light of the Vatican Finds* (Lucerne: H. Keller's Foreign Printing Office, 1899).

11. As one example, *American Monthly* ran an article on the discovery in January 1836. Author John Stark announced that the remains were similar to drawings of sculptures found in the Mayan city of Palenque in southern Mexico, proving that the skeleton had to be of a Phoenician.

12. See Leland's complete assessment in Hurd's *History of Bristol County, Massachusetts* (Philadelphia: J.W. Lewis, 1883).

13. John Brereton, *A Briefe and True Relation of the Discouerie of the North Part of Virginia Being a Most Pleasant, Fruitfull and Commodious Soile* (London: George Bishop, 1602), p. 11.

14. Gosnold brought so much sassafras back to England that he caused a glut on the market, lowering the price and infuriating Sir Walter Raleigh, the monopoly holder of the sassafras market.

15. Lawrence C. Wroth, *The Voyages of Giovanni da Verrazzano, 1524–1528* (New Haven: Published for the Pierpont Morgan Library by Yale University Press, 1970).

16. Wroth, p. 138.

17. William Martin Beauchamp, *Metallic Ornaments of the New York Indians* (Albany: University of the State of New York, 1903).

18. Andrew R. Hilen and Henry Wadsworth Longfellow, *Longfellow and Scandinavia: A Study of the Poet's Relationship with the Northern Languages and Literature* (New Haven: Yale University Press, 1947).

19. Henry Wadsworth Longfellow, "The

Skeleton in Armor," *Knickerbocker Magazine*, January 1841.

20. Henry Wadsworth Longfellow, *The Poetical Works of Longfellow: Cambridge edition* (Boston: Houghton Mifflin, 1975).

21. Rasmus Björn Anderson, *America Not Discovered by Columbus: A Historical Sketch of the Discovery of America by the Norsemen, in the Tenth Century* (Chicago: S.C. Griggs, 1874).

22. See a summary of his work in "Twentieth Report of the Curator," *Twentieth Annual Report of the Trustees of the Peabody Museum of American Archaeology and Ethnology III* (1887), pp. 535–570. The report was prompted by the museum's acquisition of several of the tinkling cones, returned from Copenhagen by naturalist Samuel Kneeland.

23. The metallurgical analysis was performed by no less than Jöns Jacob Berzelius, the Swedish chemist who developed modern chemical notation system and is considered one of the fathers of modern chemistry.

24. Helen B. Camp, *Archaeological Excavations at Pemaquid, Maine, 1965–1974* (Augusta: Maine State Museum, 1976).

25. Warren King Moorehead, *A Report on the Archæology of Maine; Being a Narrative of Explorations in that State, 1912–1920, Together with Work at Lake Champlain, 1917* (Andover, MA: Andover Press, 1922).

26. Ruth H. Whitehead, "The Protohistoric Period in the Maritime Provinces," *Prehistory of the Maritime Provinces: Past and Present Research*, edited by Michael Deal and Susan Blair (Fredericton, New Brunswick: Council of Maritime Premiers–Maritime Committee on Archaeological Cooperation, 1991), Vol. 8, pp. 227–258.

27. Rasmus Björn Anderson, "Book III. The Norsemen in America" in *The Norse Discovery of America; A Compilation in Extensó of All the Sagas, Manuscripts, and Inscriptive Memorials Relating to the Finding and Settlement of the New World in the Eleventh Century*, edited by James W. Buel (London: Norroena Society, 1906); Rasmus Björn Anderson and Albert O. Barton, *Life Story of Rasmus B. Anderson* ([s.n.], Madison, Wis., 1915).

28. Reeves, pp. 299–301.

29. Anderson (1915), pp. 190–191.

30. Henry Wadsworth Longfellow, *Tales of a Wayside Inn* (Boston: Ticknor and Fields, 1863).

31. Joseph and Sara Thorp were the children of Wisconsin state senator Joseph Thorp, lumber baron and supporter of Rasmus Anderson's Scandinavian Studies Department at the university.

32. Anderson (1915), p. 206.

33. Eleanor Tufts, "An American Victorian Dilemma, 1875: Should a Woman Be Allowed to sculpt a man?" *Art Journal* 51 (1), 1992, pp. 21–56.

34. Even if those legs were encased in granite trousers. The resulting furor raised Whitney's profile significantly in public awareness.

35. Although a highly respected and well-known sculptor at that time, John Quincy Adams Ward is best remembered in modern-day Boston for sculpting the *Good Samaritan* statue, a monument in Boston Gardens "to commemorate the discovery that the inhaling of ether causes insensibility to pain. First proved at the Mass. General Hospital in Boston."

36. Thomas Gold Appleton, correspondence December 13, 1878.

37. Thomas Gold Appleton, *Faded Leaves* (Boston: Printed for the author, Roberts Brothers, 1872).

38. Thomas J. Schlereth, "Columbia, Columbus, and Columbianism," *Journal of American History* 79 (3), 937–68 (1992).

39. "Monuments," *American Art Review* 1, 320 (1880).

40. Richard R. John, "Eben Norton Horsford, the Northmen, and the Founding of Massachusetts," *Essays in Cambridge History* 45 (Proceedings, 1980–1985), 116–44 (1998).

41. "Our Next Public Statue," *Evening Transcript*, January 17, 1887.

42. Elizabeth Rogers Paine, "Anne Whitney, Sculptor," *Art Quarterly* 25 (1962).

43. Horsford (1890), p. 6. Horsford quotes a report by a committee of the Massachusetts Historical Society that compares the sagas to Homeric poems as literature, not historical documents. See "Proceedings of the Massachusetts Historical Society" 18 (May 1880), pp. 79–81, for the full litany of arguments against the statue.

44. Anderson (1874).

45. Henry Cabot Lodge, Review of *America Not Discovered by Columbus...* by Rasmus Björn Anderson, *North American Review* 120 (1), 1875, pp. 194–6).

46. Thomas Gold Appleton, *correspondence* December 16, 1881.

47. Lewis I. Sharp and John Quincy Adams Ward, *John Quincy Adams Ward, Dean of American Sculpture: With a Catalogue Raisonné* (Newark: University of Delaware Press, 1985).

48. Eben Norton Horsford, *The Theory and Art of Bread-Making: A New Process Without the Use of Ferment* (Cambridge: Welch Bigelow and Company Printers, 1861); Eben Norton Horsford, *Report on Vienna Bread* (Washington, DC: Government Printing Office, 1875).

49. Previous forms of chemical leavening agents contained baking soda and cream of tartar, which were unreliable and inconsistent. Professor Horsford's Phosphatic Baking Powder replaced the cream of tartar with calcium biphosphate. The product is still available commercially as Rumford Baking Powder.

50. By this point, Ole Bull had arranged for the purchase of the Dighton Rock, which nearly ended up as part of the statue's display. See Chapter Three.

51. Eben Norton Horsford, "John Cabot's Landfall, Site of Norumbega," *Journal of the American Geographical Society of New York* 17, 1885, pp. 45–78.

52. Another poet who wrote of the Norse in

New England, John Greenleaf Whittier, wrote a dedicatory poem for the 1886 opening of Norumbega Hall at Wellesley College, named in honor of Horsford, who, in Whittier's words, was "one of the most munificent patrons of that noble institution."

53. Sharp, p. 198 and Paine, p. 254. Both sources list Whitney's fee as $11,000. A January 17, 1887, Boston *Evening Transcript* article lists the total cost for the statue and pedestal as $19,000, a significant drop from the original estimate of $40,000.

54. Rafn had suggested that etymological evidence of the Norse could be found among the place names of the Natives. Rafn used this same method to locate Vinland in Narragansett Bay.

55. Horsford does not offer an explanation why these explorers would choose to name a new land after Norway when they were from Iceland and Greenland, neither of which was under Norwegian control at the time.

56. Eben Norton Horsford, *Discovery of America by Northmen Address at the Unveiling of the Statue of Leif Eriksson, Delivered in Faneuil Hall, Oct. 29, 1887* (Boston: Houghton Mifflin, 1888).

57. Headley, p. 41.

58. Originally, Leif would have been gazing toward the Charles River, which Horsford believed to be the location of Vinland. The statue was repositioned when moved ca. 1919.

59. Tufts, p. 55.

60. The stern was removed during a 1919 repositioning.

61. Anderson (1906), p. 300.

62. Joseph T. Gilbert was the business partner of Joseph Thorp, Sr., who was the father of both Ole Bull's wife, Sara Thorp Bull, and Longfellow's son-in-law, Joseph Thorp, Jr.

63. Because of the less elaborate dedication ceremony, the Milwaukee statue was actually unveiled to the public several weeks before the one in Boston.

64. Whitney actually exhibited three pieces at the Exposition. In addition to the Leif Eriksson Statue, she also displayed a bust of Lucy Stone in the Women's Building and *Roma*, a bronze statue shown in the Fine Arts Palace.

65. Hubert Howe Bancroft, *The Book of the Fair; An Historical and Descriptive Presentation of the World's Science, Art, and Industry, as Viewed Through the Columbian Exposition at Chicago in 1893* (New York: Bounty Books, 1894).

66. Justin Winsor, *Narrative and Critical History of America* (Boston: Houghton Mifflin, 1884).

67. Winsor, Vol.1, p. 59.

68. Winsor, Vol.1, p. 98.

69. Eben Norton Horsford, *The Defences of Norumbega and a Review of the Reconnaissances of Col. T.W. Higginson, Professor Henry W. Haynes, Dr. Justin Winsor, Dr. Francis Parkman, and Rev. Dr. Edmund F. Slafter; A Letter to Judge Daly* (Boston: Houghton Mifflin, 1891a).

70. Eben Norton Horsford, *The Landfall of Leif Eriksson, A.D. 1000, and the Site of his Houses in Vineland* (Boston: Damrell and Upham, 1892); Eben Norton Horsford, *Sketch of the Norse Discovery of America, at the Festival of the Scandinavian Societies Assembled May 18, 1891, in Boston on the Occasion of Presenting a Testimonial to Eben Norton Horsford in Recognition of the Finding of the Landfall of Leif Eriksson, the Site of his Vineland Home, and of the Ancient Norse city of Norumbega, in Massachusetts, in the 43rd degree* ([Boston?, 1891b); Eben Norton Horsford and E.H. Clement, *The Discovery of the Ancient City of Norumbega. A communication to the president and council of the American Geographical Society at their special session in Watertown, November 21, 1889* (Boston: Houghton Mifflin, 1890).

71. Eben Norton Horsford, *The Problem of the Northmen. A letter to Judge Daly ... on the opinion of Justin Winsor, that "Though Scandinavians may have reached the shores of Labrador, the soil of the United States has not one vestige of their presence."* (Cambridge, MA: J. Wilson and Son, 1890).

72. Eben Norton Horsford and Cornelia Horsford, *Leif's House in Vineland* (Boston: Damrell and Upham, 1893).

73. Eben Norton Horsford, *The Indian Names of Boston, and Their Meaning* (Cambridge: J. Wilson and Son, 1886).

74. Richard Hakluyt, *The Principall Nauigations, Voiages, and Discoueries of the English Nation* (London: George Bishop and Ralph Newberie, 1589).

75. André Thevet, *La Cosmographie Universelle d'André Thevet, cosmographe du roy illustrée de diverses figures des choses plus remarquables veues par l'auteur, & incogneuës de noz anciens & modernes* (Paris: Chez Guillaume Chandiere, 1575).

76. Samuel Eliot Morison, *The European Discovery of America: The Northern Voyages, A.D. 500–1600* (New York: Oxford University Press, 1971).

77. Morison (1971), pp. 467–468.

78. Bert Salwen, "The Reliability of Andre Thevet's New England Material," *Ethnohistory* 10 (2), 183–5 (1963).

79. Salwen, p. 184.

80. B. F. DeCosta, "Translation: The Cosmography of the Fraudulent Thevet," *Magazine of American History* 8, 130–8 (1882).

81. B. F. DeCosta, *The Pre-Columbian Discovery of America by the Northmen: Illustrated by Translations from the Icelandic Sagas* (J. Munsell, 1868).

82. B. F. DeCosta, *Ancient Norombega, or The voyages of Simon Ferdinando and John Walker to the Penobscot River. 1579-1580. Revised from the N.E. Historical and Genealogical Register, April, 1890* (Albany: J. Munsell's Sons (Boston: Printed by D. Clapp & Son, 1890).

83. DeCosta (1890), p. 5.

84. Horsford (1891a), pp. 27–34.

85. Horsford uses the term "mösurr wood" to be identical to "masur wood," which was used to create communion vessels. From it is derived the mazer, a flat round drinking bowl. According to Horsford's theory, the burls that grow on the sides of maple trees were a valued commodity because

of the ease with which they could be worked into the mazers.

86. After several moves during road widening, the plaque is now located at Memorial Drive and Gerry's Landing Road in Cambridge. The tablet reads, "On this spot in the year 1000 Leif Eriksson built his house in Vineland."

87. The bridge has since been replaced by the Galen Street Bridge. The tablet reads, "Outlook upon the Stone Dam and Stone-walled Docks and Wharves of Norumbega, the Seaport of the Norsemen in Vineland. Erected by Eben Norton Horsford, December 31, 1892."

88. Henry W. Haynes, "Progress of American Archaeology During the Past Ten Years," *American Journal of Archaeology* 14 (1), 1900.

89. Horsford's 1890 book refuting Winsor was addressed to New York State Supreme Court Chief Justice Charles Daly, president of the American Geographical Society.

90. John, p. 129. John points out that Winsor's antagonism was understandable. In addition to being a direct descendant of Pilgrims, he was the author of a Columbus biography. Additionally, Winsor was corresponding secretary of the Massachusetts Historical Society and an officer at Harvard University, two organizations that perceived themselves as "the Puritans' principal intellectual conservator."

91. Edwin M. Bacon, *Walks and Rides in the Country Round about Boston; Covering Thirty-Six Cities and Towns, Parks and Public Reservations, Within a Radius of Twelve Miles from the State House* (Boston: Published for the Appalachian Mountain Club by Houghton Mifflin, 1898); Elizabeth G. Shepard, *A Guide-book to Norumbega and Vineland; or, The Archeological Treasures along Charles River* (Boston: Damrell and Upham, 1893).

92. There was also another local landmark named Norumbega Park, located directly across the river in the Auburndale section of Newton, MA. This trolley park was a 27-acre wooded area with a small zoo, canoeing facilities, an amphitheater, and a locally renowned ballroom. The privately owned park opened in 1897, eight years after Horsford's tower was erected. The park closed in 1963 after years of decline. Half the park property is now the site of a large hotel, and the remaining part is owned by the city of Newton under the name of the Norumbega Park Conservation Land.

93. Gerard Fowke, "Points of Difference between Norse Remains and Indian Works Most Closely Resembling Them," *American Anthropologist* New Series, 2 (3), 550–62 (1900).

94. Fowke, p. 562.

95. Brian Regal, "Cornelia Horsford and the Adventures of Leif Erikson: Viking Settlements in the Bay State," *Historical Journal of Massachusetts* 48 (2), Summer 2020, p. 53.

96. Cornelia Horsford, *An Inscribed Stone* (Cambridge: J. Wilson and Son, 1895), pp. 9–10.

97. Horsford (1895), pp. 10–11.

98. "The Vikings in New York," *New York Herald*, August 4, 1895.

99. Horsford (1895), p. 10.

100. Horsford (1895), p. 14.

101. By 1895, Chenoweth had started his own engineering business and may have felt the Inwood Stone overshadowed his engineering accomplishments, such as designing the foundation for the Statue of Liberty and serving as the engineer in charge of the Croton aqueduct.

102. Cornelia Horsford, *Graves of the Northmen* (Boston: Damrell and Upham, 1893); Cornelia Horsford, *Dwellings of the Saga-time in Iceland, Greenland, and Vineland* (Washington, DC: Judd & Detweiler Printers, 1898); Cornelia Horsford, *Vinland and Its Ruins. Some of the Evidence that Northmen Were in Massachusetts in Pre-Columbian Days* (New York: Appleton, 1899).

103. Cornelia Horsford, "Dwellings of the Saga-time in Iceland, Greenland, and Vineland," *National Geographic* 9 (3) (1898).

104. Cornelia Horsford, "Vinland and Its Ruins," *Popular Science Monthly*, 12 (December 1899).

105. Regal, p. 55.

106. Juul Dieserud, "Norse Discoveries in America," *Bulletin of the American Geographical Society* 33 (1), 1–18 (1901).

107. In 2006, Sylvester Manor became the 243-acre historic plantation and nonprofit Sylvester Manor Educational Farm.

Chapter Three

1. Charles C. Willoughby, Review of *Dighton Rock*, by Edmund Burke Delabarre, *American Anthropologist* 31 (3), 1929, pp. 518–21.

2. Considered one of the major British empiricists of the time, Berkeley developed a school of philosophy known as immaterialism, which simply states that matter does not exist—physical objects are composed solely of ideas.

3. Berkeley sent the new town a gift of a church organ. Insisting their Puritanical roots disallowed music in the church service, the town refused the gift. The organ was given to Trinity Church in Newport, where Berkeley had preached during his stay. The original organ facade remains in the church to this day, with the rest of the parts of Berkeley's gift now in the Museum of Newport History.

4. D. Hamilton Hurd, *History of Bristol County, Massachusetts with Biographical Sketches of Many of Its Pioneers and Prominent Men* (Philadelphia: J.W. Lewis, 1883).

5. Edmund Burke Delabarre, *Dighton Rock: A Study of the Written Rocks of New England* (New York: Walter Neale, 1928).

6. Edmund Burke Delabarre, "A Possible Pre-Algonkian Culture in Southeastern Massachusetts," *American Anthropologist* 27 (3), 1925, pp. 359–69; Edmund Burke Delabarre, "A Prehistoric Skeleton from Grassy Island," *American Anthropologist* 30 (3), 1928, pp. 476–80.

7. Cotton Mather, *The wonderful works of God commemorated. Praises bespoke for the God in heaven in a thanksgiving sermon; delivered on Decemb. 19. 1689. Containing just reflections upon the excellent things done by the great God, more generally in creation and redemption, and in the government of the world; but more particularly in the remarkable revolutions of providence which are every where the matter of present observation. With a postscript giving an account of some very stupendous accidents, which have lately happened in France. / By Cotton Mather. ; To which is added a sermon preached unto the convention of the Massachusetts-Colony in New-England, with a short narrative of several prodigies, which New-England hath of late had the alarms of heaven in* (Boston: S. Green, 1690).

8. Over the subsequent centuries, there were questions about the identity, if not the existence, of John Danforth. Because of his role in the early history of Dighton Rock, Delabarre (1928) devotes several pages (pp. 29–36) to confirming who Danforth actually was.

9. Cotton Mather, "An Extract of Several Letters from Cotton Mather, D.D. to John Woodward, M.D. and Richard Waller, esq," *Philosophical Transactions of the Royal Society of London* 29, 1714, pp. 62–79.

10. Delabarre (1928), pp. 50–54, notes at least four trips while Stiles was in Newport. His observations and drawings are part of Stiles' travel notes known as the "Itineraries," housed at Beinecke Library.

11. Sewall, a professor of Hebrew and Oriental Languages at Harvard, had made a life-size drawing of the rock in 1768, a reduced copy of which was sent to Court de Gébelin. Sewall himself actually thought the rock was Indian. Delabarre (1928), pp. 55–56.

12. Antoine Court de Gébelin, *Monde Primitif, Analysé et Comparé avec Le Monde Moderne* (Paris: Chez l'auteur, 1781).

13. Court de Gébelin is primarily remembered for an essay in *Monde Primitif* suggesting an ancient Egyptian origin for tarot cards, giving rise to a school of esotericism based on the cards beyond that of their association with divination.

14. Ezra Stiles, *The United States Elevated to Glory and Honor: a sermon preached before His Excellency Jonathan Trumbull, Esq. L.L.D., Governor and Commander in Chief, and the Honorable the General Assembly of the State of Connecticut, Convened at Hartford, at the Anniversary Election, May 8th, 1783* (Printed by Thomas & Samuel Green, New-Haven, 1783).

15. Michael Lort, "Account of an Antient Inscription in North America," *Archaeologia* 8, 1787, pp. 290–301.

16. Stiles believed in a literal interpretation of the Bible, including the Great Flood and the earth's subsequent repopulation by the descendants of Noah: Japheth, Shem, and Ham. Japheth and Shem were blessed; Japheth's territories would enlarge, and they would dwell in the house of Shem (Shem being the ancestor of Abraham, David, and Jesus). Ham, through his son Canaan, was cursed to be the servant of Japheth and Shem. The Canaanites spent a great deal of the Old Testament being conquered and/or dispersed.

17. Lort, pp. 290–291 footnote.

18. In Electronic Irish Records (ed. Stewart, B.) (Princess Grace Irish Library, Monaco, 2001). PGIL-EIRData also notes that the controversial Vallancey never actually learned Irish, for all his published work on the topic.

19. Philip Johan von Strahlenberg, *An Historico-Geographical Description of the North and Eastern Parts of Europe and Asia: But More Particularly of Russia, Siberia, and Great Tartary; Both in their Ancient and Modern State: Together with an Entire New Polyglot-Table of the Dialects of 32 Tartarian Nations and a Vocabulary of the Kalmuck-Mungalian tongue* (London: Printed for J. Brotherton, J. Hazard, W. Meadows, T. Cox, T. Astley, S. Austen, L. Gilliver and C. Corbet, 1738).

20. Charles Vallancey, "Observations on the American Inscription," *Archaeologia* 8, 1787, pp. 302–6.

21. John Finch developed one of the earliest cataloged collections of North American fossils, donating it to the Academy of Natural Sciences of Philadelphia.

22. John Finch, "On the Celtic Antiquities of America," *American Journal of Science and Arts* VII, 1824, pp. 149–61.

23. Edward Augustus Kendall, *Travels Through the Northern Parts of the United States, in the Years 1807 and 1808* (New York: Printed and published by I. Riley, 1809).

24. Kendall's reference predates the creation of Ingraham's Captain Kyd, so it is not a reference to the fictional pirate character. Kyd is an early variant spelling of Kidd in genealogical records, so despite the spelling, this is probably a reference to William Kidd.

25. Kendall (vol. 2), p. 221.

26. Kendall (vol. 2), pp. 223–224.

27. Charles M. Skinner, *Myths and Legends of Our Own Land* (Philadelphia: J.B. Lippincott, 1896).

28. Delabarre (1928), p. 141. Delabarre cites an 1850 Taunton newspaper that the treasure seekers were such a nuisance to the property owner that he threatened to "blow the rock up."

29. See Taylor's "The Early Republic's Supernatural Economy: Treasure Seeking in the American Northeast, 1780–1830." *American Quarterly* 38, 1986, pp. 6–34. Taylor notes that pirate gold protected by supernatural forces was a widespread motif in the region's folklore. He hypothesized that treasure hunters were not so much motivated by greed as reacting sociologically to the shift toward the Industrial Revolution.

30. Delabarre (1928), pp. 74–76, 330.

31. Delabarre (1928), pp. 76–83, 336.

32. Carl Christian Rafn, *Antiquitates*

Americanæ sive scriptores septentrionales rerum ante-columbianarum in America (Hafniæ, typis officinæ Schultzianæ, Copenhagen, 1837).

33. North Ludlow Beamish, *The Discovery of America by the Northmen in the Tenth Century With Notices of the Early Settlements of the Irish in the Western Hemisphere* (London: T. and W. Boone, 1841).

34. And probably a little concerned for the stone's safety after the 1850 Taunton newspaper article that had the owner planning to demolish the rock to discourage treasure hunters.

35. Delabarre (1828), pp. 27, 99.

36. The short-lived (1852–1853) experiment's original settlements are now part of Ole Bull State Park in Potter County, Pennsylvania.

37. Delabarre (1928), pp. 99–100.

38. Delabarre (1928), p. 27. Delabarre also dryly notes that the club had immediately started plans to move the rock to Boston to rest near their statue.

39. "The Dighton Rock Puzzle," *New York Times*, January 6, 1890.

40. John Lathrop, "John Lathrop, D.D., to Judge Davis" in *Proceedings of the Massachusetts Historical Society 1867–1869* (Boston: Massachusetts Historical Society, 1868), Vol. X, pp. 114–116.

41. Henry Rowe Schoolcraft, *Historical and Statistical Information Respecting the History, Condition and Prospects of the Indian Tribes of the United States* (Philadelphia: J.B. Lippincott, 1854).

42. Schoolcraft mentions that the translation work was done off a copy of the markings while he was on Michilimackinac Island in Michigan, now known as Mackinac Island. This means the translation was done by a member of the Ojibwe Nation. Although the Wampanoag and Ojibwe languages are Algonquin, they are separate dialects—how accurate his interpretation is can be debated.

43. Garrick Mallery, *Picture-writing of the American Indians* (New York: Dover Publications, 1972).

44. Garrick Mallery, "Dangers of Symbolic Interpretation [abstract]," *Transactions of the Anthropological Society of Washington* 1, 1882, pp. 70–79.

45. Mallery (1972), pp. 86–87.

46. Delabarre was a general experimental psychologist who founded the laboratory at Brown University in 1892. He also was one of the founders of the American Psychological Association and served as director of Harvard's psychological lab.

47. Edmund Burke Delabarre, "Early Interest in Dighton Rock," *The Publications of the Colonial Society of Massachusetts* XVIII (1916); Edmund Burke Delabarre, "Middle Period of Dighton Rock History," *The Publications of the Colonial Society of Massachusetts* XIX (1917); Edmund Burke Delabarre, "Recent History of Dighton Rock," *The Publications of the Colonial Society of Massachusetts* XX (1919).

48. Edmund Burke Delabarre, "A Petroglyphic Study of Human Motives," *Scientific Monthly* 41 (5), 1935, pp. 421–9.

49. Delabarre (1928), pp. 167–174.

50. Delabarre (1928), p. 174.

51. George Patterson, "The Portuguese on the North East Coast of America," *Proceedings and Transactions of the Royal Society of Canada for the Year 1890*, 1891, p. 164.

52. Louisbourg Institute Archaeology Artifact Database, Provenience Record Number 1B6A13.1 The information itself may be incorrect, but the reference does suggest the mindset of the cataloguers at the time the cannon was acquisitioned.

53. Champlain, Samuel de, et al. *The Works of Samuel de Champlain* (Champlain Society, Toronto, 1922), Volume 1, pp. 234–236.

54. Robert Grant Haliburton, *A Search in British North America for Lost Colonies of Northmen and Portuguese.* (Royal Geographic Society Proceedings 7 (1), January 1885.

55. The Danforth drawing of the inscriptions was sent to England by Isaac Greenwood ca. 1730, along with a brief description of the carving that includes a passing mention of the tradition.

56. Kendall (vol. 2), p. 230.

57. The Center of Acadian Studies at the University of Moncton in New Brunswick, Canada, has an alternative demise for the brothers Corte Real. They record an oral legend of a phantom ship with sails on fire that is sighted off Heron Island on New Brunswick's northern coast when a storm is about to hit the area. It is Miguel Corte Real's ship, which caught fire during a battle with the local natives. Apparently, Miguel stumbled across a tribe who had previously captured and tortured Gaspar in revenge for his abducting the tribal leaders and bringing them to Portugal as slaves. http://collections.ic.gc.ca/vaisseaufantome/

58. Delabarre (1928), pp. 76–78.

59. Olaf Strandwold, *Norse Runic Inscriptions Along the Atlantic Seaboard* (Prosser, WA: published by the author, 1939).

60. William H. Babcock, *Early Norse Visits to North America* (Smithsonian Institute, Washington, DC, 1913).

61. Olaf Strandwold, *Norse Inscriptions on American Stones* (Weehauken, NJ: Magnus Björndal, 1948).

62. Strandwold, for comparison, includes an engraving of the Nybble Stone that he credits as being copied from George Stephens' *Handbook of the Old-Northern Runic Monuments of Scandinavia and England.* Stephens had, in turn, copied it from *The Bautil*, a 1750 collection of runestone images by Swedish national antiquarian, Johan Göransson.

63. Delabarre died on March 16, 1945. In his will, he left a small parcel of land near Dighton Rock to the Old Colony Historical Society of Taunton.

64. See Chapter Four.

65. Herbert C. Pell, "The Old Stone Mill, Newport," *Rhode Island History* 7 (4), 1948, pp. 105–19.

66. Various sources confirm this refusal without elaboration as to why. The current thought is that

Manuel was attempting to keep at least one male heir of the Corte Real bloodline safe and sound.

67. Joseph Dâmaso Fragoso, "O Emblema da Ordem de Cristo Gravado na Pedra de Dighton," *Mundo Lusíada*, 1 (8), 1951, pp. 207–208.

68. There had been a Dighton Rock Park established in 1896 on the Dighton side of the Taunton River, owned by the local streetcar company (with direct trolley service from Fall River, Taunton, and Dighton). This park was a Victorian diversion, with excursion boats, a ballroom, amusements, clambakes, and vaudeville shows. It finally burned to the ground in 1921 after several years of decline. The former park grounds are now residential housing. See Lane's *History of the town of Dighton, Massachusetts* (Dighton, MA: Town of Dighton, 1962).

69. Old Colony Historical Society transferred ownership of the Dighton Rock to the Commonwealth of Massachusetts at the same time.

70. At one point, Fragoso compared his ordeal to the suffering of Christian martyrs. It was not his most controversial comment. See Fragoso, *A Historical Report of Twenty-eight Years of Patriotic and Dramatic Efforts to Save Dighton Rock* (New Bedford, MA: published by the author, 1954). His "editorial comments" antagonized and insulted just about every participant in plans to save the Dighton Rock in the previous 20 years.

71. "Quo Warranto?" *Boston Globe*, April 19, 1956.

72. Fingold was running for governor at the time. If the Dighton Rock was damaged, the resulting scandal would eliminate his chances to win, particularly in the Fall River area, which had been monitoring the situation closely. Fingold died of a heart attack right before the 1958 Democratic primary, which he was expected to win easily.

73. Manuel Luciano da Silva, *Portuguese Pilgrims and Dighton Rock: The First Chapter in American History* (Bristol, RI: published by the author, 1971).

74. As further proof, in 1983, the Massachusetts legislature declared Dighton Rock the official state "Explorer Rock." That same year, covering all bases, the official state "Historical Rock" was designated in Plymouth.

75. Edward J. Lenik, *Picture Rocks: American Indian Rock Art in the Northeast Woodlands* (Hanover, NH: University Press of New England, 2002).

76. Lenik (2002), pp. 131–134.

77. da Silva, p. 58.

78. da Silva, pp. 59–63.

79. Rev. Timothy J. Goldrick, "Cross of Christ Placed Atop Oldest Diocesan Church," *Standard-Times*, January 01, 2005.

Chapter Four

1. Locally, the structure was/is referred to as "The Old Stone Mill" or some similar variation. For consistency, this chapter will refer to the structure generically as a tower.

2. Before Touro Park's creation, the property was privately owned. Judah Touro's will, executed in 1854, left the funds to the city of Newport, specifically to purchase of the Old Stone Mill.

3. Morton's record of the history of the Plymouth colony was published in 1669. Easton wrote his notes in the margins on pp. 94–95. The book is now in the collection of the Redwood Library and Athenæum of Newport, RI.

4. The quotes from Easton are reproduced on p. 166 of Means, Phillip Ainsworth, *Newport Tower* (New York: Henry Holt, 1942).

5. Nearby Touro Synagogue, dedicated in 1762, is the oldest synagogue in the United States and a National Historic Site. Judah Touro's father Isaac was the first Hazan at the temple, which was named after an 1854 bequest from Judah.

6. Charles Timothy Brooks, *The Controversy Touching the Old Stone Mill, in the Town of Newport, Rhode-Island. With Remarks, Introductory and Conclusive* (Newport: C.E. Hammett Jr., 1851).

7. Governor Arnold (ca. 1615–1678) should not be confused with the infamous Revolutionary War figure of the same name. Governor Benedict Arnold was the second great grandfather of Major General Benedict Arnold.

8. Esq. Hubbard, Edwin, "Early Records of the Arnold Family," *New England Historical and Genealogical Register* 33 (3), 429 (1879).

9. The will has been reproduced in several publications, including Brooks (pp. 73–84).

10. Brooks, pp. 85–88.

11. Means (1942), pp. 21–22.

12. Means (1942), pp. 21–22.

13. William C. Gibbs, a native of Newport, was governor from 1821 to 1824.

14. Benson John Lossing, *The Pictorial Fieldbook of the Revolution; or, Illustrations, by Pen and Pencil, of the History, Biography, Scenery, Relics, and Traditions of the War for Independence* (New York: Harper & Brothers, 1855).

15. Reprint of a *Boston Journal* article in the Lake Shore Observer (Dunkirk, NY, December 21, 1885).

16. J.S., "Antiquities of North America," *American Monthly*, January 1836.

17. Carl Christian Rafn, *Antiqvitates Americanæ; Sive, Scriptores Septentrionales Rerum Ante-Columbianarum in America* (typis officinæ Schultzianæ, Hafniæ, 1837).

18. Carl Christian Rafn, Thomas H. Webb, John M'Caul, et al., *Supplement to the Antiquitates Americanæ* (At the secretary's office of the Society, Copenhagen, 1841).

19. Means (1942) discusses the correspondence in his book, most notably pp. 50–56. Webb later revised his opinion on the tower's origins, which appears to have irritated Means to no end.

20. Henry Wadsworth Longfellow, "The Skeleton in Armor," *Knickerbocker Magazine*, January 1841.

21. Brooks, pp. 44–51.

22. Means (1942) devotes over ten pages to the debate, pp. 64–75.

23. John Gorham Palfrey and Francis Winthrop Palfrey, *History of New England* (Boston: Little Brown, 1858).

24. Palfrey (vol. 1), pp. 53–57.

25. Palfrey (vol. 1), pp. 57–59.

26. James Fenimore Cooper, *Red Rover*, Mohawk ed. (New York: Putnam's, 1850).

27. An August 9, 1876 article in the *New York Times* complained that the Norse origin of "that ugly edifice" was a fraud perpetrated by the tourist industry in Newport, concocted 30 years before as a countermeasure to the tourism generated by sea serpent sightings off the coast of Cape Ann, Massachusetts. And that subsequent "discoveries" at the tower were solely to perpetuate the tourism boom.

28. Post mills had a wooden body that housed milling equipment and the sail. The body rested across a central vertical post. The entire structure was rotated into the wind by pivoting on the vertical post.

29. F. J. Allen, "The Ruined Mill, or Round Church of the Norsemen, at Newport, Rhode Island, U.S.A., Compared with the Round Church at Cambridge and Others in Europe," *Proceedings of the Cambridge Antiquarian Society, with Communications Made to the Society* Vol. XXII, 1921, pp. 90–107.

30. Means (1942), pp. 184–187.

31. Elisha Stephen Arnold, *The Arnold Memorial* (Rutland, VT: Tuttle, 1935).

32. Hjalmar Rued Holand, *Westward from Vinland: An Account of Norse Discoveries and Explorations in America, 982–1362* (New York: Duell Sloan & Pearce, 1940).

33. Philip Ainsworth Means, "The Mysterious Runic Stone," *New York Times*, May 26, 1940.

34. Hjalmar Rued Holand, *America, 1355–1364: A New Chapter in Pre-Columbian History* (New York: Duell Sloan and Pearce, 1946).

35. Means (1942), pp. 265–267, 283.

36. A double-splayed window is a type of window where the opening is positioned in the center of the wall thickness with the surrounding wall cut away. Small splayed windows are found in buildings expecting use as a defensive stronghold, such as castles, towers, and signal towers.

37. Allen, pp. 104–105.

38. Count Morozzo, *Repertory of Arts and Manufacturers* 2 (1795), pp. 416–432. Referred to in K.N. Palmer, *Dust Explosion and Fires* (1973), pp. 7–8, as cited in *Prevention of Grain Elevator and Mill Explosions* (National Materials Advisory Board, Washington, D.C., 1982), p. V.

39. Means (1942), p. 284.

40. F. Stokhuyzen, *The Dutch Windmill* (New York: Universe Books, 1963).

41. Stokhuyzen, pp. 46–48.

42. Edward Adams Richardson, "Builder of the Newport Tower," *American Society of Civil Engineers Transactions* 86 (Paper no. 3091), 73–95 (1960).

43. Richardson, pp. 12–13.

44. Suzanne Carlson, "Loose Threads in a Tapestry of Stone: The Architecture of the Newport Tower," *NEARA Journal* 35 (1), 2001.

45. Rock of Cashel is a group of medieval buildings set on an outcrop of limestone in County Tipperary, Ireland. Formerly the seat of the Kings of Munster, it was visited by St. Patrick in 450 AD, and Brian Boru was crowned King of Ireland here in the 10th century. The extant buildings include a round tower, a 13th-century Gothic cathedral, a 15th-century castle, and Cormac's Chapel, built in 1127 as a small cruciform-shaped chapel to house the body of King Cormac.

46. Means (1942), p. 286.

47. Means (1942), pp. 298–302.

48. "Philip A. Means, 52, Inca Lore Expert," *New York Times*, November 25, 1944, p. 13.

49. Philip Ainsworth Means, Alice Dalgliesh, *Tupak of the Incas* (New York: Scribner, 1942).

50. Both archaeologists were also involved in excavations at the America's Stonehenge site. Hencken, in 1939, disputed Goodwin's ninth-century Irish monastery theory. Bird, in 1945, questioned Hencken's results and, in 1955, arranged for graduate student Gary Vescelius to excavate at the site. See Chapter Five.

51. William Simpson Godfrey, *Digging a Tower and Laying a Ghost: The Archaeology and Controversial History of the Newport Tower* (Cambridge, MA: Harvard University, 1951).

52. Johs Hertz, "Round Church or Windmill? New Light on the Newport Tower," *Newport History: Journal of the Newport Historical Society* 68 part 2 (235), 1997, pp. 55–91.

53. Hertz, pp. 84, ff 56.

54. The settlement at Newport developed around a spring-fed pond capable of driving a mill. See Bayles, *History of Newport County, Rhode Island* (1888), p. 483.

55. Nicholas Esson (Easton) and Richard Drummer are both mentioned as building mills in 1638, the year prior to the town's grant of proprietorship. *History of Newport County, Rhode Island*, p. 23.

56. William S. Godfrey Jr., "The Archaeology of the Old Stone Mill in Newport, Rhode Island," *American Antiquity* 17 (2), 1951, pp. 120–9.

57. William S. Godfrey Jr., "The Newport Tower II," *Archaeology* 3 (Summer 1950), and "The Newport Puzzle," *Archaeology* 2, Autumn 1949.

58. Frederick J. Pohl, "Plaster Under the Newport Tower," *American Antiquity* 19 (3), 1954, pp. 275–7.

59. Godfrey (1951), p. 126.

60. See "The Early Republic's Supernatural Economy: Treasure Seeking in the American Northeast, 1780–1830," *American Quarterly* 38, 1986, pp. 6–34, for more on the treasure hunter phenomenon in New England.

61. William S. Godfrey Jr., "Answer to 'Plaster under the Tower,'" *American Antiquity* 19 (3), January 1954.

62. Hertz, p. 81.

63. Hertz (1997), p. 74.

64. Hjalmar Rued Holand, "The Age of the Newport Tower," *Archaeology* 4, Autumn 1951.

65. See Holand (1951), p. 155 (cites the relevant portion).

66. The Rhenish-Danish-Norwegian foot is a catchall term for three separate measurements close enough in tolerance to be indistinguishable to two decimal places. The *rheinfuß*, the Danske *fod*, and the Norske *fot* can all be calculated as 12.35 English inches.

67. Also covered in Hjalmar Rued Holand, "The Newport Mystery" *Rhode Island History* 12, 1953, pp. 56–59.

68. In addition to the letters in *Archaeology* and *Antiquity*, the questions spilled into the mainstream press. An October 31, 1950, article in *The News* (Newport, RI) quotes Holand calling Godfrey's excavations "a most superficial piece of work."

69. William S. Godfrey, Jr., "Reply to Holand," *American Antiquity* 18 (4), 1953, pp. 395–396.

70. William S. Godfrey, Jr., "Vikings in America: Theories and Evidence," *American Anthropologist* 57 (1), 1955, pp. 35–43.

71. Arlington H. Mallery, "The Pre-Columbian Discovery of America: A Reply to W.S. Godfrey," *American Anthropologist* 60 (1), 1958, pp. 141–152.

72. Arlington Mallery had developed a theory that an Iron Age culture had existed in pre-Columbian North America. Mallery excavated a number of Ohio sites which he claimed were smelting furnaces utilized by Norse and Celts for trans-Atlantic trade. See Mallery, Arlington H. and Mary Roberts Harrison, *The Rediscovery of Lost America* (New York: Dutton, 1979).

73. "Excavation at Old Stone Mill by Celtic Theorist Approved," *Newport Daily News*, November 9, 1954.

74. Arlington H. Mallery, Gardner C. Easton, and John Howieson, *Interim Report*, 1955.

75. "Old Stone Mill Weakened by '49 Excavations, Ohio Engineer Claims in Report to Council," *Newport Daily News*, October 20, 1955.

76. Godfrey was a member of the Beloit College faculty from 1951 to 1973 and served as executive secretary of the American Anthropological Association, which used Beloit College as a base of operations. The Godfrey Anthropology Building on campus was dedicated to Godfrey upon completion in 1975.

77. Hertz, p. 76.

78. Mallery (1958), pp. 147–148.

79. Arlington H. Mallery, Gardner C. Easton, and John Howieson, *Preliminary Report* (1956).

80. Means (1942), pp. 93, 288–289.

81. Camille Enlart, "Le Problème de la Vieille Tour de Newport (Rhode-Island)," *Revue de l'art chrétien* LX, pp. 309–320 (1910).

82. Mallery never quite got the reporters to stop referring to the hypothetical ambulatory as a "wooden shed" or "lean-to."

83. "Study Underway at Old Stone Mill in Attempt to Rebuild Original Edifice," *Newport Daily News*, November 19, 1954.

84. As towers became progressively taller to elevate the sails above any obstructions to the wind, such as neighboring structures or forests, a stage was added for accessing the sails. If the tower was originally several stories taller, this horizontal shelf could also have been utilized to anchor the stage for a windmill and build upward, not down and out. See Stokhuyzen for further discussion on the mechanical components and design requirements of a windmill.

85. *Newport Daily News* (November 9, 1954).

86. Mallery (1958), pp. 149–150.

87. P. H. Loffelt, John Romeyn Brodhead, and J.C. Jonge, *Niev Nederlandt* (New York: Sarony, 1841).

88. William Wood, *New England's Prospect* [1635] (Amherst: University of Massachusetts Press, 1635, rep 1977).

89. This map was rediscovered in 1841 in the Royal Archives at The Hague. It was presented to the Dutch legislature in 1616 in hopes of obtaining a trade monopoly. It shows the extent of the discoveries made by Captain Cornelius Hendricks in a small ship named *The Restless*. Hendricks had commanded *The Tiger*, a trade vessel sent to New Netherlands in 1613. However, the vessel caught fire and was beached. *The Restless* was built from the remnants and sailed back to the Netherlands.

90. "The Commodities of the Island called Manati Ore Long Isle Within the Continent of Virginia," *Collections of the New-York Historical Society* 2, 1869, pp. 214–218.

91. Frederick J. Pohl, "Was the Newport Tower Standing in 1632?" *New England Quarterly* 18 (4), 1945, pp. 501–506.

92. Plowden, p. 217.

93. Pohl discusses this matter further in *The Lost Discovery; Uncovering the Track of the Vikings in America* (New York: Norton, 1952), pp. 181–186.

94. Wood, p. 16.

95. "I did it the rather, because there hath some relations heretofore past the Presse, which have beene very imperfect; as also because there hath beene many scandalous and false reports past upon the Country, even from the sulphurious breath of every base ballad-monger." Wood, William, *New England's Prospects*. As cited by Graham Roebuck, "'This innocent worke': Adam and Eve, John Smith, William Wood and the North American Plantations," *Early Modern Literary Studies* 1, 1995.

96. Giovanni da Verrazzano, Adriaen Block, and John Smith are all recorded as exploring Narragansett Bay.

97. William Cronon, *Changes in the Land: Indians, Colonists, and the Ecology of New England*, 1st ed. (New York: Hill and Wang, 1983).

98. Cronon, p. 49.

99. Morton, T. "New English Canaan" Tracts and other papers relating principally to the Origin, Settlement, and Progress of the colonies in North America, from the discovery of the country to the year 1776. As cited by Cronon, p. 49.

100. Paul H. Chapman, *The Man Who Led Columbus to America* (Atlanta: Judson Press, 1973).

101. Paul H. Chapman, *The Norse Discovery of America* (Atlanta: One Candle Press, 1981).
102. Chapman (1981), pp. 72–73.
103. The section of the Mercator map reproduced in Chapman's book is not particularly detailed, but similar towers at Ipedra and Medano are still visible.
104. Richardson, pp. 7–9.
105. Richardson, pp. 9–12.
106. Richardson, p. 13.
107. Richardson, p. 22.
108. Hjalmar Rued Holand, "An English Scientist in America 130 Years Before Columbus," *Transactions of the Wisconsin Academy of Sciences, Arts and Letters* XLVIII, 1959.
109. Holand's article contradicts his previous theory that Knutson used Newport as the base camp by suggesting that Nicholas allowed the Knutson expedition to sail directly from Greenland to the Maritime Provinces and into Hudson Bay.
110. William S. Penhallow, "Astronomical Alignments in the Newport Tower" in *Across Before Columbus?: Evidence for Transoceanic Contact with the Americas Prior to 1492*, edited by Donald Y. Gilmore and Linda S McElroy (Edgecomb, ME: New England Antiquities Research Association NEARA, 1998), pp. vi, 313.
111. Means (1942). Penhallow specifically used figures 5, 6, 7, 8, and 16, rendered by John Howland Rowe as part of an unpublished report on the tower Rowe did while an undergraduate at Brown University.
112. Penhallow (1994), p. 52.
113. William S. Penhallow, "Some Thoughts on the Newport Tower," *NEARA Journal* 36 (2), 2002, pp. 31–8.
114. Hertz, p. 77.
115. Strandwold (1948).
116. Strandwold (1948), p. 31.
117. O. G. Landsverk and Alf Mongé, *Norse Medieval Cryptography in Runic Carvings* (Glendale, CA: Norseman Press, 1967).
118. Landsverk, pp. 127–130.
119. Rafn (1841).
120. The Spirit Pond, Kensington, and Heavener runestones, respectively.
121. Barry Fell, *Saga America* (New York: Times Books, 1980).
122. Keeler had spent a great deal of time studying the Cuna Indians of the San Blas Islands in Panama, who have the highest rate of genetic albinism in the world. Keeler also helped document the Cuna culture, eventually publishing five books on the topic, and the first book on the Cuna alphabet. Keeler's interest in pre-Columbian visits to America grew from short-lived theories that the Cuna albinism was actually European genetic infiltration.
123. Clyde Keeler, "The Newport Round Church: Description and Analysis," *Epigraphical Society Occasional Publications* 13 (329) (1985).
124. Pell, pp. 105–11).

125. Manuel Luciano da Silva, "Review of the History of the Portuguese Templars," *Stonewatch: Newsletter of the Gungywamp Society* 12 (2), 1993, p. 4.
126. See Chapter Three for more on the Corte Real theory.
127. Pell, p. 115.
128. Hjalmar Rued Holand, "The Newport Mystery (2)," *Rhode Island History* 12 (3), 1953, pp. 83–9.
129. Manuel Luciano da Silva, *Portuguese Pilgrims and Dighton Rock: The First Chapter in American History* (Bristol, RI: published by the author, 1971).
130. da Silva, p. 78.
131. Stokhuyzen, p. 7.
132. The computer-drawn detailed map was included in the report sent to the Newport city council. This is the report used by Penhallow (1994).
133. John Hale, Jan Heinemeier, Lynne Lancaster, et al., "Dating Ancient Mortar," *American Scientist* 91 (2), 2003, pp. 130–8.
134. See Hertz for an abridged English language version of the final report by Jan Heinemeier and Högne Jungner. The report, "C14-datering af kalkmørtel," appeared in *Arkæologiske udgravninger i Danmark* 1994 (Copenhagen 1995).
135. The oldest surviving house in Newport, the Wanton-Lyman-Hazard House, was built ca. 1696 and is a National Historic Landmark. The Newport Historical Society purchased the property in 1927 and continues to use the house as a museum.
136. David P. Barron, "Danes Announce Carbon Dating on Newport Tower," *Stonewatch: Newsletter of the Gungywamp Society* 12 (1), 1993, pp. 1, 8.
137. The primary evidence is a 1668 document that refers to a road that "leads to Georg Lawtons mill," which Lawton family research indicates could be Mill Road, which passes Touro Park. See the family genealogical newsletter, Lawton Ledger 2 (1), March 1996; 3 (4), December 1997. The difficulty remains in determining if the reference is to a windmill or a mill driven by water.
138. "The Old Stone Mill," *Newport Daily News*, August 17, 1979.
139. See Chapter Seven for more on Henry Sinclair.
140. "Stone Tower Theory Raises Questions," *Newport Daily News*, February 19, 1996.
141. Hertz, p. 78.
142. Hertz, p. 78.
143. Bill Strubbe and Richard Flavin, "Written in Stone," *Historic Traveler*, 5 (2), February 1999.
144. Means (1942), pp. 265–267, 283.
145. Andrew Sinclair, *The Sword and the Grail* (New York: Crown, 1992).
146. James P. Whittall and Mark Stoughton, "Ground Penetrating Radar Survey, Newport Tower Site, Touro Park, Newport, Rhode Island, 1994." *Early Sites Research Society Bulletin*, June 1995.
147. Dan Welch, "Report of the Ground-Penetrating Radar Survey, Touro Park, Newport, Rhode

Island, June 12, 2001," *NEARA Journal* 36 (2), 2002, pp. 25–27.

148. Andre J. de Bethune, "On the Carbon 14 Analyses of Mortar from the Newport Tower: Theoretical Considerations," *Newport History: Journal of the Newport Historical Society* 69, part 1 (238), 1998, pp. 19–26.

149. James L. Guthrie, "Radiocarbon Dating of the Newport Tower Mortar," *NEARA Journal* 36 (2), 2002, pp. 39–40.

150. J. Huston McCulloch, "Newport Tower Radiocarbon Dates: Some Reservations about the Newport Tower C-14 Dates," *Midwestern Epigraphic Journal* 15, 2001, pp. 79–92.

151. Hertz, p. 93.

152. Heinemeier and Jungner, p. 36. Cited by McCulloch.

153. Guthrie, p. 40.

154. James Egan, *Elizabethan America: The John Dee Tower of 1583, a Renaissance Horologium in Newport, Rhode Island*.

155. Christopher Knight and Robert Lomas. *The Book of Hiram: Freemasonry, Venus and the Secret Key to the Life of Jesus*. (London: Element, 2005). The authors theorize that the worship of Venus began in prehistory and continued with civilization and that the worship is prevalent in Biblical references. The Templars recovered the knowledge that Jesus was among the Venus-worshippers, becoming a founding tenet of Freemasonry.

156. The "egg" is not centered at the top of the arch, so it is not a keystone, and it is a stretch to consider it ovate enough to be egg-shaped.

157. Wolter's article originally ran in *Ancient American* #77 (February 2008) as "Venus Alignments in the Newport Tower, RI." It has since appeared as "A Templar Temple in Rhode Island" in *Unlocking the Prehistory of America*, Joseph Frank, ed. NY: Rosen Publishing, 2014.

158. Strong, *The Renaissance Garden in England*, pp. 11, 101.

159. *The Arnold Memorial*, pp. 54–55.

160. Gavin Menzies, *1421: The Year China Discovered America*, 1st U.S. ed. (New York: William Morrow, 2003).

161. Menzies, p. 288.

162. For example, *Archaeology* magazine's Eric Powell prominently features Menzies in an article on "Seductions of Pseudoarchaeology: Bogus Books" (56:3, May-June 2003) placing him at the same lofty level in pseudoarchaeology as Erich von Däniken.

163. "In the Wake of Zheng He: Regarding '1421, The Year China Discovered America.'" The web page was formerly at www.neara.org/Misc Reports/1421.htm and has since expired. Copy on file.

Chapter Five

1. William B. Goodwin, *The Truth About Leif Ericsson* (Boston: Meador, 1941).

2. Goodwin (1946).

3. Gerald S. Hawkins, *Stonehenge Decoded* (Garden City, NY: Doubleday, 1965).

4. Goodwin (1946), p. 62. The stone louvers have been removed out of safety concerns.

5. Goodwin (1946), pp. 96–97. Goodwin's interpretation of the Y-chamber was that it was the private chapel and quarters of the abbot.

6. Goodwin (1946), p. 39.

7. See Lambert, *America's Stonehenge: An Interpretive Guide* (Kingston, NH: Sunrise, 1996) for diagrams, maps, and photographs of specific site features discussed.

8. Many of the diseases prevalent in New England were waterborne—cholera, typhoid, hepatitis, and the one that killed Jonathan Pattee in 1849, dysentery.

9. The structure is built with a glacial erratic boulder as one wall and is too small for any storage or housing functions. As the name suggests, it is theorized that it is a shelter for a sentry. Although it has been excavated numerous times (in 1955, 1959, 1969, and 1981), no clues have been found to suggest its function.

10. Local tradition has the stone being shipped to Lawrence, MA, during the construction of a dam for the textile industry. Pattee shows up in town records as providing stone for a new crypt at nearby Pine Grove cemetery.

11. 2000–1000 BP.

12. Robert E. Stone, "Preliminary Survey: No. Salem Rock Shelter," *New Hampshire Archeological Society Miscellaneous Papers* (1961).

13. Geochron Laboratories, Inc., "Report of Analytical Work, Radiocarbon Age Determination—Sample GX20670" (Cambridge, MA: Geochron Laboratories, 1995).

14. Seth Jonathan Mallon Pattee (1815–1900) was the only son who lived to adulthood. His daughter Anna McNeil was the last Pattee to own the property, selling it in 1927.

15. It has been alternately suggested that the house was not built by Jonathan Pattee. Instead, Pattee may have utilized a farmhouse already on the property, built by his grandfather, Seth Pattee, Sr. See Goudsward (2002), pp. 55–57.

16. Edgar Gilbert, *History of Salem, N.H.* (Concord, NH: Rumford Printing, 1907).

17. Gilbert, opposite p. 417.

18. *Architectural Heritage of Haverhill* (Haverhill, MA: Trustees of the Haverhill Public Library, 1976).

19. Sarah E. Johansen, "Survey of Seth Mallon Pattee House," 1974.

20. In 1927, he was elected to the Walpole Society, an exclusive group of antique collectors whose ranks included such noted collectors as Henry Francis du Pont, whose collection would become Winterthur Museum.

21. William B. Goodwin, *correspondence to Harral Ayres*, 1936.

22. Clay Perry, *Underground New England* (Brattleboro, VT: Stephen Daye Press, 1939).

23. Clay Perry, *New England's Buried Treasure* (New York: Stephen Daye Press, 1946).

24. Wesley S. Griswold, "Stone Village Mystery," *Hartford Courant*, June 19, 1938.

25. Hugh O. Hencken, "The 'Irish Monastery' at North Salem, N.H.," *New England Quarterly* 12 (3), 1939, pp. 429–42.

26. Hencken, pp. 434–435.

27. George Woodbury, "Tourists Can Take It From Here: 'Mystery Caves'—Ancient Ruins or Codger's Retreat?" *New Hampshire Sunday News*, July 13, 1958.

28. In Goodwin's defense, this was not a deliberate attempt at plagiarism. Prior to photocopier technology, Goodwin would have his secretary type up copies of materials he wished to keep on file. These file copies are indistinguishable from the book's manuscript, and it would not take much for the materials to become confused in the rush to publish.

29. Goudsward (2002), pp. 81–86.

30. Goodwin (1946), pp. 208–214.

31. The "Virginia Dare Stones" or "Roanoke Stones" were 46 stones written in Elizabethan text. Chronicling the flight and demise of the lost Roanoke Colony survivors, the stones were found scattered from Virginia to Georgia.

32. Boyden Sparkes, "Writ on Rocke," *Saturday Evening Post*, April 26, 1941.

33. Frederick J. Pohl, "To Perpetuate a Linguistic Hoax," *Anthropological Journal of Canada* 18 (2), 1980, pp.14–5.

34. Samuel Eliot Morison, *The European Discovery of America: The Northern Voyages, A.D. 500–1600* (New York: Oxford University Press, 1971).

35. Morison (1971), pp. 30, 89, and 107. The text includes references to Goodwin as a "paladin of lost causes" and the "father of archaeological lost causes."

36. Morison (1971), pp. 32–62.

37. James Deetz, *In Small Things Forgotten* (Garden City, NY: Anchor Press/Doubleday, 1977).

38. Lambert, p. 30 as an example.

39. Stone, Robert, "Mystery Hill: New Information on the Status of Its Structures in 1938." *NEARA Journal* 11 (1976), pp. 18–22. A previously unknown 1938 visit to the site resulted in diagrams of the site in the early stages of Goodwin's ownership that indicate all the major site components are still in the same position as they were when Goodwin arrived.

40. Daniel's 1977 review of Barry Fell's *America B.C.* in the *New York Times* included such quaint terms as "ignorant rubbish" and "deluded scholar." In a subsequent defense of his review, he elaborates with terms such as "self-deluded," "cranks," "fuddy-duddies," "nonsensical," "fantasy," and "archaeological fiction."

41. Seán P. Ó Ríordáin and Glyn Edmund Daniel, *New Grange and the Bend of the Boyne* (New York: F.A. Praeger, 1964).

42. One of the other grad students on the project was David H. Kelley, who would author a 1976 text establishing the phonetic character of Mayan glyphs.

43. Vescelius was reported to have an excavation in Peru waiting for him that he could not start until his contract in New Hampshire was completed. Godfrey's work in Newport was part of his doctoral dissertation, and under a timetable.

44. Gary S. Vescelius, "1955 North Salem, N.H. Site Excavations," North Salem, NH: *Early Sites Foundation*, 1955.

45. Ezra Scollay Stearns, *Genealogical and Family History of the State of New Hampshire* (New York: Lewis, 1908).

46. Walter Harriman, *History of Warner, New Hampshire* (Warner, NH: Republican Press Association, 1879).

47. The area encompassing Salem, NH, was originally part of Haverhill, MA. The fourth division of land in Haverhill brought property, including America's Stonehenge, into the possession of Peter's grandchildren, Seth and Richard. Both land parcels were north of the long disputed state border when Salem, NH, was incorporated in 1750 from Massachusetts.

48. Marie Lollo Scalisi, Virginia M. Ryan, "Peter Pattee of Haverhill Massachusetts: A 'Journeyman Shoemaker' and His Descendants," *New England Historical and Genealogical Register* 146, 147, 1992–1993, pp. 315–36, 73–86, 174–87.

49. Aside from the Huguenot confusion in Stearns, there is also a theory that Peter was an illegitimate son of Sir William Petty. This first appears in print in Harriman's error-riddled sketch of Asa Pattee in the Warner, NH, history.

50. Richard L. Burger and Thomas F. Lynch, "Gary S. Vescelius (1930–1982)," *Andean Past* 1, 1987.

51. Frank Glynn, "Further Report on Metal Fragment," unpublished typescript on file, America's Stonehenge Research Department.

52. Barry Fell, *America B.C.: Ancient Settlers in the New World* (New York: Quadrangle/New York Times Book, 1976).

53. Barry Fell, "Iberian-Punic Stele," *The Epigraphic Society of Occasional Publications*, 2 (44, part 2), 1975a.

54. Fell (1976), pp. 90–91.

55. Barry Fell, "Romano-Celtic Phase at Mystery Hill, New Hampshire, in New England," *The Epigraphic Society Occasional Publications (ESOP)* 3 (54), 1975b.

56. William A. Haviland and Marjory W. Power, "Visions in Stone: A New Look at the Bellows Falls Petroglyphs," *Northeast Anthropology* 50 (Fall 1995), pp. 91–107.

57. See Chapter Six.

58. America's Stonehenge Tour Guide Map.

59. Hawkins' book was reviewed by R.J.C. Atkinson for *The New York Review of Books* (June 23, 1966). Atkinson, considered one of the foremost experts on Stonehenge, took a dim view of Hawkins' assertion that the site was a megalithic astronomical observatory, an opinion Atkinson repeated

in *Nature* and *Antiquity*. This prompted a terse exchange of letters in the August 18, 1966 issue of *The New York Review of Books*.

60. David Stewart-Smith, *Ancient and Modern Quarry Techniques* (Nashua, NH: Gamemasters, 1989).

61. Stewart-Smith, pp. 14–16.

62. Edward Hitchcock, Report on the Geology, Mineralogy, Botany, and Zoology of Massachusetts (Amherst, MA: Press of J.S. and C. Adams, 1833), p. 17. Metal drills cut inch-wide holes 2–3 inches into the rock. Metal wedges are then driven into the holes. Hitchcock reports slabs up to 50–60 feet long can be separated this way.

63. Jonathan Pattee died intestate in 1849, and his son Seth J.M. Pattee was awarded the estate. Town records show several loads of stone sold by Seth J.M. Pattee for such projects as the new graveyard's tomb. Local tradition also has large amounts of stone hauled to Lawrence, MA, for the construction of bridges and dams. Jonathan's will was found in 1863. Jonathan had actually left the property to his grandson George. George sued his father in 1863 to regain control of his inheritance.

64. Lambert, p. 23.

65. Goodwin (1946), p. 60, passingly mentions the "two huts we dug out" as part of the evidence of the original length of the Y-chamber. An architectural rendering of the area by Vincent Fagin on p. 61 includes two beehives at the location. On p. 192, Goodwin refers to the same location as having three huts of unknown function.

66. Lambert (p. 80) includes a topographic map of the main site that shows the start of the walls that extend out in all directions.

67. Precession, or more accurately, Precession of the Equinoxes, causes a slow circular motion that changes which star is the pole star as seen from Earth. Thuban was the pole star while the Egyptians built the pyramids, but the motion of precession tilted the Earth's axis away from Thuban toward Polaris, the current pole star. In a few centuries, there will be no pole star as Polaris moves out of alignment. In 6000 years, Deneb will be the pole star, and 13,000 years from now, Earth's rotation will point north at Vega.

68. Mark Feldman, *The Mystery Hill Story* (North Salem, NH: Mystery Hill Press, 1977), pp. 60–63.

69. Carbon dating results are reported in dates BP (before present) and calculated from a base year of 1950. For a rough conversion to dates BC, subtract 1950 from the date. So 3475 BP ± 210 is roughly the same as 1525 BC ± 210 years. Accurate conversion between C-14 dates (or radiocarbon dates) and calendar dates requires the application of additional non-linear corrections to compensate for varying historical rates of C-14 production in the upper atmosphere.

70. Harold Krueger, "Report of Analytical Work, Radiocarbon Age Determination: Sample GX2310" (Cambridge, MA: Geochron Laboratories, 1974).

71. Harold Krueger, "Report of Analytical Work, Radiocarbon Age Determination: Sample GX1608" (Cambridge, MA: Geochron Laboratories, 1969).

72. Hencken (1939), p. 441.

73. James P. Whittall II, "2995± 180 at Mystery Hill," *NEARA Newsletter* 4 (3), 1969, p.50.

74. David Stewart-Smith, the Mystery Hill Research Committee chairman, was quick to point out in his *1995 Field Season Report* that this 5440 BC date is anomalous and may indicate a pre-inhabitation brush fire or a mid-archaic fire pit. As intriguing as the date is, there is no correlation to the stone structures.

75. G.A Jones, "Data Report #95–029: Radiocarbon Results" (Woods Hole, MA: Woods Hole Oceanographic Institution, 1995).

76. Louis Winkler and Robert E. Stone, *Mystery Hill: Its Construction and Use 2000 BC–1600 AD* (North Salem, NH: Mystery Hill Research Dept. 1999, n.p.)

77. Zenith stars pass overhead and dip below the horizon. Grazing-circumpolar stars also pass overhead, but never drop below the horizon, although they come close enough to be lost to sight due to atmospheric dimming.

78. Apparent Magnitude is a logarithmic measure of the brightness of an object as seen from the earth. The brighter the object, the lower the number.

79. Harald Meller, "Star Search," *National Geographic* 205 (1), 2004, pp. 77–87.

80. James P. Whittall II, "Precolumbian Parallels between Mediterranean and New England Archeology," *Epigraphic Society Occasional Publications* 3 (52), 1975.

81. Dennis Stone, *America's Stonehenge Souvenir Book* ([North Salem, NH]: [n.p.], 2019), [p. 40].

82. George E. Lankford, "The Great Serpent in Eastern North America." In *Ancient Objects and Sacred Realms*. ed. F. Kent Reilly III and James F. Garber. (Austin: University of Texas Press, 2010), p. 109. He further cites T. Smith, *The Island of the Anishnaabeg* (1995), pp. 97–8. T. Smith summarizes previous studies and observes descriptions are "invariably of a water serpent, usually horned and always of an immense size."

83. Edward J. Lenik, "Mythic Creatures: Serpents, Dragons, and Sea Monsters in Northeastern Rock Art." *Archaeology of Eastern North America*, 38, 2010, p. 17.

84. See Goodwin (1946), p. 94 or Lambert, p. 40 for the image.

85. Mark Hedden, "Passamaquoddy Shamanism and Rock-Art in Machias Bay, Maine" In *The Rock-art of Eastern North America: Capturing Images and Insight*. ed. Carol Diaz-Granados and James R. Duncan. (Tuscaloosa: The University of Alabama Press, 2004), p. 319.

86. Kathleen J. Bragdon, "The Shamanistic 'Text' in Southern New England." In *The Written and the Wrought: Complementary Sources in Historical Anthropology: essays in honor of James Deetz*, ed. Mary Ellin D'Agostino. Berkeley, CA: Kroeber Anthropological Society Papers 79, 1995.

87. Mark Warhus, Mark. *Another America: Native American Maps and the History of Our Land* (New York: St. Martin's Press, 1997), p. 3.

88. Mallery (1972), pp. 338, 339, 341.

89. See Daniel G. Brinton, *The Myths of the New World: A Treatise on the Symbolism and Mythology of the Red Race of America* (New York: Leypoldt and Holt, 1868), pp. 117–126 for examples of how widely this archetype was known.

90. George E. Lankford, *Reachable Stars: Patterns in the Ethnoastronomy of Eastern North America* (Tuscaloosa, AL: The University of Alabama Press, 2007).

Chapter Six

1. R.A. Stewart Macalister, "External Evidenced Affecting the Problem of the Age of Ogham Writing in Ireland," *Man* 2, 1902, pp. 6–7.

2. J.M. Mancini, "Discovering Viking America," *Critical Inquiry* 28 (7), 2002.

3. Fell (1976).

4. Fell (1982); Barry Fell, *Saga America* (New York: Times Books, 1983).

5. Peter H.J. Castle, "Howard Barraclough Fell" (obituary), *Yearbook of the Academy Council of The Royal Society of New Zealand* (1996).

6. David H. Kelley, *Deciphering the Maya Script* (Austin, TX: University of Texas Press, 1976).

7. David H. Kelley, "Proto-Tifinagh and Proto-Ogham in the Americas," *Review of Archaeology* 11 (1), 1990.

8. Warren L. Cook, *Ancient Vermont: Proceedings of the Castleton Conference, Castleton State College, October 14–15, 1977* (Rutland, VT: Published for the College by Academy Books, 1978).

9. Fell's presentation was transcribed for inclusion in the publication. Cook, pp. 70–84.

10. Cook, pp. 21–25.

11. Goodwin (1946), pp. 385–386, 397–401.

12. Other organizations had reported and recorded stone chambers in Vermont in the 1950s and 1960s, most notably the Early Sites Research Society and New England Antiquities Research Association. However, this work was sporadic and inconclusive.

13. Byron E. Dix, "An Early Calendar Site in Central Vermont," *ESOP* 3 (51), 1976, pp. 1–89.

14. Fell (1975b).

15. Gerald S. Hawkins, *Beyond Stonehenge*, (New York: Harper & Row, 1973).

16. James W. Mavor, *Voyage to Atlantis* (New York: Putnam, 1969).

17. James W. Mavor, "The Riddle of Mzorah," *Almogaren* 7, 1976, pp. 89–121.

18. James W. Mavor and Byron E. Dix, *Manitou: The Sacred Landscape of New England's Native Civilization* (Rochester, VT: Inner Traditions International, 1989).

19. Byron E. Dix and James W. Mavor, "Heliolithic Ritual Sites in New England," *NEARA Journal* 16 (3), 1982, pp. 63–84.

20. Dix (1982), p. 71.

21. Dix (1982), pp. 72–73.

22. Mavor (1989), pp. 16–17.

23. Mavor (1989), pp. 332–342.

24. Cook, pp. 9–12, 123–129.

25. Giovanna Neudorfer, *Vermont's Stone Chambers: An Inquiry into Their Past* (Montpelier, VT: Vermont Historical Society, 1980).

26. Neudorfer, p. 9. In the ensuing 45 years, a number of these chambers have been destroyed and several new ones uncovered, making any specific inventory somewhat tentative.

27. Neudorfer, p. 13.

28. A *megalithic yard* was a unit of measurement coined by Alexander Thom. Thom surveyed megalithic structures across the British Isles. He found they had all used the same unit of measure: 2 feet 8.64 inches (82.966 cm).

29. Byron E. Dix, "Possible Evidence of the Megalithic Yard at Calendar Site II, Vermont," *NEARA Journal* 11 (2), 1976c, p. 25.

30. Neudorfer, pp. 48–49.

31. Neudorfer, pp. 30–34. Neudorfer also notes two of these structures were identified by Fell as Celtic temples.

32. Personal communication with author, January 21, 2004.

33. "Origin of Caves Cleared Up by Kin of Builder," *Haverhill Evening Gazette*, August 17, 1934.

34. Goudsward (2002).

35. Goudsward (2002), pp. 61–62.

36. Byron E. Dix, "A Second Early Calendar Site in Central Vermont," *ESOP* 3 (61), 1976b, pp. 1–167.

37. Cook, p. 7.

38. Fell as transcribed in Cook, p. 71.

39. Mavor (1989), pp. 240–242.

40. Mavor (1989), p. 242.

41. Dix (1982), p. 78.

42. Fell as transcribed in Cook, pp. 72–73.

43. Fell (1976), pp. 134–135.

44. Francisco Marco Simón, "Religion and Religious Practices of the Ancient Celts of the Iberian Peninsula," *e-Keltoi: Journal of Interdisciplinary Celtic Studies* 6 (2005), pp. 287–345.

45. Fell (1976), pp. 143–145. Fell would later find the same symbol at the America's Stonehenge site.

46. Leonard A. Curchin, "Literacy in the Roman Provinces: Qualitative and Quantitative Data from Central Spain," *The American Journal of Philology* 116 (3), 1995, pp. 461–476.

47. Francisco Beltran Lloris, "Writing, Language and Society: Iberians, Celts, and Romans in Northeastern Spain in the 2nd and 1st centuries BC," *Bulletin of the Institute of Classical Studies* 43, 1999, pp. 131–51; Fiona A. Rose, "Text and Image in Celtiberia: The Adoption and Adaptation of Written Language into Indigenous Visual Vocabulary," *Oxford Journal of Archaeology* 22 (2), 2003, pp. 133–154.

48. Fell uses the Sanskrit terms of *yoni* and *lingua* to indicate the ceremonial representations of vulvae and penises.

49. Cook, p. 7.

50. Cook p. 7 also notes additional sites in Vermont. Fell (1976), pp. 244–245, prefers the term "petromantic" to include both animated and anthropomorphic stones.

51. Warren W. Dexter and Donna Martin, *America's Ancient Stone Relics: Highlighting Vermont's Link to Bronze Age Mariners* (Rutland, VT: Academy Books, 1995).

52. Mavor (1989), pp. 8–9.

53. Fell (1976), pp. 68–74.

54. The epilogue of her book specifically laments the fact that common ground was never established, and as such, no dialogue was possible. Neudorfer, p. 62.

55. Neudorfer, pp. 58–59.

56. Mavor (1989), pp. 21–22. The Goddard committee also included James Mavor, Byron Dix, and James Whittall. Mavor and Dix left the committee before the start of a test excavation because they felt the scope of the study was too narrow.

57. Cook, pp. 139–146.

58. Anne Ross and Peter Reynolds, "Ancient Vermont," *Antiquity* 52 (205), 1978, pp. 100–7.

59. Cook, p. 114.

60. Cook, p. 133.

61. William R. McGlone, Phillip M. Leonard, James L. Guthrie et al., *Ancient American Inscriptions: Plow Marks or History?* (Sutton, MA: Early Sites Research Society, 1993); James P. Whittall Jr., *Myth Makers: Epigraphic Illusion in America* (Rowley, MA: Early Sites Research Society, 1990).

62. Whittall (1990), p. 3. For an example of petromanteia, see the Manana Island inscription in Chapter Eight.

63. McGlone, Appendix C (pp. 365–381).

64. James P. Whittall, Jr., "The Problem of Epigraphic Delusion" in *Myth Makers: Epigraphic Illusion in America*, edited by James P. Whittall, Jr. (Rowley, MA: Early Sites Research Society, 1990), p. 90.

65. John Finch, "On the Celtic Antiquities of America," *American Journal of Science and Arts* VII, 1824, pp. 149–161.

66. Finch, p. 152.

67. A rocking stone is a large rock resting upon another or bedrock that is so well balanced on a pivot point that it can be moved with minimal force. In Finch's time, prior to the introduction of glacial theory, rocking stones were considered manmade or the result of erosion.

68. Finch, p. 157.

69. Barry Fell was equally impressed, believing the boulder to be the largest dolmen in North America. He featured it prominently in his third book, including a color photo on the cover. Fell (1982), pp. 63, 68–69.

70. Mavor (1989), pp. 103–109.

71. Mavor (1989), pp. 108–110.

72. For a discussion of British sites compared to other locations in Europe and Asia, see Walhouse's "On Non-Sepulchral Rude Stone Monuments" in *The Journal of the Anthropological Institute of Great Britain and Ireland* 7, 1878, pp. 21–43.

73. Mavor (1989), pp. 112–113. The rock in Dunkeld is known locally as Craigiebarns Rocking Stone. It has local folklore traditions of Druidic ceremonies associated with it.

74. Cyrus M. Tracy, *Studies of the Essex Flora: A Complete Enumeration of All Plants Found Growing Naturally Within the Limits of Lynn, Mass., and the Towns Adjoining, Arranged According to the Natural System, with Copious Notes as to Localities and Habits* (Lynn, MA: Stevenson & Nichols Printers, 1858).

75. Elizabeth Hope Cushing, "So Near the Metropolis: Lynn Woods, a Sylvan Gem in an Urban Setting," *Arnoldia* 48 (4), 1998, pp. 37–51.

76. N. S. Emerson, *The History of Dungeon Rock, Completed Sept. 17th, 1856*, 2d ed. (Boston: Adams, 1859); Richard G. Provenzano, *Pirates' Glen & Dungeon Rock: The Evolution of a Legend*, 1st ed. (Saugus, MA: Saugus Historical Society, 1983).

77. Leonard M. Keene, "Lynn Woods Mega-Geometry," *NEARA Journal* 15 (2), 1980; "Mega-Geometry Update Essex County, MA," *NEARA Journal* 16 (1), 1981; "Lynn Woods Grooved Stone," *NEARA Journal* 16 (2), 1981.

78. Cushing, p. 43.

79. Joseph Mason Rowell, "Excursion to Nunnery pasture," 1856.

80. In Greek mythology, Phaeton was the son of Helios, who unsuccessfully attempted to drive the chariot of the Sun God across the sky. Rowell noted in his report that he thought the outline of the boulder was roughly the profile of an ancient chariot, inspiring the connection between the errant sun chariot and a boulder appearing to fly off a ledge.

81. "Secretary's Report, April 16, 1866," *Proceedings of the Essex Institute* 5 (1866-7).

82. Joseph Henry, "January 1858–December 1865, The Smithsonian Years" in *The Papers of Joseph Henry*, ed. by Marc Rothenberg (Washington, DC: Smithsonian Institution Press distributed by Braziller New York, 1972), Vol. 10.

83. Henry, p. 103. Letter dated August 18, 1859.

84. Henry also mentions the ladder in his letter, p. 103.

85. D. Hamilton Hurd, *History of Essex County, Massachusetts, With Biographical Sketches of Many of Its Pioneers and Prominent Men* (Philadelphia: J.W. Lewis, 1888).

86. Goodwin (1946).

87. Robert Ellis Cahill, *New England's Ancient Mysteries* (Salem, MA: Old Saltbox Publishing House, 1993).

88. Cahill, p. 22.

89. Tom Dalton, "Boulders May Tell Ancient Tale," *Daily Evening Item*, May 4, 1987.

90. Dalton, p. 2. Whittall felt that the second dolmen, although smaller, was a more interesting site due to additional stone structures and walls associated with the location.

91. Taylor Armerding, "Let's Not Lose a Sense of Place," *North Shore Sunday*, March 16, 1997.

92. R.D. Flavin, *Dolmen Doldrums*, http://www.flavinscorner.com/dolmen.htm (last access April 24, 2005).
93. Goodwin (1946), pp. 158–159.
94. "Indian Carvings on River Bank Made More Visible," *Brattleboro Daily Reformer*, August 9, 1961.
95. Samuel Williams, *The Natural and Civil History of Vermont* (Burlington, VT: Samuel Mills, 1809).
96. Benjamin Homer Hall, *History of Eastern Vermont, from Its Earliest Settlement to the Close of the Eighteenth Century* (New York: Appleton, 1858).
97. Henry Rowe Schoolcraft, *Historical and Statistical Information Respecting the History, Condition and Prospects of the Indian Tribes of the United States* (Philadelphia: J.B. Lippincott, 1854).
98. William A. Haviland and Marjory W. Power, "Visions in Stone: A New Look at the Bellows Falls Petroglyphs," *Northeast Anthropology* 50 (Fall 1995), pp. 91–107.
99. Haviland, p. 98.
100. Schoolcraft 6, plate 48. This rendering was provided by A.C. Hamlin, who also provided Schoolcraft with the Monhegan Island inscription.
101. Lenik (2002).
102. Haviland (p. 94) and Lenik (2002) (p. 93) mention, among other damage, blasting the river channel to facilitate the passage of logs to local mills, construction of a retaining wall built for a railroad bed, and dumping of sand and salt laden snow off the banks.
103. Delabarre (1928), pp. 264–266.
104. Goodwin (1946), p. 159. Goodwin is referring to the New England Power Company plant and dam. The dam still powers a hydroelectric plant.
105. Stanley J. Trczinski, "The Bellows Falls Petroglyphs," *NEARA Newsletter* 3 (1), 1968, pp. 21–2.
106. Thompson, Zadock, *History of Vermont, Natural, Civil, and Statistical*, 2:208 (Burlington, VT: For the author, by C. Goodrich, 1842).
107. See Lenik (2002) for more on the Brattleboro carvings, pp. 105–107.
108. The article in question ran in numerous regional newspapers. The author's file copy is from the *Iowa City Daily Press*, Monday, April 29, 1907.
109. Lenik (2002), pp. 87–103.
110. Susan Smallheer, "Rockingham, Abenaki Tribe get national grant to study petroglyphs," *Brattleboro Reformer*, April 21, 2022.
111. Pratt Pond, Jr. (pseud. Daniel Fiske), "Upton Traditions: A Deserted Haunt of Unknown Origin," *Milford Journal*, April 26, 1893.
112. Malcolm Pearson, "Was It a Cave?" In *Upton, Massachusetts*, edited by William George Poor (Milford, MA: Charlescraft Press, 1935), pp. 149–150.
113. Donald Blake Johnson, *Upton's Heritage: The History of a Massachusetts Town*, [1st]. ed. (Canaan, NH: Phoenix, 1984).
114. Pearson, quoted in Cahill, pp. 41–42.
115. Strandwold (1939); Strandwold (1948).
116. Goodwin was a resident of Seattle from 1889–1899, not including some time in the Yukon panning for gold. His wife Mary was a Seattle native and still had relatives in the area.
117. William B. Goodwin, *The Truth About Leif Ericsson* (Boston: Meador, 1941).
118. Goodwin (1946), p. 31.
119. "Old Caves at Salem, N.H., Laid to Robbers, Indians," *Boston Globe*, October 24, 1935.
120. Pearson would supervise Goodwin's restorations and excavations at Mystery Hill, eventually inheriting it in 1950.
121. Goodwin (1941). Chapter 11 is a five-page précis of what would become *The Ruins of Great Ireland in New England*. Goodwin suggests (pp. 164–165) that the placement of the Irish stone chambers gave him the territorial limits of Vinland, aiding him in finally pinpointing Portsmouth, NH.
122. Goodwin initially identified the site as a *clochan* or a stone hut with a corbelled roof similar to a beehive hut. Unlike the beehives, clochans are not necessarily round and are occasionally found in groupings with their walls connected. In this case, the structure appeared to have a deliberate external stone placement to resemble a turtle. Goodwin was not entirely convinced of the European origins of the effigy, discussing the possibility that it was a clan totem for the Merrimac Indians (Goodwin (1946), pp. 102–108). Frank Glynn excavated a side chamber in the mound in 1951. He believed he found evidence that he believed indicated a Neolithic burial site. See *NEARA Newsletter* 4(4), 1969, for his report.
123. Clay Perry, *New England's Buried Treasure* (New York: Stephen Daye Press, 1946).
124. Goodwin (1946), p. 41.
125. In addition to the cost of the work crew at Mystery Hill, Goodwin had underwritten Strandwold's first book and several of the visits to the East Coast that allowed Strandwold to examine the inscriptions in person for his second book.
126. David H. Kelley and John Glass, reprint of "1955 report to Early Sites Foundation," *Early Sites Research Society Bulletin* 1 (1), 1973, pp. 17–21.
127. Kelley (1973), p. 19.
128. Salvatore Michael Trento, *Field Guide to Mysterious Places of Eastern North America*, (New York: Holt, 1997).
129. Trento, p. 130. Trento also remarks on the magnetic field in the area of the chamber, as he does with all the sites in the book. Trento believes that site selection is based on geomagnetic aberrations.
130. Kelley (1973), p. 20. The fragment is extremely fragile and broke into three pieces while being packed for further study.
131. Byron E. Dix and James W. Mavor, "Possible Astronomical Alignments, Date and Origin of the Pearson Stone Chamber," *Early Sites Research Society Bulletin* 8 (1), 1980, pp. 1–16.

132. Mavor (1989), pp. 45-46.
133. Mavor (1989), pp. 47-52.
134. Lawrence C. Wroth, *The Voyages of Giovanni da Verrazzano, 1524-1528* (New Haven: Published for the Pierpont Morgan Library by Yale University Press, 1970).
135. Mavor (1989), p. 54.
136. Meagher, Jonathan. *The Upton Chamber Mystery: An Analysis of Competing Theories Concerning the Chamber's Origins and the Chamber's Historical Significance*. Unpublished report on file with the Upton Historical Commission, 2004, 4-36. The Morris letter is quoted from Jones, *America's Icemen: An Illustrative History of the United States Natural Ice Industry, 1665-1925* (Humble, TX: Jobeco Books, 19840, pp. 75-76.
137. Eunice Kim, "Town Explores Its Options for Saving Cave: Upton Historical Commission Doesn't Want 'Treasure' Developed," *Milford Daily News*, August 22, 2004.
138. Kathryn Wagner, "Historical Commission Works to Save Cave," *Milford Daily News*, September 24, 2004.
139. Dudek, Martin. *Archaeological Site Examination for the Upton Chamber Masonry Rehabilitation and Drainage Improvement Project, 18 Elm Street (Assessor's Parcel 28, Town of Upton, Worchester County, Massachusetts,* 2012. Available online at https://www.uptonma.gov/historical-commission/pages/heritage-park
140. The GPR results are included in Dudek as Appendix VIII.
141. S.A. Mahan et al. "Construction ages of the Upton Stone Chamber: Preliminary findings and suggestions for future luminescence research." *Quaternary Geochronology* 30-B, October 2015.

Chapter Seven

1. Hodgman, *History of the Town of Westford* (1883), p. 237. Nason, *A Gazetteer of the State of Massachusetts* (1874), p. 542.
2. Strandwold (1939); Strandwold (1948).
3. Goodwin (1941).
4. Goodwin (1946).
5. Goodwin (1946), p. 54.
6. Goodwin (1946), pp. 362, 363.
7. Clay Perry, *New England's Buried Treasure* (New York: Stephen Daye Press, 1946).
8. Clay Perry, *Underground New England* (Brattleboro, VT: Stephen Daye Press, 1939).
9. Perry (1946), p. 245.
10. Goodwin (1946) was rushed due to his failing health and because a paper supply suddenly became available, a rare commodity in the waning days of World War II rationing.
11. T.C. Lethbridge, *Merlin's Island: Essays on Britain in the Dark Ages* (London: Methuen, 1948).
12. Lethbridge (1948), Chapter 4. Eleven years before the publication of *Merlin's Island*, Lethbridge had published *Umiak*, a brief study of the similarities between the umiak, a skin-covered boat used by Eskimos, and the skin-covered curragh used in Britain.
13. T.C. Lethbridge, *Herdsmen and Hermits: Celtic Seafarers in the Northern Seas* (Cambridge: Bowes & Bowes, 1950).
14. Lethbridge (1948), p. 91.
15. James P. Whittall II, *T.C. Lethbridge-Frank Glynn Correspondence 1950-1966* (Rowley, MA: Early Sites Research Society, 1988).
16. Lethbridge, in *Herdsman and Hermits* (p. 128), had already expressed a suspicion that Henry Sinclair could have made it to America.
17. The "Byfield Viking Graves" were photographed by Pearson in the 1930s. See Chapter Nine.
18. Lawrence F. Willard, "Westford's Mysterious Knight," *Yankee*, 22 (4), April 1958.
19. The Fisher family was prominent in Westford society, contributing teachers, judges, and elected officials to the community. The family home was on Depot Road at Main Street, less than one-quarter mile from the Knight.
20. Lethbridge-Glynn Correspondence, p. 30. This "improvement" is also recorded in Hodgman.
21. Lethbridge-Glynn Correspondence, pp. 31-32.
22. William S. Fowler, "The Westford Indian Rock," *Massachusetts Archaeological Society Bulletin* 21,1960, pp. 21-2.
23. Sinclair remarks that on his first visit to Westford, the division was still unabated, nearly 50 years after Frank Glynn first began stripping away the lichen.
24. Frank Glynn, "A Unique Punched Portrait in Massachusetts," *Eastern States Archaeological Federation Bulletin*, 1957.
25. Frederick J. Pohl, *Prince Henry Sinclair: His Voyage to the New World in 1398* (New York: Clarkson N. Potter, 1974).
26. Iain Moncrieffe, *The Highland Clans* (New York: Clarkson N. Potter, 1967).
27. Moncrieffe, p. 161.
28. Frederick J. Pohl, *The Sinclair Expedition to Nova Scotia in 1398* (Pictou Nova Scotia: Pictou Advocate Press, 1950).
29. Pohl (1974), p. 160.
30. John Burke, *A General and Heraldic Dictionary of the Peerage and Baronetage of the British Empire*, 106 ed. (London: Burke's Peerage, 1999).
31. Nicolò Zeno, *The Discovery of the Islands of Frislandia, Eslanda, Engronelanda, Estotilanda, and Icaria; Made by Two Brothers of the Zeno Family, Namely Messire Nicolò, the Chevalier, and Messire Antonio. With a Map of the Said Islands (English Translation)* (Venice, 1558).
32. Carlo Zeno (1334-1418) was a Venetian admiral who commanded a fleet that lay siege to the Genoese-occupied city of Chioggia in 1380. The victory was the first time shipboard cannons were employed and was a turning point in the struggle between the two great maritime republics.
33. Fred. W. Lucas, trans., "The Zeno Narrative," *New Orkney Antiquarian Journal* 2, 2002, pp. 19-28.

34. Pohl (1974), pp. 97–98. Pohl suggests that this Antonio Zeno was Nicolò's son, not the brother of the same name.

35. Brian Smith, "Earl Henry Sinclair's Fictitious Trip to America," *New Orkney Antiquarian Journal* 2, 2002, p. 92.

36. Smith also points out that Andrea da Mosto, director of the State Archives of Venice, published an article in 1933 discussing the problem that Nicolò Zeni was a common name in Venice in that period.

37. Johann Reinhold Forster, *History of the Voyages and Discoveries Made in the North* (London: Printed for G.G.J. and J. Robinson, 1786).

38. C. C. Zahrtmann, "Remarks on the Voyages to the Northern Hemisphere, Ascribed to the Zeni of Venice," *Journal of the Royal Geographic Society of London* 5, 102–28 (1835).

39. Fred. W. Lucas and Niccolò Zeno, *The Annals of the Voyages of the Brothers Nicolò and Antonio Zeno, in the North Atlantic About the End of the Fourteenth Century, and the Claim Founded Thereon to a Venetian Discovery of America; A Criticism and an Indictment* (London: H. Stevens Sons and Stiles, 1898).

40. Samuel Eliot Morison, *The European Discovery of America* (New York: Oxford University Press, 1971).

41. Morison also takes another shot at William Goodwin, incorrectly claiming that Goodwin, a "paladin of lost causes," found the image of Sinclair himself on a rock in Westford.

42. Pohl (1950), p. 9.

43. Pohl (1974), pp. 86–87.

44. William Herbert Hobbs, "The Fourteenth-Century Discovery of America by Antonia Zeno," *Scientific Monthly*, 72:1, January 1951.

45. Arlington Mallery, in *Rediscovery of Lost America*, argues that the Zeno Map rendering of Greenland, although inaccurate at first glance, is an accurate outline of the coasts beneath the ice cover.

46. Arlington H. Mallery and Mary Roberts Harrison, *The Rediscovery of Lost America* (New York: Dutton, 1979).

47. Pohl (1952), pp. 210–213.

48. Hobbs quotes the passage in his *Scientific Monthly* article (p. 30).

49. A number of researchers, most notably Pohl, note parallels between Sinclair's visit and the Mi'kmaq folk figure Glooscap. Pohl (1974), pp. 133–154.

50. Andrew Sinclair, *The Sword and the Grail* (New York: Crown, 1992).

51. Sinclair, pp. 144–147.

52. Means (1942).

53. Pell, pp. 105–19.

54. Manuel Luciano da Silva, *Portuguese Pilgrims and Dighton Rock: The First Chapter in American History* (Bristol, RI: published by the author, 1971).

55. Sinclair, p. 136.

56. Provenience Record Number 1B6A13.1, Louisbourg Institute Archaeology Artifact Database (Fortress of Louisbourg National Historic Site).

57. George Patterson, "The Portuguese on the North East Coast of America," *Proceedings and Transactions of the Royal Society of Canada for the Year 1890*, 1891, p. 164.

58. Forster, p. 179.

59. Charles Wingate Chase, *History of Haverhill, Massachusetts* (Haverhill, MA: George Wingate Chase, 1861).

60. N.A.M. Rodger, *The Safeguard of the Sea: A Naval History of Britain, 660–1649* (New York: W.W. Norton, 1998).

61. Lincoln P. Paine, *Ships of the World: An Historical Encyclopedia* (Boston: Houghton Mifflin, 1997).

62. Patricia Trainor O'Malley and Paul H. Tedesco, *A New England City: Haverhill, Massachusetts* (Northridge, CA: Windsor, 1987).

63. Elizabeth Lane, the tireless "Keeper of the Knight," who maintained the Westford Library's collection on the carving, recalled a persistent local rumor of a rock with "1399" carved into the face. This rock is alleged to be located in the immediate vicinity of the juncture of the Concord and Merrimack Rivers. It may or may not be associated with the Sinclair voyage, but 1399 would be the approximate date of the journey.

64. Billerica, Massachusetts: 1:25,000-scale metric topographic map. Massachusetts Dept. of Public Works (Reston, VA: U.S. Geological Survey, 1987).

65. Pohl (1974), p. 164. Pohl cites Moncrieffe's interpretation of the emblems on the shield as proof of the rank of the effigy.

66. Hodgman, p. 4.

67. For more on the evolution of the Knights Templar into the Masons and the subsequent association with the Westford site, see David Goudsward, *The Westford Knight and Henry Sinclair* (Jefferson, NC: McFarland, 2020), chapters 12–14.

68. Tim Wallace-Murphy and Marilyn Hopkins, *Templars in America: From the Crusades to the New World*. (Boston: Weiser Books, 2004).

69. Wallace-Murphy, p. 93.

70. Dan Brown, *The Da Vinci Code*, 1st ed. (New York: Doubleday, 2003); *The Da Vinci Code*, feature film produced by Brian Grazer and John Calley, USA (distributed by Sony Pictures; released 2006).

71. Goudsward (2020), especially the epilogue. The nadir of Westford references is a book that identifies the carving as a schematic of a time gate in a global earth energy–consciousness grid used by both the Celts and the Templars.

72. Frank Glynn, "A Second Mediaeval Marker at Westford Massachusetts," *Eastern States Archaeological Federation Bulletin* 26 (14), 1967.

73. Frank Glynn, "Another Possible Medieval Marker in Westford, Mass.," *NEARA Journal* 2 (2), 1967, pp. 21–2.

74. Mapped and measured by James Whittall of the Early Sites Research Society, the site was subsequently destroyed for home construction.

75. This "Apple Post," located left of the barn, was relocated 50 feet from the right side during barn renovations in the mid-1990s. See Harde and Day, *The New Old Houses of Westford* (Westford, MA: Westford Historical Commission, 2004), p. 53 for a photograph of the original location.

76. After the 1996 death of the last of the Gould family property owners, Bernice Gould Picking, the farm was purchased by her family, selling the farm and 21 acres to a private partnership to operate as a working farm. The remaining land became walking trails known as the Snake Meadow Brook Trail under the stewardship of the Westford Conservation Trust. For more on the complicated history of boundaries in this section of Westford and why carved stones were used, see Goudsward (2020), pp. 170–173.

77. Wolter and Lemcke, "Petrographic Analysis of Rock." A copy is on file in the Westford Knight Collection at Westford's J.V. Fletcher Library.

78. Wolter, *The Hooked X: Key to the Secret History of North America* (St. Cloud, MN: North Star Press of St. Cloud, 2009), p. 178. Such navigation skills would be useful as support for Wolter's theory of secret transatlantic voyages during the Middle Ages.

79. Brydall, "The Monumental Effigies of Scotland, from the Thirteenth to the Fifteenth Century," *Proceedings of the Society of Antiquaries of Scotland* 29, p. 329. Brydall, p. 337, also notes that most Scottish effigies monuments are carved of stone, brightly colored, and gilt, not monochromatic bronze.

Chapter Eight

1. William H. Babcock, *Early Norse Visits to North America* (Washington, DC: Smithsonian Institute, 1913).

2. Babcock's *Cian of the Chariots* (Boston: Lothrop, 1898) is sometimes credited as the first Arthurian historical novel written by an American author.

3. The 1922 Rover started the trend in England with a standing Viking on the radiator cap. This quickly crossed over to the U.S. with the 1924 Chrysler Six and 1929–1931 Pontiacs.

4. Along with Norse items excavated at L'Anse aux Meadows, butternuts were found. Also called white walnuts or oilnuts, the northern limit for butternuts is now northeastern New Brunswick. New Brunswick is also the northern limit for wild grapes, so the only thing between the Norse and the New England coast was Nova Scotia.

5. "Indian Relics," *Essex Gazette*, May 1, 1830.

6. Whittier was the editor of the *Essex Gazette* at the time of the rock's discovery and probably wrote the original 1830 newspaper report.

7. Whittier would compose other poems that had Scandinavian themes, including "The Conquest of Finland" (1856), "Kallundborg Church" (1865), "Norumbega" (1869), and "King Volmer and Elsie" (1870). Also of note is "Norumbega Hall" (1886), written in honor of the dedication of Norumbega Hall at Wellesley College, named in honor of Eben Norton Horsford, trustee and benefactor of the college.

8. John Greenleaf Whittier, *The Complete Poetical Works of John Greenleaf Whittier*, Cambridge ed. (Boston: Houghton Mifflin, 1894).

9. John Greenleaf Whittier, "The Double-Headed Snake of Newbury," *Atlantic Monthly* 3 (15), 1859.

10. The letter is reprinted on p.195 of Coffin's *A Sketch of the History of Newbury, Newburyport, and West Newbury, from 1635 to 1845* (Boston: Samuel G. Drake, 1845).

11. The ledge with the inscription is actually in neighboring West Newbury, which had been set off from Newbury in 1819.

12. George I. Pool, "An Antiquity Discovered in the Valley of the Merrimack," *New England Historical and Genealogical Register* 8, 1854, p. 184.

13. The Dighton Rock has so many layers of inscriptions superimposed on each other that it would be difficult not to find something that matched.

14. Delabarre (1928).

15. Delabarre (1928), p. 279.

16. Dow, editor of the journal *Old-Time New England* for Boston's Society for the Preservation of New England Antiquities, lived in nearby Topsfield, MA.

17. The original 1854 article included a footnote from the editor noting they had elected not to reproduce a profile sketch of the rock with the article because there was "nothing peculiar in the appearance..."

18. Delabarre (1928), p. 280.

19. Strandwold (1948), pp. 27–29.

20. Strandwold (1948), p. 27.

21. Johannes Brøndsted, *Norsemen in North America Before Columbus* (Washington, DC: Smithsonian Institution, 1954); *Problemet om nordboer i Nordamerika før Columbus: en bedømmelse af det amerikanske materiale* (København: Bianco Lunos bogtrykkeri, 1951).

22. See Chapter Twelve.

23. Brøndsted (1954), pp. 397–398.

24. Rod Doherty, "'Old Hanging Rock' again reveals its Nordic legend," *Newburyport Daily News*, August 1976.

25. Laurie D. Williams, "Rediscovery of the 'Whittier Runestone' in Massachusetts," *NEARA Journal* 11 (2), 1976, pp. 22–4.

26. Williams, p. 23.

27. "Local Discoveries Indicate Norsemen Were Here First," *Newburyport Daily News*, October 11, 1957.

28. "Long Hunt for Relics Starts," *Newburyport Daily News*, May 1, 1930.

29. See Chapter Ten.

30. "Thorvald's Stone Riddle is Solved," *Boston Globe*, June 26, 1938.

31. "Norse Markings on Hampton Rock Made

by Explorer 'Bui,'" *Newburyport Daily News,* June 27, 1938.

32. Wallace B. Ordway, "Markings on Byfield Stones Spur Scientific Speculation," *Newburyport Daily News,* December 15, 1948.

33. Charles Michael Boland, *They All Discovered America* (Garden City, NY: Doubleday, 1961).

34. When Frank Glynn began searching for the sword carving that would become the Westford Knight (Chapter Seven), Pearson thought he meant the Byfield stones. Having not visited either site in decades, he dutifully repeated Boland's book as the carving having been destroyed.

35. O. G. Landsverk and Alf Mongé, *Norse Medieval Cryptography in Runic Carvings* (Glendale, CA: Norseman Press, 1967).

36. O. G. Landsverk, *Runic Records of the Norsemen in America* (NY: E.J. Friis, 1974). p. 15. He dismissively refers to Strandwold's two publications as "brochures."

37. Wallace, p. 9. Wallace includes a recent (c.2000) photograph of the stone Strandwold translated as "Overland route, øn set the stone," Strandwold (1942), pp. 35–36.

38. William Jenks, *The Comprehensive Commentary on the Holy Bible: Containing the Text According to the Authorized Version* (Brattleboro, VT: Fessenden, 1835).

39. William Jenks, "Abstract of Presentation on the Mananas Island Inscription," *Proceedings of the American Academy of Arts and Sciences* 6, 1851, pp. 267–8.

40. Lenik (2002).

41. Jenks (1851), p. 267.

42. The station was operated by civilian employees from 1855 to 1956 and then by Coast Guard personnel until automated in 1986.

43. For 40 years, Manana was also home to a hermit. During the Depression, Ray Phillips left New York City, went to Monhegan Island, bought one-sixth of Manana Island, and built a shack from driftwood. He lived there, tending sheep and geese until his death in May 1975 at age 83. His ashes are buried on the island.

44. Ida Sedgwick Proper, *Monhegan, the Cradle of New England* (Portland, ME: Southworth Press, 1930).

45. David B. Quinn, *North America from Earliest Discovery to First Settlements: the Norse Voyages to 1612,* 1st Harper Torchbook ed. (New York: Harper & Row, 1978).

46. Samuel Eliot Morison, *The Maritime History of Massachusetts, 1783–1860* (Boston: Houghton Mifflin, 1961).

47. Proper, pp. 5–6.

48. A.C. Hamlin, "Supposed Runic Inscriptions," *Proceedings of the American Association for the Advancement of Science* 10 (Part 2), 1857, pp. 214–216.

49. Hamlin, p. 214.

50. Henry Rowe Schoolcraft, *History of Indian Tribes of the United States: Their Present Condition and Prospects, and a Sketch of their Ancient Status* (Philadelphia: J.B. Lippincott, 1857).

51. Schoolcraft, pp. 608–609.

52. Sir Daniel Wilson, *Prehistoric Man; Researches into the Origin of Civilisation in the Old and the New World* (London: Macmillan, 1876).

53. Wilson, p. 98.

54. Schoolcraft's volume VI discusses the Dighton Rock in several places. He states unequivocally that the Dighton inscription was a Native American mnemonic. Apparently, Jenks is referring to an earlier draft of the text where Schoolcraft is less adamant in his opinion.

55. Jenks (1851), pp. 267–268.

56. George Hickes, et al., *Linguarum Vett Septentrionalium Thesaurus Grammatico-criticus et Archæologicus* (Oxoniæ: E Theatro Sheldoniano, 1705).

57. Based on the timeline of the Hamlin casting and Schoolcraft's volume, it appears that Jenks was responsible for both Hamlin's casting and the inclusion of the inscription in Schoolcraft's tome.

58. G. H. Stone, "The Inscription Rocks on the Island of Monhegan," *Science* 6 (132), 1885, p. 124.

59. In the article, Stone actually reserved identification of the type of gabbro, apparently planning to publish a more in-depth report that was never completed.

60. Stone, p. 124.

61. E.C.E. Lord, "Notes on the Geology and Petrography of Monhegan Island, Maine." *American Geologist* 26 (6), 1900, p. 330.

62. Lord, pp. 344–345. Lord uses the archaic term *beerbachyte* for the aplitic gabbro.

63. Hornblende registers at 5 to 6 on the scale. Plagioclases such as gabbro range from 6 to 6.5 on the same scale.

64. B. F. DeCosta, *The Pre-Columbian Discovery of America by the Northmen* (Albany: J. Munsell, 1868).

65. DeCosta, p. LVII.

66. Garrick Mallery, *Picture-writing of the American Indians* (New York: Dover, 1972).

67. Mallery, p. 759.

68. Samuel Adams Drake, *The Pine-tree Coast* (Boston: Estes & Lauriat, 1891).

69. Drake, p. 217. Drake also suggests that the islanders believe the inscription to be natural, as opposed to what they might say publicly during tourist season.

70. John Campbell, "Recently Discovered Relics of the American Mound-Builders," *Transactions of the Royal Society of Canada* (Section II) (1898).

71. The Davenport Tablets are three inscribed tablets first uncovered in 1874 near Davenport, Iowa. The authenticity remains questionable and debated.

72. John Campbell, "Hittites in America," *Canadian Naturalist* 9 (5 & 6), 1873.

73. Campbell (1893), p. 10 cites *Mémoires de la Société Royale des Antiquaires du Nord* as his source for the image used in translation. Hamlin's 1857 article in *Proceedings of the American Association for the Advancement of Science* was discussed at the 1859 annual meeting, and *Mémoires*

included reproductions of the runes from the original.
74. Wilson, p. 98.
75. Delabarre (1928), pp. 284–285.
76. Herman Wirth, *Der Aufgang der Menschheit; untersuchungen zur geschichte der religion, symbolik und schrift der atlantischnordischen rasse* (Jena, Germany: E. Diederichs, 1928).
77. Franz Wegener, *Das Atlantidische Weltbild: Nationalsozialismus und neue Rechte auf der Suche nach dem versunkenen Atlantis* (Gladbeck: KFVR-Kulturförderverein Ruhrgebiet, 2000).
78. Strandwold (1939), pp. 10–11.
79. This would be the same *Mémoires de la Société Royale des Antiquaires du Nord* issue used by Campbell for his Hittie translation.
80. Strandwold (1948), pp. 33–34.
81. Several years earlier, Pohl had arranged for an excavation in search of Leif Ericsson's winter quarters, only to see the results interpreted counter to his theories. See Chapter Twelve.
82. Frederick J. Pohl, *Atlantic Crossings Before Columbus* (New York: Norton, 1961).
83. Pohl (1961), pp. 196–198.
84. James P. Whittall, Jr. "The Monhegan Inscriptions," *Early Sites Research Society Bulletin* 4 (1), 1976, pp. 1–7.
85. Fell (1976).
86. Monroe Oppenheimer and Willard Wirtz, "A Linguistic Analysis of Some West Virginia Petroglyphs," *West Virginia Archeologist* 41 (1), 1989, pp. 1–6.
87. Fell, p. 58.
88. Whittall (1975). Fell regularly sent reports to Whittall for use in his organization's newsletter and vice versa. Because of differing publishing timetables, minor revisions and elaborations often differ from one issue to the other.
89. Fell (1976), pp. 100–101.
90. Arthur Frederick, "Discovery Shakes Theory of New World," *Sunday Record*, January 16, 1977.
91. Suzanne Carlson, "Manana Revisited," *NEARA Journal* 27 (3/4), 1993, pp. 84–5.
92. Carlson, p. 85.
93. Carlson, p. 84.
94. Charles C. Willoughby, "Prehistoric Burial Places In Maine." *Archaeological and Ethnological Papers of the Peabody Museum* 1(6), July 1898.
95. Edward J. Lenik, *Making Pictures in Stone: American Indian Rock Art of the Northeast* (Tuscaloosa: University of Alabama Press, 2009).
96. Bruce J. Bourque, *Twelve Thousand Years: American Indians in Maine* (Lincoln: University of Nebraska Press, 2004).
97. Strandwold (1948), pp. 43–44.
98. Strandwold (1939), pp. 12, 48.
99. Goodwin (1941), p. 433.
100. Goodwin (1941), pp. 420, 431.
101. Lindley S. Hanson and Dabney W. Caldwell, *Reconnaissance surficial geology of the Sebec [15-minute] quadrangle.* (Maine Geological Survey, Open-File Map 80-10, map, scale 1:62,500. Maine Geological Survey Maps (1980), p. 633.
102. Goodwin (1941), pp. 432–3.
103. Strandwold (1948), p. 45.

Chapter Nine

1. Goodwin (1941), p. 445. Pp. 409–412 are Pearson's report and photographs.
2. Strandwold (1948), p. 32.
3. Personal communication with author, August 11, 2004.
4. Goodwin (1941), pp. 41–78.
5. See Chapter Ten.
6. See Chapter Twelve.
7. O. G. Landsverk and Alf Mongé, *Norse Medieval Cryptography in Runic Carvings* (Glendale, CA: Norseman Press, 1967).
8. O. G. Landsverk, *Runic Records of the Norsemen in America* (New York: E.J. Friis, 1974).
9. Landsverk (1974), p. 169.
10. As of the publication of the 1974 book, Mongé had not actually examined the stones himself.
11. Cyrus Gordon was a linguist who studied various languages, including Akkadian, Hebrew, Latin, and Scandinavian, and was a specialist in the Semitic language of Ugarit, an ancient city of western Syria on the Mediterranean. During World War II, like Alf Mongé, he was a codebreaker for the Army Signal Corps.
12. Cyrus Herzl Gordon, *Riddles in History* (New York: Crown, 1974).
13. Gordon (1974), p. 135, 135n94.
14. Landsverk (1974), pp. 201–211.
15. Like his predecessor, Haugen also had a connection to Ole Bull. Haugen and his daughter Camilla Cai collaborated on a biography entitled *Ole Bull: Norway's Romantic Musician and Cosmopolitan Patriot* (Madison: University of Wisconsin Press, 1993).
16. Einar Haugen, "The Rune Stones of Spirit Pond Maine," *Man in the Northeast* 4, 62–80 (1972).
17. Landsverk (1974), pp. 201–222.
18. Holand was almost singlehandedly responsible for keeping Minnesota's Kensington Rune Stone controversy alive. He purchased it in 1907 and spent the rest of his life trying to prove its authenticity. The debate continues to this day, unabated and inconclusive.
19. Hjalmar R. Holand, *The Kensington Stone: A Study in Pre-Columbian American History.* (Ephraim, WI: n.p., 1932). Holand being accused of accidentally creating a how-to guide for runic forgeries would also come into play over the Narragansett Rune Stone. See Chapter Thirteen.
20. Hjalmar R. Holand, *The Kensington Rune Stone: The Oldest Native Document of American History* (Menasha, WI: n.p., 1919). The booklet was reprinted from an earlier *Wisconsin Magazine of History* article.
21. Aslak Liestøl, "Cryptograms in Runic Carvings: A Critical Analysis," *Minnesota History* 41 (1), 1968, pp. 34–42.

22. O. G. Landsverk, "The Spirit Pond Cryptography," *Man in the Northeast* 6, 1973, pp. 67–74.

23. Haugen's most recent publication, a compilation of his essays on Norwegian linguistic topics, had recently been published. *The Ecology of Language, Language Science and National Development* (Stanford, CA: Stanford University Press, 1972).

24. Einar Haugen, "Comment on O.G. Landsverk's 'The Spirit Pond Cryptography,'" *Man in the Northeast* 6, 1973, pp. 75–6.

25. Hans Karlgren, review of *Norse Medieval Cryptography in Runic Carvings* by O.G. Landsverk and Alf Mongé, *Scandinavian Studies* 40 (4), 1968, pp. 326–30.

26. Erik Wahlgren, "American Runes: from Kensington to Spirit Pond," *Journal of English and Germanic Philology* 81, 1982, pp. 157–85.

27. Erik Wahlgren, *The Vikings and America* (New York: Thames and Hudson, 1986).

28. Wahlgren (1982), p. 164.

29. Wahlgren (1982), p. 160.

30. *The Spirit Pond Runestones* (Milford, NH: New England Antiquities Research Association, 1972).

31. Calvin Trillin, "Runes," *The New Yorker*, February 5, 1972.

32. Wahlgren (1982), p. 167n13.

33. Wahlgren (1982), p. 177.

34. Holand, Hjalmar Rued, *Westward from Vinland: An Account of Norse Discoveries and Explorations in America*, pp. 982–1362 (New York: Duell Sloan & Pearce, 1940). Wahlgren cites p. 173 in the 1969 reprint.

35. James P. Whittall II, "A 'Runic' Amulet," *Early Sites Research Society Bulletin* 3 (1), 1975, pp. 1–5.

36. Erik Wahlgren, "Cryptopuzzle," *Biblical Archaeologist* 43 (2), 1980, p. 74.

37. Wahlgren (1980), p. 74. He specifically notes the Landsverk and Mongé translation of the term "sailing ship," which Old Icelandic had no word for, since there were no other types of ships.

38. Wahlgren's later remarks were prompted by a series of articles debating the authenticity of the Paraiba Stone, an inscribed stone found in Brazil in the last century. This stone purportedly proved that Hebrew and Phoenician traders had developed trade routes with the New World in Biblical times. Cyrus Gordon had used Landsverk's work on the Spirit Pond stones to prove the Paraiaba's authenticity by finding it had a cryptograms in the text.

39. Paul H. Chapman, *The Norse Discovery of America* (Atlanta: One Candle Press, 1981).

40. Paul H. Chapman, *Spirit Pond Runestones: A Study in Linguistics* (San Francisco: Epigraphic Society, 1994).

41. Chapman (1994), p. 17. Chapman also felt that the inscription of the amulet that was found at a later date was proof. He felt that the carvings were similar enough in style to suggest the same creator, and both included Ogham with the runes.

42. Suzanne Carlson, "The Spirit Pond Inscription Stone: Rhyme and Reason," *NEARA Journal* 28 (1), 1993.

43. Donal Buchanan, "A New Look at the Spirit Pond Runestones," *Epigraphic Society Occasional Publications* 21, 1992, pp. 138–164; Paul H. Chapman, "An In-depth Examination of the Spirit Pond Runestones," *Epigraphic Society Occasional Publications* 21, 192, pp. 114–137.

44. Several of the stones also traveled to a Smithsonian Institute exhibit, "Vikings: The North Atlantic Saga." The stones were on display as examples of hoaxes associated with Viking interest.

45. Richard Nielsen and Scott F. Wolter, *The Kensington Rune Stone: Compelling New Evidence* (Minneapolis, MN: Lake Superior Agate, 2006).

46. Nielsen and Wolter, pp. 49–92, Appendix C.

47. See Chapter Seven for a brief overview of the resurgence of the Templars as a modern secret society among the conspiracy inclined.

48. See Chapter Thirteen for more on the Narragansett Rune Stone. Wolter also conveniently found a hooked X at the Westford Knight site in 2014 during a brief examination while filming an episode of the third season of *America Unearthed*, a cable television program he hosted. The episode (3:13) title was "The Templars' Deadliest Secret: Evidence Exposed." Everyone else sees pareidolic scratches on the ledge. See p. 182 for a comparison of the hooked X marks.

49. Richard Nielsen, "An Old Norse Translation of the Spirit Pond Runic Inscriptions of Maine," *Epigraphic Society Occasional Publications* 22, 1993, pp. 158–200.

50. Scott F. Wolter, *The Hooked X* (St. Cloud, MN: North Star Press of St. Cloud, 2009), pp. 71–85.

51. Wolter (2009), p. 73.

52. Richard Nielsen, "The Runes and Language of the Spirit Pond Stones and the Narragansett Inscription Can be Found in Modern Books," *The Epigraphic Society Occasional Papers* 27, 2009.

53. Scott F. Wolter, *Akhenaten to the Founding Fathers: The Mysteries of the Hooked X* (St. Cloud, MN: North Star Press of St. Cloud, 2013), p.4.

Chapter Ten

1. Peter Randall, *Hampton, a Century of Town and Beach, 1888–1988* (1989), pp. 307–8.

2. Edmund F. Slafter. *Voyages of the Northmen to America*. Boston: Prince Society, 1877; Edmund Slafter, "The Discovery of America by the Northmen, in the Tenth and Eleventh Centuries." *Proceedings of the New Hampshire Historical Society* 2 (June 1888–June 1895).

3. The original article ran in the *Beverly Citizen* on September 14 and 21, 1889. The broadside is reproduced in Delabarre (1928), p. 280.

4. Joseph Dow, *History of the Town of Hampton, New Hampshire* (1893).

5. Lovell's first attempt at a weekend destination was the Hampton Beach Casino Ballroom, which remains a local landmark.

6. Several other ancient sites discussed in this book had affiliations with their local trolley park/pleasure resort, including Dighton Rock Park, owned and operated by the Dighton, Somerset & Swansea Street Railway Company. Commonwealth Avenue Street Railway's Norumbega Park was in Auburndale, Massachusetts, across the Charles River from Eben Horsford's stone tower in Weston. The Hudson, Pelham & Salem Railway opened Canobie Lake Park in 1902. Less than ten miles away from America's Stonehenge, the location of Canobie Lake Park was unrelated to the Stonehenge location of Mystery Hill, but the popularity and accessibility of the new park did funnel picnickers away from the site, minimizing the damage already occurring. Canobie Lake Park is one of the few survivors and is now an amusement park.

7. [Lamprey's article on the stone near Hampton]. *Philadelphia Times*, July 27, 1902.

8. William H. Babcock. *Early Norse Visits to North America* (Washington, DC: Smithsonian Institute, 1913).

9. Olaf Strandwold. *The Yarmouth Stone, Mystic Characters on Yarmouth Stone Yield Startling Evidence of Norse Discoveries* (Prosser, WA: Prosser Printing Company, 1934).

10. Strandwold (1939). Despite the title, the booklet covers more Scandinavian runic material than North American. The latter is limited to Nova Scotia and Northern New England.

11. Babcock, p. 49.

12. William D. Cram. *Official Pictorial Magazine: 1638–Hampton Tercentenary–1938.* (Concord, NH: Rumford Press, 1938). pp. 14, 59.

13. William D. Cram. "Thorvald's Grave" (Little Stories of Old New England). *Hampton Union & Rockingham County Gazette*, December 2, 1937.

14. "Norse Markings on Hampton Rock Made by Explorer 'Bui.'" *Newburyport Daily News*, June 27, 1938. The article was carried regionally in other newspapers, including *The Boston Globe*. The material is also covered in Strandwold (1939).

15. Goodwin (1946), p. 59, 352, 392. The illustration in *Ruins* is misleading, placing the cross and metal in such a way as to infer an interconnectedness. Goodwin also notes a pair of brass "Mass spoons" found near Hampton Falls.

16. Because of the haste in which the book was put together, there is no way to tell what Goodwin's final thoughts on Hampton were. What are obviously preliminary, earlier thoughts appear sporadically in the book, eliminating any sort of chronology in his thinking. So, although at various points, the text suggests that he thought it was Norse, there is no certainty as it whether that was his final opinion.

17. James W. Tucker. "The Vikings In Hampton" (Our Town column). *Hampton Union*, July 26, 1951.

18. James W. Tucker. "Our Town column." *Hampton Union*, May 14, 1959.

19. Graham Griffith. "Old Norse Explorer Spinning in Grave." *The Portsmouth Herald*, July 21, 1967.

20. David V. Craig. "Thorwald's Grave: Fact or Legend?" *New Hampshire Profiles* 23 (1), January 1974, pp. 70–79.

21. William B. Goodwin, *correspondence with Frances Healy* (September 9, 1938), NEARA archives.

22. Strandwold (1939), pp. 16, 74.

23. Goodwin (1941), pp. 427–8. Goodwin did not even bother to remove Strandwold's original pagination.

24. Willard Du Lue. "Hampton Falls Woman Owns Norseman's Rock." *Boston Globe*, August 13, 1952.

25. Gertrude Johnson. "The Healey Stone." *Early Sites Research Society Bulletin* 3 (2), May 1975.

26. Barry Fell. [notes from Fell's Libyan Trip.] *Early Sites Research Society News-Letter* #32, January 1978.

27. James P. Whittall II. "A Libyan Lithic Measure," *Early Sites Research Society Bulletin* 6 (1), May 1978.

28. Fell (1980), Chapter 11 "Arabs before Islam."

Chapter Eleven

1. In the early 1900s, Speck also recorded the Mohegan Pequot language from Fidelia Hoscott Fielding, the last person fluent in the language. After Fielding died in 1908, Speck translated her diaries.

2. Frank Gouldsmith Speck, *Native Tribes and Dialects of Connecticut, a Mohegan-Pequot Diary* (Washington, DC: 1928); Frank Gouldsmith Speck, *Notes on the Mohegan and Niantic Indians* (New York: American Museum of Natural History, 1909).

3. Speck (1909), p. 202.

4. Prior to the Shepard novel, Gungywamp Hill appears on maps as a geographic reference without any indication of anything out of the ordinary.

5. Odell Shepard and Willard Shepard, *Holdfast Gaines* (New York: Macmillan, 1946).

6. Shepard won the 1937 prize for his biography of Bronson Alcott.

7. David P. Barron, "Necrology: Willard Odell Shepard," *Stonewatch* 8 (1) (1988a).

8. William Scranton Simmons, *Spirit of the New England Tribes: Indian History and Folklore, 1620–1984* (Hanover: University Press of New England, 1986); William S. Simmons, "The Mystic Voice: Pequot Folklore from the Seventeenth Century to the Present" in *The Pequots in Southern New England: The Fall and Rise of an American Indian Nation*, edited by Laurence M. Hauptman and James Wherry (Norman, OK: University of Oklahoma Press, 1990).

9. Michael A. Persinger, "Limitations of Human Verbal Behavior in the Context of UFO-Related Stimuli" in *UFO Phenomena and the Behavioral*

Scientist, edited by Richard F. Haines (Metuchen, NJ: Scarecrow Press, 1979), pp. 165–187; Michael A. Persinger, "Possible Infrequent Geophysical Sources of Close UFO Encounters: Expected Physical and Behavioral-Biological Effects" in *UFO Phenomena and the Behavioral Scientist*, edited by Richard F. Haines (Metuchen, NJ: Scarecrow Press, 1979), pp. 396–433.

10. This luminosity is well documented, although the cause is debated. Current wisdom is that it is caused by gas ionization triggered by the piezoelectric effect in quartz-bearing rock.

11. Michael A. Persinger, "Religious and Mystical Experience as Artifacts of Temporal Lobe Function: A General Hypothesis," *Perceptual and Motor Skills* 57, 1255–62 (1983).

12. Persinger lists several phenomena associated with TLTs: a sense of divine guidance, déjà vu, recurring vivid dreams, memory blanks, and distortions in the serial order of events (precognition).

13. John S. Derr and Michael A. Persinger, "Geophysical Variables and Behavior: LIV. Zeitoun (Egypt) Apparitions of the Virgin Mary as Tectonic Strain-induced Luminosities," *Perceptual and Motor Skills* 68, 1989, pp. 123–8.

14. Similarly, America's Stonehenge is also positioned on a faultline near a swamp. The bedrock is heavily laced with quartz and a pluton of newer rock with a trace percentage of magnetite ends on the hill. See Goudsward (2002), pp. 19–21.

15. John A. Burke, "Scientific Instrument Survey of the Gungywamp Complex," *Stonewatch* 13 (4), 9 (1995).

16. David P. Barron and Sharon Mason, *The Greater Gungywamp: A Guidebook* (Noank, CT: The Gungywamp Society, 1990).

17. The YMCA owned a significant part of the property, part of a bequest in 1942. In 1985, the YMCA attempted to sell the parcel, finally being allowed in 1989 to sell 100 acres of the land in North Groton. The remaining tract of YMCA land is now the "The Gungywamp Preserve," part of the Great Oak Greenway, creating one of the largest trail systems in southeastern Connecticut.

18. Barron (1990), p. 3. Barron places the number at 300 acres for his guidebook's purposes.

19. Barron (1990), pp. 7–10.

20. Stewart-Smith's position on restorations is to rebuild the structures only to a status that can be documented with photographs, with a mason's mark and date carved into the stone.

21. David P. Barron, "Mystery of the Gungywamp Light Show," *Stonewatch* 7 (3), 1988b, pp. 1, 5–6.

22. Barron (1990), pp. 7–10.

23. James P. Whittall II, "Vernal Equinox Light Channel," *Early Sites Research Society Bulletin* 18 (1), 1991a, pp. 23–25.

24. Whittall (1991a), p. 25.

25. James P. Whittall II, "The Gungywamp Complex, Groton, Connecticut," *Early Sites Research Society Bulletin* 4 (1), 1976, pp. 15–27.

26. Barron (1990), pp. 11–12.

27. Paulette J. Buchanan, "More Conclusive Research on the Rows of Standing Stones & Other Sites in the Gungywamp," *Stonewatch* 21 (1), 2004.

28. Barron (1990) includes site maps. The smaller chamber ruins appear to be isolated by stone walls, suggesting grazing areas.

29. David P. Barron, "'Adam's Dwelling' Excavation Finished," *Stonewatch* 13 (1), 1 (1994); Paulette J. Buchanan, "Adams Dwelling Update," *Stonewatch* 16 (2), 4 (1998); James P. Whittall II, "Colonial 'Half-House' Excavated in Gungywamp Complex," *Stonewatch* 8 (3), 6–7 (1989).

30. Alfred M. Bingham, "Squatter Settlements of Freed Slaves in New England," *Connecticut Historical Society Bulletin* 41 (3), 1976, pp. 65–80.

31. His best-known book was a biography of his father, Hiram Bingham III, the explorer who rediscovered the lost Incan ruins of Machu Picchu.

32. Robert Alexander Douglas-Lithgow, *Dictionary of American-Indian Place and Proper Names in New England; With Many Interpretations, etc.* (Salem, MA: Salem Press, 1909).

33. Vance R. Tiede, "The Chi-Rho Controversy Rages On: View 1," *Stonewatch* 20 (1), 2003, pp. 1–2; Paulette J. Buchanan, "The Chi-Rho Controversy Rages On: Response to Vance R. Tiede's Viewpoint," *Stonewatch* 20 (1), 2003, pp. 2–4.

34. Barron (1990), p. 42

35. David P. Barron, "Geologist Spots Chi Rhos," *Stonewatch* 3 (1), 1982, p. 2.

36. Paulette J. Buchanan, "Chi Rho Site: Vogt Ruins," *Stonewatch* 14 (1), 1995, p. 10.

37. Paulette J. Buchanan, "New Research Findings," *Stonewatch* 19 (1), 2002, pp. 1–2.

38. The society's website at www.gungywamp.com is now defunct. The final version included a 300-word mission statement. A full two-thirds of the text was devoted to disavowing any connection to a "religious/spiritual or paranormal interpretation" or "pre-Columbian Celtic or Norse (Viking) occupation." David Barron was not necessarily a believer in any of the listed theories but was a staunch advocate of exploring all avenues of research.

39. Goodwin (1946).

40. David Goudsward, "Great Ireland Revisited: Goodwin's Culdee Monks 45 Years Later," *Stonewatch* 10 (3), 1992, pp. 6–7.

41. Goodwin (1946), p. 343.

42. Goodwin (1946), pp. 102–108, 198–200.

43. Nancy Edwards, *The Archaeology of Early Medieval Ireland* (Philadelphia: University of Pennsylvania Press, 1990).

44. James W. Mavor, "Astronomy and Shamanism Among Culdee Monks," *Early Sites Research Society Bulletin* 12 (1), 1985, pp. 2–17.

45. W.A. Craigie, "The Gaels in Iceland," *Proceedings of the Society of Antiquaries of Scotland* 31, 1897, pp. 247–64.

46. Mavor (1985), p. 14.

47. David Goudsward, "A Possible Origin for the Gungywamp Chi Rhos," *Stonewatch* 13 (1), 1994, pp. 4–5.

48. Lactantius, a contemporary of Constantine the Great, in his *Death of the Persecutors* (ca. 315), says that on the night before the battle (28 Oct 312), Constantine experienced a vision in which God instructed him to mark his men's shields with a Chi bisected with a Rho. The historian, Eusebius of Caesarea, tells a similar tale in his *Vita Constantini*, with the Lord appearing with a Chi Rho in his hand, declaring "In hoc vinces!" (By this, conquer). Subsequent retellings changed the phrase to "In Hoc Signo Vinces," (By this sign, you shall conquer), which has become the motto of various military and religious groups over the centuries.

49. Arians denied that Jesus was of the same substance as God. Instead, they believed that he was only the highest of created beings—not quite human and not quite divine.

50. Donatists believed that the rites and sacraments of the Church were only as sacred as the administering clergy. By their reasoning, the sanctity of the rites could not be guaranteed because it depended on the priest's moral character.

51. Gregory Telepneff, *The Egyptian Desert in the Irish Bogs: The Byzantine Character of Early Celtic Monasticism* (Etna, CA: Center for Traditionalist Orthodox Studies, 1998).

52. Telepneff, pp. 30–32. Telepneff notes that the concept of renunciation of home and family dates back to the Old Testament mandate to Abraham in Genesis 12:1–9.

53. Barron (1988b), p. 6.

54. Jack Hitt, "How the Gungywampers Saved Civilization," *GQ*, January 1998.

55. Stephen C. McCluskey, "Gregory of Tours, Monastic Timekeeping, and Early Christian Attitudes to Astronomy," *Isis* 81 (1), 1990, pp. 8–22.

56. Vance R. Tiede, "Solar Orientation of Irish Early Christian Oratories [abstract]," *HAD News: The Newsletter of the Historical Astronomy Division of the American Astronomical Society* (33), December 2001, p. 1363; "The Sun of Truth & The Oratory: Solar Metaphors from Early Christian Ireland," *Memorie della Società Astronomica Italiana (Journal of the Italian Astronomical Society)*, Special Number 1, 2002.

57. The Celtic Church used an 84-year cycle that the Roman Church had superseded with a 19-year cycle for calculating the paschal moon. Both these saints were associated with the controversy over determining the date of Easter. St. Patrick's Day also marked the vernal equinox and the arrival of the paschal full moon, the lunar event used to calculate the date of Easter. St. Aidan was a Culdee monk who refused to adopt the 19-year cycle for calculating the paschal moon.

58. Gerald S. Hawkins, *Stonehenge Decoded* (Garden City, NY: Doubleday, 1965).

59. Gerald S. Hawkins, "Astro-archaeology." *Vistas in Astronomy* 10, 1968, pp. 45–54.

60. Gerald S. Hawkins, *Beyond Stonehenge* (New York: Harper & Row, 1973).

61. Vance R. Tiede, "Orientation of Stone Chamber One" in *The Greater Gungywamp: Twentieth Anniversary Edition*, edited by David P. Barron and Sharon Mason (Noank, CT: The Gungywamp Society, 1998), pp. 54–57.

62. Old Celtic calendars observed these days as cross quarters, halfway between an equinox and a solstice. Modern calendars define the start of a season on the solstice or equinox; the Celtic calendar recognized those days as the midway point, with the seasons actually beginning and ending on the cross quarter.

63. Tiede (1998), p. 56.

64. John Pynchon, "Letters of John Pynchon, 1654–1700" in *The Pynchon Papers*, edited by Carl Bridenbaugh (Boston: Colonial Society of Massachusetts, 1982), Vol. 1.

65. The eldest son of John Winthrop, first governor of the Massachusetts Bay Colony, Winthrop the Younger would serve as governor of the Colony of Connecticut, 1657 and 1659–1676.

66. Winthrop was interested in bog iron and established iron works at Lynn and Braintree, Massachusetts, in 1633 and at New Haven, Connecticut, in 1657. There is no record of whether Winthrop was associated with the iron works found in the Gungywamp.

67. Alicia Larson, "A Gungywamp Historical Research Update," *Stonewatch* 8 (2), 1989, pp. 9, 13.

68. Alicia Larson, "Alicia Larson Supports Pynchon Papers Relating to Gungywamp," *Stonewatch* 10 (4), 1992, p. 5.

69. Barron (1990), pp. 23–24.

70. Iron Thunderhorse, "An Amerindian View of Bird Effigy in Complex," *Stonewatch* 14 (3), 1996, p. 5.

71. David E. Philips, *Legendary Connecticut* (East Haven, CT: Curbstone Press, 1992).

72. James W. Mavor and Byron E. Dix, *Manitou: The Sacred Landscape of New England's Native Civilization* (Rochester, VT: Inner Traditions International, 1989).

73. Mavor and Dix, p. 332. Mavor and Dix also believe that the two rows of standing stones are associated with the Manitou (p. 337).

74. See Chapter Twelve.

75. Frederick J. Pohl, "Cockaponsett Carvings in Connecticut." *Anthropological Journal of Canada* 16 (4), 1978.

76. Frederick J. Pohl, "Cockaponsett Carvings." *Epigraphic Society Occasional Publications* 6 (134), 1979.

77. John Gallagher, "Inscriptions and other features at Cockaponset." *Epigraphic Society Occasional Publications* 6 (137), 1979.

78. Barry Fell, "A Fifth-century Moroccan Emigration to North America." *Epigraphic Society Occasional Publications* 3 (46), 1976; Barry Fell, "Arabic Dialect in Ancient Moroccan Inscriptions." *Epigraphic Society Occasional Publications* 3 (48), 1976.

79. Norman Totten, "Implications of the Figuig Decipherment." *Epigraphic Society Occasional Publications* 3 (47), 1976.

80. John Gallagher, "Fifth Century Christian

Church Found in Connecticut." *On Site* 1 (3), June 1987.

81. Telepneff, pp.30–31

82. John Gallagher, "Connecticut's 5th Century Church." *Ancient American* 8 (54), December 2003. Also reprinted in *Unearthing Ancient America* (Franklin Lakes, NJ: New Page Books, 2009).

83. Boland, p. 38.

84. Boland, pp. 37–38. The "Phoenician ship," Boland claimed, is only visible when the waters of Lake Assawompset are low. Lenik (2002) disagrees with Boland entirely. Lenik notes it is located in an area known for multiple examples of Native American petroglyphs and colonial graffiti. Lenik further notes the "ship" stylistically fits with other Native metal-tool carvings of the Historic Contact period (pp. 127–28).

85. See Goudsward (2020), chapter 15 "The Tor Bay Runic Axe."

86. The website was removed after his death. Archival copy on file.

Chapter Twelve

1. G. M. Gathorne-Hardy, *The Norse Discoverers of America: The Wineland Sagas Translated and Discussed* (Oxford: Clarendon Press, 1921).

2. Rafn (1837).

3. Vilhjalmur Stefansson and Rudolph Martin Anderson, *My Life With the Eskimo* (New York: Macmillan, 1913).

4. Vilhjalmur Stefansson, *Greenland* (Garden City, NY: Doran, 1942).

5. J.R.L. Anderson, *Vinland Voyage* (New York: Funk & Wagnalls, 1967).

6. The Vinland Map in Yale University's Beinecke Library is either a 15th-century map that is the oldest known map depicting North America or a 20th-century fraud. The map shows Europe and an area to the west marked "Vinland." In 1965, Yale University Press published "The Vinland Map and the Tartar Relation," a detailed study that leaned toward the map's authenticity. Ink analysis and C-14 tests on the paper have only continued the debate.

7. Brad Lynch, "Did Vikings Make History on Cape Cod?" *Barnstable Patriot*, March 8, 2001.

8. Marcia Kozubek, "Wind Farm Would Scuttle Viking Studies, Researcher Says." *The Yarmouthport Register*, April 8, 2004.

9. Commonwealth of Massachusetts Board of Underwater Archaeological Resources [notes on Good's permit renewal]. Final minutes of public meeting, September 30, 2021.

10. F. W. Tupper, *Thomas Tupper and His Descendants* (Tupper Family Association of America, 1945).

11. Fell (1975a).

12. Strandwold (1948).

13. Lenik (2002).

14. Edmund B. Delabarre, "The Indian Petroglyph at the Aptucxet Trading Post in Bourne, Massachusetts," *Old-Time New England* 26 (3), January 1936, p.112. In a later article, ""Miguel Cortereal: The First European to Enter Narragansett Bay," *Rhode Island Historical Society Collections* 29 (1), October 1936, p. 116, Delabarre equates the handshake with the iconography of the William Penn wampum belt and figures carved on Dighton Rock at the extreme left-hand end.

15. Strandwold (1948), p. 25.

16. James P. Whittall II, "The Inscribed Stone from Comassakumkanit," *ESOP* 2 (44) (1975).

17. Fell (1975a). The two pages of translation notes were also reprinted in Fell (1976).

18. Fell (1976), pp. 95, 160–1.

19. Elizabeth Reynard, *The Narrow Land: Folk Chronicles of Old Cape Cod* (Boston: Houghton Mifflin, 1968 [rep.]).

20. Both Fell and Whittall were reprinted in *Early Sites Research Society Bulletin* 3:2 (May 1975). The ESRS version includes a Malcolm Pearson photograph not found in the ESOP version, but does not include introductory remarks by Fell.

21. Nigel Davies, *Voyagers to the New World* (New York: William Morrow, 1979).

22. Lenik (2002), p. 139.

23. Gosnold would later reassign the name to the larger island that currently bears the name, less than three miles to the north.

24. Charles Edward Banks, *The History of Martha's Vineyard, Dukes County, Massachusetts* (Edgartown, MA: Dukes County Historical Society, 1966).

25. A turn-of-the-century lawsuit brought by the last two adults on the island. They sued the local school district, demanding a schoolhouse for their offspring, the last two children on the island. They lost the suit.

26. See *Washington Post*, May 23, 1915, for one example, where submarine K6 went aground in heavy fog.

27. It is still not clear whether the actual kidnappers were involved or if it was a red herring, but at one point the Coast Guard was actively searching for a white yacht off Nomans Land Island in April of 1932.

28. Edward Francis Gray, *Leif Eriksson, Discoverer of America A.D. 1003* (New York: Oxford University Press, 1930).

29. B. F. DeCosta, *The Pre-Columbian Discovery of America by the Northmen: With Translations from the Icelandic Sagas*, 2nd ed. (Albany, NY: Joel Munsell's Sons, 1890).

30. John Fiske, *New France and New England* (Boston: Houghton Mifflin, 1902), p. 54. Fiske relates how Samuel de Champlain unexpectedly encountered shoals where the island had been, damaging their rudder and forcing them to make harbor at Chatham for repairs.

31. The 400-ton rock was known as "Haystack Rock" or "Whale Rock" and had been a landmark for passing ships.

32. Delabarre (1928).

33. Delabarre (1928), p. 375. Delabarre does

not mention Gray by name, the location, or the inscription's content in the reference. He merely cautioned that experts had not inspected the carvings and thought it would turn out to be recent. Strandwold (1948), p. 40, includes a photo of a plaster casting of the Nomans Land runes taken by Delabarre in 1931, suggesting Delabarre's reticence was based on more than a cursory examination.

34. Gray, p. 163.
35. Gray, p. 164.
36. Gray, p. 164. Craigie was also suspicious of the fact that the inscription contained everything a modern researcher would want to find—name, date, and place.
37. Gray, pp. 168–169.
38. F. S. Cawley and S.E. Morison, review of *Leif Eriksson, Discoverer of America, A.D. 1003* by Edward Francis Gray, *New England Quarterly* 4 (3), 554–60 (1931).
39. Cawlcy, p. 555.
40. Cawley, p. 559.
41. Correspondence with the author, 2004.
42. Annie Moulton Wood and Cameron E. Wood, *Noman's Land; Isle of Romance* (New Bedford, MA: Reynolds Printing, 1931).
43. Edmund Burke Delabarre and Charles W. Brown, "The Runic Rock on No Man's Land Massachusetts: Geological Notes," *New England Quarterly* 8 (3), 365–77 (1935a).
44. Delabarre (1935), pp. 421–9.
45. Delabarre (1935), p. 422.
46. Delabarre (1935a). As with his article in *Scientific Monthly* (1935), Delabarre enumerates the possible suspects and their motivation for doing so.
47. Daniel Ricketson, *The History of New Bedford, Bristol County, Massachusetts: Including a History of the Old Township of Dartmouth and the Present Townships of Westport, Dartmouth, and Fairhaven, From Their Settlement to the Present Time* (New Bedford: Published by the author, 1858).
48. Strandwold (1939), p. 14.
49. Strandwold (1948), p. 40. As with his Monhegan Island inscription translations, Strandwold's greatest weakness was his reliance on other people's images.
50. Peter S. McGhee, "Bertrand Woods Noman's," *Vineyard Gazette*, August 1966.
51. The August 24, 1954, edition of the *Newport News* [RI] reported that Curtis Bacon, an amateur archaeologist from New York, had rediscovered the stone. Although erosion had taken its toll, Bacon was hopeful that ultraviolet light would enhance the inscription. This was before the arrival of the 1954 hurricane season and three hurricanes in two months that further eroded the shore and altered the landscape, hiding the stone once again.
52. Kenneth M. Jungersen, "The Search for Vinland," *Oceans* 18 (5), 1985.
53. "Vineyarders Draw Bead on Navy Target Island," *Boston Globe*, April 5, 1987.
54. "Noman's Land: It's for the Birds—Duck!" *Los Angeles Times*, December 10, 1989.

55. Mavor is also the author of several archaeology texts, including *Voyage to Atlantis* (1969) and *Manitou* (1989).
56. Nielsen and Wolter, pp. 312–15.
57. Hickey, Jim. "Historic Preservation Commissions Doubt Rune Rock Credibility," *Vineyard Gazette*, July 5, 2007.
58. "Vikings in America." *America Unearthed*. H2 Channel, season 2, episode 4, December 21, 2013.
59. "Vikings in America." *Expedition Unknown*. Travel Channel, season 4, episode 2, January 3, 2018.
60. Hjalmar R. Holand, "A Fourteenth-Century Runic Inscription from Martha's Vineyard," *Scandinavian Studies* 21, 79–88 (1949).
61. Holand (1949), pp. 86–87.
62. Hjalmar Rued Holand, *The Kensington Stone, A Study in Pre-Columbian American History* (Ephraim, WI: Private Printing, 1932).
63. Holand (1949), p. 80.
64. The fifth rune is the one Holand believed proved the authenticity of the Kensington Rune Stone.
65. Hjalmar Rued Holand, *America, 1355–1364: A New Chapter in Pre-Columbian History* (New York: Duell Sloan and Pearce, 1946).
66. Morse reprinted the letter in a semi-annual publication he edited. Goodwin, William B. "An Ancient Norse Relic," *The Chronicle* 228, 1938, pp. 36–39.
67. Goodwin had just purchased the axe, the impetus of the letter. Goodwin (1938), pp. 38–39, says Olaf Strandwold translates the axe runes as an invocation to Tyr. By the time of publication of Strandwold's book in 1939, the translation was "Engr inscribed (this to) Aelu." See Strandwold (1939), pp. 17, 76, 78, for additional details. After Goodwin died in 1950, the axe remained in the family. The current whereabouts are unknown. See Goudsward (2020), chapter 15, "The Tor Bay Runic Axe."
68. Goodwin (1938), p. 37.
69. Goodwin (1941).
70. Goodwin (1946).
71. Goodwin (1946), p. 175.
72. The local assessment, according to early newspaper reports, was that the structure was a shelter built for hogs.
73. Goodwin (1946) refers to the site by this name (p. 390). The site has acquired a number of different names over the years, none of which seem to remain attached for any length of time.
74. In 1998, the town of Gay Head officially changed its name to Aquinnah, which in the Wampanoag language means, "The shore or end of the island."
75. "Has Quitsa a Cromlech?" *Vineyard Gazette*, August 19, 1927.
76. Gray, pp. xvi, 122–124.
77. Frederick Johnson, "The Dolmen of Martha's Vineyard," *Bulletin of the Massachusetts Archaeological Society* 6 (2), January 1945, pp. 29–32.

78. The artifacts included four small pieces of plate glass, a rubber gasket from a Mason jar, and an iron gate hinge.

79. Johannes Brøndsted, *Problemet om nordboer i Nordamerika før Columbus: en bedømmelse af det amerikanske materiale* (København: Bianco Lunos bogtrykkeri, 1951); Johannes Brøndsted, *Norsemen in North America Before Columbus* (Washington, DC: Smithsonian Institution, 1954).

80. English translation of Brøndsted (1951), pp. 99–100.

81. James P. Whittall II, "The Quista Dolmen," *NEARA Newsletter* 6 (1), March 1971, p. 16.

82. Whittall refers to it as the "fire and water method," but the process is the same. A large fire is built on the rock to superheat it. If the rock didn't crack from uneven heat expansion, it was doused with water, and the sudden contraction of the rock adding to the stress level would cause it to crack.

83. Johnson, p. 31. Johnson also believes that the capstone was split from this boulder lying northwest of the structure but wouldn't commit to whether the split was natural or not.

84. Squibnocket triangles are usually associated with the Late Archaic to Middle Woodland Period (6000–1000 BP). A relatively common projectile point in southern New England, this point predates the European explorers, the Vikings Exploration Age, and the Dolman construction period.

85. Barry Fell, *Bronze Age America*, 1st ed. (Boston: Little, Brown, 1982).

86. Fell (1982), p. 60. There is no indication that Fell actually attempted a translation of the ogham.

87. James W. Mavor and Byron E. Dix, *Manitou: The Sacred Landscape of New England's Native Civilization* (Rochester, VT: Inner Traditions International, 1989).

88. An embrasure is a U- or V-shaped recess in an otherwise linear stone row. A stone row, in the authors' context, is a length of stone wall that does not ostensibly have a colonial origin as a property boundary. Mavor, pp. 83–88.

89. Mavor, p. 159.

90. "Editorial: Runes and Research," *Martha's Vineyard Gazette*, August 24, 1954.

91. Huntington, Gale. *An Introduction to Martha's Vineyard and a Guided Tour of the Island* (Oak Bluffs, MA: Martha's Vineyard Print. Co., 1969).

92. *Grænlendinga Saga* was preserved in a manuscript compiled about A.D. 1387 called *Flateyjarbók*, or Flat Island Book, after the location in Iceland where it was found, ca. 1650.

93. "Saga of Erik the Red," in several manuscripts. The most commonly cited versions are the *Hauksbók* and the *Skalholtsbók*. Erik's Saga has Leif blown off course and discovering the new lands himself.

94. M. L. Fernald, "Notes on the Plants of Wineland the Good," *Rhodora* 12 (134), 1919, pp. 17–38; "The Natural History of Ancient Vinland and Its Geographic Significance," *Bulletin of the American Geographical Society* 47 (9), 1915.

95. Fernald (1915), p. 686.

96. Pohl (1952); Frederick J. Pohl, *The Vikings on Cape Cod: Evidence from Archaeological Discovery* (Pictou, Nova Scotia: Pictou Advocate Press, 1957); Frederick J. Pohl, *The Viking Settlements of North America* (New York: C.N. Potter, 1972).

97. Pohl (1957), pp. 11–16.

98. Edward Rowe Snow, *Famous New England Lighthouses* (Boston: Yankee, 1945).

99. Pohl (1952), pp. 52–54.

100. Pohl notes that Monomoy Island would still be attached to the Cape Cod mainland at Chatham at this time, making the start of the northward cape eight nautical miles from Great Point.

101. Abner Morse, *Traces of the Ancient Northmen in America: Being a Paper Read Before the New England Historical Genealogical Society August, 1861: Also Supplement to Same* (Boston: Mudge Printers, 1887); Abner Morse, *Further Traces of the Ancient Northmen in America: With Geological Evidences of the Location of their Vineland* (Boston: H.W. Dutton, 1861).

102. William B. Hovgaard, *The Voyages of the Norsemen to America* (New York: American-Scandinavian Foundation, 1914).

103. A. S. Packard, "Who First Saw the Labrador Coast?" *Journal of the American Geographical Society of New York* 20 (2), 1888, pp. 197–207.

104. Gray (1930) felt his geography was valid, with or without the runes, and placed the winter camp on Nomans Land Island.

105. Pohl (1957), p. 37.

106. Pohl (1972), pp. 207–208. Known locally as Blue Rock, it was directly opposite the 1840 site where Abner Morse had found a hearth he identified as Scandinavian. Pohl felt a narrow spot in the river was an ideal spot for a small boat to fish. Assuming Morse was correct, the salmon taken from the river were smoked and dried less than 100 feet from where they were caught.

107. Including trips to Martha's Vineyard to join Hjalmar Holand in search of the Priester Runestone.

108. Frederick J. Pohl, "Leif Ericsson's Visit to America," *American-Scandinavian Review* 36, 1948, pp. 17–29.

109. Morton M. Hunt, "The Secret of the Vanished Explorer," *Saturday Evening Post*, June 12, 1951.

110. Morton M. Hunt, "Saga of Leif the Lucky and Mr. Pohl," *Reader's Digest*, September 1951.

111. The remaining 18 members began work on several alternative spots picked out the day before by Pohl and Society president Howard Mandell. They located a burial pit and a large native hearth. These substantial discoveries were overshadowed by the Norse ship dig.

112. Pohl (1957), pp. 47–48.

113. See Pohl (1957), p. 51 or Pohl (1972), p. 198 for a diagram of the wooden artifacts.

114. Donald Allan, "Cape Cod Diggers Find 'Norse Relics,'" *New York Times*, May 11, 1952.

115. Donald W. Linebaugh, *The Man Who Found*

Thoreau: Roland W. Robbins and The Rise of Historical Archaeology in America (Hanover, NH: University Press of New England, 2005).

116. Robbins, as documented in his 1959 book, *Hidden America*, also visited the America's Stonehenge site and removed several roof slabs from the entrance to the Oracle Chamber. Robbins was not authorized to be on the site, let alone undertake excavations, and was physically removed from the site by owner Malcolm Pearson. The current whereabouts of these vandalized slabs remain unknown.

117. Donald Allan, "Cape Cod Timbers are Not Viking; 'Artifacts' Are Only a Century Old," *New York Times*, May 12, 1952.

118. Benjamin L. Smith, "A Report on the Follins Pond Investigation," *Massachusetts Archaeological Society Bulletin* 14 (2), January 1953, pp. 82–88.

119. Pohl (1961).

120. Frederick J. Pohl, "The Ship's Shoring at Follins Pond," *Massachusetts Archaeological Society Bulletin* 16 (3), April 1955, pp. 53–60.

121. Frederick J. Pohl, "Can the Ship's Shoring at Follins Pond be Radiocarbon Dated?" *Massachusetts Archaeological Society Bulletin* 17 (3), April 1956, pp. 49–50.

122. Pohl (1961), pp. 119–122.

123. Pohl arranged another excavation at Follins Pond in 1964 that uncovered what he believed was Karlsefni's palisade. Pohl (1972), pp. 222–229.

124. Pohl (1957), p. 43. Pohl sarcastically mentions two housing developments on the north side of the pond that were kind enough to name the streets after the saga characters.

125. Paula Peters, "Window on the Past," *Cape Cod Times*, January 7, 2001.

126. Nigel Warren, *Metal Corrosion in Boats* (Dobbs Ferry, NY: Sheridan House, 2006), pp. 39–40.

127. Josef Berger, writing as Jeremiah Digges, *Cape Cod Pilot* (Provincetown, MA: Modern Pilgrim Press, 1937) pp. 76–78.

Chapter Thirteen

1. Delabarre (1928).

2. Rafn, Carl Christian. *Antiqvitates Americana; sive, Scriptores Septentrionales Rerum Ante-Columbianarum in America* (Copenhagen: Typis Officinæ Schultzianæ, 1837).

3. Delabarre (1928), p. 235.

4. Delabarre (1928), p. 191. He notes the group rechristened the rock in 1919. By the publication of the 1921 annual automobile travel guide *Handbook of New England* (p. 493), the new name was faltering. Ironically, Delabarre's dismissal of the name in 1928 is the last significant reference to the "Lief's Rock" [sic] and/or "Leif's Rock" name.

5. Delabarre (1928), chapter XI.

6. Strandwold (1948), p.39.

7. Bengst Odenstedt, *On the Origin and Early History of Runic Script* (Stockholm: Almqvist & Wiksell, 1990).

8. Fell (1976), p. 99.

9. Fell (1976), p. 100.

10. Charles Devine, Tom Hardie, and Jon Woodson, "A Newly-Located Inscription from Narragansett Bay, Rhode Island," *NEARA Journal* 20 (1–2), Summer/Fall 1985.

11. Devine, p. 30. Landsverk and Alf Mongé were best known for their runic puzzle work on the Spirit Pond Stones. See Chapter Nine.

12. Donal Buchanan, "Report on The Narragansett Inscription," *NEARA Journal* 20 (1–2) Summer/Fall 1985. p. 32.

13. Paul Chapman, "Narragansett Bay Runestone Translation," *NEARA Journal* 21(1), Summer 1986. p. 4.

14. Paul Chapman, "America's Oldest Historical Record?" *NEARA Journal* 19 (1–2), Summer/Fall 1985. pp. 24–27.

15. Suzanne O. Carlson, "The Narragansett Stone Reconsidered," *NEARA Journal* 25 (3–4), 1991 Winter/Spring, 1991, pp. 80–83.

16. Cahill, p. 85. Cahill was the former sheriff of Essex County, which was centered in Salem, which remains a tourism destination.

17. Cahill's booklets were popular and that popularity cannot be emphasized sufficiently. As late as 2014, Rhode Island newspapers used the "four victorious near the river" translation as if it were the uncontested translation.

18. David P. Barron, "Narragansett Stone—A Brief Visit," *Stonewatch* 12 (2), winter 1993.

19. Ian Kirby, "The Narragansett Runic Inscription, Rhode Island," *Beowulf and Beyond* (Frankfort: Peter Lang, 2007).

20. Nielsen and Wolter.

21. Wolter (2009), pp. 171–3. Wolter also identifies a mason mark at Rosslyn Chapel (p.150–1) as a hooked X. See Goudsward (2020), Chapter 18 for more on Rosslyn mason marks.

22. Nielsen (2009).

23. Janet Freedman and Dave Beutel, "Report on the Inscribed Rock at Pojac Point," Rhode Island Coastal Resources Management Council, February 27, 2012.

24. *Holy Grail in America*, History Channel, September 21, 2009.

25. Richard C. Dujardin, "As theories of its origin abound, what does future hold for Narragansett Rune Stone?" *The Providence Journal*, July 6, 2013. This is one of the few media reports that mention the identity of the new neighbor. The privacy-loving prime suspect was Timothy Mellon, "heir to the Mellon family fortune, a founder of the Heritage Foundation and the CEO of Pan Am Systems."

26. Chris Church, "TV show renews interest in missing rune stone," *The Independent (Narragansett, RI)*, March 23, 2013.

27. "Tracking the Templars," *America Unearthed*. H2 Channel, season 1, episode 11, March 2, 2013.

28. The airport scene is a recreation, although not identified as such. Jason Colavito, the skeptic/journalist who has devoted much time to debunking Wolter's claims, points this out in *Unearthing the Truth* (2013), p.156. As Colavito notes, the stone was stolen sometime in June, with Wolter commenting on the theft to Rhode Island newspapers in August. The airport scene was "filmed in the autumn—as shown by the colors on the trees and Wolter's heavy clothes—pretends it just happened and he just learned of the theft."

29. "RI Attorney General And RI Department Of Environmental Management Joint Investigation Leads to The Return of the Narragansett Rune Stone." *States News Service*, April 26, 2013.

30. Elizabeth McNamara, "Narragansett Rune Stone Returned; To Be Tested," *East Greenwich Patch*, April 26, 2013.

31. Chris Church, "Rock of Ages: The mysterious rune stone is now an official tourist attraction," *The Independent (Narragansett, RI)*, November 6, 2015.

Bibliography

Abrams, Marc D. "Eastern White Pine Versatility in the Presettlement Forest." *BioScience* 51 (11):967(12), 2001.

Aldhouse-Green, Miranda J. *The Sun Gods of Ancient Europe*. London: B.T. Batsford, 1991.

Allan, Donald. "Cape Cod Diggers Find 'Norse Relics.'" *New York Times*, May 11, 1952.

_____. "Cape Cod Timbers are Not Viking; 'Artifacts' Are Only a Century Old." *New York Times*, May 12, 1952.

Allen, F.J. "The Ruined Mill, or Round Church of the Norsemen, at Newport, Rhode Island, U.S.A., Compared with the Round Church at Cambridge and Others in Europe." *Proceedings of the Cambridge Antiquarian Society, with Communications Made to the Society* Vol. XXII, 1921.

Anderson, J.R.L. *Vinland Voyage*. New York: Funk & Wagnalls, 1967.

Anderson, Rasmus Björn. *America Not Discovered by Columbus: A Historical Sketch of the Discovery of America by the Norsemen, in the Tenth Century*. Chicago: S.C. Griggs, 1874.

_____. Norumbega. In *The Norse Discovery of America: A Compilation in Extenso of all the Sagas, Manuscripts, and Inscriptive Memorials Relating to the Finding and Settlement of the New World in the Eleventh Century*, edited by R.B. Anderson. London: Norroena Society, 1906.

Anderson, Rasmus Björn, and Albert O. Barton. *Life Story of Rasmus B. Anderson*. [N.p.] Madison, WI, 1915.

Appleton, Thomas Gold. Correspondence. In *John Quincy Adams Ward Papers*, edited by N.-Y. H. Society, New York, December 13, 1878.

_____. Correspondence. In *John Quincy Adams Ward Papers*, edited by N.-Y. H. Society, New York, December 16, 1881.

_____. *Faded Leaves*. Boston, MA: Printed for the author by Roberts Brothers, 1872.

"Architectural Heritage of Haverhill." Haverhill, MA: Trustees of the Haverhill Public Library, 1976.

Armerding, Taylor. "Let's Not Lose a Sense of Place." *North Shore Sunday*, March 16, 1997.

Arnold, Elisha Stephen. *The Arnold Memorial*. Rutland, VT: Tuttle, 1935.

Atkinson, R.J.C. "Stonehenge." *New York Times Review of Books*, August 18, 1966.

_____. "Stonehenge in Darkness." *The New York Review of Books*, June 23, 1966.

Babcock, William Henry. *Cian of the Chariots: A Romance of the Days of Arthur*. Boston: Lothrop, 1898.

_____. *Early Norse Visits to North America*. Vol. 59, *Smithsonian Miscellaneous Collections*. Washington, D.C.: Smithsonian Institute, 1913.

Bacon, Edwin M. *Walks and Rides in the Country Round about Boston; Covering Thirty-Six Cities and Towns, Parks and Public Reservations, Within a Radius of Twelve Miles from the State House*. Boston: Appalachian Mountain Club by Houghton Mifflin, 1898.

Baker, Elizabeth Feaster. *Henry Wheaton, 1785–1848*. Philadelphia: University of Pennsylvania Press, 1937.

Bancroft, Hubert Howe. *The Book of the Fair; An Historical and Descriptive Presentation of the World's Science, Art, and Industry, As Viewed Through the Columbian Exposition at Chicago in 1893*. New York: Bounty Books, 1894.

Banks, Charles Edward. *The History of Martha's Vineyard, Dukes County, Massachusetts*. Edgartown, MA: Dukes County Historical Society, 1966.

Barron, David P. "'Adam's Dwelling' Excavation Finished." *Stonewatch* 13 (1), 1994.

_____. "Danes Announce Carbon Dating on Newport Tower." *Stonewatch* 12 (1), 1993.

_____. "Geologist Spots Chi Rhos." *Stonewatch: Newsletter of the Gungywamp Society* 3, 1982.

_____. "Mystery of the Gungywamp Light Show." *Stonewatch* 7 (3):1, 1988.

_____. "Narragansett Stone—A Brief Visit." *Stonewatch* 12 (2), winter 1993.

_____. "Necrology: Willard Odell Shepard." *Stonewatch* 8 (1), 1988.

Barron, David P., and Sharon Mason. *The Greater Gungywamp: A Guidebook*. Noank, CT: The Gungywamp Society, 1990.

Bassett, Mike. "Leominster Rock Ready to Roll." *Sentinel and Enterprise*, February 6, 2003.

Bayles, Richard M. ed. *History of Newport County, Rhode Island. From the Year 1638 to the Year 1887, Including the Settlement of Its Towns, and Their Subsequent Progress*. New York: L.E. Preston, 1888.

Beamish, North Ludlow. *The Discovery of America by the Northmen in the Tenth Century with Notices of the Early Settlements of the Irish in the Western Hemisphere*. London: T. and W. Boone, 1841.

Beauchamp, William Martin. *Metallic Ornaments of the New York Indians, New York State Museum. Bulletin 73. Archeology. [no.] 8*. Albany: University of the State of New York, 1903.

Beltran Lloris, Francisco. "Writing, Language and Society: Iberians, Celts, and Romans in Northeastern Spain in the 2nd and 1st centuries BC." *Bulletin of the Institute of Classical Studies* 43, 1999.

Berger, Josef (writing as Jeremiah Digges). *Cape Cod Pilot*. Provincetown, MA: Modern Pilgrim Press, 1937.

"B. F. Clyde's Cider Mill, Established 1898, Old Mystic, Connecticut, National Mechanical Engineering Site Dedication, October 29, 1994." *National Mechanical Engineering Site Dedication October 29, 1994*. Old Mystic, CT: American Society of Mechanical Engineers, 1994.

Bigelow, Paul. *Wrights and Privileges: The Mills and Shops of Pelham, Massachusetts, from 1740 to 1937*. Athol, MA: Haley's, 1993.

Billerica, Massachusetts: 1:25,000-scale metric topographic map. Massachusetts Dept. of Public Works, Reston, VA: U.S. Geological Survey, 1987.

Bingham, Alfred M. "Squatter Settlements of Freed Slaves in New England." *Connecticut Historical Society Bulletin* 41 (3):65–80, 1976.

Boland, Charles Michael. *They All Discovered America*. Garden City, NY: Doubleday, 1961.

Bourque, Bruce J. *Twelve Thousand Years: American Indians in Maine*. Lincoln: University of Nebraska Press, 2004.

Bragdon, Kathleen J. "The Shamanistic 'Text' in Southern New England." In *The Written and the Wrought: Complementary Sources in Historical Anthropology: essays in honor of James Deetz*. ed. Mary Ellin D'Agostino. Berkeley, CA: Kroeber Anthropological Society Papers 79 (1995).

Brate, Erik. *Östergötlands runinskrifter*. Stockholm, Sweden: P.A. Norstedt, 1911–1918.

Brereton, John, and Edward Hayes. *A Briefe and True Relation of the Discouerie of the North Part of Virginia: Being a Most Pleasant, Fruitfull and Commodious Soile : Made This Present Yeere 1602, by Captaine Bartholomew Gosnold, Captaine Bartholowmew Gilbert, and Divers Other Gentlemen ... : Whereunto Is Annexed a Treatise, Conteining Important Inducements for the Planting in Those Parts, and Finding a Passage That Way to the South Sea, and China*. London: George Bishop, 1602.

Bright, Pascal A. "The Making of Tar in Hocking County." *Ohio Archaeological and Historical Quarterly* 41 (2), 1932.

Brinton, Daniel G. *The Myths of the New World: A Treatise on the Symbolism and Mythology of the Red Race of America*. New York: Leypoldt and Holt, 1868.

Brøndsted, Johannes. *Norsemen in North America Before Columbus, Publication 4162*. Washington, D.C.: Smithsonian Institution, 1954.

_____. *Problemet om Nordboer i Nordamerika før Columbus: en bedømmelse af de Amerikanske materiale, Aarbøger for nordisk oldkyndighed og historie*. København: Bianco Lunos bogtrykkeri, 1951.

Brooks, Charles Timothy. *The Controversy Touching the Old Stone Mill, in the Town of Newport, Rhode Island. With Remarks, Introductory and Conclusive*. Newport, RI: C.E. Hammett Jr., 1851.

Brown, Dan. *The Da Vinci Code*. New York: Doubleday, 2003.

Brydall, Robert. "The Monumental Effigies of Scotland, from the Thirteenth to the fifteenth Century." *Proceedings of the Society of Antiquaries of Scotland* 29 (May 13, 1895).

Buchanan, Donal. "A New Look at the Spirit Pond Runestones." *Epigraphic Society Occasional Publications* 21, 1992.

_____. "Report on The Narragansett Inscription." *NEARA Journal* 20 (1–2) Summer/Fall 1985.

Buchanan, Paulette J. "Adams Dwelling Update." *Stonewatch* 16 (2), 1998.

_____. "The Chi-Rho Controversy Rages On: Response to Vance R. Tiede's Viewpoint." *Stonewatch* 20 (1), 2003.

_____. "Chi Rho Site: Vogt Ruins." *Stonewatch* 14 (1), 1995.

_____. "More Conclusive Research on the Rows of Standing Stones & Other Sites in the Gungywamp." *Stonewatch* 21 (1), 2004.

_____. "New Research Findings." *Stonewatch* 19 (1), 2002.

Burger, Richard L., and Thomas F. Lynch. "Gary S. Vescelius (1930–1982)." *Andean Past* 1, 1987.

Burke, James. *Connections*. Boston, MA: Little, Brown, 1978.

Burke, John. *A General and Heraldic Dictionary of the Peerage and Baronetage of the British Empire*. London: Burke's Peerage, 1999.

Burke, John A. "Scientific Instrument Survey of the Gungywamp Complex." *Stonewatch* 13 (4), 1995.

Cahill, Robert Ellis. *New England's Ancient Mysteries*. Salem, MA: Old Saltbox Publishing House, 1993.

Camp, Helen B. *Archaeological Excavations at Pemaquid, Maine, 1965–1974*. Augusta: Maine State Museum, 1976.

Campbell, John. *Hittites in America*. Montreal: 1873.

_____. "Recently Discovered Relics of the American Mound-Builders." *Transactions of the Royal Society of Canada* (Section II) 1898.

Carlson, Suzanne. "Loose Threads in a Tapestry of Stone: The Architecture of the Newport Tower." *NEARA Journal* 35 (1), 2001.

_____. "Manana Revisited." *NEARA Journal* 27 (3/4), 1993.

_____. "The Narragansett Stone Reconsidered," *NEARA Journal* 25 (3–4), Winter/Spring 1991.

_____. "The Spirit Pond Inscription Stone: Rhyme and Reason." *NEARA Journal* 28 (1), 1993.

Carlton, Craig. "Making Tar." In *Foxfire 4*, edited by E. Wigginton. Garden City, NY: Anchor Press, 1977.

Castle, Peter H.J. "Howard Barraclough Fell" (obituary). *Yearbook of the Academy Council of The Royal Society of New Zealand*, 1996.

Cawley, F. S., and S.E. Morison. Review of *Leif Eriksson, Discoverer of America, A.D. 1003* by Edward Francis Gray. *New England Quarterly* 4 (3), 1931.

Champlain, Samuel de, Henry Percival Biggar, Hugh Hornby Langton, William Francis Ganong, John Home Cameron, John Squair, tran., and William Dawson LeSueur. *The Works of Samuel de Champlain*. Toronto: Champlain Society, 1922.

Chapman, Paul H. "America's Oldest Historical Record?" *NEARA Journal* 19 (1–2), Summer/Fall 1985.

———. "An In-depth Examination of the Spirit Pond Runestones." *Epigraphic Society Occasional Publications* 21, 1992.

———. *The Man Who Led Columbus to America*. Atlanta, GA: Judson Press, 1973.

———. "Narragansett Bay Runestone Translation." *NEARA Journal* 21(1), Summer 1986.

———. *The Norse Discovery of America*. Atlanta, GA: One Candle Press, 1981.

———. "Spirit Pond Runestones: A Study in Linguistics." San Francisco: Epigraphic Society, 1994.

"Charles Vallancey." Princess Grace Irish Library 2001. Available from http://www.pgil-eirdata.org/html/pgil_datasets/index.htm. [cited 13 April 2004].

Chase, Charles Wingate. *History of Haverhill, Massachusetts*. Haverhill, MA: George Wingate Chase, 1861.

Church, Chris. "Rock of Ages: The mysterious rune stone is now an official tourist attraction." *The Independent (Narragansett, RI)*, November 6, 2015.

———. "TV show renews interest in missing rune stone." *The Independent (Narragansett, RI)*, March 23, 2013.

Coffin, Joshua. *A Sketch of the History of Newbury, Newburyport, and West Newbury, from 1635 to 1845*. Boston: Samuel G. Drake, 1845.

Colavito, Jason. *Unearthing the Truth*. Albany, NY: JasonColavito.com Books, 2013.

Cole, Benjamin. "Mysterious Stone Finds New Home." *Sentinel and Enterprise*, 24 June 2002.

Colligan, Douglas. "Brawl Over a '2000-year-old' Archaeological Site." *Science Digest*, January 1973.

"The Commodities of the Island Called Manati Ore Long Isle Within the Continent of Virginia." *Collections of the New-York Historical Society* 2, 1869.

Cook, Warren L. *Ancient Vermont: Proceedings of the Castleton Conference, Castleton State College, October 14–15, 1977*. Rutland, VT: Academy Books, 1978.

Cooper, James Fenimore. *Red Rover*. New York: Putnam's, 1850.

Court de Gébelin, Antoine. *Monde Primitif, Analysé et Comparé avec le Monde Moderne*. Paris: Chez l'auteur, 1781.

Craig, David V. "Thorwald's Grave: Fact or Legend?" *New Hampshire Profiles*. XXIII (1), January 1974.

Craigie, W.A. "The Gaels in Iceland." *Proceedings of the Society of Antiquaries of Scotland* 31, 1897.

Cram, William D. "Thorvald." *Official Pictorial Magazine: 1638–Hampton Tercentenary–1938*. [Concord, NH]: Rumford Press, 1938.

———. "Thorvald's Grave" (Little Stories of Old New England column). *Hampton Union & Rockingham County Gazette*, December 2, 1937.

Cronon, William. *Changes in the Land: Indians, Colonists, and the Ecology of New England*. New York: Hill and Wang, 1983.

"Crushing Truth." *New York Times*, August 9, 1876.

Curchin, Leonard A. "Literacy in the Roman Provinces: Qualitative and Quantitative Data from Central Spain." *The American Journal of Philology* 116 (3), 1995.

Cushing, Elizabeth Hope. "So Near the Metropolis: Lynn Woods, a Sylvan Gem in an Urban Setting." *Arnoldia* 48 (4), 1998.

Dalton, Tom. "Boulders May Tell Ancient Tale." *Daily Evening Item*, May 4, 1987.

da Mosto, Andrea. "I Navigatori Nicolò e Antonio Zeno." In *Ad Alessandro Luzio*. Firenze: Le Monnier, 1933.

Daniel, Glyn Edmund. Comments by readers and additional comments by Daniel Glynn. *New York Times*, May 1, 1977.

———. Reviews of *America B.C.* by Barry Fell and *They Came Before Columbus* by Ivan Van Sartima. *New York Times*, March 13, 1977.

da Silva, Manuel Luciano. *Portuguese Pilgrims and Dighton Rock: the First Chapter in American History*. Bristol, RI: [published by the author] 1971.

———. Review of the history of the Portuguese Templars. *Stonewatch* 12 (2), 1993.

Davies, Nigel. *Voyagers to the New World*. New York: William Morrow, 1979.

de Bethune, Andre J. "On the Carbon 14 Analyses of Mortar from the Newport Tower: Theoretical Considerations." *Newport History: Journal of the Newport Historical Society* 69, part 1 (238), 1998.

DeCosta, B.F. *Ancient Norombega, or The Voyages of Simon Ferdinando and John Walker to the Penobscot River, 1579–1580*. Revised from the N.E. Historical and Genealogical Register, April, 1890. Albany: J. Munsell, 1890.

———. *The Pre-Columbian Discovery of America by the Northmen: Illustrated by Translations from the Icelandic Sagas*. Albany: J. Munsell, 1868.

———. *The Pre-Columbian Discovery of America by the Northmen: With Translations from the Icelandic Sagas*. 2nd ed. Albany: Joel Munsell, 1890.

———. "Translation: The Cosmography of the Fraudulent Thevet." *Magazine of American History* 8, 1882.

Deetz, James. *In Small Things Forgotten*. Garden City, NY: Anchor Press/Doubleday, 1977.
Delabarre, Edmund Burke. *Dighton Rock: A Study of the Written Rocks of New England*. New York: Walter Neale, 1928.
_____. "Early Interest in Dighton Rock." *The Publications of the Colonial Society of Massachusetts* XVIII, 1916.
_____. "The Indian Petroglyph at the Aptucxet Trading Post in Bourne, Massachusetts." *Old-Time New England* 26 (3), January 1936.
_____. "Middle Period of Dighton Rock History." *The Publications of the Colonial Society of Massachusetts* XIX, 1917.
_____. "Miguel Cortereal: The First European to Enter Narragansett Bay." *Rhode Island Historical Society Collections* 29 (1), October 1936.
_____. "A Petroglyphic Study of Human Motives." *Scientific Monthly* 41 (5), 1935.
_____. "A Possible Pre-Algonkian Culture in Southeastern Massachusetts." *American Anthropologist* 27 (3):359–369, 1925.
_____. "A Prehistoric Skeleton from Grassy Island." *American Anthropologist* 30 (3), 1928.
_____. "Recent History of Dighton Rock." *The Publications of the Colonial Society of Massachusetts* XX, 1919.
Delabarre, Edmund Burke, and Charles W. Brown. "The Runic Rock on No Man's Land, Massachusetts: Geological Notes." *New England Quarterly* 8 (3), 1935a.
Delabarre, Edmund Burke, and Harris H. Wilder. "Indian Corn-Hills in Massachusetts." *American Anthropologist* 22 (3), 1920.
Derr, John S., and Michael A. Persinger. "Geophysical Variables and Behavior: LIV. Zeitoun (Egypt) Apparitions of the Virgin Mary as Tectonic Strain-induced Luminosities." *Perceptual and Motor Skills* 68, 1989.
Devine, Charles, Tom Hardie, and Jon Woodson. "A Newly-Located Inscription from Narragansett Bay, Rhode Island." *NEARA Journal* 20 (1–2), Summer/Fall 1985.
Dexter, Warren W. *Ogam Consaine and Tifinag Alphabets: Ancient Uses*. Rutland, VT: Academy Books, 1984.
Dexter, Warren W., Barry Fell, and Elizabeth Sincerbeaux. "An Ogam Consaine Inscription at Royalton, Vermont." *The Epigraphic Society Occasional Publications* 12 (297), 1984.
Dexter, Warren W., and Donna Martin. *America's Ancient Stone Relics: Highlighting Vermont's Link to Bronze Age Mariners*. Rutland, VT: Academy Books, 1995.
Deyo, Simeon L. ed. *History of Barnstable County, Massachusetts*. New York: Blake, 1890.
Dieserud, Juul. "Norse Discoveries in America." *Bulletin of the American Geographical Society* 33 (1), 1901.
"The Dighton Rock Puzzle." *New York Times*, January 6, 1890.
Dix, Byron E. "An Early Calendar Site in Central Vermont." *The Epigraphic Society Occasional Publications* 3 (51), 1976.
_____. "A Second Early Calendar Site in Central Vermont." *The Epigraphic Society Occasional Publications* 3 (61), 1976.
_____. "Possible Evidence of the Megalithic Yard at Calendar Site II, Vermont." *NEARA Journal* 11 (2), 1976.
Dix, Byron E., and James W. Mavor. "Heliolithic Ritual Sites in New England." *NEARA Journal* 16 (3), 1982.
_____. "Possible Astronomical Alignments, Date and Origins of the Pearson Stone Chamber." *Early Sites Research Society Bulletin* 8 (1), 1980.
Doherty, Rod. "'Old Hanging Rock' Again Reveals Its Nordic Legend." *Newburyport Daily News*, August 1976.
Douglas-Lithgow, Robert Alexander. *Dictionary of American-Indian Place and Proper Names in New England; With Many Interpretations, etc.* Salem, MA: Salem Press, 1909.
Dow, Joseph Dow. *History of the Town of Hampton, New Hampshire, from Its Settlement in 1638, to the Autumn of 1892*. Salem, MA: Salem Press Publishing and Printing Company, 1894.
Drake, Samuel Adams. *The Pine-tree Coast*. Boston: Estes & Lauriat, 1891.
Du Lue, Willard. "Hampton Falls Woman Owns Norseman's Rock." *Boston Globe*, August 13, 1952.
Dujardin, Richard C. "As theories of its origin abound, what does the future hold for Narragansett Rune Stone?" *The Providence Journal*, July 6, 2013.
Earle, Alice Morse. *Home Life in Colonial Days*. New York: Macmillan, 1898.
"Editorial: Runes and Research" *Martha's Vineyard Gazette*, August 24, 1954.
Edwards, Nancy. *The Archaeology of Early Medieval Ireland*, Middle Ages series. Philadelphia: University of Pennsylvania Press, 1990.
Egan, James Alan. *Elizabethan America: The John Dee Tower of 1583, a Renaissance Horologium in Newport, Rhode Island*. Newport, RI: Cosmopolite Press, 2011.
Eiríkr, Magnússon. *The Story of the Ere-Dwellers (Eyrbyggja Saga), with the Story of the Heath-Slayings (Hei_arvíga saga) as appendix*, The Saga library; vol. 2. London: B. Quaritch, 1892.
Ellis, Marietta. "Introduction to Soap Making," *Vita Technical Bulletin*. Mount Rainier, MD: Volunteers in Technical Assistance, 1981.
Emerson, N.S. *The History of Dungeon Rock, Completed Sept. 17th, 1856*. Boston: Adams, 1856.
Enlart, Camille. "Le Problème de la Vieille Tour de Newport (Rhode-Island)." *Revue de l'art Chrétien* LX, 1910.
Evans, John Davies. *The Prehistoric Antiquities of the Maltese Islands: A Survey*. London: Athlone Press, Univ. of London, 1971.
"Excavation at Old Stone Mill by Celtic Theorist Approved." *Newport Daily News*, November 9, 1954.

Falnes, Oscar J. "New England Interest in Scandinavian Culture and the Norsemen." *New England Quarterly* 10 (2), 1937.

Feldman, Mark. *The Mystery Hill Story*. North Salem, NH: Mystery Hill Press, 1977.

Fell, Barry. *America B.C.: Ancient Settlers in the New World*. New York: Quadrangle/New York Times Books, 1976.

_____. "Arabic Dialect in Ancient Moroccan Inscriptions." *Epigraphic Society Occasional Publications* 3 (48), 1976.

_____. *Bronze Age America*. Boston: Little, Brown, 1982.

_____. "A Fifth-century Moroccan Emigration to North America." *Epigraphic Society Occasional Publications* 3 (46), 1976.

_____. "An Iberian-Punic Stele of Hanno." *The Epigraphic Society Occasional Publications* 2 (44, part 2), 1975a.

_____. [notes from Fell's Libyan Trip.] *Early Sites Research Society News-Letter* #32, January 1978.

_____. "Romano-Celtic Phase at Mystery Hill, New Hampshire, in New England." *The Epigraphic Society Occasional Publications* 3 (54), 1975b.

_____. *Saga America*. New York: Times Books, 1980.

Fenn, Elizabeth A., and Peter H. Wood. "Part 1: Natives & Newcomers: North Carolina before 1770." In *The Way We Lived in North Carolina*, edited by J.A. Mobley. Chapel Hill: University of North Carolina Press, 2003.

Fernald, M.L. "The Natural History of Ancient Vinland and Its Geographic Significance." *Bulletin of the American Geographical Society* 47, 1915.

_____. "Notes on the Plants of Wineland the Good." *Rhodora* 12 (134), 1910.

Fessenden, Thomas G., ed. "Receipt For Cold Soap." *New England Farmer and Horticultural Journal, Containing Essays, Original and Selected, Relating to Agriculture and Domestic Economy; With Engravings, and the Prices of Country Produce*. VIII, 1829.

Finch, John. "On the Celtic Antiquities of America." *American Journal of Science and Arts* VII, 1824.

Fiske, John. *New France and New England*. Boston: Houghton Mifflin, 1902.

Fitzhugh, William W., and Elisabeth I. Ward. *Vikings: The North Atlantic Saga*. Washington, D.C.: Smithsonian Institution, 2000.

Flavin, R.D. *Dolmen Doldrums* [2000]. Available from http://www.flavinscorner.com/dolmen.htm. [cited April 24, 2005].

Fleming, Robin. "Picturesque History and the Medieval in Nineteenth-Century America." *The American Historical Review* 100 (4), 1995.

Fleming, Stuart J. *Authenticity in Art: The Scientific Detection of Forgery*. London: Institute of Physics, 1975.

Forster, Johann Reinhold. *History of the Voyages and Discoveries Made in the North*. London: Printed for G.G.J. and J. Robinson, 1786.

Fowke, Gerard. "Points of Difference Between Norse Remains and Indian Works Most Closely Resembling Them." *American Anthropologist* New Series, 2 (3), 1900.

Fowler, William S. "The Westford Indian Rock." *Massachusetts Archaeological Society Bulletin* 21, 1960.

Fragoso, Joseph Dâmaso. *A Historical Report of Twenty-eight Years of Patriotic and Dramatic Efforts to Save Dighton Rock*. New Bedford, MA: Joseph D. Fragoso, 1954.

_____. *In Honor of Portugal, The Portuguese Navy and the Dighton Rock*. New Bedford, MA: Joseph D. Fragoso, 1958.

_____. "O Emblema da Ordem de Cristo Gravado na Pedra de Dighton." *Mundo Lusíada*, 1:8 (1951): 207–208.

Frederick, Arthur. "Discovery Shakes Theory of New World." *Sunday Record*, January 16, 1977.

Freedman, Janet, and Dave Beutel. "Report on the Inscribed Rock at Pojac Point." A Coastal Resources Management Council report dated Feb. 27, 2012, submitted to the Rhode Island Historic Preservation and Conservation Commission.

Gallagher, John. "Connecticut's 5th Century Church." *Ancient American* 8 (54), December 2003. Also reprinted in *Unearthing Ancient America*, ed. Frank Joseph. Franklin Lakes, NJ: New Page Books, 2009.

_____. "Fifth Century Christian Church Found in Connecticut." *On Site* 1 (3), June 1987.

_____. "Inscriptions and other features at Cockaponset." *Epigraphic Society Occasional Publications* 6 (137), 1979.

Gathorne-Hardy, G.M. *The Norse Discoverers of America: The Wineland Sagas Translated and Discussed*. Oxford: Clarendon Press, 1921.

Geochron Laboratories, Inc. "Report of Analytical Work, Radiocarbon Age Determination—Sample GX20670." Cambridge, MA: Geochron Laboratories, Inc., 1995.

Gilbert, Edgar. *History of Salem, N.H.* Concord, NH: Rumford Printing, 1907.

Gilmore, Donald Y., and Linda S. McElroy. *Across Before Columbus? Evidence for Transoceanic Contact with the Americas Prior to 1492*. Edgecomb, ME: New England Antiquities Research Association Publications, 1998.

Glynn, Frank. "Another Possible Medieval Marker in Westford, Mass." *NEARA Journal* 2 (2), 1967.

_____. Communication regarding Maltese sites. Clinton, CT, 27, February 1967.

_____. "Further report on metal fragment." Unpublished typescript, America's Stonehenge Research Dept., North Salem, NH, 7, May 1965.

_____. "A Second Mediaeval Marker at Westford Massachusetts." *Eastern States Archaeological Federation Bulletin* 26 (14), 1967.

_____. "A Unique Punched Portrait in Massachusetts." *Eastern States Archaeological Federation Bulletin*, 1957.

"Godfrey Denies Stones Removed In 1948–49

Stone Mill Excavations." *Newport Daily News*, October 31, 1955.

"Godfrey Priester Dies." *Vineyard Gazette*, June 1, 1962.

Godfrey Jr., William S. Answer to "Plaster under the Tower." *American Antiquity* 19 (3), January 1954.

_____. "The Archaeology of the Old Stone Mill in Newport, Rhode Island." *American Antiquity* 17 (2), 1951.

_____. "Digging a Tower and Laying a Ghost: The Archaeology and Controversial History of the Newport Tower." Cambridge, MA: Harvard University, 1951.

_____. "The Newport Puzzle." *Archaeology*, Autumn 1949.

_____. "The Newport Tower." *Archaeology*, Summer 1950.

_____. Reply to Holand. *American Antiquity* 18 (4), 1953.

_____. "Vikings in America: Theories and Evidence." *American Anthropologist* 57 (1), 1955.

Goldrick, Rev. Timothy J. "Cross of Christ Placed Atop Oldest Diocesan Church." *Standard-Times*, January 01, 2005.

Goodwin, William B. "An Ancient Norse Relic." *The Chronicle* 228, 1938.

_____. Correspondence to Frances Healey. Hartford, CT, September 9, 1938.

_____. Correspondence to Harral Ayres. Hartford, CT, July 27, 1936.

_____. *The Lure of Gold.* Boston, MA: Meador, 1940.

_____. *The Ruins of Great Ireland in New England.* Boston: Meador, 1946.

_____. *Spanish and English Ruins in Jamaica.* Boston: Meador, 1946.

_____. *The Truth About Leif Ericsson and the Greenland Voyages.* Boston: Meador, 1941.

Göransson, Johan. *Bautil; det är: Alle Svea ok Götha rikens runstenar, upreste ifrän verldenes år 2000 til Christi år 1000; för detta, efter glorvördigast i åminnelse konung Gustaf Adolfs ok konung Karl XI: tes befallning afritade ok til största delen uti former inskurne; men nu, efter.* Stockholm, 1750.

Gordon, Cyrus Herzl. *Riddles in History.* New York: Crown, 1974.

Goudsward, David. "Great Ireland Revisited: Goodwin's Culdee Monks 45 Years Later." *Stonewatch* 10 (3), 1992.

_____. "The Pattees in England: An Overview and a New Theory." *Pattee Family Research Newsletter* 1 (4), 1990.

_____. "A Possible Origin for the Gungywamp Chi Rhos." *Stonewatch* 13 (1), 1994.

_____. *The Westford Knight and Henry Sinclair.* 2nd ed. Jefferson, NC: McFarland & Co, 2020.

Goudsward, David, and Robert Stone. *America's Stonehenge: The Mystery Hill Story.* Wellesley, MA: Branden Books, 2002.

Graves, Robert. *The White Goddess: A Historical Grammar of Poetic Myth.* New York: Farrar Straus and Giroux, 1966.

Gray, Edward Francis. *Leif Eriksson, Discoverer of America A.D. 1003.* New York: Oxford Univ. Press, 1930.

Greene, J.R. *The Creation of Quabbin Reservoir: the Death of the Swift River Valley.* Privately published, 2001.

Griffith, Graham. "Old Norse Explorer Spinning in Grave." *The Portsmouth Herald*, July 21, 1967.

Griswold, Wesley S. "Stone Village Mystery." *Hartford Courant*, June 19, 1938.

Groenlendinga, áttr., Magnus Magnusson, ed., trans., and Pálsson Hermann. *The Vinland Sagas, the Norse Discovery of America.* Baltimore: Penguin Books, 1965.

Guthrie, James L. "Radiocarbon Dating of the Newport Tower Mortar." *NEARA Journal* 36 (2), 2002.

Gutstein, Morris Aaron. *The Story of the Jews of Newport; Two and a Half Centuries of Judaism, 1658–1908.* New York: Bloch, 1936.

Haines, Richard F. *UFO Phenomena and the Behavioral Scientist.* Metuchen, NJ: Scarecrow Press, 1979.

Hakluyt, Richard C. *The Principall Nauigations, Voiages, and Discoueries of the English Nation.* George Bishop and Ralph Newberie, 1589.

Hale, John, Jan Heinemeier, Lynne Lancaster, Alf Lindroos, and Asa Ringbom. "Dating Ancient Mortar." *American Scientist* 91 (2), 2003.

Haliburton, Robert Grant. *A Search in British North America for Lost Colonies of Northmen and Portuguese,* Royal Geographic Society Proceedings 7 (1), January 1885.

Hall, Benjamin Homer. *History of Eastern Vermont, From Its Earliest Settlement to the Close of the Eighteenth Century.* New York: Appleton, 1858.

Hamlin, A.C. "Supposed Runic Inscriptions." *Proceedings of the American Association for the Advancement of Science* 10 (Part 2), 1857.

Hanson, Lindley S., and Dabney W. Caldwell, *Reconnaissance surficial geology of the Sebec [15-minute] quadrangle,* Maine: Maine Geological Survey, Open-File Map 80–10, map, scale 1:62,500. Maine Geological Survey Maps (1980).

Harde, Ellen, and Marilyn Day. *The New Old Houses of Westford.* Westford, MA: Westford Historical Commission, 2004.

Harper, J.R. "Two Seventeenth Century Copper-Kettle Burials." *Anthropologica* 4, 1957.

Harriman, Walter. *History of Warner, New Hampshire.* Warner, NH: Republican Press Association, 1879.

"Has Quitsa a Cromlech?" *Vineyard Gazette*, August 19, 1927.

Hattendorf, Ingrid M. From the Collection: William S. Godfrey's Old Stone Mill Archaeological Collection part 2 (235):109–111, *Newport History: Journal of the Newport Historical Society* 68, 1997.

Haugen, Einar. Comment on O.G. Landsverk's

"The Spirit Pond Cryptography." *Man in the Northeast* 6, 1973.

_____. *The Ecology of Language, Language Science and National Development*. Stanford, CA: Stanford Univ. Press, 1972.

_____. "The Rune Stones of Spirit Pond, Maine." *Man in the Northeast* 4, 1972.

Haviland, William A., and Marjory W. Power. "Visions in Stone: A New Look at the Bellows Falls Petroglyphs." *Northeast Anthropology* 50 (Fall 1995), 1995.

Hawkins, Gerald S. "Astro-archaeology." *Vistas in Astronomy* 10, 1968.

_____. *Beyond Stonehenge*. New York: Harper & Row, 1973.

_____. "Stonehenge." *New York Times Review of Books*, August 18, 1966.

_____. *Stonehenge Decoded*. Garden City, NY: Doubleday, 1965.

Haynes, Henry W. "Progress of American Archaeology During the Past Ten Years." *American Journal of Archaeology* 14 (1), 1900.

Headley, Janet A. "Anne Whitney's Leif Eriksson: A Brahmin Response to Christopher Columbus." *American Art* 17 (2), 2003.

Hedden, Mark, "Passamaquoddy Shamanism and Rock-Art in Machias Bay, Maine." In *The Rock-art of Eastern North America: Capturing Images and Insight*. ed. Carol Diaz-Granados and James R. Duncan. Tuscaloosa: The University of Alabama Press, 2004.

Hencken, Hugh. "The 'Irish Monastery' at North Salem, New Hampshire." *New England Quarterly* 12 (3), September 1939.

_____. "What Are Pattee's Caves?" *Scientific American* 163, November 1940.

Henry, Joseph. "January 1858–December 1865, The Smithsonian Years." In *The Papers of Joseph Henry*, edited by Marc Rothenberg. Washington, D.C.: Smithsonian Institution Press, 1972.

Hermann, Pálsson and Paul Geoffrey Edwards, ed. *The Book of Settlements; Landnámabók, University of Manitoba Icelandic Studies, vol. 1*. Winnipeg: University of Manitoba, 1972.

Hertz, Johs. "Round Church or Windmill? New Light on the Newport Tower." *Newport History: Journal of the Newport Historical Society* 68, part 2 (235), 1997.

Hickes, George, Humphrey Wanley, Jónsson Runólfur, Andrew Fountaine. *Linguarum Vett Septentrionalium Thesaurus Grammatico-criticus et Archæologicus*. Oxoniæ: E Theatro Sheldoniano, 1705.

Hickey, Jim. "Historic Preservation Commissions Doubt Rune Rock Credibility," *Vineyard Gazette*, July 5, 2007.

Hilen, Andrew R., and Henry Wadsworth Longfellow. *Longfellow and Scandinavia; a Study of the Poet's Relationship with the Northern Languages and Literature, Yale Studies in English*. New Haven: Yale Univ. Press, 1947.

Hitchcock, Edward. *Report on the Geology, Mineralogy, Botany, and Zoology of Massachusetts*. Amherst, MA: Press of J.S. and C. Adams, 1833.

Hitt, Jack. "How the Gungywampers Saved Civilization." *Gentlemen's Quarterly*, January, 128–135, 1998.

Hobbs, William Herbert. *The Fourteenth-Century Discovery of America by Antonia Zeno*. *Scientific Monthly*, January 1951.

Hockensmith, Charles D. Euro-American Petroglyphs Associated with Pine Tar Kilns and Lye Leaching Devices in Kentucky. *Tennessee Anthropologist* XI (2), 1986.

Hodgman, Edwin R. *History of the Town of Westford in the County of Middlesex, Massachusetts: 1659–1883*. Lowell: Morning Mail, 1883. Reprint 2003.

Holand, Hjalmar Rued. "The Age of the Newport Tower." *Archaeology*, Autumn, 1951.

_____. *America, 1355–1364; A New Chapter in Pre-Columbian History*. New York: Duell Sloan and Pearce, 1946.

_____. "An English Scientist in America 130 Years Before Columbus." *Transactions of the Wisconsin Academy of Sciences, Arts and Letters* XLVIII, 1959.

_____. "A Fourteenth-Century Runic Inscription from Martha's Vineyard." *Scandinavian Studies* 21, 1949.

_____. *The Kensington Stone, a Study in Pre-Columbian American History*. Ephraim: WI. Private Printing, 1932.

_____. "The Newport Mystery." *Rhode Island History* 12 (2), 1953.

_____. "The Newport Mystery (2)." *Rhode Island History* 12 (3), 1953.

_____. *Westward from Vinland; An Account of Norse Discoveries and Explorations in America, 982–1362*. New York: Duell Sloan & Pearce, 1940.

Holy Grail in America, History Channel, September 21, 2009.

Horsford, Cornelia. *Dwellings of the Saga-time in Iceland, Greenland, and Vineland*. Washington, D.C.: Judd & Detweiler Printers, 1898.

_____. *Graves of the Northmen*. Boston: Damrell and Upham, 1893.

_____. *An Inscribed Stone*. Cambridge: J. Wilson and Son, 1895.

_____. "Vinland and Its Ruins." *Popular Science Monthly*, December 1899.

Horsford, Eben Norton. *The Defences of Norumbega and a Review of the Reconnaissances of Col. T.W. Higginson, Professor Henry W. Haynes, Dr. Justin Winsor, Dr. Francis Parkman, and Rev. Dr. Edmund F. Slafter; A Letter to Judge Daly*. Boston: Houghton Mifflin, 1891.

_____. *Discovery of America by Northmen Address at the Unveiling of the Statue of Leif Eriksen, Delivered in Faneuil Hall, Oct. 29, 1887*. Boston: Houghton Mifflin, 1888.

_____. *The Indian Names of Boston, and Their Meaning*. Cambridge: J. Wilson and Son, 1886.

_____. "John Cabot's Landfall, Site of Norumbega."

Journal of the American Geographical Society of New York 17, 1885.

———. *The Landfall of Leif Erikson, A.D. 1000, and the Site of his Houses in Vineland.* Boston: Damrell and Upham, 1892.

———. *The Problem of the Northmen. A Letter to Judge Daly ... on the opinion of Justin Winsor, that "Though Scandinavians may have reached the shores of Labrador, the soil of the United States has not one vestige of their presence."* Cambridge: J. Wilson and Son, 1890.

———. "Report on Vienna Bread," In *U.S. Commission to the Vienna Exhibition, 1873. Reports. 1875-76.* Washington, D.C.: Government Printing Office, 1875.

———. *Sketch of the Norse Discovery of America, at the festival of the Scandinavian societies assembled May 18, 1891, in Boston on the occasion of presenting a testimonial to Eben Norton Horsford in recognition of the finding of the landfall of Leif Erikson, the site of his Vineland home, and of the ancient Norse city of Norumbega, in Massachusetts, in the 43rd degree,* [Boston, MA], 1891.

———. *The Theory and Art of Bread-making: A New Process Without the Use of Ferment.* Cambridge: Welch Bigelow and Company Printers, 1861.

Horsford, Eben Norton, and E.H. Clement. *The Discovery of the Ancient City of Norumbega. A communication to the president and council of the American Geographical Society at their special session in Watertown, November 21, 1889.* Boston: Houghton Mifflin, 1890.

Horsford, Eben Norton, and Cornelia Horsford. *Leif's House in Vineland,* Boston: Damrell and Upham, 1893.

Hovgaard, William B. *The Voyages of the Norsemen to America, Scandinavian monographs, vol. I;* New York: American-Scandinavian Foundation, 1914.

Howe, Ann. "Good-by Columbus, says local archaeologist." *The Sunday Sun* [Lowell, MA], December 19, 1982.

Hubbard, Edwin. "Early Records of the Arnold Family." *New England Historical and Genealogical Register* 33 (3), 1879.

Hunt, Morton M. "Saga of Leif the Lucky and Mr. Pohl." *Reader's Digest* 59 (9), 1951.

———. "The Secret of the Vanished Explorer." *Saturday Evening Post,* June 12, 1951.

Huntington, Gale. *An Introduction to Martha's Vineyard and a Guided Tour of the Island.* [Oak Bluffs, MA]: Martha's Vineyard Print. Co., 1969.

Hurd, D. Hamilton. *History of Bristol County, Massachusetts with Biographical Sketches of Many of Its Pioneers and Prominent Men.* Philadelphia: J.W. Lewis, 1883.

———. *History of Essex County, Massachusetts, with Biographical Sketches of Many of Its Pioneers and Prominent Men.* Philadelphia: J.W. Lewis, 1888.

"Indian Carvings on River Bank Made More Visible." *Brattleboro Daily Reformer,* August 9, 1961, 12.

"Indian Relics." *Essex Gazette,* May 1, 1830.

"Indian Sculpture Is Lost." *Iowa City Press,* April 29, 1907.

Iron, Thunderhorse. "An Amerindian View of Bird Effigy in Complex." *Stonewatch* 14 (3), 1996.

Jenks, William. "Abstract of Presentation on the Mananas Island Inscription." *Proceedings of the American Academy of Arts and Sciences* 6, 1851.

———. *The Comprehensive Commentary on the Holy Bible; Containing the Text According to the Authorized Version.* 5 vols. Brattleboro, VT: Fessenden, 1835.

Johansen, Sarah E. "Survey of Seth Mallon Pattee House." In *Pattee Family Research Archives.* North Salem, NH: Mystery Hill Research Department, 1974.

Johanson, Lars. *Discoveries on the Turkic Linguistic Map.* Stockholm, Sweden: Svenska Forskningsinstitutet i Istanbul, 2001.

John, Richard R. "Eben Norton Horsford, the Northmen, and the Founding of Massachusetts." *Essays in Cambridge History* 45 (Proceedings, 1980–1985), 1998.

Johnson, Donald Blake. *Upton's Heritage: The History of a Massachusetts Town.* [1st]. ed. Canaan, NH: Phoenix, 1984.

Johnson, Frederick. "The Dolmen of Martha's Vineyard." *Bulletin of the Massachusetts Archaeological Society* 6 (2), January 1945.

Johnson, Gertrude. "The Healey Stone." *Early Sites Research Society Bulletin* 3 (2), May 1975.

Jones, G.A. "Data Report #95–029: Radiocarbon Results Carbondating Samples #8923, #8924." Woods Hole, MA: Woods Hole Oceanographic Institution, 1995.

Jones, Joseph C. *America's Icemen: An Illustrative History of the United States Natural Ice Industry, 1665–1925.* Humble, TX: Jobeco Books, 1984.

"J.S." "Antiquities of North America." *American Monthly,* January 1836.

Judge, Joseph. "The Island of Landfall." *National Geographic* 170 (5), November 1986.

Jungersen, Kenneth M. "The Search for Vinland." *Oceans* 18 (5), 1985.

Karlgren, Hans. Review of *Norse Medieval Cryptography in Runic Carvings* by O.G. Landsverk and Alf Mongé. *Scandinavian Studies,* 1968.

Keeler, Clyde. "The Newport Round Church: Description and Analysis." *Epigraphic Society Occasional Publications* 13 (329), 1985.

Keene, Leonard M. "Lynn Woods Grooved Stone." *NEARA Journal* 16 (2), 1981.

———. "Lynn Woods Mega-Geometry." *NEARA Journal* 15 (2), 1980.

———. "Mega-Geometry Update Essex County, MA." *NEARA Journal* 16 (1), 1981.

Kelley, David H. *Deciphering the Maya Script.* Austin, TX: Univ. of Texas Press, 1976.

———. "Proto-Tifinagh and Proto-Ogham in the Americas." *Review of Archaeology* 11 (1), 1990.

Kelley, David. H., and John Glass. Report to Early Sites Foundation. Unpublished manuscript, 1955.

_____. Reprint of "1955 Report to Early Sites Foundation." *Early Sites Research Society Bulletin* 1 (1), 1955.

Kendall, Edward Augustus. *Travels Through the Northern Parts of the United States, in the Years 1807 and 1808*. New York: Printed and published by I. Riley, 1809.

Kim, Eunice. "Town Explores Its Options for Saving Cave: Upton Historical Commission Doesn't Want 'Treasure' Developed." *Milford Daily News*, August 22, 2004.

Kirby, Ian. "The Narragansett Runic Inscription, Rhode Island," in *Beowulf and Beyond*. Frankfort: Peter Lang, 2007.

Knight, Christopher, and Robert Lomas. *The Book of Hiram: Freemasonry, Venus and the Secret Key to the Life of Jesus*. London: Element, 2005.

Kozubek, Marcia. "Wind Farm Would Scuttle Viking Studies, Researcher Says." *The Register*, April 8, 2004.

Krueger, Harold. "Report of Analytical Work, Radiocarbon Age Determination: Sample GX1608." Cambridge: Geochron Laboratories, 1969.

_____. Report of Analytical Work, Radiocarbon Age Determination: Sample GX2310. Cambridge: Geochron Laboratories, 1974.

LaBaree, Leonard Woods. "Naming a Continent." *New York Times*: January 14, 1945.

Lambert, Joanne Dondero. *America's Stonehenge: An Interpretive Guide*. Kingston, NH: Sunrise Publications, 1996.

Landsverk, O.G. *Runic Records of the Norsemen in America*. New York: E.J. Friis, 1974.

_____. "The Spirit Pond Cryptography." *Man in the Northeast* 6, 1973.

Landsverk, O. G., and Alf Mongé. *Norse Medieval Cryptography in Runic Carvings*. Glendale, CA: Norseman Press, 1967.

Lane, Helen H. *History of the Town of Dighton, Massachusetts*. Dighton, MA: Town of Dighton, 1962.

Lankford, George E. "The Great Serpent in Eastern North America." In *Ancient Objects and Sacred Realms*. ed. F. Kent Reilly III and James F. Garber. Austin: University of Texas Press, 2010.

_____. *Reachable Stars: Patterns in the Ethnoastronomy of Eastern North America*. Tuscaloosa: The University of Alabama Press, 2007.

Larson, Alicia. "Alicia Larson Supports Pynchon Papers Relating to Gungywamp." *Stonewatch* 10 (4), 1992.

_____. "A Gungywamp Historical Research Update." *Stonewatch* 8 (2), 1989.

Lathrop, DD, John. Letter to Judge Davis. In *Proceedings of the Massachusetts Historical Society 1867–1869*. Boston: Massachusetts Historical Society, 1868.

Lenik, Edward J. *Making Pictures in Stone: American Indian Rock Art of the Northeast*. Tuscaloosa: University of Alabama Press, 2009.

_____. "Mythic Creatures: Serpents, Dragons, and Sea Monsters in Northeastern Rock Art." *Archaeology of Eastern North America*, 38, 2010.

_____. *Picture Rocks: American Indian Rock Art in the Northeast Woodlands*. Hanover, NH: University Press of New England, 2002.

Lethbridge, T.C. *Herdsmen and Hermits: Celtic Seafarers in the Northern Seas*. Cambridge: Bowes & Bowes, 1950.

_____. *Merlin's Island: Essays on Britain in the Dark Ages*. London: Methuen, 1948.

_____. *Umiak: The European Ancestry of the 'Women's Boat.'* London: self-published, 1937.

Liestøl, Aslak. "Cryptograms in Runic Carvings: A Critical Analysis." *Minnesota History* 41 (1), 1968.

Lightman, Andrew. "Historical Commission Gets OK to Buy Cave." *Milford Daily News*, March 23, 2005.

_____. "Town Taking New Pass at Cave." *Milford Daily News*, February 24, 2005.

Linebaugh, Donald W. *The Man Who Found Thoreau: Roland W. Robbins and the Rise of Historical Archaeology in America*. Hanover, NH: University Press of New England, 2005.

"Local Discoveries Indicate Norsemen Were Here First." *Newburyport Daily News*, October 11, 1957.

Lodge, Henry Cabot. [Review of *America Not Discovered by Columbus ...* by Rasmus Björn Anderson]. *North American Review* 120 (1), 1875.

Loffelt, P. H., John Romeyn Brodhead and J.C. Jonge. *Nieu Nederlandt*. New York: Sarony, 1841.

"Long Hunt for Relics Starts." *Newburyport Daily News*, May 1, 1930.

Longfellow, Henry Wadsworth. *The Poetical Works of Longfellow: Cambridge edition*. Boston: Houghton Mifflin, 1975.

_____. "The Skeleton in Armor." *Knickerbocker Magazine*, January 1841.

_____. *Tales of a Wayside Inn*. Boston: Ticknor and Fields, 1863.

Lord, E.C.E. "Notes on the Geology and Petrography of Monhegan Island, Maine." *American Geologist* 26 (6), 1900.

Lort, Michael. "Account of an Antient Inscription in North America." *Archaeologia* 8, 1787.

Lossing, Benson John. *The Pictorial Field-book of the Revolution; or, Illustrations, by Pen and Pencil, of the History, Biography, Scenery, Relics, and Traditions of the War for Independence*. New York: Harper & Brothers, 1855.

Louisbourg Institute Archaeology Artifact Database. Provenience Record Number 1B6A13.1: Fortress of Louisbourg National Historic Site.

Löve, Áskell. "The Plants of Vineland the Good." *The Icelandic Canadian*, 1951.

Lucas, Fred. W. (trans.). "The Zeno Narrative." *New Orkney Antiquarian Journal* 2, 2002.

Lucas, Fred. W., and Niccolò Zeno. *The Annals of the Voyages of the Brothers Nicolò and Antonio Zeno, in the North Atlantic About the End of the Fourteenth Century, and the Claim Founded Thereon to a Venetian Discovery of America; A

Criticism and an Indictment. London: H. Stevens Sons and Stiles, 1898.

Lynch, Brad. "Did Vikings Make History on Cape Cod?" *Barnstable Patriot*, March 8, 2001.

Macalister, R.A. Stewart. "External Evidence Affecting the Problem of the Age of Ogham Writing in Ireland." *Man* 2, 1902.

Mahan, Shannon A., F.W. Martin, and Catherine Taylor. "Construction ages of the Upton Stone Chamber: Preliminary findings and suggestions for future luminescence research." *Quaternary Geochronology* 30 part B, October 2015.

Mallery, Arlington H. "The Pre-Columbian Discovery of America: A Reply to W.S. Godfrey." *American Anthropologist* 60 (1), 1958.

Mallery, Arlington H., Gardner C. Easton, and John Howieson. *Interim Report.* Newport, RI, 1955.

_____. *Preliminary Report.* Newport, RI, 1956.

Mallery, Arlington Humphrey, and Mary Roberts Harrison. *The Rediscovery of Lost America.* New York: Dutton, 1979.

Mallery, Garrick. "Dangers of Symbolic Interpretation" [abstract]. *Transactions of the Anthropological Society of Washington* 1, 1882.

_____. *Picture-writing of the American Indians.* New York: Dover, 1972.

Mancini, J.M. "Discovering Viking America." *Critical Inquiry* 28 (7), 2002.

Marco Simón, Francisco. "Religion and Religious Practices of the Ancient Celts of the Iberian Peninsula." *e-Keltoi: Journal of Interdisciplinary Celtic Studies* 6, 2005.

Mason, O.T. "Notes and News: 'The Skeleton in Armor.'" *American Anthropologist* 1 (2), 1888.

Mavor, James W. "Astronomy and Shamanism Among Culdee Monks." *Early Sites Research Society Bulletin* 12 (1), 1985.

_____. "The Riddle of Mzorah." *Almogaren* 7, 1976.

_____. *Voyage to Atlantis.* New York: Putnam, 1969.

Mavor, James W., and Byron E. Dix. *Manitou: The Sacred Landscape of New England's Native Civilization.* Rochester, VT: Inner Traditions International, 1989.

McCallum, Kent. *Old Sturbridge Village: A Visitor's Guide.* Sturbridge, MA: The Village, 1996.

McCluskey, Stephen C. "Gregory of Tours, Monastic Timekeeping, and Early Christian Attitudes to Astronomy." *Isis* 81 (1), 1990.

McCulloch, J. Huston. "Newport Tower Radiocarbon Dates: Some Reservations about the Newport Tower C-14 Dates." *Midwestern Epigraphic Journal* 15, 2001.

McGhee, Peter S. "Bertrand Woods Noman's." *Vineyard Gazette*, August 1966.

McGlone, William R., et al. *Ancient American Inscriptions: Plow Marks or History?* Sutton, MA: Early Sites Research Society, 1993.

McNamara, Eileen. "Legislators Push Their Pet Rocks." *Boston Globe*, April 23, 1983.

McNamara, Elizabeth. "Narragansett Rune Stone Returned; To Be Tested." *East Greenwich Patch*, April 26, 2013.

Meagher, Jonathan. *The Upton Chamber Mystery: An Analysis of Competing Theories Concerning the Chamber's Origins and the Chamber's Historical Significance.* Unpublished report on file with the Upton Historical Commission, 2004.

Means, Philip Ainsworth. "The Mysterious Runic Stone." *New York Times*, May 26, 1940.

_____. *Newport Tower.* New York: Holt, 1942.

_____. *Tupak of the Incas.* New York: Scribner's, 1942.

Meller, Harald. "Star Search." *National Geographic* 205 (1):77–87, 2004.

Menzies, Gavin. *1421: The Year China Discovered America.* New York: William Morrow, 2003.

Miller, June White. Malcolm Pearson. *NEARA Journal* 21 (3), 1987.

Mims, Tilda. "Turpentining: One of the South's Oldest Forest Industries." *Alabama's Treasured Forests* 18 (2):12–13, 1999.

"Minutes of Public Meeting." Commonwealth of Massachusetts Board of Underwater Archaeological Resources. January 30, 2003.

Moncrieffe, Iain. *The Highland Clans.* New York: Clarkson N. Potter, 1967.

"Monuments." *American Art Review* 1, 1880.

Moorehead, Warren King. "Ancient remains at Pemaquid." *Old Time New England*, January 1924.

_____. *A Report on the Archeology of Maine; Being a Narrative of Explorations in That State, 1912–1920, Together with Work at Lake Champlain, 1917.* Andover, MA: The Andover Press, 1922.

Morison, Samuel Eliot. *The European Discovery of America: the Northern Voyages, A.D. 500–1600.* New York: Oxford University Press, 1971.

_____. *The Maritime History of Massachusetts, 1783–1860.* Boston: Houghton Mifflin, 1961.

Morse, Abner. *Further Traces of the Ancient Northmen in America: with Geological Evidences of the Location of Their Vineland.* Boston: H.W. Dutton, 1861.

_____. *Traces of the Ancient Northmen in America: Being a Paper Read before the New England Historic Genealogical Society August, 1861: Also Supplement to Same.* Boston: Mudge Printers, 1887.

Neudorfer, Giovanna. *Vermont's Stone Chambers: An Inquiry into Their Past.* Montpelier, VT: Vermont Historical Society, 1980.

Newport Correspondent for the Boston Journal. The Old Stone Mill. *Lake Shore Observer*, December 21, 1885.

Nielsen, Richard. "The Runes and Language of the Spirit Pond Stones and the Narragansett Inscription Can be Found in Modern Books," *The Epigraphic Society Occasional Papers* 27 (2009).

Nielsen, Richard, and Scott F. Wolter. *The Kensington Rune Stone: Compelling New Evidence.* Minneapolis, MN: Lake Superior Agate, 2006.

Nielson, Helge. "Trelleborgenes geometri og måleenheder. Eksempler på modulanalyse med datamat" (The geometry and units of measure of the Trelleborg ring-forts. An example of module analysis by computer). In *Ti år med RECAU*, edited by Steen Larsen. Århus, Denmark: Århus Universitet/RECAU, 1981.

Noman's Land: It's for the Birds—Duck!" *Los Angeles Times*, December 10, 1989.

"Norse Markings on Hampton Rock Made by Explorer 'Bui.'" *Newburyport Daily News*, June 27, 1938.

Odenstedt, Bengt. *On the Origin and Early History of the Runic Script: Typology and Graphic Variation in the Older Futhark.* Stockholm: Almqvist & Wiksell, 1990.

"Old Caves at Salem, N.H., Laid to Robbers, Indians." *Boston Globe*, October 24, 1935.

"The Old Stone Mill." *Newport Daily News*, August 17, 1979.

"Old Stone Mill Weakened By '49 Excavations, Ohio Engineer Claims In Report To Council." *Newport Daily News*, October 20, 1955.

Olson, Julius E. Review of *The problem of the Northmen and the Site of Norumbega* by Eben Norton Horsford; with a response by Horsford. Cambridge, MA, 1891.

O'Malley, Patricia Trainor, and Paul H. Tedesco. *A New England City: Haverhill, Massachusetts.* Northridge, CA: Windsor, 1987.

Oppenheimer, Monroe, and Willard Wirtz. "A Linguistic Analysis of Some West Virginia Petroglyphs." *West Virginia Archeologist* 41 (1), 1989.

Ordway, Wallace B. "Markings on Byfield Stones Spur Scientific Speculation." *Newburyport Daily News*, December 15, 1948.

"Origin of Caves Cleared Up by Kin of Builder." *Haverhill Evening Gazette*, August 17, 1934.

Ó Ríordáin, Seán P., and Glyn Edmund Daniel. *New Grange and the Bend of the Boyne.* New York: F.A. Praeger, 1964.

"Our Next Public Statue." *Evening Transcript*, January 17, 1887.

Packard, A.S. "Who First Saw the Labrador Coast?" *Journal of the American Geographical Society of New York* 20 (2), 1888.

Paine, Elizabeth Rogers. "Anne Whitney, Sculptor." *Art Quarterly* 25, 1962.

Paine, Lincoln P. *Ships of the World: An Historical Encyclopedia.* Boston: Houghton Mifflin, 1997.

Palfrey, John Gorham, and Francis Winthrop Palfrey. *History of New England.* Boston: Little, Brown, 1858.

Patterson, George. "The Portuguese on the North East Coast of America." *Proceedings and Transactions of the Royal Society of Canada for the Year 1890*, 1891.

Pearson, Malcolm. "Was It a Cave?" In *Upton, Massachusetts*, edited by W.G. Poor. Milford, MA: Charlescraft Press, 1935.

Pell, Herbert C. "The Old Stone Mill, Newport." *Rhode Island History* 7 (4), 1948.

Pendery, Steven R. "The Newport Tower: Revisiting New England's Fantastic Archaeology" in *Archaeology of Eastern North America: Papers in Honor of Stephen Williams*, Ed. James B. Stoltman. Jackson: Mississippi Department of Archives and History, 1993. (Archaeological Report No. 25).

Penhallow, William S. "Astronomical Alignments in the Newport Tower." *NEARA Journal* 29 (1/2), 1994.

———. "Some Thoughts on the Newport Tower." *NEARA Journal* 36 (2), 2002.

Perry, Clay. *New England's Buried Treasure.* New York: Stephen Daye Press, 1946.

———. *Underground New England.* Brattleboro, VT: Stephen Daye Press, 1939.

Persinger, Michael A. "Limitations of Human Verbal Behavior in the Context of UFO-Related Stimuli." In *UFO Phenomena and the Behavioral Scientist*, ed. by R.F. Haines. Metuchen, NJ: Scarecrow Press, 1979.

———. "Possible Infrequent Geophysical Sources of Close UFO Encounters: Expected Physical and Behavioral-Biological Effects." In *UFO Phenomena and the Behavioral Scientist*, edited by R.F. Haines. Metuchen, NJ: Scarecrow Press, 1979.

———. "Religious and Mystical Experience as Artifacts of Temporal Lobe Function: A General Hypothesis." *Perceptual and Motor Skills* 57, 1983.

Peters, Paula. "Window on the Past." *Cape Cod Times*, January 7, 2001.

"Philip A. Means, 52, Inca Lore Expert." *New York Times*, November 25, 1944.

Philips, David E. *Legendary Connecticut.* Willimantic, CT: Curbstone Press, 1992.

Picard, Dennis D. "A Short Note on Cider Making in 19th Century New England and the Lyford-Hutchins Mill." In *Papers and Articles: OSV Research Paper.* Sturbridge, MA: Old Sturbridge Village, 1985.

Pohl, Frederick J. *Atlantic Crossings Before Columbus.* New York: Norton, 1961.

———. "Can the Ship's Shoring at Follins Pond be Radiocarbon Dated?" *Massachusetts Archaeological Society Bulletin* 17 (3), 1956.

———. "Cockaponsett Carvings." *Epigraphic Society Occasional Publications* 6 (134), 1979.

———. "Cockaponsett Carvings in Connecticut." *Anthropological Journal of Canada* 16 (4), 1978.

———. "Leif Ericsson's Visit to America." *American-Scandinavian Review* 36, 1948.

———. *The Lost Discovery; Uncovering the Track of the Vikings in America.* New York: Norton, 1952.

———. "Plaster Under the Newport Tower." *American Antiquity* 19 (3), 1954.

———. *Prince Henry Sinclair: His Voyage to the New World in 1398.* New York: Clarkson N. Potter, 1974.

———. "The Ship's Shoring at Follins Pond." *Massachusetts Archaeological Society Bulletin* 16 (3):53–60, 1955.

———. *The Sinclair Expedition to Nova Scotia in 1398.* Pictou, Nova Scotia: Pictou Advocate Press, 1950.

———. "To Perpetuate a Linguistic Hoax." *Anthropological Journal of Canada* 18 (2), 1980.

_____. *The Viking Settlements of North America*. New York: Clarkson N. Potter, 1972.

_____. *The Vikings on Cape Cod: Evidence from Archaeological Discovery*. Pictou, Nova Scotia: Pictou Advocate Press, 1957.

_____. "Was the Newport Tower Standing in 1632?" *New England Quarterly* 18 (4), 1945.

Pond Jr., Pratt (pseud. Daniel Fiske). "Upton Traditions: A Deserted Haunt of Unknown Origin." *Milford Journal*, April 26, 1893.

_____. "Upton Traditions: A Deserted Haunt of Unknown Origin" [reprint]. *Early Sites Research Society Bulletin* 1 (1), 1973.

Pool, George I. "An Antiquity Discovered in the Valley of the Merrimack." *New England Historical and Genealogical Register* 8, 1854.

Poor, William George. *Upton, Massachusetts*. Milford, MA: Charlescraft Press, 1935.

Porters, Frank. "Problem for Archaeologists." *Haverhill Evening Gazette*, August 15, 1934.

Prevention of Grain Elevator and Mill Explosions. Washington, D.C.: National Materials Advisory Board, 1982.

Proper, Ida Sedgwick. "Monhegan, the Cradle of New England." Portland, ME: Southworth Press, 1930.

Provenzano, Richard G. *Pirates' Glen & Dungeon Rock: The Evolution of a Legend*. Saugus, MA: Saugus Historical Society, 1983.

Putnam, Frederick Ward. "Twentieth Report of the Curator." *Twentieth Annual Report of the Trustees of the Peabody Museum of American Archaeology and Ethnology* III (7), 1887.

Pynchon, John. "Letters of John Pynchon, 1654–1700." In *The Pynchon Papers*, ed. by C. Bridenbaugh. Boston: Colonial Society of Massachusetts, 1982.

Pynchon, John, Carl Bridenbaugh, and Juliette Tomlinson. *The Pynchon Papers*. 2 vols. (Publications of the Colonial Society of Massachusetts, v. 60–61.) Boston: Colonial Society of Massachusetts, 1982.

Quinion, Michael B. *Cidermaking, Shire Album 95*. Aylesbury, UK: Shire, 1982.

Quinn, David B. *North America from Earliest Discovery to First Settlements: The Norse Voyages to 1612*. New York: Harper & Row, 1978.

"Quo Warranto?" *Boston Globe*, April 19, 1956.

Rafn, Carl Christian. *Antiquitates Americanæ sive scriptores septentrionales rerum antecolumbianarum in America*. Copenhagen: Hafniæ, typis officinæ Schultzianæ, 1837.

_____. *Antiquités américaines d'après les monuments historiques des Islandais et des anciens Scandinaves. Publiées sous les auspices de la Société royale des Antiquaires du Nordmericanae*. Copenhagen: Secrétariat de la Société, 1845.

Rafn, Carl Christian, Thomas H. Webb, and John M'Caul. *Supplement to the Antiquitates Americanæ*. Copenhagen: At the secretary's office of the Society, 1841.

Randall, Peter E. *Hampton, a Century of Town and Beach, 1888–1988*. [Hampton, NH:] published by the author, 1989.

Reynard, Elizabeth. *The Narrow Land: Folk Chronicles of Old Cape Cod*. Boston: Houghton Mifflin, 1934.

"RI Attorney General and RI Department of Environmental Management Joint Investigation Leads to the Return of the Narragansett Rune Stone." *States News Service*, April 26, 2013. Academic OneFile, http://link.galegroup.com/apps/doc/A327792403/AONE?u=gale15691 &sid=AONE&xid=fe986b31. Accessed 22 Nov. 2018.

Richardson, Edward Adams. "Builder of the Newport Tower." *American Society of Civil Engineers Transactions* 86 (Paper no. 3091), 1960.

Ricketson, Daniel. *The History of New Bedford, Bristol County, Massachusetts: including a history of the old township of Dartmouth and the present townships of Westport, Dartmouth, and Fairhaven, from their settlement to the present time*. New Bedford, MA: published by the author, 1858.

Rixson, Denis. *The West Highland Galley*. Edinburgh: Birlinn, 1998.

Robertson, Marion. *Rock Drawings of the Micmac Indians*. Halifax, Nova Scotia: Nova Scotia Museum, 1973.

Rodger, N.A.M. *The Safeguard of the Sea: A Naval History of Britain, 660–1649*. New York: W.W. Norton, 1998.

Roebuck, Graham. "'This Innocent Worke': Adam and Eve, John Smith, William Wood and the North American Plantations." *Early Modern Literary Studies* 1 (1), 1995.

Rose, Fiona A. "Text and Image in Celtiberia: The Adoption and Adaptation of Written Language into Indigenous Visual Vocabulary." *Oxford Journal of Archaeology* 22 (2), 2003.

Ross, Anne, and Peter Reynolds. "Ancient Vermont." *Antiquity* 52 (205), 1978.

Rowell, Joseph Mason. "Excursion to Nunnery pasture." Lynn, MA. June 20, 1856.

Salwen, Bert. "The Reliability of Andre Thevet's New England Material." *Ethnohistory* 10 (2), 1963.

Scalisi, Marie Lollo and Virginia M. Ryan. "Peter Pattee of Haverhill Massachusetts: A 'Journeyman Shoemaker' and His Descendants." *New England Historical and Genealogical Register* Vol. 4, no. 4 (October 1992); Vol. 147, no. 1 (January 1993); Vol. 147, no. 2 (April 1993).

Schlereth, Thomas J. "Columbia, Columbus, and Columbianism." *Journal of American History* 79 (3), 1992.

Schoolcraft, Henry Rowe. *Historical and Statistical Information Respecting the History, Condition and Prospects of the Indian Tribes of the United States*. US Bureau of American Ethnology. Bulletin 152. Philadelphia: J.B. Lippincott, 1854.

_____. *History of Indian Tribes of the United States: Their Present Condition and Prospects, and a Sketch of their Ancient Status*. Philadelphia: J.B. Lippincott, 1857.

_____. *Personal Memoirs of a Residence of Thirty Years with the Indian Tribes on the American Frontiers: With Brief Notices of Passing Events, Facts, and Opinions, A.D. 1812 to A.D. 1842.* Philadelphia, PA: Lippincott, Grambo, 1851.

Secretary's Report. *Proceedings of the Essex Institute* 5 (1866–7). April 16, 1866.

Shammas, Carole. "How Self-Sufficient Was Early America?" *Journal of Interdisciplinary Studies* 13 (2), 1982.

Sharp, Lewis I., and John Quincy Adams Ward. *John Quincy Adams Ward, Dean of American Sculpture: With a Catalogue Raisonné.* Newark, DE: Univ. of Delaware Press, 1985.

Shepard, Elizabeth G. *A Guide-book to Norumbega and Vineland; or, The Archæological Treasures along Charles River.* Boston: Damrell & Upham, 1893.

Shepard, Odell, and Willard Shepard. *Holdfast Gaines.* New York: Macmillan, 1946.

Shipley, Marie A. *The Norse Colonization in America by the Light of the Vatican Finds.* Lucerne: H. Keller's Foreign Printing Office, 1899.

Shoumatoff, Alex. *Westchester, Portrait of a County.* New York: Coward McCann & Geoghegan, 1979.

Simmons, William S. "The Mystic Voice: Pequot Folklore from the Seventeenth Century to the Present." In *The Pequots in Southern New England: The Fall and Rise of an American Indian Nation*, ed. L.M. Hauptman and J. Wherry. Norman: University of Oklahoma Press, 1990.

Simmons, William Scranton. *Spirit of the New England Tribes: Indian History and Folklore, 1620–1984.* Hanover, NH: University Press of New England, 1986.

Sinclair, Andrew. *The Sword and the Grail.* New York: Crown, 1992.

Sivulka, Juliann. *Stronger Than Dirt: A Cultural History of Advertising Personal Hygiene in America, 1875–1940.* Amherst, NY: Humanity Books, 2001.

Skinner, Charles M. *Myths and Legends of Our Own Land.* Philadelphia: J.B. Lippincott, 1896.

Slafter, Edmund F. "The Discovery of America by the Northmen, in the Tenth and Eleventh Centuries." *Proceedings of the New Hampshire Historical Society* 2 (June 1888–June 1895).

_____. *Voyages of the Northmen to America.* Boston: Prince Society, 1877.

Smallheer, Susan. "Rockingham, Abenaki Tribe get national grant to study petroglyphs." *Brattleboro Reformer*, April 21, 2022.

Smith, Benjamin L. "A Report on the Follins Pond Investigation." *Massachusetts Archaeological Society Bulletin* 14 (2), 1953.

Smith, Brian. "Earl Henry Sinclair's Fictitious Trip to America." *New Orkney Antiquarian Journal* 2, 2002.

Smith, R.W. Correspondence on cider mill, Monroe, NY. September 14, 1953.

_____. "Memorandum No.16: Cider Mill." Monroe, NY: Museum Village of Old Smith's Clove, 1960.

Snow, Edward Rowe. *Famous New England Lighthouses.* Boston: Yankee, 1945.

Sparkes, Boyden. "Writ on Rocke." *Saturday Evening Post*, April 26, 1941.

Speck, Frank Gouldsmith. "Native Tribes and Dialects of Connecticut, a Mohegan-Pequot Diary." *Bureau of American Ethnology Annual report*; v. 43: Washington, D.C.: Smithsonian Institution, 1928.

_____. *Notes on the Mohegan and Niantic Indians.* Anthropological papers of the American Museum of Natural History. New York: American Museum of Natural History, 1909.

Spofford, Jeremiah. *A Historical and Statistical Gazetteer of Massachusetts.* Haverhill, MA: E.G. Frothingham, 1860.

Starr, Harris Elwood. "Ezra Stiles." *Dictionary of American Biography.* New York: Scribner's, 1936.

Stearns, Ezra Scollay. *Genealogical and Family History of the State of New Hampshire.* New York: Lewis, 1908.

Stefansson, Vilhjalmur. *Greenland.* Garden City, NY: Doran, 1942.

Stefansson, Vilhjalmur, and Rudolph Martin Anderson. *My Life with the Eskimo.* New York: Macmillan, 1913.

Stephens, George. *Handbook of the Old-northern Runic Monuments of Scandinavia and England.* London: Williams and Norgate, 1884.

Stewart-Smith, David. *Ancient and Modern Quarry Techniques, America's Stonehenge at Mystery Hill.* Monograph Series. Nashua, NH: Gamesmasters, 1989.

Stiles, Ezra. "Itineraries." In *Ezra Stiles Papers.* New Haven, CT: Yale University, 1760–94.

_____. *The United States Elevated to Glory and Honor: A Sermon Preached before His Excellency Jonathan Trumbull, Esq. L.L.D., Governor and Commander in Chief, and the Honorable the General Assembly of the State of Connecticut, Convened at Hartford, at the Anniversary Election, May 8th, 1783.* New Haven, CT: Thomas & Samuel Green, 1783.

Stokhuyzen, F. *The Dutch Windmill.* New York: Universe Books, 1963.

Stone, Dennis. *America's Stonehenge Souvenir Book*, [North Salem, NH]: [n.p.], 2019.

Stone, G.H. "The Inscription Rocks on the Island of Monhegan." *Science* 6 (132), 1885.

Stone, Robert. "Mystery Hill: New Information on the Status of Its Structures in 1938." *NEARA Journal* 11 (2), 1976.

_____. "The NEARA Symbol." *NEARA Newsletter* 2 (3), 1967.

_____. "Preliminary Survey: No. Salem Rock Shelter." *New Hampshire Archeological Society Miscellaneous Papers*, 1961.

"Stone Tower Theory Raises Questions." *Newport Daily News*, February 19, 1996.

Strahlenberg, Philip Johan von. *An Historico-geographical Description of the North and Eastern Parts of Europe and Asia: But More Particularly of Russia, Siberia, and Great Tartary; Both in*

Their Ancient and Modern State: Together with an Entire New Polyglot-table of the Dialects of 32 Tartarian Nations and a Vocabulary of the Kalmuck-Mungalian Tongue. London: Printed for J. Brotherton, J. Hazard, W. Meadows, T. Cox, T. Astley, S. Austen, L. Gilliver and C. Corbet, 1738.

Strandwold, Olaf. *Norse Inscriptions on American Stones*. Weehauken, NJ: Magnus Björndal, 1948.

_____. *Norse Runic Inscriptions along the Atlantic Seaboard*. Prosser, WA: [published by author], 1939.

_____. *The Yarmouth Stone, Mystic Characters on Yarmouth Stone Yield Startling Evidence of Norse Discoveries* (Prosser, WA: Prosser Printing Company, 1934).

Strubbe, Bill, and Richard Flavin. "Written in Stone." *Historic Traveler*, February 1999.

"Study Underway at Old Stone Mill In Attempt To Rebuild Original Edifice." *Newport Daily News*, November 19, 1954.

"Submarine is Ashore." *Washington Post*, May 23, 1915.

Swauger, James L. "Petroglyphs, Tar Burner Rocks, and Lye Leaching Stones." *Pennsylvania Archaeologist* 51 (1–2), 1981.

Sylvester, Herbert Milton. *The Land of St. Castin*. Boston: W.B. Clarke, 1909.

Taylor, Alan. "The Early Republic's Supernatural Economy: Treasure Seeking in the American Northeast, 1780–1830." *American Quarterly* 38 (1), 1986.

Telepneff, Gregory. *The Egyptian Desert in the Irish Bogs: the Byzantine Character of Early Celtic Monasticism*. Etna, CA: Center for Traditionalist Orthodox Studies, 1998.

"The Templars' Deadliest Secret: Evidence Exposed." *America Unearthed*. H2 Channel, season 3, episode 13, January 31, 2015.

Thevet, André. *La Cosmographie Universelle d'André Thevet, cosmographe du roy illustrée de diverses figures des choses plus remarquables veues par l'auteur, & incogneuës de noz anciens & modernes. CIHM/ICMH Microfiche series no. 40484*. Paris: Chez Guillaume Chandiere, 1575.

Thompson, Zadock. *History of Vermont, Natural, Civil, and Statistical*. Burlington, VT: For the author, by C. Goodrich, 1842.

"Thorvald's Stone Riddle is Solved." *Boston Globe*, June 26, 1938.

"'Thorwald Rock' Still Remains Unmoved as Scientists Study On." *Hampton Union & Rockingham County Gazette*, July 28, 1938.

Tiede, Vance R. "The Chi-Rho Controversy Rages On." *Stonewatch* 20 (1), 2003.

_____. "Orientation of Stone Chamber One." In *The Greater Gungywamp: Twentieth Anniversary Edition*, D.P. Barron and S. Mason, eds. Noank, CT: The Gungywamp Society, 1998.

_____. "Solar Orientation of Irish Early Christian Oratories" [abstract]. *HAD News: The Newsletter of the Historical Astronomy Division of the American Astronomical Society* (33), December 2001.

_____. "The Sun of Truth & The Oratory: Solar Metaphors from Early Christian Ireland." *Memorie della Società Astronomica Italiana (Journal of the Italian Astronomical Society)*. Special Number 1, 2002.

"The Times They Are A-Changin'!" *Stonewatch* 20 (1), 2003.

Totten, Norman. "Epigraphic Research in America: Reply to Archaeologists Denunciations." *The Epigraphic Society Occasional Publications* 9 (215), 1981.

_____. "Implications of the Figuig Decipherment." *Epigraphic Society Occasional Publications* 3 (47), 1976.

"Tracking the Templars." *America Unearthed*. H2 Channel, season 1, episode 22, March 2, 2013.

Tracy, Cyrus M. *Studies of the Essex Flora: A Complete Enumeration of All Plants Found Growing Naturally within the Limits of Lynn, Mass., and the Towns Adjoining, Arranged According to the Natural System, with Copious Notes as to Localities and Habits*. Lynn, MA: Stevenson & Nichols Printers, 1858.

Trczinski, Stanley J. "The Bellows Falls Petroglyphs." *NEARA Newsletter* 3 (1), 1968.

Trento, Salvatore Michael. "A Bogus Inscription on Cape Cod, Massachusetts," *NEARA Journal* 14 (1), Summer 1979.

_____. *Field Guide to Mysterious Places of Eastern North America*. New York: H. Holt, 1997.

_____. *The Search for Lost America: The Mysteries of the Stone Ruins*. Chicago: Contemporary Books, 1978.

Tucker, James W. "Our Town column." *Hampton Union*, May 14, 1959.

_____. "The Vikings in Hampton" (Our Town column). *Hampton Union*, July 26, 1951.

Tufts, Eleanor. "An American Victorian Dilemma, 1875: Should a woman be allowed to sculpt a man?" *Art Journal* 51 (1), 1992.

Tupper, F.W. *Thomas Tupper and His Descendants*: Tupper Family Association of America, 1945.

Vallancey, Charles. *Collectanea de Rebus Hibernicis*. Dublin, Ireland: L. White, 1781.

_____. *An Essay on the Antiquity of the Irish Language; Being a Collation of the Irish with the Punic Language*. 3rd ed. London: Printed for R. Ryan, 1818.

_____. "Observations on the American Inscription." *Archaeologia*, 1787.

Vescelius, Gary S. "Excavation at Pattee's Caves." *Eastern States Archeology Bulletin* 15, 1956.

_____. "1955 North Salem, N.H. Site Excavations." In *Early Sites Foundation*. North Salem, NH, 1955.

_____. "North Salem, N.H., Site Excavations." North Salem, NH: Mystery Hill, 1955.

"Vikings in America." *America Unearthed*. H2 Channel, season 2, episode 4, December 21, 2013.

"Vikings in America." *Expedition Unknown*. Travel Channel, season 4, episode 2, January 3, 2018.

"Vineyarders Draw Bead on Navy Target Island." *Boston Globe*, April 5, 1987.

Wagner, Kathryn. "Historical Commission Works to Save Cave." *Milford Daily News*, September 24, 2004.

Wahlgren, Erik. "American runes: From Kensington to Spirit Pond." *Journal of English and Germanic Philology* 81, 1982.

_____. "Cryptopuzzle." *Biblical Archaeologist* 43 (2), 1980.

_____. *The Vikings and America, Ancient Peoples and Places*. New York: Thames and Hudson, 1986.

Wallace, Birgitta Linderoth. "Vikings in North America—New and Old," *Viking Heritage Magazine*, April 2003.

Wallace-Murphy, Tim, and Marilyn Hopkins. *Templars in America: From the Crusades to the New World*. Boston: Weiser Books, 2004.

Warhus, Mark. *Another America: Native American Maps and the History of Our Land*. New York: St. Martin's Press, 1997.

Warren, Nigel. *Metal Corrosion in Boats*. Dobbs Ferry, NY: Sheridan House, 2006.

Waters, Frank, and Oswald White Bear Fredericks. *Book of the Hopi*. New York: Viking Press, 1963.

Wegener, Franz. *Das Atlantidische Weltbild: Nationalsozialismus und neue Rechte auf der Suche nach dem versunkenen Atlantis*. Gladbeck, Germany: KFVR-Kulturförderverein Ruhrgebiet, 2000.

Welch, Dan. "Report of the Ground-Penetrating Radar Survey, Touro Park, Newport, Rhode Island, June 12, 2001." *NEARA Journal* 36 (2), 2002.

Wheaton, Henry. *Elements of International Law: with a Sketch of the History of the Science*. London: B. Fellowes, 1836.

_____. *History of the Northmen; or, Danes and Normans, from the Earliest Times to the Conquest of England by William of Normandy*. London: Murray, 1831.

Whitehead, Ruth H. "The Protohistoric Period in the Maritime Provinces." In *Prehistory of the Maritime Provinces: Past and Present Research*, ed. M. Deal and S. Blair. Fredericton, New Brunswick: Council of Maritime Premiers Maritime Committee on Archaeological Cooperation, 1991.

Whittall, J.P., ed. *The Spirit Pond Runestones*. Milford, NH: n.p., 1972.

Whittall II, James P. "Colonial 'Half-House' Excavated in Gungywamp Complex." *Stonewatch* 8 (3), 1989.

_____. Correspondence regarding similarities at Misrah Sinjura and Mystery Hill. Westford, MA, January 3, 1970.

_____. "The Gungywamp Complex, Groton, CT." *Early Sites Research Society Bulletin* 4 (1), 1976.

_____. "The Inscribed Stone from Comassakumkanit." *The Epigraphic Society Occasional Publications* 2 (44), 1975.

_____. "A Libyan Lithic Measure." *Early Sites Research Society Bulletin* 6 (1), May 1978.

_____. "The Monhegan Inscriptions." *Early Sites Research Society Bulletin* 4 (1), 1976.

_____. "Precolumbian Parallels between Mediterranean and New England Archeology." *Epigraphic Society Occasional Publications* 3 (52), 1975.

_____. "The Problem of Epigraphic Delusion." In *Myth Makers: Epigraphic Illusion in America*. Rowley, MA: Early Sites Research Society, 1990.

_____. "The Quista Dolmen." *NEARA Newsletter* 6 (1), March 1971.

_____. "A Report on the Pearson Stone Chamber." *Early Sites Research Society Bulletin* 7 (1), 1979.

_____. "A 'Runic' Amulet." *Early Sites Research Society Bulletin* 3 (1), 1975.

_____. *T.C. Lethbridge–Frank Glynn Correspondence 1950–1966*. Rowley, MA: Early Sites Research Society, 1998.

_____. "2995±180 at Mystery Hill." *NEARA Newsletter* 4 (3), 1969.

_____. "Vernal Equinox Light Channel." *Early Sites Research Society Bulletin* 18 (1), 1991.

Whittall Jr., James P., and David P. Barron. "Double Ring of Stones, The Gungywamp Complex." *Early Sites Research Society Bulletin* 18 (1), 1991.

Whittall Jr., James P., and Mark Stoughton. "Ground Penetrating Radar Survey, Newport Tower Site, Touro Park, Newport, Rhode Island, 1994." *Early Sites Research Society Bulletin*, 1995.

Whittier, John Greenleaf. "The Double-Headed Snake of Newbury." *Atlantic Monthly* 3 (15), 1859.

_____. *Narrative and Legendary poems, Riverside Edition. The writings of Whittier*. Boston: Houghton Mifflin, 1888.

Wigginton, Eliot. "Water Systems, Fiddle Making, Logging, Gardening, Sassafras Tea, Wood Carving, and Further Affairs of Plain Living." *Foxfire 4*. Garden City, NY: Anchor Books, 1977.

Wildung, Frank. Inventory of items at Hadley Farm Museum, Hadley, Massachusetts, for the Massachusetts Society for Promoting Agriculture. Shelburne VT: Shelburne Museum, 1960.

Willard, Lawrence F. "Westford's Mysterious Knight." *Yankee*, April 1958.

Williams, Laurie D. "Rediscovery of the 'Whittier Runestone' in Massachusetts." *NEARA Journal* 11 (2), 1976.

Williams, Samuel. *The Natural and Civil History of Vermont*. Burlington, VT: Samuel Mills, 1809.

Willoughby, Charles C. "Prehistoric Burial Places in Maine." *Archaeological and Ethnological Papers of the Peabody Museum* 1(6), July 1898.

Willoughby, Charles C. Review of *Dighton Rock* by Edmund Burke Delabarre, *American Anthropologist* 31(3), 1929.

Wilson, Sir Daniel. *Prehistoric Man; Researches into the Origin of Civilisation in the Old and the New World*. London: Macmillan, 1876.

_____. *The Vinland of the Northmen*. CIHM/ICMH Microfiche series no. 27466, 1890.

Wilson, James, Grant Wilson, and John Fiske. Ezra Stiles. In *Appleton's Cyclopedia of American Biography*. New York: D. Appleton, 1889.

Winkler, Louis, and Robert E. Stone. *Mystery Hill: Construction and Use 2000 BC–AD 1600*. North

Salem, NH: Mystery Hill Research Department, 1999.

Winsor, Justin. *Narrative and Critical History of America*. Boston: Houghton Mifflin, 1884.

Wirth, Herman. *Der Aufgang der Menschheit; untersuchungen zur geschichte der religion, symbolik und schrift der atlantischnordischen rasse*. Jena, Germany: E. Diederichs, 1928.

Wolter, Scott F. *Akhenaten to the Founding Fathers: The Mysteries of the Hooked X*. St. Cloud, MN: North Star Press of St. Cloud, 2013.

———. *The Hooked X: Key to the Secret History of North America*. St. Cloud, MN: North Star Press of St. Cloud, 2009.

———. "Venus Alignments in the Newport Tower, RI." *Ancient American* 12, no. 77 (February 2008).

Wolter, Scott F., and Blake Lemcke. "Petrographic Analysis of Rock." St. Paul, MN: American Petrographic Services, 2007.

Wood, Annie Moulton, and Cameron E. Wood. *Noman's Land; Isle of Romance*. New Bedford, MA: Reynolds Printing, 1931.

Wood, William. *New England's Prospect* (1635). Ed. A.T. Vaughan. Amherst: University of Massachusetts Press, 1977.

Woodbury, George. "Tourists Can Take It from Here: 'Mystery Caves'—Ancient Ruins or Codger's Retreat?" *New Hampshire Sunday News*, July 13, 1958.

Wroth, Lawrence C. *The Voyages of Giovanni da Verrazzano, 1524–1528*. New Haven, CT: Yale Univ. Press, 1970.

Wylie, J.A. *History of the Scottish Nation*. London: Hamilton, Adams, 1886.

Wytfliet, Corneille. *Histoire Universelle des Indes Occidentales*. Douay, France: Chez Francois Fabri, 1607.

Zahrtmann, C.C. "Remarks on the Voyages to the Northern Hemisphere, Ascribed to the Zeni of Venice." *Journal of the Royal Geographic Society of London* 5, 1835.

Index

Numbers in ***bold italics*** indicate pages with illustrations

America B.C. 81, 82, 84, 86, 156, 162, 198*n*40; *see also* Fell, Barry
America Unearthed (television series) 138, 168, 183, 208*n*48, 216*n*28
America's Stonehenge, North Salem, New Hampshire 63–80; alignments 65, 74, ***75***–76, 77, 78, 80; inscriptions 64–65, 71–74, ***72***, 157; Native Americans 65, 66; Oracle Chamber 10, ***64***; Pattee family 9, 10, 63, 65, 66, 67, 69–71, 75, 76, 185*n*15, 186*n*37, 186*n*38, 197*n*10, 197*n*14, 197*n*15, 199*n*63; sacrificial table 7–11, ***8***; vandalism 10–11, 15; zoomorphic carvings 78–80; *see also* Goodwin, William B.; Whittall, James P.
amphisbaena *see* Whittier, John Greenleaf poetry
Anderson, Rasmus B. 19, 20–22, 24, 134
Andover, Massachusetts clochán (Turtle Mound) 95, 151, 202*n*122
Antiquitates Americanae see Rafn, Carl Christian
Appleton, Thomas Gold 22, 23
Aquidneck Island, Rhode Island *see* Sakonnet Stones
Assawompset Pond, Massachusetts (Phoenician ship carving) 157, 212*n*84
astronomical alignments *see* America's Stonehenge; Cachão da Rapa; Calendar One; Gungywamp; Newport Tower; Pearson Chamber; Sky Disk of Nebra; Stonehenge

Babcock, William H. 39, 111, 140, 149
Barron, David 148, 149, ***150***, 181, 210*n*38
Bellows Falls, Vermont petroglyphs 91–93, ***92***
Bird, Junius 51, 70, 71, 96, 194*n*50
Bjorndal, Magnus 57, 116
Boland, Charles Michael 116, 154, 157–158
Bourne, Massachusetts inscribed stone 130, 160–162, ***161***
Brønsted, Johannes 113, 171
Buchanan, Donal 135, 179–180
Bull, Ole 20–22, ***21***, 23, 24, 35, 172, 188*n*50, 192*n*36
Byfield, Massachusetts Viking graves 101, 114–117, ***118***

Calendar One, South Royalton, Vermont 82–84, ***83***, 86, 87
Calendar II, South Woodstock, Vermont ***85***–86

Cannon Rock *see* Phaeton Rock, Lynn Massachusetts
Carlson, Suzanne 50, 123, 136–137, 181
Castleton State College, Vermont 82, 87
Ceilie Dei see Culdee Monks
Celt-Iberian origin 72–73, 77, 81–82, 86, 87, 123, 179; *see also* Ogham
Celtic church 151–153, 157, 211*n*57; *see also* Culdee monks
Celtic origin 3, 81, 88, 156, 157, 211*n*62
Chapman, Paul 55, 135–136, 180
Chatfield Stone, Sebec Lake, Maine 126–128, ***127***
Cheney, Harry A. 125–126, 141
Chenoweth, Alexander C. *see* Inwood Stone
cider presses 6–7
Cockaponset carvings, Connecticut 154–158, ***155***
Cook, Warren 82, 85, 87
Corte Real family 37, 38, 39, 58, 192*n*57, 192*n*66; Miguel as creator of Dighton Rock 38, 39, 42, 58, 105
Crane, Joshua 163, 165, 166
cryptograms, runic 57, 117, 131, 133, 134, 135, 179, 180, 208*n*38
Culdee monks 8, 11, 68, 69, 91, 100, 116, 151–152, 169; *see also* Celtic church

Danville, New Hampshire beehive ii
Da Silva, Manuel Luciano 40–43, 58, 105, 163
DeCosta, B.F. 26–27, 28, 121
Delabarre, Edmund Burke 32, 35, 36–37, 38–39, 41–42, 93, 113, 121, 140, 161, 164, 165–166, 177–178, 192*n*46, 192*n*63, 212*n*33
Dighton Rock 18, 32–43, ***34***, 36, ***42***; 46, 88; 112, 120, 164, 177; Celtic 33–34; Native American 32–33, 34, 36, 41; Norse 35–36, 38–39, 128; Phoenician 33, 35; Portuguese 36–37, 38, 39–42, 58, 105
Dix, Byron 80, 82, 83, 84, 85–86, 87, 88, 96–97, 154, 172
"The Double-Headed Snake" *see* Whittier, John Greenleaf poetry

Early Norse Visits to North America see Babcock, William H.
Early Sites Foundation 9–10, 70, 96
Early Sites Research Society 59, 90, 96, 146, 181, 200fn12

233

Elliot, Walter 130–131, 133
Ellsworth, Maine runestone 123–*125*
entoptic phenomena 74, 92-3
Eriksson, Leif 17, 18, 27, 159, 169, 170, 173; Ward statue 22, 23, 24, 188n35; Whitney statue *see* Whitney, Anne; *see also* Nomans Land Island, Massachusetts; Yarmouth, Massachusetts
Eriksson, Thorvald 28, 130, 166, 176; *see also* Thorvald's Grave, Hampton, New Hampshire

Fell, Barry 3, 57, 717–4, 81–82, 85, 86, 87, 122–123, 146, 150, 151, 152, 156–157, 162, 172, 179, 201n69; *see also America B.C.*
Finch, John 22, 88, 191n21
Follins Pond excavations *see* Yarmouth, Massachusetts
Fortress of Louisbourg, Nova Scotia 37, 105
Foxboro, Massachusetts table stone 14, 185n1
Fragoso, Joseph 39–40, 41, 193n70

Glynn, Frank 15, 65, 71, 77, 96, 100, 101–102, 103, 107, 109, 143
Gnupsson, Erik (Bishop Henricus) 28, 46, 57, 117, 131, 133, 134
Godfrey, William S., Jr. 50–53, 54, 59, 60, 70, 195n76
Goodwin, William B. 11, 14, 82, 90, 91, 93, 94–95, 96, 99–100, 113, 115, 126, 127–128, 129–130, 140–141, 142–143, 144–145, 146, 158, 169–*170*, 186n20, 186n27, 186n50, 202n116; at America's Stonehenge 8–9, 10, 63, 64, 66, 67–70, 75, 78, 95, 116, 151; *Ruins of Great Ireland* 69, 70, 82, 99, 100, 101, 116, 186n49, 198n28, 202n121, 203n10, 209n16; Tor Bay runic axe 158, 169, 213n67; *Truth About Leif Ericsson* 128, 130, 145, 202n121
Gosnold, Bartholomew 16, 163, 165, 171, 187n14
Gray, Edward F. 163, 164, 165, 166, 170, 174
Gungywamp Complex, Groton, Connecticut 147–154; alignments 149–150, 151; Chi Rhos *150*–151, 152; similarities to Irish oratories 152–153

Hadley, Massachusetts sacrificial table *13*
Hamlin, A.C. 93, 119, 120, 121, 122
Hampton, New Hampshire *see* Thorvald's Stone
Hanging Rock *see* Whittier Runestone
Haugen, Einar 133–135
Haverhill, Massachusetts 17, 71, 105, 112, 198n47
Hawkins, Gerald 63, 74, 83, 153
Healey Stone, Hampton Falls, New Hampshire 144–145, *145*
Heavener Rune Stone *see* Oklahoma inscriptions
Hencken, Hugh 8–9, 51, 68, 69, 76
Hendrick, Cornelius 54, 163
Henrikus, Bishop *see* Gnupsson, Eric
Herjólfsson, Bjarni 17, 173
Hertz, Johannes 51, 52, 53, 57, 58, 59, 60
Holand, Hjalmar 49, 52, 56, 58, 115, 116, 168–169, 207n18; use of Holand texts to carve hoax inscriptions 134, 135, 138, 182, 183, 207n19
"hooked X" rune *136*, 137, 138, *180*, 181–*182*; *see also* Nielsen, Richard
Horsford, Cornelia 29–31

Horsford, Eben Norton 22, 23–24, 25- 26, 27–28, 189n55, 189n85
Hvitramannaland see Great Ireland

Iberian Punic *see* Celt-Iberian
Indians *see* Native Americans
inscriptions, foreign: Cachão da Rapa rock shelter, Portugal 87; El-Hadj-Mimoun, Morocco 156–157; Nybble Stone, East Gotland, Sweden 39; Old Swedish 137; Paraiba Stone, Brazil 208n38; Tunisian 146; Vånga stone, Västergötland, Sweden 179
inscriptions, North American *see* America's Stonehenge; Assawompset Pond; Bellows Falls petroglyphs; Bourne Stone; Byfield Viking graves; Calendar I and II; Chatsfield Stone; Dighton Rock; Ellsworth runestone; Gungywamp Chi Rhos; Healey Stone; Inwood Stone; Kensington Rune Stone; Monhegan Island; Mount Mineral Petroglyph; Newport Tower; Narragansett rune stone; Nomans Land Island inscription; Oak Bluffs runes; Oklahoma inscriptions; Popham Beach Stone; Preister Runestone; Sakonnet Stones; Spirit Pond Stone; Thorvald's Grave; Tyngsboro map stone; Virginia Dare stones; Westford ship stone; Weston Stone; Whittier Runestone; Worrell, William; Yarmouth, Nova Scotia
Inwood Stone, Manhattan, New York 30, 190n101

Jenks, William 117–118, 120, 206n57

Karlsefni, Thorfinn 28, 35, 128, 131, 136, 174, 176, 215n123
Kelley, David H. 81–82, 96, 198n42
Kendall, Edward 34–35, 38
Kensington Rune Stone 1; 49, 56, 61, 108, 111, 114, 131, 134, 135, 137, 168–169, 207n18
Kirby, Ian 181, 182, 183
Knights Templar 58, 59, 60, 61, 105, 106, 137, 138, 197n155
Knutson, Paul 56, 169, 196n109

Landsverk, O.G. 57, 117, 131, 133, 134–135, 136, 179, 180
Leif Eriksson, Discoverer of America A.D. 1003 see Gray, Edward F.
Leifsbudir *see* Yarmouth, Massachusetts
Lenik, Edward 41, 78, 93, 124, 161, 162
Lethbridge, T.C. 100–101, 102, 107, 203n12
Longfellow, Henry Wadsworth 19, 20, 21–22, 23, 24, 46,111, 112, 172; "The Skeleton in Armor" 19, 46, 112
lye stones 3, 4–6, 9, 13
Lynn, Massachusetts dolmen *see* Phaeton Rock

Mallery, Arlington 52–54, 104, 195n72
Mallery, Garrick 36, 79, 121
Malta 77; Misrah Sinjura sacrificial table 15
Manana Island, Maine *see* Monhegan Island, Maine inscription
Mather, Cotton 32–33, 36, 112

Index

Mavor, James W. 80, 83, 84, 85–86, 87, 88, 96–97, 151–152, 154, 167, 172, 201n56
Means, Philip Ainsworth 45, 48–49, 50, 53, 56, 58, 60, 104
Merrimack River 3, 79, 80, 105, 107, 112, 115, 116
Monroe, New York 13–14
Mongé, Alf 57, 117, 131, 133, 134, 135, 136
Monhegan Island, Maine inscription 117–123, *124*
Morison, Samuel Eliot 26, 68, 69, 104, 119, 165, 198n35, 201n41
Mount Mineral petroglyph, Shutesbury, Massachusetts 15–*16*
Mystery Hill *see* America's Stonehenge

Narragansett Bay, Rhode Island 19, 44, 54, 55, 56, 111, 177
Narragansett rune stone 179–*184*; hooked X 137, 138, *180*, 181, *182*
Native Americans 10, 11, 12, 18–19, 20, 26, 32, 34, 38, 66, 68, 78, 80, 84, 86, 88, 106, 124, 126, 142, 147, 148, 159, 160, 186n50; Algonquin 3, 34, 36, 68, 78, 79, 151, 154, 160; inscriptions as Native 33, 36, 38–39, 79, 91–92, 99, 101, 120, 121, 162, 177, 178; Mi'kmaq 20, 104, 153, 154; Narragansett 34, 97; Wampanoag 36, 41, 160, 167, 168, 178
Neudorfer, Giovanna 84–85, 87
Newport, Rhode Island Tower 18, 19, 35, 44–62, *47*, 70; alignments 61; colonial origin 44–45, 46–47, 48, 51, 59; inscriptions 57; 169; Norse origin 18, 19, 39, 46, 48–49, 50, 52–53, 55, 56, 57, 59–60, 61, 104, 140, 172, 194n37; Portuguese origin 39, 58, 105; prospect tower origin 61–62
Nielsen, Richard 137, 138, 167, 181, 182 208 213 215
Nomans Land Island, Massachusetts 114, 163–168; inscription *164*–166
"The Norsemen" *see* Whittier, John Greenleaf poetry
North Salem, New Hampshire *see* America's Stonehenge
North Salem, New York dolmen 88
Northmen's Rock *see* Sakonnet Stones
Norumbega 23, 24, 27, 55
Norumbega Tower *see* Weston, Massachusetts
Notown table stone (Leominster, Massachusetts) 11–*12*

Oak Bluffs, Martha's Vineyard, Massachusetts 172–173
Ogham 72–73; 81–82, 86, 123, 136, 172
Oklahoma inscriptions 57, 117, 131
Old Smith's Clove *see* Monroe, New York
Orkney Islands 59–60, 103, 104, 105, 109, 152; Oephir church 49, 60, 104

Pearson, Malcolm 9, 57, 63, 64, 68, 70, 94, 95, 96, 97, 99, 100, 101, 125–126, 141, 144–145, 165, 180, 206n34; photography 39, *47*, 82, *92*, *95*, 115, *117*, *118*, 122, *124*, *127*, 129, *132*, *142*, *145*, *161*, *170*, 178, 179, *180*
Pearson Chamber, Upton, Massachusetts 94–98, *95*, 125, 129
Pell, Herbert 39, 58, 105

petroglyphs *see* inscriptions
Phaeton Rock, Lynn Massachusetts dolmen 88–91, *89*
Pohl, Frederick J. 69, 122, 168; Cockaponset carvings 154–156, 157, 158; Newport Tower 51–52, 53, 54, 55; Westford Knight 102, 103, 104, 106; Yarmouth, Massachusetts 173–174, 175, 176, 214n100, 214n106, 215n124
Popham Beach stone, Maine 129, *130*, 131
Powell, Bernard 154, 157, 158
Priester Runestone, North Tisbury, Massachusetts 168–*169*
Punic script *see* Celt-Iberian

Quitsa dolmen 169–172, *170*

Rafn, Carl Christian 17, 19, 23, 35, 46, 57;120, 159; 166, 177, 189n54; *Antiquitates Americanae* 17, 30, 35, 46, 112, 177
Ruins of Great Ireland in New England see Goodwin, William B.
runes *see* inscriptions

sacrificial tables *see* America's Stonehenge; Foxboro; Hadley; Malta; Monroe; Notown
Sakonnet Stones, Aquidneck Island, Rhode Island 177–179, *178*
Schoolcraft, Henry 36, 92, 93, 119–120, 122
Shutesbury, Massachusetts carving 15–*16*
Sinclair, Henry 59–60, 99, 102–103, 104, 105–106, 109, 155
"The Skeleton in Armor" *see* Longfellow, Henry Wordsworth
Sky Disk of Nebra 77
Spirit Pond rune stones, Phippsburg, Maine 117, 130–138, *132*, *136*, 180, 181–182
Stefansson, Vilhjalmur 96, 159
Stone, Dennis 63, 78, 80
Stone, Robert 15, 63, 66, 71, 72, 74, *75*, 77–78, 85
Stonehenge, Wiltshire, England 2, 74, 83, 153
Strandwold, Olaf 38–39, 57, 94, 99, 101, 113, 114, 115–116, *117*, *118*, 122, 123, 124–125, 126, 128, 129, 130, 131, 140–142, 144–145, 161, 166, 178–179, 192n62

tar kilns 3, 4, 6, 13
They All Discovered America see Boland, Charles Michael
Thorvald's Grave, Hampton New Hampshire 115, 125–126, 139–*144*, *142*, 176
Tiede, Vance 152–153
Tisbury, Massachusetts *see* Priester rune stone
Truth About Leif Ericsson see Goodwin, William B.
Tyngsboro, Massachusetts map stone 79–80

Upton, Massachusetts chamber *see* Pearson Chamber
Upton, Massachusetts Magunco Stone 125–126

Verrazzano, Giovanni da 19, 55, 97, 119, 165
Vescelius, Gary 9–10, 70–71
Virginia Dare stones hoax 69

Wahlgren, Erik 1, 135, 182
Waquoit Bay, Massachusetts 159–160
Westford, Massachusetts knight effigy 99–110, *102*, *109*, 126, 155, 204*n*71; Glynn, Frank 100–102, 103, 107, 109; Pohl, Frederick J. 102, 103, 104, 106; *see also* Sinclair, Henry
Westford, Massachusetts ship stone 107–109, *108*
Weston Massachusetts Norumbega Tower 27–29, *29*
Weston Stone 29–31, *30*
White Man's Land *see* Great Ireland
Whitney, Anne 22, 23–24; 25; Eriksson statue 20–*25*, 35, 111
Whittall, James P. 15, 87, 90–91, 96, 122, 123, 135, 146, 149, 162, 171, 181; at America's Stonehenge 71, 72, 76; at Newport Tower 56, 59–60
Whittier, John Greenleaf poetry 112, 205*n*6, 205*n*7, 188*n*52
Whittier Runestone (Hanging Rock), West Newbury, Massachusetts 112–114, *113*, 115, 116, 118
Wolter Scott 61, 108, 137–138, 167, 168, 18, 183, 184, 208*n*48; *see also* hooked X
Worrell, William H. 1–2

Yarmouth, Massachusetts (Leifsbudir) 173–176

Zeno Narrative 103, 104, 105, 107; *see also* Sinclair, Henry

www.ingramcontent.com/pod-product-compliance
Ingram Content Group UK Ltd.
Pitfield, Milton Keynes, MK11 3LW, UK
UKHW050533150426
5217IPUK00026B/1912